Production Planning and Scheduling:

MATHEMATICAL PROGRAMMING APPLICATIONS

Kenneth D. Lawrence / Stelios H. Zanakis

Industrial Engineering and Management Press
Institute of Industrial Engineers

Industrial Engineering and Management Press,
25 Technology Park/Atlanta, Norcross, Georgia 30092

Published 1984
Printed in the United States of America

ISBN 0-89806-047-8

Contents

CHAPTER 3. PRODUCTION PLANNING UNDER MULTIPLE GOALS AND OBJECTIVES

Preface

The objective of this volume is to present, in an organized manner, a comprehensive, integrated treatment of the use of mathematical programming approaches in the fields of production planning and scheduling. This interface is receiving more and more attention, as documented in chapter 1 of this volume. Therefore, although of limited scope, this volume should appeal to a variety of students and practitioners in both fields.

University courses in these two areas are somehow neglecting this interface. Most production management courses and textbooks do not include mathematical programming approaches to production problems, considering them too rigorous or beyond their introductory scope. On the other hand, many mathematical programming courses and texts tend to emphasize the optimization methodology, rarely paying more than scant attention to practical problems of using mathematical programming in an expanding field like production management.

This volume, it is hoped, will narrow this gap. It may be used to supplement either a production management or mathematical programming text in a corresponding course at the upper-undergraduate or graduate level. It may broaden the reader's awareness and understanding of operations planning/scheduling problems and provide a reference of characteristic applications of mathematical programming approaches in the field of production management. It should be useful to students, teachers, and practitioners (analysts and managers) in the fields of *industrial and systems engineering, management science, operations research, systems analysis,* and *production management.*

The emphasis of this volume is *not* in mathematical programming algorithms but, rather, in building and using such models in production planning and scheduling. Mathematically sound or practically effective solution procedures are outlined in several articles—not as an aim in itself but to operationalize the models.

Prior familiarity (not expertise) in mathematical programming—mainly linear—is helpful but not necessary. To reduce the need for this familiarity and, primarily, to help the reader raise critical concerns when studying the application articles, this volume starts with a review on building, solving, validating, implementing, and using mathematical programming models. This focus should increase the appeal of this volume to practice-oriented people.

Chapter 2 starts with a brief review of production planning and classical solution approaches, presents a case study, and concludes with two sets of articles illustrating models/approaches and real applications, respectively. Many of these applications demonstrate the considerable savings possible by integrating new production systems with other business functions.

Chapter 3 presents an introduction to multiple objective linear and goal programming as applied to production planning and scheduling, followed by articles illustrating characteristic applications.

Undoubtedly, many interesting and worth-reading articles could be included in a book like this. However, space limitations made including applications in all areas of production/operations management impossible. The most popular subject—namely, mathematical programming applications in production planning and scheduling—was selected.

The choice of articles was guided by our desire to include different modeling approaches to major production planning/scheduling problems, different solution techniques, some implementation realities, and some integrated planning systems (a need expressed in recent surveys [Taylor 1979]). Applications-oriented articles rather than articles on extensive algorithmic and computational development were often preferred. Naturally, candidate articles were limited to those that we were aware of or able to find after considerable literature search of major periodicals in the field. Not all good articles could be included in a single book. We hope that the articles included will contribute toward achieving our objectives.

1. An Overview
of Mathematical Programming

Mathematical programming—especially linear programming—is one of the best developed and most widely used techniques of operations research (OR). Results of surveys of U.S. companies concur that:

1. The most often used OR techniques are regression analysis, linear programming, simulation, and PERT/CPM (Ledbetter and Cox 1977a, Taylor 1979, Ledbetter and Cox 1977b, Gaither 1975). Other mathematical-programming techniques (nonlinear, dynamic, and integer) are being used much less frequently.
2. The greatest areas of application of mathematical programming and other OR techniques seem to be the fields of production management (Fabozzi and Valente 1976, Ledbetter and Cox 1977a) and, especially, production planning and control (Gaither 1975). The usage has nearly tripled in the last twenty years (from about 30 percent to 85 percent of *major* U.S. companies [Ledbetter and Cox 1977a] and 52 percent of *all* U.S. manufacturers [Gaither 1975]).

Therefore, the interface of mathematical programming (especially linear) and production management is of particular interest to practitioners, students, and educators. To provide better coverage in the space available, this volume will address the area of production planning and scheduling. The term *production planning and scheduling* refers to the development and use of systematic procedures for best planning (longer time) and scheduling (shorter time horizon) the use of production resources (material, equipment, manpower, and capital). This area also accounts for the majority of mathematical-programming applications in the field of production management (Ledbetter and Cox 1977a, Gaither 1975).

Historically, *production management* has evolved in the manufacturing environment, where goods are produced with the aid of productive resources. This transformation process requires design, planning, and control of production operations. Similar needs exist in the rapidly growing service sector (hospitals, banks, municipalities, government, etc.). For example, manpower scheduling is needed for factory workers as well as for nurses, bank tellers, telephone operators, airport personnel, etc. Applications of mathematical programming to the many service sectors cannot be adequately covered here. This book will focus on business and industrial applications. However, it is recognized that, in general, production is viewed in a broader sense as the process by which goods and services are created—that is, the operation phase of an organization. This phase requires efficient use of all (limited) resources, and this is where mathematical programming can help.

Mathematical programming is a methodology for determining the optimum allocation of limited resources among competing alternatives, under various constraints imposed by the nature of the problem under study.

A mathematical-programming approach to developing a production management system involves the following general steps:

1. Defining the production problem and the objectives of the system.
2. Building the model—conceptual model selection (linear, integer, nonlinear single versus multiple objectives), decision-variable definition, constraint (goal) determination, data collection, model formulation, and simplification.
3. Solving the mathematical-programming model—selection and use of an appropriate algorithm and computer code.

4. Validating the model—comparisons against historical data and/or results obtained in step 1.
5. Implementation—translating (incorporating) these developments into the production system and using them to assist managers in making decisions.

These steps require different skills, methods, and information and present various difficulties as explained in the subsequent sections. The first and last steps are the least-structured phases, involving behavioral and organizational interfaces with the real (outside-the-model) world. Student training in these respects is important but extremely difficult and is considerably aided by case studies, applied articles, and student participation in real-world team projects (Zanakis 1979). The second step, model building, is more of an art than a science, requiring not only training in OR but also understanding, insight, and some intuition about the nature of the problem. Finally, the steps of solving and validating a model are rather mechanical in nature and are usually handled effectively by an experienced analyst.

TYPES OF MATHEMATICAL-PROGRAMMING PROBLEMS

The general (nonlinear) mathematical-programming problem with a single objective has the form:

Optimize $f(x_1, x_2, \ldots, x_n)$

subject to

$$\left. \begin{aligned} g_i(x_1, x_2, \ldots, x_n) &= b_i \quad i = 1, \ldots, m \\ x_1, x_2, \ldots, x_n &\epsilon R \end{aligned} \right\} \quad (1)$$

The decision (controllable) variables $x_1, x_2, \ldots, x_n$ must usually lie within some region R (for example, nonnegative) that, along with the m constraints $g_i(x_1, \ldots, x_n) = b_i$ constitutes the area of feasible solutions. Of these, the optimal solution is the one that maximizes or minimizes (as the case might be) the objective function—for example, maximize profit or minimize cost—subject to technological (capacities, material, etc.), financial, marketing, administrative, social, and other restrictions.

Some simple modeling manipulations should be noted here. Minimizing $f(x_1, \ldots, x_n)$ is equivalent to maximizing $-f(x_1, \ldots, x_n)$ and vice versa. If needed, inequality constraints may be converted to equality by adding a slack W_i (≥ 0) or substructing a surplus $V_i (\geq 0)$ variable:

$$g_i(x_1, \ldots, x_n) \leq b_i \longleftrightarrow g_i(x_1, \ldots, x_n) + W_i = b_i$$

$$g_i(x_1, \ldots, x_n) \geq b_i \longleftrightarrow g_i(x_1, \ldots, x_n) - V_i = b_i$$

or

$$-g_i(x_1, \ldots, x_n) \leq -b_i \longleftrightarrow -g_i(x_1, \ldots, x_n) + U_i = -b_i \quad (V_i = U_i)$$

Similarly, an equality constraint is equivalent to two opposite inequalities:

$$g_i(x_1, \ldots, x_n) = b_i \longleftrightarrow g_i(x_1, \ldots, x_n) \leq b_i$$

and

$$g_i(x_1, \ldots, x_n) \geq b_i$$

These conversions are needed because some mathematical-programming methods (algorithms) accept only one type of constraint.

Three special cases of nonlinear programming are quadratic, separable, and geometric programming. The first has linear constraints and a second-degree polynomial for objective function. In separable programming, lack of cross-product terms permits separation of all functions to a sum of single variable functions, $h(x_1, \ldots, x_n) = h_1(x_1) + \ldots + h_n(x_n)$, which then can be linearized by piecewise approximations. Finally, in geometric programming the objective function is the sum of polynomial terms, i.e.

$$f(x_1, \ldots, x_n) = \sum_{i=1}^{k} c_i x_1^{a_{i1}} x_2^{a_{i2}} \ldots x_n^{a_{in}}.$$

Many engineering design problems are amenable to geometric programming formulation.

If all (some) decision variables $x_1, \ldots, x_n$ are allowed to take on only discrete values (for example, $R = \{0,1,2, \ldots \}$), (1) represents an all (mixed) *integer* programming problem. A special case of integer programming is when all decision variables can be either 0 or 1. Many yes ($x = 1$) no ($x = 0$) types of management problems can be modeled this way—for example, selecting competing project investments (capital budgeting).

The simplest and most often used form of mathematical programming is that in which the objective function and all constraints are linear. *Linear programming* has the form:

Optimize $f = c_1 x_1 + \ldots + c_n x_n$

subject to

$$\left. \begin{array}{l} a_{i1}x_1 + \ldots + a_{in} x_n = b_i \quad i = 1, \ldots, m \\ x_j \geqslant 0 \quad j = 1, \ldots, n \end{array} \right\} \quad (2)$$

where

b_i's = limits on resources
a_{ij}'s = technological coefficients
c_j's = costs (to minimize f),
revenues or profits (to maximize f)

Dynamic programming models are custom-made for the solution of mathematical-programming problems with a sequence of multistage phases (for example, time-dependent optimization problems).

Heuristic programming refers to simple (common-sense) rules for obtaining good (near-optimal) solutions to large, complex optimization problems. These may be general or custom-made.

Multiobjective mathematical programming is concerned with decision-making problems in which there are several conflicting objectives. Contrasting with single-objective methods, which employ a unique measure of effectiveness leading to identification of an optimal alternative, multiobjective methods are used to generate and evaluate more than a single alternative.

Koopmans was the first to introduce the idea of the vector maximization problem:

Maximize $[f_1(\bar{x}), f_2(\bar{x}) \ldots, f_k(\bar{x})]$

subject to   (3)

$$g_i(\bar{x}) \leq b_i \quad i = 1,2 \ldots ,m$$

where

$\bar{x} = n$ dimensional vector of decision variables.

Although much theoretical work has been undertaken in solving the multiple-objective formulation of the vector maximization problem, the vast majority of such work has had little or no practical impact for the industrial practitioner. These works are characterized for the most part by algorithms that, if computerization is available, are able to solve only extremely small problems. The only multiple-objective method that has enjoyed any substantial use in practice is goal programming.

Goal programming, instead of trying to maximize or minimize the objective criterion directly, minimizes the deviations between goals and achievable limits dictated by the set of system constraints in a pre-emptive order of priority.

Minimize $\bar{Z} = [h_1(\bar{d}), \ldots ,h_r(\bar{d}), \ldots ,h_k(\bar{d})]$

subject to   (4)

$$g_i(x_1, \ldots , x_n) + d_i^- - d_i^+ = b_i \quad i = 1, 2, \ldots , m$$

where

$$\bar{Z} = \text{vector of } k \text{ priority achievement functions}$$
$$h_r(\bar{d}) = \sum_{i \in I_r} (w_{ir}^- d_i^- + w_{ir}^+ d_i^+),$$
separated by commas
$I_r = $ set of goals in the rth priority level
$d_i^-, d_i^+ = $ underachievement and overachievement from goal level b_i
$w_{ir}^-, w_{ir}^+ = $ weight of underachievement and overachievement of the ith goal in the rth priority (usually 0 or 1).

All previous forms of mathematical programming assume that all coefficients are reasonably known with certainty. Incorporating probabilities in the coefficients or in the entire constraint results in *stochastic* and *chance-constrained programming,* respectively, which are more difficult to solve than their deterministic counterpart.

The schematic graph below summarizes the various types of mathematical programming models.

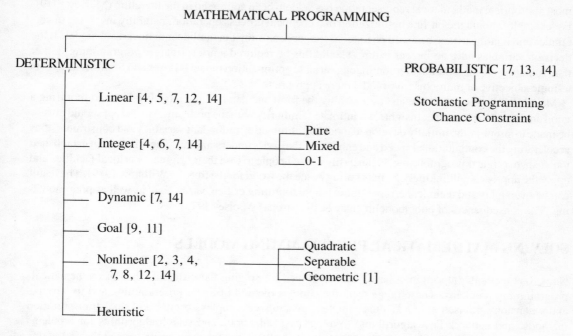

Note: Numbers within the brackets refer to items in the bibliography on mathematical programming at the end of this chapter.

BUILDING MATHEMATICAL PROGRAMMING MODELS

Once the problem has been carefully determined and the objectives of the study (or system) explicitly stated, a conceptual model may be developed. This should recognize existing realities in input data availability, solution methodologies/packages, and implementation potential of resulting changes. Two major points must be addressed simultaneously at this point:

1. The desirable *detail* of the model
2. The *form* of the model.

A dilemma that often surfaces when dealing with real and complex problems is which to sacrifice—detail or breadth? To put it another way, should we aim for the optimal solution of a simplified representation or for a good solution of an accurate representation? The answer depends on the particular situation and is guided by this rule: *A model should be detailed to the degree that it produces useful and acceptable results for management.* The model results will be useful if they improve existing operations or provide considerable insight into new operations. In any case, management will accept and trust the model results only if these results and their sensitivity can be reasonably explained in logical nontechnical terms. A manager will not blindly accept a solution simply because the analyst proved that it is optimal (optimal to what problem?).

Simple models are useful for gaining valuable insights into the operation of the system (Geoffrion 1976), thus quickly gaining management's trust and support and paving the road for more elaborate models (usually strategic) requiring more time and resources that management would otherwise be willing to commit. Large models of tactical or operational problems may be prohibitively expensive to run on a routine (frequent) basis. In such cases, a large model may be occasionally run to validate or update the operational use of simple (approximate) models and gain management's confidence (Ignall, Kolessar, and Walker 1978).

Model detail is, of course, related to the availability of input data (existing or reasonably obtainable) and to the form of the model. The form of the model is affected by the nature of the problem, the type of solution codes available, and the imagination of the analyst. Comparing alternative model forms and selecting the most appropriate mathematical representation has seldom been addressed in the literature (Mulvey 1979). For example, should the on-line optimization of a chemical process operation, naturally involving uncertainties and nonlinearities, be based on a stochastic, or deterministic, nonlinear or linearized model? If the decision variables have an integer nature, should this be required a priori (integer programming) rather than rounding off the solution of a continuous variable optimization model (Glover and Sommer 1975)? Is a single-objective or multiobjective model more appropriate?

Model building is more than just establishing the form and detail of the model. It is an art requiring a good analytical background, insight, and intimate familiarity with the problem. An attempt should always be made to simplify the initially developed model by eliminating redundant variables and constraints, thus accelerating the computational speed and enhancing the user's understanding. The blind use of established tools, such as linear programming, "can easily cause people to lose their original or critical faculties and apply the approach unthinkingly..., thus failing to see the wood for the trees" (Williams 1979). The result can be oversights and technical errors—for example, omitting critical variables—as well as poor modeling. The consequences of poor modeling may be disastrous (Woolsey 1973).

SOLVING MATHEMATICAL PROGRAMMING MODELS

Numerous methods (algorithms) have been developed for solving the different types of mathematical-programming problems. These range from the simplex method of linear programming and its variants and extensions (revised simplex, dual simplex, generalized simplex, primal and dual transportation methods, and network flow algorithms) to a variety of algebraic and search algorithms for problems other than linear programming. The bibliography on mathematical programming texts at the end of this chapter gives sources of detailed descriptions of these methods. This section is concerned with some tactical problems in using such methods.

The first—and often overlooked—question an analyst should raise is whether a near-optimal (heuristic) solution is acceptable and/or preferable. This could be the case when (1) measurement errors and subjective estimates raise questions on the usefulness of an exact solution to a problem with inexact data and (2) the optimization problem is too large to permit determination of an optimal solution in reasonable time. The best heuristic procedure is usually not obvious. These alternatives include general heuristics for a certain problem class (for example, integer programming problems [Zanakis 1977]), heuristics specifically developed for the problem in question, or premature stopping of exact algorithms (for example, branch and bound) when a satisfactory solution has been obtained. Zanakis and Evans (1981) give a detailed account of why, when, and how to use and validate heuristics.

Even when an exact algorithm is used, the true optimum may not be obtained, because the procedure fails to converge or terminates in a local rather than in the global optimum. Nonlinear programming algorithms can guarantee the optimal solution only to a convex problem—that is, a U-shaped (convex) objective function to be minimized over a constrained space in which any two points specify a straight line segment lying entirely on or within the constrained space. The chance of obtaining the global optimum to a nonconvex programming problem is improved by starting the optimization procedure from different initial points and selecting the best final solution produced.

All mathematical programming algorithms employ an algebraic or search (iterative) procedure for moving, by means of some criterion, through a sequence (preferably a few) of improved intermediate solution points to a final solution. Having a good initial feasible solution to start the iterative procedure not only expedites computations but also establishes a benchmark for justifying the accuracy/time tradeoffs of an optimal solution and provides some additional insight into the problem and its optimum. A good initial solution may be known from the practical experience of the problem or obtained by using some so-called quick-and-dirty heuristic.

Sometimes, superimposing upper and lower bounds on the decision variables may expedite convergence by drastically reducing the size of the space to be searched. Methods treating them as bounds will be more efficient than methods treating them as constraints—for example, using upper-bounded rather than the regular simplex methods for solving bounded-variable linear programming (LP) problems or using 0-1 rather than integer programming algorithms with the additional constraint that all decision variables
$x_j \leq 1$.

Partitioning or decomposing a structured optimization problem into a series of subproblems may permit solving a problem that is otherwise too large to solve. Data storage requirements are reduced by using direct-access storage devices and recalling into the core only the elements needed at each iteration (for example, column-generation schemes). These techniques and the rapid growth of powerful computers have enabled analysts to solve very large mathematical-programming problems. Solutions of linear-programming problems with a couple of million variables and several hundred thousand constraints have been reported since the early 1970s. Further details on the computational aspects of mathematical-programming algorithms are available from White (1973), and the bibliography at the end of this chapter gives additional sources.

The solution of a mathematical programming problem in practice does not end with the determination of an optimum solution. It is followed by a sensitivity or postoptimality analysis, model validation, and results interpretation.

Sensitivity of the optimal solution to intentional modifications (for example, different conditions and policies) or unintentional changes (for example, errors) affecting some or all problem coefficients increases the reliability and acceptance of the model. Comparing the model results with past performance and logically interpreting the optimum solution (Geoffrion 1976) are essential to successful implementation. Forrester pointed out in 1961: "The validity of a model should be judged by its suitability for a particular purpose. A model is sound and dependable if it accomplishes what is expected of it." Many models are being developed every day, but few are actually used by decision makers, for "the prime asset of model-building is the breadth of its practice, [while] the prime liability is the narrowness of its implementation" (Roberts 1976).

USING MATHEMATICAL PROGRAMMING MODELS

While the vast majority of literature in mathematical programming involves theory, problem formulation solution technique, and the interpretation of solutions, the problems of solution acceptance and implementation have been given scant attention. Although these areas have been given such minimal exposure, they are extremely crucial and are typically the areas critical to the success or failure of the entire project (Rivett 1968).

Mathematical-programming models have enjoyed the widest and most prominent use in business operation planning. It is common in the oil industry to schedule daily refinery operations through the use of mathematical programming models. Large-scale manufacturing activities are also planned using such models. For these problem structures that are well-understood and that involve a large number of interacting variables, these models have proved to be powerful aids to decision-making for particular subunits of companies. Many of these models are directly linked to the company's computerized information system. For example, a production planning model may obtain cost coefficients or demand forecasts directly from disk files and also provide data for regular manufacturing and distribution reports.

For a mathematical-programming problem solution technique to work effectively within a company—and, therefore, within a formal organizational structure—it needs to be fitted into the context of the organization. It needs to be fitted into the long-range strategic and policy framework as an integral part of the structure of the company.

The decisions that face a manufacturing operation can typically be classified into three categories of decision-making: *strategic* planning, *tactical* planning, and *operations* control (Keen and Morton 1978).

Strategic planning concerns itself with the establishment of managerial policies and with the development of resources necessary for the company to satisfy its requirements, as established by its managerial goals. Such strategic decisions include major investments in production facilities, the sizes and locations of new plants, and distribution facilities. These decisions are those that structure the company's growth and competitive abilities.

Tactical planning concerns itself with the effective allocation of resources, storage distribution, workforce, production facility, and managerial resources to satisfy the demand and technical requirements of the company; the costs and revenues associated with the operation of the company are taken into account. Typically, the situation involves multiple plants, distribution centers or warehouses, with products requiring multistage production processes to serve large market areas with random patterns. The decisions to be made within this multiperiod planning horizon usually address the utilization of workforce, the allocation of aggregate capacity resources to production, and the selection of distribution channels and transportation alternatives.

Finally, the *operations* control planning decision is examined. After the aggregate allocation of resources has been made, actual period-by-period scheduling decisions must be made. The process requires the disaggregation of tactical planning decisions into details consistent with the operation of the company. These decisions involve assigning customer orders to specific machines, dispatching and processing orders, and controlling inventory.

For the most part, the role of mathematical programming in supporting strategic and operational decision-making has been limited. In the case of strategic decisions, the great degree of uncertainty and the high risk associated with such decisions have severely limited the application of mathematical programming. In the case of operational planning, the excessive amount of detailed information necessary to resolve these problems almost totally precludes the use of mathematical-programming methodology. Thus, mathematical-programming models find their widest use in the tactical arena of planning (Ackoff 1970, Driebeck 1969).

Basically, the computerized mathematical-programming model is a specialized form of decision-support system that aids management in the decision-making process. Such systems assist managers in their decision process and support, rather than replacing managerial judgment. They also improve the effectiveness of decisions. The payoff of these model structures has been in generating better solutions for the problem. The relevance for managers has been the provision of detailed recommendations and new methodologies for handling complex problems (Aronofsky, Dutton, and Tayyabkhan 1978).

Among the factors that appear to be most crucial in the successful implementation of a mathematical-programming modeling system project (Harvey 1970) are:

1. Definite and well-formulated management goals and objectives
2. A cooperative effort between all groups within the organization of the company
3. A simple user interface
4. Flexibility in report generation from the system
5. The ability to interface with the company's other systems.

To give a better appreciation of each of these critical areas, a brief discussion of each follows.

1. For a mathematical-programming model project to be successful, the goals and objectives of the model must be specific, and they must be understood by various groups within the company. It should be clearly understood that the mathematical-programming model does not make the decisions but that it is only an analytical tool to help operational managers to evaluate various alternatives.
2. Typically, to build, develop, and implement a mathematical-programming model for production planning, cooperation from various groups within the organization is needed. This cooperation should start with the project's inception and continue through its implementation. Making the user of the system an integral part of the total process effort is essential for success.

3. Many mathematical-programming models have died slow and painful deaths because of the difficulties in getting information into the "black box." Therefore, it is essential that, in addition to being informative, the interface be simple and to the point.
4. Once a system is successful, there normally are many requests for additional detailed and summary reports. Therefore, it is essential to be able to produce these reports quickly and efficiently.
5. The mathematical-programming system should not be designed or implemented as an independent or closed system. It should have the capability of receiving information from other systems. Moreover, it should also be capable of easily passing its results on to other systems of the company.

It must be recognized that decision-makers will use models only if they are simple, robust, easy to control, adaptive to change, complete on important issues, and easy to communicate (Little 1970).

The development and maintenance of the data base is a major, ongoing task for a large-scale mathematical-programming model. A specialized group within the organization is needed to provide and regularly update the data for the model. Since data will come from many departments or systems, specialized procedures or systems will be needed to standardize and coordinate the flow of data. Moreover, many off-line changes to the model structure may be needed (technological changes in production processes, etc.). Thus, it is best to make the data base for the mathematical-programming model an integral part of the computerized system of the company.

The golden rule for building, solving, and using models in practice has been summarized earlier (Zanakis et al. 1980):

> Managers want to improve their current operation as cheaply and quickly as possible, care little about an optimal solution to a problem with usually inexact dates, and will not accept a new solution they do not understand.

REFERENCES

Ackoff, R. 1970. *The concept of corporate planning*. New York: Wiley.

Aronofsky, J., J. Dutton, and M. Tayyabkhan. 1978. *Managerial planning with linear programming in process industry operations*. New York: Wiley.

Driebeck, N. 1969. *Applied linear programming*. Reading, Mass.: Addison Wesley.

Fabozzi, F. J., and J. Valente. 1976. Mathematical programming in American companies: A sample survey. *Interfaces* 7(1):93-98.

Gaither, N. 1975. The adoption of operations research techniques by manufacturing organizations. *Decision Sciences* 6 (October): 797-815.

Geoffrion, A.M. 1976. The purpose of mathematical programming is insight, not numbers. *Interfaces* 7(1):81-92.

Glover, F., and D.C. Sommer. 1975. Pitfalls of rounding in discrete management decision problems. *Decision Sciences* (April): 211-220.

Harvey, A. 1970. Factors making for implementation success and failure. *Management Science* 14.

Ignall, E.J., P. Kolessar, and W.E. Walker. 1978. Using simulation to develop and validate analytic models: Some case studies. *Operations Research* 26(2):237-253.

Keen, P., and M. Morton. 1978. *Decision support systems: An organizational perspective*. Reading, Mass.: Addison-Wesley.

Ledbetter, W.N., and J.F. Cox. 1977a. Operations research in production management: An investigation of past and present utilization. *Production & Inventory Management* (3rd Quarter): 84-92. (This article also compares the results of 1958, 1964, and 1976 surveys).

————. 1977*b*. Are OR techniques being used? *Industrial Engineering* (February): 19-21.

Little, J.D.C. 1970. Models and managers: The concept of a decision calculus. *Management Science* 16(8):B466-485.

Mulvey, J.M. 1979. Strategies in modeling: A personnel scheduling example. *Interfaces* 9(3):66-76.

Rivett, B. 1968. *Concepts of operational research.* London: Watts.

Roberts, E.B. 1976. On modeling. *Technological Forecasting and Social Change* 9:231-238.

Taylor, S.G. 1979. The APICS process industry survey: Implications for education and research. W. AIDS conference proceedings, Reno, 202-204.

White, W.W. 1973. A status report on computing algorithms for mathematical programming. *Computing Surveys* 5(3):135-166.

Williams, H.P. 1979. Four examples of artless modelling. *Omega* 7(2):163-165.

Woolsey, R.E.D. 1973. A novena to St. Jude, or four edifying case studies in mathematical programming. *Interfaces* 4(1):33-39.

Zanakis, S.H. 1977. Heuristic 0-1 linear programming: An experimental comparison of three methods. *Management Science* 24(1):91-104.

————. 1979. Real world student class projects disclose: Negligence or pitfall in inventory control? *Decision Line* (March).

Zanakis, S.H., L.M. Austin, D.C. Nowading, and E.A. Silver. 1980. From teaching to implementing inventory management: Problems of translation. *Interfaces* 10(6):103-110.

Zanakis, S.H., and J. R. Evans. 1981. Heuristic optimization: Why, when and how to use it. *Interfaces* 11(5):84-91.

SELECTED BIBLIOGRAPHY ON MATHEMATICAL PROGRAMMING

1. Beightler, C. S., and D. T. Phillips. 1976. *Applied Geometric Programming.* New York: Wiley.

2. Beightler, C.S., D.T. Phillips, and D.J. Wilde. 1979. *Foundations of Optimization.* 2nd ed. Englewood Cliffs, N.J.: Prentice-Hall.

3. Beveridge, G.S.G., and R.S. Schechter. 1970. *Optimization: Theory and Practice.* New York: McGraw-Hill.

4. Bradley, S.P., A.C. Hax, and T.L. Magnanti. 1977. *Applied Mathematical Programming.* Reading, Mass: Addison-Wesley.

5. Dantzig, G. P. 1963. *Linear Programming and Extensions.* Princeton: Princeton University Press.

6. Garfinkel, R. S., and G. L. Nemhauser. 1972. *Integer Programming.* New York: Wiley.

7. Hillier, F. S., and G. J. Lieberman. 1974. *Introduction to Operations Research.* 2nd ed. San Francisco: Holden-Day.*

8. Himmelblau, D. 1972. *Applied Nonlinear Programming.* New York: McGraw-Hill.

9. Ignizio, J. P. 1976. *Goal Programming and Extensions.* Lexington, Mass.: Lexington Books.

10. Kuester, J., and J. Mize. 1973. *Optimization Techniques with FORTRAN.* New York: McGraw-Hill.

11. Lee, S. M. 1972. *Goal Programming for Decision Analysis.* Philadelphia: Auerbach.

12. McMillan, C., Jr. 1975. *Mathematical Programming.* 2nd ed. New York: Wiley.

---

*General Operations Research textbooks.

13. Sengupta, J.K. 1972. *Stochastic Programming: Methods and Applications.* New York: Academic Press.

14. Wagner, H.M. 1975. *Principles of Operations Research with Applications to Managerial Decisions.* 2nd ed. Englewood Cliffs, N.J.: Prentice-Hall.*

SELECTED BIBLIOGRAPHY ON PRODUCTION PLANNING AND SCHEDULING

Bedworth, D. D. 1973. *Industrial Systems: Planning Analysis and Control.* New York: Ronald.

Buffa, E. 1972. *Operations Management: Problems and Models.* 3rd ed. New York: Wiley.

————. 1979. *Modern Production Management: Managing the Operations Function.* 6th ed. New York: Wiley.

Buffa, E., and W. H. Taubert. 1972. *Production-Inventory Systems: Planning and Control.* Homewood, Ill.: Irwin.

Colley, J. L., Jr., R. D. Landel, and R. R. Fair. 1977. *Production Operations Planning and Control: Text & Cases.* San Francisco: Holden-Day.

Fabrycky, W. J., P. M. Ghare, and P. E. Torgensen. 1972. *Industrial Operations Research.* Englewood Cliffs, N.J.: Prentice-Hall.

Gavet, J. W. 1968. *Production and Operations Management.* New York: Harcourt-Brace & World.

Johnson, L. A., and D. C. Montgomery. 1973. *Operations Research in Production Planning, Scheduling & Inventory Control.* New York: Wiley.

Starr, M. 1978. *Operations Management.* Englewood Cliffs, N.J.: Prentice-Hall.

Zimmerman, H. J., and M. G. Sovereign. 1974. *Quantitative Models for Production Management.* Englewood Cliffs, N.J.: Prentice-Hall.

---

*General Operations Research textbooks.

2. Production Planning and Scheduling

OVERVIEW OF PRODUCTION PLANNING AND SCHEDULING

The Nature of the Production Planning Problem

Production planning may be defined as the intermediate-range matching of variable and fixed inputs of the production process to meet future demand requirements. The standard objective is meeting customer demand at minimum cost. Intermediate-range planning is facilitated by aggregating the many products of the typical company into a single unit of output, commonly referred to as the aggregate production unit. Measures of aggregate output include tons for steel mills, cases for bottling plants, barrels for a refinery, and machine hours for a job shop. When correctly implemented, plans for the aggregate product can be disaggregated at a later stage in the planning process into detailed plans for individual products.

Aggregate production planning cannot be effective if it is separated from the other decision processes of the organization. It provides a major interface of production with the marketing and financial functions. The coordination of aggregate production planning with marketing is essential since it determines a production plan that meets the variation in the demand. Unless this function is properly met, there will be constant arguments between the production and marketing functions regarding meeting orders and the adequacy of lead time and capacity. Additionally, to plan labor, raw materials, and seasonal inventories effectively, it is essential that production be interfaced with financial planning. If such an interface is not effective, sudden layoffs or shortages may result when the company's financial position does not allow for these expenditures. For the company's aggregate plan to be successful and, thus, help to promote a profitable organization, cooperation and coordination between production, marketing, and finance must exist. The mere exchange of information between these areas is not enough to ensure a successful aggregate production plan.

The aggregate planning problem in its most general form consists of determining, for each period, the required size of the workforce, rate of production, and inventory level, given a product demand forecast for each period. Generally, the solution to the aggregate planning problem has been determined by minimizing the expected total cost over the given planning horizon. Typically, the cost components considered include (1) cost of payroll (regular and overtime), (2) cost of changing production rate, (3) cost of carrying inventory, and (4) cost of demand shortage (this estimate is usually complicated by the existence of intangibles).

The complexity underlying the aggregate production planning problem arises from the variable pattern of the product demand per period. Developing a solution to this problem requires a simultaneous process to investigate several simple strategies usually offered to the aggregate production structure:

1. Adjusting the size of the workforce by hiring and firing in response to demand fluctuations. Excessively used, this short-term strategy will create labor-union problems and lower the company's goodwill image.
2. Changing the production rate by working overtime or undertime with the same workforce.
3. Absorbing demand fluctuations through changes in inventory level or backlog of orders without changing production rates. Deferring customer demand (backlogging), whenever possible, will reduce pick loads.
4. Increasing or decreasing the aggregate amount of outside contracting to absorb demand fluctuations.

The best production planning strategy may be a combination of these strategies.

Developing decision-support systems to solve the aggregate production planning problem involves satisfying a number of data requirements. Before such system forecasts can be developed, the demand for products must be in place. Additionally, a single overall measure of production output and sales for different products to be scheduled by the aggregate production plan must also be developed. Finally, the costs associated with the aggregate production plan must be identified and measured.

A crucial aspect of the aggregate planning process concerns the dynamic nature of the decision process. The present decision in the planning model is just one of a sequence of decisions and does not establish a permanent production policy. Errors in the forecasts of products for a past period, for which decisions had been developed, will help in modifying decisions for future periods.

Within a company, various motives underlie the aggregate planning processes. The company's general and financial management prefer to keep inventory levels at a minimum. Operations management prefers long production runs, with smooth production and workforce levels. Market management prefers large inventory levels, with the majority of the finished items available on demand to the customer. Satisfying these conflicting objectives will require overcoming the parochial interests of different department managers and fine-tuning a model's results to account for nonquantifiable factors.

Simple Mathematical Programming Methods for Solving the Aggregate Planning Problem

Basically, the methodologies that have been used in the solution of the aggregate production problem are of two classes: heuristic decision rules and mathematical-programming models. Before the various mathematical-programming models for the aggregate production planning problem are considered, a short discussion of the decision rules will be given.

The decision rules are basically of two types. The first of these involves the approximation of such decision rules by heuristically derived equations. The values of the rule parameters are obtained either by regression analysis on historical data or by a combination of simulation and trial-and-error methods using grid searches. The second type of solution methodology does not estimate the form of the decision rule equations but obtains the specific values of the decisions by searching the response surface formed by the criterion function.

The Transportation Method for Solving the Aggregate Production Planning Problem

The transportation method of solving the aggregate production planning problem was proposed by Bowman (1956). This formulation is simple and easy to understand. This model structure has as its objective the assignment of units of production to periods such that the total cost of production and inventory are minimized while satisfying demand levels within available production capacity constraints.

Bowman's model for aggregate production planning is demonstrated in the following case study developed and used regularly in the production management and operations research classes at Florida International University.

A Case on Production Planning. Sikan Manufacturing Company produces two major products, designated as A and B, in a facility used exclusively for these two products. In the past, significant increases in demand necessitated the use of overtime and outside subcontracting. An outside commitment has already been made for the upcoming quarter to subcontract a total of 50 units for products A and/or B. Because of union pressures, the company has agreed to limit outside subcontracting to a total of 30 units for each subsequent quarter. Detailed information is given in the table on the next page (data have been rounded to make computations easier).

TABLE 1

DATA FOR SIKAN CO.

Quarter	Available Capacity, Units			Demand, Units	
	Regular	Overtime	Subcontract	A	B
1st	130	40	50	60	50
2nd	100	60	30	110	120
3rd	120	70	30	70	130
4th	100	60	30	95	125
Initial inventory, units				10	10
Desirable ending 4th quarter inventory, units				15	25
Regular cost, $/unit				10	8
Overtime cost, $/unit				12	10
Subcontracting cost, $/unit				15	12
Cost to carry one unit in inventory for one quarter, $/unit and quarter				1	2*

*Bulky item

An annual production plan by quarter is needed that minimizes costs for the upcoming year.

This problem can be modeled in the classical transportation format as shown in table 2. The rows indicate quarter and type of production, and the columns denote type of product and quarter of consumption. Cell costs reflect production plus inventory cost per unit—for example, one unit of product B, produced in period 1 with overtime to satisfy the demand for period 4, will cost: $10 (production) + 3 quarters storage × $2 (inventory holding) = $16. Note that the portion of the table below the main diagonal is not feasible, since no backlogs are permitted. An arbitrarily high cost ($100) has been assigned for the last three quarters (columns) of row 1—subcontracting, to avoid violation of the outside commitment to subcontract the production of 50 units of A and/or B during the first quarter. Finally, the requirements for the first (last) quarter have been adjusted by subcontracting (adding) the corresponding starting (ending) inventory.

Starting with the least-cost-method solution (assign as many units as possible to cells in order of increasing costs—excluding zeros), the modified distribution method (MODI) produced, after four iterations, the optimal solution shown in table 2. The corresponding production plan, summarized for management use, is presented in table 3.

MODI reveals that the optimal solution is not unique. Examination of the shadow (dual) prices—not shown here—reveals that the most limiting (expensive) resource is regular production capacity, particularly in later quarters. For example, if an extra unit of regular capacity is added to quarter 4, the total optimal cost will be reduced by $5. This stresses the importance of shifting capacity from the most expensive subcontracting to the cheapest regular capacity, particularly during later periods. Similarly, lifting the subcontracting commitment in quarter 1 will save $3 per unit. This type of postoptimal analysis is very useful to management.

TABLE 2

TRANSPORTATION TABLEAU FOR SIKAN CO. PRODUCTION PLANNING
MODI OPTIMAL SOLUTION CIRCLED, TOTAL COST = $8,050

Produced in Quarter	Supply / Production	Q1 A	Q1 B	Q2 A	Q2 B	Q3 A	Q3 B	Q4 A	Q4 B	Slack, Units	Capacity, Units
1	Regular	10 (40)	8	11 (90)	10	12	12	13	14	0	130
1	Overtime	12	10	13	12	14	14	15 (40)	16	0	40
1	Subcontracted	15 (10)	12 (40)	100	100	100	100	100	100	100	50
2	Regular			10	8 (100)	11	10	12	12	0	100
2	Overtime			12 (20)	10 (20)	13	12	14 (20)	14	0	60
2	Subcontracted			15	12	16	14	17	16	30 / 0	30
3	Regular					10	8 (110)	11 (10)	10	0	120
3	Overtime					12 (70)	10	13	12	0	70
3	Subcontracted					15	12 (20)	16	14	10 / 0	30
4	Regular							10	8 (100)	0	100
4	Overtime							12 (40)	8 (20)	0	60
4	Subcontracted							15	12 (30)	0	30
	Requirements, Units	50	40	110	120	70	130	110	150	40	820 / 120

TABLE 3

PRODUCTION PLAN, SIKAN MANUFACTURING CO.

MODI SOLUTION SUMMARY

	Quarter	1 A	1 B	2 A	2 B	3 A	3 B	4 A	4 B
	Product	A	B	A	B	A	B	A	B
Production	Regular	130	—	—	100	10	110	—	100
Production	Overtime	40	—	40	20	70	—	40	20
Production	Subcontracted	10	40	—	—	—	20	—	30
Production	Total	180	40	40	120	80	130	40	150
Requirements		60	50	110	120	70	130	95	125
Inventory	Beginning	10	10	130	—	60	—	70	—
Inventory	Ending	130	—	60	—	70	—	15	25
Production cost*	Regular	$1,390	—	—	800	110	880	—	800
Production cost*	Overtime	$ 600	—	520	200	840	—	480	200
Production cost*	Subcontracted	$ 150	480	—	—	—	240	—	360
Production cost*	Sub-total	$2,140	480	520	1,000	950	1,120	480	1,360
Total Cost		$8,050							

*The production costs include inventory holding costs of $1/unit-quarter for product A and $2/unit-quarter for product B.

The transportation approach to solving production planning problems is simple to understand and straightforward. However, it becomes quite involved if many products and time periods are in the planning horizon; and, it cannot accommodate other types of restrictions as the linear-programming method does. For instance, it does not provide for interdependencies over time or between products, or other resource constraints; nor does it provide for penalty cost for lost sales. Backordering, however, can be handled by adding the backorder cost to the production cost per unit in the lower part of the table.

Sadleir (1970) has used the transportation model in a multiplant footwear company to determine where (but not when) to produce each style. Then to address the question of when to produce, heuristic procedures were employed to smooth this production plan over the time horizon. In practice, implementing the transportation model results may be precluded because of the operating manager's short-term objectives, such as maximizing existing company resources and satisfying multiple conflicting objectives (Stainton 1977).

Linear Programming Approaches to Aggregate Production Planning

Numerous linear-programming formulations of aggregate production planning have been developed. Compared with the Bowman transportation problem formulation the linear-programming formulations are able to include the production level change costs, as well as shortage costs. Generally, the objective function that is used is concerned with minimizing total cost, which is represented by a linear function of payroll (regular or overtime), hiring, layoff, setup, and inventory costs. These costs are assumed to be linear or, sometimes, quadratic. The early Haussmann-Hess (1960) LP model considered quadratic hiring/layoff, overtime, and shortage costs of the Holt-Modigliani-Simon type. These costs were linearized by introducing a positive and a negative component in each. This was in fact a linear goal-programming approach, although this concept had not yet been introduced.

The model's decision variables are expressed in terms of production rates, workforce, and inventory levels. Constraints of typical LP models include (1) production capacity (regular and overtime) in each period, (2) the amount of production capacity that can be added or removed, (3) restrictions on inventories, and (4) restrictions to ensure that all demands are met. Standard units are required to achieve comparability of inputs and outputs in aggregation. Typical of such standards are the man-hours required.

Wide varieties of linear-programming models have been developed and tailored to suit the particular aggregate production planning problems of organizations. Typically, these linear-programming models have the following set of comparable characteristics:

1. Demand is unknown but deterministic
2. The cost of regular-time production is piecewise linear
3. The cost changes in production rate are usually taken to be piecewise linear
4. Production and inventory levels are bounded
5. Cost of inventory can vary from period to period
6. Backorders or lost sales are not always permitted.

These model structures allow for the direct incorporation of operational and economic constraints, as well as for the inclusion of many product categories. For a detailed treatment of linear and general cost models for production planning, see Johnson and Montgomery (1977) and the paper by Bitran and Hax in this volume.

An important benefit of the linear-programming model is the ability to perform sensitivity analyses using parametric programming techniques. These sensitivity analyses allow for the evaluation of the effects in changes in cost parameters and resource or demand levels and for measuring the effects of uncertain conditions. Furthermore, with the extension of integer variables, a more realistically set-up cost structure can easily be added. Finally, the linear-programming model structure allows for the use of commercial linear programming packages that readily handle large amounts of often-changing data and can solve large realistic problems. Moreover, results can be output in a usable and nontechnical format and provide simple sensitivity analysis through the simplex dual solution—a standard feature of many LP packages.

REFERENCES

Bowman, E. H. 1956. Production scheduling by the transportation method of linear programming. *Operations Research* 4(1).

Haussmann, F., and S. W. Hess. 1960. A linear programming approach to production and employment scheduling. *Management Technology* (1): 45-51.

Johnson, L. A., and D. C. Montgomery. 1977. *Operations research in production planning, scheduling and inventory control*. New York: Wiley.

Sadleir, C. D. 1970. Use of the transportation method of linear programming in production planning: A case study. *Operational Research Quarterly* 21:393-402.

Stainton, R. S. 1977. Production scheduling with multiple criteria objectives. *Operational Research Quarterly* 28:285-292.

MODELS AND METHODS OF PRODUCTION PLANNING
AND SCHEDULING

"The Role of Mathematical Programming in Production Planning," by Gabriel R. Bitran and Arnoldo C. Hax, presents an extensive account of developments and solutions of mathematical-programming models in production planning. First it presents linear cost models with fixed and variable workforces along with their advantages and disadvantages. The authors then survey uncapacitated and capacitated lot-size models and efficient linear-programming and heuristic procedures for solving these problems. Nonlinear, heuristic, search, and simulation methods are briefly stated for copying with nonlinear or discontinuous cost behavior.

The authors propose a top-down three-level hierarchical production planning system: aggregate annual planning by product type; shorter-period disaggregation to families, minimizing setup costs; and further allocation to individual items that maximize the length of production runs. The first-level model is a linear-programming model that minimizes the aggregate production, inventory, and labor costs. The family disaggregation (nonlinear) model and the item disaggregation (knapsack) subproblem are solved optimally by using special algorithms developed by the authors earlier. Mechanisms are also examined for linking these subproblems, to avoid introducing potential infeasibilities by the rolling-horizon concept and to produce good, not necessarily optimal, final results.

The authors performed a series of simulated experiments, with data from a tire manufacturer, to examine the effects of forecast errors, setup costs, capacity, and planning horizon. These experiments also provide insights on the deviation of production plans obtained using the proposed hierarchical system from the optimal results to a few small problems. It appears that this hierarchical planning system produces quite good results when high setup costs are not present.

"Effective Shift Allocation in Multiproduct Lines: A Mixed Programming Approach," by Stelios H. Zanakis and Kenneth D. Lawrence, presents a model for effectively allocating production shifts and products to a set of production lines under various resource restrictions. The concept of effectiveness is encountered when the profit motive is removed from the decision-making process (for example, a marketing department may aim at satisfying all customer demands as much as possible; or, in military operations, particular emphasis is placed on maximizing system effectiveness at any cost).

The basic scenario underlying the model structure deals with allocating scarce resources of manpower, material, and money to several products. Each product can be made at several production lines, each having different production and setup costs. An aggregate production plan that will assure a maximum level of system effectiveness in fulfilling given requirements—that is, a maximum ratio of units available to units required—is sought for a certain time period.

Of two mixed-integer programming models developed for this problem, the first seeks to satisfy as large a percentage of demand as possible for the least-effective item, given the existing level of available production resources. This model structure contains a constraint set that:

1. Limits the measure of system effectiveness to 100 percent
2. Ensures that for each line the number of production shifts does not exceed the maximum available
3. Ensures that the availability of all resources is obeyed
4. Prevents total costs from exceeding the available budget
5. Imposes a fixed-charge setup cost only to non-idle lines, using a set of 0-1 inequalities.

The second model structure is similar to the first, except it minimizes the total deviation from the goal of perfect satisfaction of all demands. The authors use an example to illustrate those models and, finally, discuss briefly multiple-goal extensions of the model.

"The Assignment of Men to Machines: An Application of Branch-and-Bound," by J. G. Miller and W. L. Berry, discusses the use of semi-automatic equipment that requires partial operator attendance in machine shops and textile mills. After which jobs are to be performed in each machine has been decided, the next problem, which this paper addresses, is determining the number of operators required, their machine assignments, and the sequence of servicing each machine.

The authors present a nonlinear 0-1 programming model that minimizes the total machine- and labor-idleness cost. Constraints include assigning one operator per machine and production-volume limitations at each machine.

The complexity of the problem necessitated several simplifying assumptions: (1) No differences exist in productivity or idle cost between operators, (2) idle time on all machines costs the same, (3) transportation time between machines is negligible, and (4) machines are serviced independently in a cyclic, not segmented, sequence.

A cleverly designed branch-and-bound algorithm solves this difficult optimization problem. Solution times increase exponentially to prohibitive amounts for problems with more than twenty machines. This computational burden, along with the foregoing simplifying assumptions, restricts the practical value of this model to small production facilities. Nevertheless, the model and algorithmic developments have great educational value and could provide a vehicle for testing the accuracy of future heuristic optimization procedures for solving large problems of this type that arise in industry.

"Production and Sales Planning with Limited Shared Tooling at the Key Operation," by G. D. Brown, A. M. Geoffrion, and G. H. Bradley, examines the problem that arises in the manufacturing of many injection-molded, extruded, cast, pressed, or stamped plastic or metal products. A dominant and expensive facility must be shared by many products, each calling for a specific tool and related machine type.

For each product and time period, the manufacturer must (a) determine the quantity to produce, sell, and stock and (b) make a tool/machine assignment. The goals are (1) to maximize total profits without exceeding tool and machine hours available or violating machine/tool compatability restrictions, (2) achieve a desirable ending inventory without backlogging, and (3) satisfy a minimum/maximum range of forecasted sales.

This paper presents a mixed-integer programming formulation and outlines an efficient solution procedure. It employs Lagrangian relaxation to generate lower bounds on the optimum value of a minimum-cost network flow subproblem. This produces several independent transportation, dynamic single-item lot-size subproblems, which are solved by using a generalized network (transshipment) code.

The authors present a practical application involving 26,000 constraints and 40,000 continuous and 12,000 integer variables. Solutions within 2 percent of the optimum are obtained routinely in about 3 minutes of computer time.

The technically sound, innovative methodology, coupled with appropriate report-writing summaries, resulted in a beneficial system that is regularly used by R. & G. Sloane Manufacturing Company.

"A Linear Programming Model for Integrating the Annual Planning of Production and Marketing," by T. A. J. Nicholson and R. D. Pullen, presents a linear-programming model for determining (1) how much of each product should be manufactured at each of several factories and for what market, (2) the product price and advertising expenditures, and (3) the need to use overtime at each plant. Thus, the model, referred to as MAPLE (marketing and product line evaluation), aims to consider decisions on production, marketing, and distribution simultaneously. The intention is not only to indicate the best plan that could be adopted but also to determine its feasibility and the areas of most fruitful future investigation.

The objective function is the total variable profit, which is to be maximized, subject to a variety of constraints. The constraints include upper and lower limits on the production and sales levels for each product line at each factory; capacity constraints on materials, supplies, base and extra production process, and distribution links; and, finally, advertising and working-capital budget limits. Sensitivity analysis and a variety of output reports enhance the value of this system for management use.

Far from just presenting a simple model with a small-scale example problem, this paper highlights an essential part of business planning—that of integrating production planning with distribution and marketing analysis. The relative inflexible data input requirements, however, may require considerable alterations to fit other situations.

"The Application of a Product Mix Linear Programming Model in Corporate Policy Making," by Jack Byrd Jr. and L. Ted Moore, presents an actual application of linear programming to analyze the coordinated production and marketing policies of a company. The model incorporates features of product mix, sequencing, and blending into a single structure. The paper is based upon the authors' consulting work for a medium-sized American corporation.

To begin modeling work, a prototype model of a hypothetical five-product plant, operating for a five-day week, was developed. This prototype model served as a vehicle for discussing the eventual plant model structure, its data requirements, and the types of information that the model would provide. This prototype model served not only as a device to convince management of the value of this planning tool, but also as a device for more quickly developing a final full-scale model.

The overall model structure consists of an objective function to maximize profit, subject to constraint sets for the following purposes:

1. Storing of raw materials
2. Material supplies needed for products
3. Blending equations
4. Materials used for products
5. Mixing equations
6. Packaging equations
7. Demand for products.

The model was run for a series of different scenarios of product demand and production capacities. The results of these model studies were used as a basis for determining policies, for packaging, and for production capacity. All of these policies were directed toward the goal of maximizing profit. Basically, this model serves as a planning and decision-making aid to management for evaluating proposed management policies with regard to such areas as pricing, inventory, and production.

The Role of Mathematical Programming in Production Planning

Gabriel R. Bitran and Arnoldo C. Hax
Massachusetts Institute of Technology[1]

INTRODUCTION

Production planning is concerned with determining production, inventory, and workforce levels to meet fluctuating demand requirements. Normally, the physical resources of the company are assumed to be fixed during the planning horizon of interest, and the planning effort is oriented toward the best utilization of those resources, given the external demand requirements. A problem usually arises because the times and quantities imposed by the demand requirements seldom coincide with the times and quantities that make for efficient use of the company's resources. Whenever the conditions affecting the production process are not stable in time (because of changes in demand, cost components, or capacity availability), production should be planned in an aggregate way to obtain effective resource utilization. The time horizon of this planning activity is dictated by the nature of the dynamic variations; for example, if demand seasonalities are present, a full seasonal cycle should be incorporated into the planning horizon. Commonly, the time horizon varies from six to eighteen months, with twelve months being a suitable figure for most planning systems.

Because it is impossible to consider every fine detail associated with the production process and still maintain such a long planning horizon, it is usually mandatory to aggregate the information being processed. This aggregation can take place by consolidating similar items into product families, different machines into machine centers, different labor skills into labor centers, and individual customers into market regions. The type of aggregation to be performed is suggested by the nature of the planning systems to be used and by the technical and managerial characteristics of the production activities. Aggregation forces the use of a consistent set of measurement units. It is common to express aggregate demand in production hours.

Once the aggregate plan has been generated, constraints are imposed in the detailed production scheduling technique, which decides the specific quantities to be produced of each individual item. These constraints normally specify production rates or total amounts to be produced per month for a given family. In addition, crew sizes, levels of machine utilization, and amount of overtime to be used are determined.

When demand requirements do not change with time, and costs and prices are also stable, it may be feasible to bypass entirely the aggregate planning process, provided the resources of the company are balanced enough to absorb the constant requirements. However, when these conditions are not met, serious inefficiencies might result from attempting to plan production by responding only to immediate requirements and ignoring the future consequences of present decisions. To understand this point, consider what happens when an order-point/order-quantity inventory control system that treats every item in isolation is applied in the presence of strong demand seasonalities. First, at the beginning of the peak season, demand starts rapidly increasing and a large number of items simultaneously trigger the order point, demanding production runs of the amount specified by the order quantities. Being unable to satisfy all these orders and still maintain an adequate service level, management may react by reducing the production-run lengths, creating multiple changeovers of small quantities. This, in turn, reduces the overall productivity (because of the high percentage of idle machine time created by the large number of changeovers), increases costs, and causes customer service levels to deteriorate. Second, items at the end of the season are produced in normal order quantities (typically large); thus, inventory that is inactive until the beginning of the next season or that must be liquidated at salvage values is created. An effective aggregate capacity planning system will prevent such inefficiencies.

1. Invited review paper.

Ways to Absorb Demand Fluctuations

There are several methods that managers can use to absorb changing demand patterns. These ways can be combined to create a large number of alternative production plans.

1. Management can change the size of the workforce by hiring and laying off, allowing changes in the production rate. Excessive use of these practices, however, can create severe labor problems.
2. While maintaining a uniform regular workforce, management can vary the production rate by introducing overtime and/or idle time or relying on outside subcontracting.
3. While maintaining a uniform production rate, management can anticipate future demand by accumulating seasonal inventories. The tradeoff between the cost incurred in changing production rates and holding seasonal inventories is the basic question to be resolved in most practical situations.
4. Management can also resort to planned backlogs whenever customers may accept delays in filling their orders.
5. An alternative that must be resolved at a higher planning level is the development of complementary product lines with demand patterns that are counterseasonal to those of the existing products. This alternative is very effective in producing a more even utilization of the company's resources, but it does not eliminate the need for aggregate planning.

Costs Relevant to Aggregate Production Planning

Relevant costs can be categorized as:

1. Basic production costs—These are the fixed and variable costs incurred in producing a given product type in a given time period. Included are direct and indirect labor costs and regular and overtime compensations.
2. Costs associated with changes in the production rate—Typical costs in this category are those involved in hiring, training, and laying off personnel.
3. Inventory holding costs—A major component of the inventory holding cost is the cost of capital tied up in inventory. Other components are storing, insurance, taxes, spoilage, and obsolescence.
4. Backlogging costs—Usually, these costs are hard to measure and include the costs of expediting, loss of customer good will, and loss of sales revenues from backlogging.

McGarrah (1963) and Holt et al. (1960) provide good discussion on the nature and structure of these cost elements.

The Role of Models in Aggregate Production Planning

Models have played an important role in supporting management decisions in aggregate production planning. Models are of great value in helping managers to:

1. Quantify and use the intangibles that are always present in the background of their thinking but that are incorporated only vaguely and sporadically in scheduling decisions.
2. Make routine the comprehensive consideration of all factors relevant to scheduling decisions, thereby inhibiting judgments based on incomplete, obvious, or easily handled criteria.
3. Fit each scheduling decision into its appropriate place in the historical series of decisions and, through the feedback mechanism incorporated in the decision rules, automatically correct for prior forecasting errors.
4. Free executives from routine decision-making activities, giving them greater freedom and opportunity for dealing with extraordinary situations.

To describe the different types of models that can be used in supporting aggregate planning decisions, it is useful to classify the models according to the assumptions they make about the structure of the cost components. In the following sections, we will extensively analyze the linear-cost and fixed-cost models that play an important role in practical applications. We conclude this paper discussing an integrated production planning system.

LINEAR-COST MODELS

Some of the first models proposed to guide aggregate planning decisions assume linearity in the cost behavior of the decision variables. These kinds of models are still popular because of the computational conveniences associated with linear programming (LP). Moreover, these models are less restrictive than they first appear, because nonlinear convex costs functions can be approximated to any degree of accuracy by piecewise linear segments.

Fixed-Workforce Model

First, consider the case in which the workforce is fixed. Hiring and firing to absorb demand fluctuations during the planning horizon are disallowed. Production rates can be fluctuated only by using overtime from the regular workforce.

The following notation is used to describe the model in mathematical terms.

Parameters:

v_{it} = unit production cost for product i in period t
c_{it} = inventory carrying cost per unit of product i in period t
r_t = cost per man-hour of regular labor in period t
o_t = cost per man-hour in overtime labor in period t
d_{it} = demand for product i in period t
k_i = man-hours required to produce one unit of product i
$(rm)_t$ = total man-hours of regular labor available in period t
$(om)_t$ = total man-hours of overtime labor available in period t
I_{io} = initial inventory level for product i
W_o = initial regular workforce level
T = time horizon, in periods
N = total number or products.

Decision Variables:

X_{it} = units of product i to be produced in period t
I_{it} = units of product i to be left over as inventory at the end of period t
W_t = man-hours of regular labor used during period t
O_t = man-hours of overtime labor used during period t.

A simple version of the fixed-workforce linear-cost model is:

$$\text{Minimize } z = \sum_{i=1}^{N} \sum_{t=1}^{T} (v_{it}X_{it} + c_{it}I_{it}) + \sum_{t=1}^{T} (r_tW_t + o_tO_t) \tag{1}$$

subject to

$$X_{it} + I_{i,t-1} - I_{it} = d_{it}, \quad t = 1, \ldots, T; \, i = 1, \ldots, N \tag{2}$$

$$\sum_{i=1}^{N} k_iX_{it} - W_t - O_t = 0, \, t = 1, \ldots, T \tag{3}$$

$$0 \leq W_t \leq (rm)_t, \quad t = 1, \ldots, T \tag{4}$$

$$0 \leq O_t \leq (om)_t, \quad t = 1, \ldots, T \tag{5}$$

$$X_{it}, I_{it} \leq 0. \quad i = 1, \ldots, N; \, t = 1, \ldots, T \tag{6}$$

The objective function (1) expresses the minimization of variable production inventory and regular and overtime labor costs. If the marginal production costs v_{it} are invariant over time, the terms $v_{it}X_{it}$ do not need to be included in the objective function (since total production is fixed). Similarly, if the payroll of regular workforce W_t constitutes a fixed commitment, the terms r_tW_t should be deleted from (1).

Constraints (2) represent the typical production-inventory balance equation. Notice that (2) and (6) imply that no backordering is allowed. The next model will show how backorders can be incorporated. Moreover, (2) assumes a deterministic demand d_{it} for every item in every time period. One way to allow for uncertainties in the demand forecast is to specify a lower bound for the ending inventory at each period: $I_{it} \geq ss_{it}$, where ss_{it} is the safety stock associated with item i in period t.[2]

Constraints (3) define the total manpower to be used at every period. This model formulation assumes that manpower availability is the only constraining resource of the production process. Expanding the number of resources being considered is trivial, provided that linearity assumptions are maintained.

Constraints (4) and (5) pose lower and upper bounds on the use of regular and overtime man-hours in every time period.

We already have indicated how constraints (6) could be changed to incorporate safety stocks. Bear in mind that if no terminal conditions are imposed on the inventories at the end of the planning horizon, the model will drive them to zero—that is, it will make $I_{iT} = 0$ for all i. If total depletion of inventories is undesirable, a target inventory constraint should be added to the model. An additional constraint should be attached if there are storage requirements that cannot be exceeded; for example, the constraint

$$\sum_{i=1}^{N} I_{it} \leq (sc)_t, \quad t = 1, \ldots, T$$

implies that the total inventory at each period cannot be greater than the storage capacity $(sc)_t$.

When it is necessary to assign products to different work centers with limited capacities, the decision variables are redefined to identify those decisions explicitly. For example, X_{ict} may denote the amount of product i produced at working center c during period t. Carrying out the resulting transformation in the overall model is straightforward.

2. The magnitude of the safety stocks depends on the quality of the demand forecasts and the level of customer service to be provided. For a good discussion of how to compute safety stocks, see Brown (1967).

Even the very simple model described by expressions (1) through (6) could present enormous computational difficulties if the individual items to be scheduled are not grouped in broad product categories. If constraints (4), (5), and (6), which merely represent upper and lower bounds for the decision variables, are ignored, the model consists of $Tx(N + 1)$ effective constraints. With complex production situations, the total number of individual items N may be several thousands. For example, if the planning model has 12 time periods and 15,000 items, the model would have about 180,000 constraints, exceeding the capabilities of a regular LP code.

In most practical applications, however, planning the allocations of the production resources at this level of detail would not be functional. First, a detailed scheduling program should take into account a large number of technological and marketing considerations that cannot be included in the overall model, because of their highly qualitative nature. Second, as expressed before, many of the planning issues to be resolved with the model deal with broad allocations of resources, and excessively detailed information will complicate rather than simplify the decision-making process. Third, aggregate forecasts are more accurate than detailed forecasts.

Common practice, therefore, is to aggregate items in family types. The criteria for aggregation are evident from the model structure: members of a single family type should share similar demand patterns d_{it}, have similar cost characteristics v_{it}, c_{it}, r_t, o_t, and should require similar unit production time k_i. Once the aggregate planning decisions have been made, these decisions impose constraints that must be observed when performing detailed item scheduling (see later discussion, "A Hierarchical Planning System").

Notice that this model, as well as any other planning model, requires definition of a planning horizon T and partitioning this time horizon into multiple time periods. Although it might be assumed that this partitioning results in T equally spaced time periods, this need not be so. Many operational planning systems are better designed if this partitioning generates uneven time periods, so that the more recent time periods carry more detailed information. Because of the uncertain environment in which this planning effort is conducted, only the first time period results are usually implemented. At the end of every time period new information, which is used to update the model and recompute the next time period plans, becomes available.

Broad technological, institutional, marketing, financial, and organizational constraints can also be included in the model formulation. This flexibility, characteristic of the LP approach to problem solving, has made this type of model very useful and popular.

A simple version of the fixed-workforce LP model, having a transportation problem structure, was first proposed by Bowman (1956).

Variable-Workforce Model

Whenever changing the workforce during the planning horizon is feasible to counteract demand fluctuations, the composition of the workforce becomes a decision variable whose values can change by hiring and firing personnel. Therefore, the corresponding hiring and firing costs should be part of the objective function. In addition, the model allows for shortages to be included; thus, a backordering cost is part of the formulation. The model decision variables are:

$$X_{it} = \text{units of product } i \text{ to be purchased at period } t$$
$$W_t = \text{man-hours of regular workforce at period } t$$
$$O_t = \text{man-hours of overtime workforce at period } t$$
$$H_t = \text{man-hours of regular workforce hired at period } t$$
$$F_t = \text{man-hours of regular workforce fired at period } t$$
$$I_{it}^+ = \text{units of ending inventory for product } i \text{ at period } t$$
$$I_{it}^- = \text{units backordered for product } i \text{ at end of period } t.$$

Using this notation with that introduced in the previous model, the cost incurred during period t includes the following components:

$$
\begin{aligned}
v_{it}\,X_{it} &= \text{variable manufacturing cost} \\
c_{it}\,I_{it}^{+} &= \text{inventory holding cost} \\
b_{it}\,I_{it}^{-} &= \text{backorder cost} \\
r_t\,W_t &= \text{regular payroll cost} \\
o_t\,O_t &= \text{overtime payroll cost} \\
h_t\,H_t &= \text{hiring cost} \\
f_t\,F_t &= \text{firing cost.}
\end{aligned}
$$

A simple version of the variable workforce model can be formulated as:

$$
\text{Minimize } z = \sum_{i=1}^{N} \sum_{t=1}^{T} (v_{it}\,X_{it} + c_{it}\,I_{it}^{+} + b_{it}\,I_{it}^{-})
$$

$$
+ \sum_{t=1}^{T} (r_t W_t + o_t O_t + h_t H_t + f_t F_t)
$$

subject to

$$
X_{it} + I_{i,t-1}^{+} - I_{i,t-1}^{-} - I_{it}^{+} + I_{it}^{-} = d_{it}, \qquad i = 1, \ldots, N; \; t = 1, \ldots, T \tag{7}
$$

$$
\sum_{i=1}^{N} k_i X_{it} - W_t - O_t \leq 0, \qquad t = 1, \ldots, T \tag{8}
$$

$$
W_t - W_{t-1} - H_t + F_t = 0, \qquad t = 1, \ldots, T \tag{9}
$$

$$
-pW_t + O_t \leq 0, \qquad t = 1, \ldots, T \tag{10}
$$

$$
X_{it}, I_{it}^{+}, I_{it}^{-} \geq 0, \qquad i = 1, \ldots, N; \; t = 1, \ldots, T
$$

$$
W_t, O_t, P_t, H_t, F_t \geq 0, \qquad t = 1, \ldots, T.
$$

Constraints (7) represent the production-inventory balance equation. Notice that this is equivalent to the old balance equation

$$
X_{it} + I_{i,t-1} - I_{it} = d_{it},
$$

except that now

$$
I_{i,t-1} = I_{i,t-1}^{+} - I_{i,t-1}^{-}
$$

and

$$
I_{it} = I_{it}^{+} - I_{it}^{-}.
$$

In the present model, the ending inventory I_{it} can be positive ($I_{it}^+ > 0$ indicates that stock remains at the end of the period) or negative ($I_{it}^- > 0$ indicates an accumulation of backorders at the end of the period). Since a cost is attached to both I_{it}^+ and I_{it}^-, those variables never will be positive simultaneously.

Constraints (8) limit production to available manpower. Constraints (9) define the change in the workforce size during period t: $W_t - W_{t-1} = H_t - F_t$. Labor has been added whenever $H_t > 0$ or has been subtracted whenever $F_t > 0$. Again, since there is a cost attached to both hiring and firing, H_t and F_t will never simultaneously have positive values in a given period.

Constraints (10) impose an upper bound on the total overtime available in period t as a function of the regular workforce size:

$$O_t \leq pW_t$$

where

p = overtime allowed to the regular workforce, percent.

Many of the comments made in the fixed work model regarding ways to expand or simplify the models and to aggregate items in item families are applicable here and are not repeated.

The first of this type of model was proposed by Haussmann and Hess (1960). Alternative approaches have been suggested, particularly those by Von Lanzenauer (1970) and O'Malley, Elmaghraby, and Jeske (1966).

Lippman, et al. (1967) have analyzed the form of the optimal policies for a single product problem assuming convex production costs, V-shaped manpower fluctuation costs, and increasing holding costs. Lippman, Rolfe, and Wagner (1967) provide an efficient algorithm to solve the special case in which all the cost functions are linear and demand requirements are monotone decreasing or increasing. The algorithm is an iterative procedure that starts by guessing the value of W_T, the regular manpower at the end of the planning horizon. It provides, next, an optimum policy for this value of W_T and checks this policy against an optimality test. If an improvement is possible, the algorithm yields a better value of W_T and the process is repeated. Convergence is guaranteed in a finite number of iterations.

Whenever costs are linear and demand requirements are nondecreasing, there exists an optimum policy such that

$$W_{t+1} \geq w_t, \qquad\qquad t = 1, \ldots, T - 1$$

$$O_{t+1} \geq O_t, \qquad\qquad t = 1, \ldots, T - 1$$

$$\frac{O_{t+1}}{W_{T+1}} \geq \frac{O_t}{W_t} \qquad\qquad t = 1, \ldots, T - 1$$

$$(W_T - W_t)O_t = 0, \qquad\qquad t = 1, \ldots, T.$$

This result is used throughout the computational process. Yuan (1967) extended this approach for a multiproduct problem.

In an early work, Hoffman and Jacobs (1954) and Antosiewicz and Hoffman (1954) considered a linear cost model for a single product, permitting changes in the production rate to be represented in the objective function. They analyzed the qualitative properties of the optimum solution and proposed simple procedures to compute that solution when demand requirements are monotone increasing. This work was extended by Johnson and Dantzig (1955).

27

Linear-programming models can be expanded easily to cover a production process having several stages. A comprehensive discussion of multistage LP models, including multiple routings, multiple sources, product mix decisions, and multiple production and distribution decisions, is given by Johnson and Montgomery (1974).

Advantages and Disadvantages of Linear-Cost Models

The overwhelming advantage of linear cost models is that they generate LPs that can be solved by readily available and efficient computer codes. Linear programs permit models with a large number of decision variables and constraints to be solved expediently and cheaply. In addition, LP lends itself very well to the performance of parametric and sensitivity analyses; this feature can be helpful in making aggregate planning decisions. The shadow-cost information can help in identifying opportunities for capacity expansions, market penetration strategies, product introductions, etc.

As indicated before, the linearity assumptions implicit in these models are less restrictive than they appear. First, cost structures might behave linearly within the range of interest of the decision variables under consideration. Second, general convex separable functions can be treated with piecewise linear approximation. Moreover, with some ingenuity, certain functions that at first seem to present nonlinear characteristics can be linearized, as indicated by Haussmann and Hess (1960) and Von Lanzenauer (1970).

The most serious disadvantage of LP models is their failure to deal with demand uncertainties in any explicit way. In some situations, this could constitute a serious drawback. However, Dzielinski, Baker, and Manne (1963) have reported favorable experiences using LP models in fairly uncertain and dynamic environments.

LOT-SIZE (FIXED COST) MODELS

Whenever the manufacturing process is characterized by batch-type (as opposed to continuous) operations production, a cost is incurred when setting up the production facilities for a given run. Including the setup cost in the planning process creates many problems. First, every item that generates a setup (or a family of items sharing a common setup) must be identified and treated independently, expanding the number of variables and constraints so that the dimensions of the model generate a large-scale system that can be handled only by using special computational techniques. Second, including setup costs produces a lot-size indivisibility, since each given batch must be run incurring a single setup, introducing integer variables in the model formulation. Finally, setup costs give rise to fixed cost components in the objective function. Moreover, the downtime characteristic of every setup operation introduces additional nonlinearities into the constraint set. The resulting large-scale, integer, non-linear programming (NLP) model is hard to resolve computationally. Review of some of the more effective approaches that have been suggested to solve this problem follows.

The Uncapacitated Lot-Size Model

The standard economic lot-size formula, also known as the economic order quantity (EOQ) formula,[3] determines the production amount for an individual item when setup and inventory holding costs identify the cost trade-offs. This formula does not account for any existing interaction between the individual items to be scheduled for production. In particular, it ignores the capacity limitations that impose some of the more critical constraints for production planning.

---

3. For a discussion on the various types of EOQ formulae that have been proposed in the literature, see Magee and Boodman (1967, chapter 14).

Moreover, the EOQ formula assumes the demand to be constant and known over the planning horizon. When the demand is known but changing during the various time periods of the planning horizon, the EOQ lot size can provide misleading recommendations. Wagner and Whitin (1958) suggested a dynamic programming (DP) model for a dynamic version of the economic lot size. Their approach is reviewed here because it plays an important role in the capacitated lot-size models to be discussed later.

A simplified version of the uncapacitated lot-size problem can be described as:

$$\text{Minimize } z = \sum_{t=1}^{T} [s_t(X_t) + c_t I_t]$$

subject to

$$X_t + I_{t-1} - I_t = d_t, \qquad t = 1, \ldots, T$$
$$X_t \geq 0, \qquad t = 1, \ldots, T$$
$$I_t \geq 0, \qquad t = 1, \ldots, T$$

where

$$\delta(X_t) = \begin{cases} 0 \text{ if } X_t = 0 \\ 1 \text{ if } X_t > 0. \end{cases}$$

And as before:

X_t = amount to be produced in period t
I_t = ending inventory at period t
s_t = setup cost in period t
c_t = inventory holding cost in period t
d_t = demand during period t.[4]

Notice that variable production costs are not included in the objective function since they are assumed to be constant throughout the planning horizon. Nor are backorders allowed. A DP solution to this problem is straightforward. The functional equation that represents the minimum-cost policy (including only setup and inventory holding costs) for periods t through $T-1$ is

$$f_t(I_{t-1}) = \min_{\substack{X_t \geq 0 \\ X_t + I_{t-1} \geq d_t}} [s_t \delta(X_t) + c_t(X_t + I_{t-1} - d_t) + f_{t+1}(X_t + I_{t-1} - d_t)]$$

In the last period T, the functional equation becomes

$$f_T(I_{T-1}) = \min_{\substack{X_T \geq 0 \\ X_T + I_{T-1} = d_T}} [s_T \delta(X_T)]$$

In this DP formulation, we have assumed that no inventory is to be left at the end of the planning horizon: $I_T = 0$. This assumption can be relaxed easily. A backward-induction process can be applied to compute the optimum lot sizes during the planning horizon. However, this is not the most effective approach to the problem.

---

4. If the initial inventory is not zero, subtract it from the demand requirements in the first period to obtain an adjusted requirement for that period. If the initial inventory exceeds the first-period demand, continue with this adjustment process until the inventory is used up and then apply the proposed algorithm.

In getting an efficient algorithm for this problem, Wagner and Whitin (1958) proved four important results about the structure of the optimal policy, assuming no initial inventory: $I_o = 0$.

(1) There is always an optimal policy such that

$$I_{t-1}X_t = 0 \qquad \text{for } t = 1, \ldots, T.$$

This statement means that costs are never reduced by having incoming stock and producing in the same time.

(2) It is enough to consider optimal policies such that for all t:

$$X_t = 0$$

or

$$X_t = \sum_{j=t}^{k} d_j$$

for some k, $1 \leq k \leq T$.

This implies that, at any given period, production either is zero or equals the sum of consecutive demands for some number of periods into the future. With a time horizon of T time periods, the total number of production sequences to be considered is 2^{T-1}. These have been called the dominant production sequences. A DP approach requires the analysis of only $T(T+1)/2$ of these sequences. This number can be reduced further by applying the following result:

(3) Whenever it is optimal to make $I_t = 0$ for any given period t, periods 1 through t and $t + 1$ through T can be considered alone.

It is advantageous at this point to reformulate the DP approach as a forward process.

The functional equation that characterizes the forward-induction procedure can be specified by letting $f(t)$ be the minimal-cost program from period 1 to t; then:

$$f(t) = \min\left\{ \min_{1 \leq j < t} \left[s_j + \sum_{h=j}^{t-1} \sum_{k=h+1}^{t} c_h d_k + f(j-1) \right], s_t + f(t-1) \right\} \qquad (11)$$

where

$$f(1) = s_1$$
$$f(0) = 0$$
$$s_j = \text{setup cost for period } j$$

$$\sum_{h=j}^{t-1} \sum_{k=h+1}^{t} c_h d_k = \text{inventory carrying cost from period } j + 1 \text{ to } t.$$

Numerical examples illustrating how to carry out the forward-induction procedures are provided in the original reference of Wagner and Whitin (1958).

The last, and most important, result of Wagner and Whitin is:

(4) Planning Horizon Theorem—If at period t^* the minimum of (11) occurs for $j = t^{**} \leq t^*$, then in periods $t > t^*$ it is sufficient to consider only $t^{**} \leq j \leq t$. In particular, if $t^* = t^{**}$, it is sufficient to consider programs such that $X_{t^*} > 0$.

If a forward DP is conducted, these results allow reducing the original problem into a succession of smaller problems by identifying periods in which the production orders are positive or, alternatively, in which the inventory levels are zero.

Wagner (1960) expanded this approach to include changing purchasing or manufacturing costs during the multiperiod planning horizon. Eppen, Gould, and Pashigian (1969) and Zabel (1964) made significant extensions to the planning horizon theorem. Zangwill (1969) showed how to treat backordering costs and provided a network representation of the problem. Another approach for the inclusion of backorders was suggested by Elmaghraby and Bawle (1972), who analyzed the uncapacitated problem when ordering must be in batches greater than one, with and without setup costs.

Subsequent sections will show how the concept of dominant production sequences has been greatly exploited for computational purposes when dealing with capacitated lot-size models.

The Capacitated Lot-Size Model

The capacitated lot-size model deals with a multi-item production planning problem under changing demand requirements during the multiperiod planning horizon. The items are competing for limited capacity, and setup costs become an important element of the total cost to be minimized.

As before, we analyze first the fixed-workforce problem when only overtime can be added to expand the manpower availability; subsequently, we examine the variable-workforce problem in which hiring and firing to change the total production rate are permitted.

Using the notation presented in the previous pages, a simple version of the fixed-workforce/capacitated fixed-cost model can be expressed as:

$$\text{Minimize } z = \sum_{i=1}^{N} \sum_{t=1}^{T} [s_{it}\delta(X_{it}) + v_{it}X_{it} + c_{it}I_{it}] + \sum_{t=1}^{T} (r_t W_t + o_t O_t) \qquad (12)$$

subject to

$$X_{it} + I_{i,t-1} - I_{it} = d_{it}, \qquad t = 1, \ldots, T, \ i = 1, \ldots, N$$

$$\sum_{i=1}^{N} [a_i\delta(X_{it}) + k_i X_{it}] - W_t - O_t \leq 0, \qquad t = 1, \ldots, T \qquad (13)$$

$$0 \leq W_t \leq (rm)_t, \qquad t = 1, \ldots, T$$
$$0 \leq O_t \leq (om)_t, \qquad t = 1, \ldots, T$$
$$X_{it}, I_{it} \geq 0, \qquad i = 1, \ldots, N, \ t = 1, \ldots, T$$

where

$$\delta(X_{it}) = \begin{cases} 0 \text{ if } X_{it} = 0 \\ 1 \text{ if } X_{it} > 0. \end{cases}$$

Most of the comments made concerning the fixed-workforce linear cost model are applicable now and will not be repeated. This model does not allow backorders, although it is easy to incorporate this feature in the model formulation.

In expression (13), the term a_i represents the setup time consumed in preparing a production run for item i. The presence of $\delta(X_{it})$ both in the objective function (12) and in the constraints (13) completely breaks the linearity conditions of our previous models and makes computing this model much more difficult. We now examine some of the methods that have been proposed to solve the model.

Fixed-Cost Model. When the downtime consumed by the setup operation is negligible, $a_i = 0$ in expression (13) and the lot-size fixed-workforce model becomes a fixed-cost LP model (also known as the fixed-charge model). Since the objective function of the fixed-charge model is concave and the constraint set is convex, the global minimum will occur at an extreme point. However, generally, many local minima also will exist at extreme points; using a simplex-type algorithm that terminates at a local minimum is not effective.

Several approaches have been suggested to deal with this problem. Exact solution methods can be classified in two categories: (1) extreme-point ranking procedures (Gray 1971 and Murty 1968) and (2) branch-and-bound solutions to mixed-integer programming (MIP) formulations of the problem (Jones and Soland 1969 and Steinberg 1970). Exact methods are computationally limited to relatively small problems and, therefore, have little practical value at present. As a result of this limitation, several heuristic approaches that generate near-optimal solutions have been proposed. Generally, these heuristics start by producing a good extreme-point solution and, by examining the adjacent extreme points, a local minimum is determined. Then, a move is made to an extreme point away from this local minimum and the process is repeated until no further improvement is obtained or a specified number of iterations have been completed. Effective heuristics have been provided by Balinski (1961), Cooper and Drebes (1967), Denzler (1969), Rousseau (1973), and Steinberg (1970).

Linear-Programming Approach. When downtime a_i required to set up a production run for every item is not negligible, the resulting large-scale nonlinear capacitated lot-size model becomes extremely hard to solve directly. In response to these computational difficulties, Manne (1958) suggested reformulation of the problem as an LP model. This approach subsequently was refined by Dzielinski, Baker, and Manne (1963), Dzielinski and Gomory (1965), and Lasdon and Terjung (1971).

The approach consists of incorporating setup costs by defining a set of possible production sequences. For a given item i, a production sequence over the planning horizon T is a set of T nonnegative integers; these identify the quantities of item i to be produced at each time period during the planning horizon so that the demand requirements for that item are met. As explained in the uncapacitated lot-size model, it is enough to consider 2^{T-1} dominant sequences for each item.

Let X_{ijt} = amount to be produced of item i by means of production sequence j in the period t; $i = 1,\ldots,N$; $j = 1,\ldots,J$; $t = 1,\ldots,T$.

And as usual, let d_{it} = demand for item i in period t.

To see how these sequences are constructed, assume only three time periods. The number of dominant sequences for item i is $2^{3-1} = 4$; these four strategies for a given item i can be defined as in table 1.

TABLE 1

AMOUNTS TO BE PRODUCED AT EACH SEQUENCE

Sequence No.	Time period		
	$t = 1$	$t = 2$	$t = 3$
$j = 1$	$X_{i11} = d_{i1} + d_{i2} + d_{i3}$	$X_{i12} = 0$	$X_{i13} = 0$
$j = 2$	$X_{i21} = d_{i1} + d_{i2}$	$X_{i22} = 0$	$X_{i23} = d_{i3}$
$j = 3$	$X_{i31} = d_{i1}$	$X_{i32} = d_{i2} + d_{i3}$	$X_{i33} = 0$
$j = 4$	$X_{i41} = d_{i1}$	$X_{i42} = d_{i2}$	$X_{i43} = d_{i3}$

$\left. \right\} X_{i11}$

Computing the total production, inventory holding, and setup costs t_{ij} for each sequence is easy. The costs in table 1 are shown in table 2.

TABLE 2

SETUP AND HOLDING COSTS FOR EACH SEQUENCE (t_{ij})

Sequence No.	t_{ij}	
$j = 1$	$t_{i1} = s_{i1} + v_{i1}(d_{i1} + d_{i2} + d_{i3}) + c_{i1}(d_{i2} + d_{i3}) + c_{i2}(d_{i3})$	
$j = 2$	$t_{i2} = (s_{i1} + s_{i3}) + v_{i1}(d_{i1} + d_{i2}) + v_{i3}d_{i3} + c_{i1}d_{i2}$	il
$j = 3$	$t_{i3} = (s_{i1} + s_{i2}) + v_{i1}d_{i1} + v_{i2}(d_{i2} + d_{i3}) + c_{i2}d_{i3}$	
$j = 4$	$t_{i4} = (s_{i1} + s_{i2} + s_{i3}) + v_{i1}d_{i1} + v_{i2}d_{i2} + v_{i3}d_{i3}$	

In general,

$$t_{ij} = \sum_{t=1}^{T} [s_{it}\delta(X_{ijt}) + v_{it}X_{ijt} + c_{it}I_{it}].$$

The total labor resources consumed by the production quantities x_{ijt} can be written as:

$$l_{ijt} = a_i\delta(X_{ijt}) + k_iX_{ijt.}$$

If we assume, to simplify matters, a prescribed workforce at every time period $(rm)_t$ that cannot be exceeded, the fixed-workforce lot-size model can be formulated as:

$$\text{Minimize } z = \sum_{t=1}^{N} \sum_{j=1}^{J} t_{ij}\theta_{ij} \tag{14}$$

subject to

$$\sum_{i=1}^{N} \sum_{j=1}^{J} l_{ijt}\theta_{ij} \leq (rm)_t, \qquad t = 1, \ldots, T \tag{15}$$

$$\sum_{j=1}^{J} \theta_{ij} = 1, \qquad i = 1, \ldots, N \tag{16}$$

$$\theta_{ij} \geq 0, \qquad i = 1, \ldots, N \quad j = 1, \ldots, J$$

where

J = total number of dominant production sequences
θ_{ij} = fraction of the jth production sequence used to produce item i.

33

Expression (14) states the objective of the model as the minimization of variable production, setup, and inventory holding costs. It is possible to expand the model to include regular and overtime labor costs, shortage costs, and hiring and firing costs. Constraints (15) prevent the total manpower in the production schedules from exceeding the maximum labor availability at each time period. It is also simple to consider several types of production resources and to include a variable workforce as a decision variable with overtime capabilities. See Dzielinski, Baker, and Manne (1963), Dzielinski and Gomory (1965), and Gorenstein (1970) for these model extensions.

Constraints (16) specify that for every item i the total fractional production must add up to unity, plus the usual nonnegativity requirements on the decision variables. Since, by the manner in which the various patterns of production in table 1 were constructed, having fractional θ's is meaningless, the natural impulse is to insist on integer values of θ_{ij}, thus restricting them to 0 or 1. Unfortunately, these integrality constraints on the θ's render a problem of any realistic size extremely difficult to compute. Worse still, the solution may be suboptimal, since the optimal schedule may not be among the pure strategies represented by the given patterns of production. This point is subtle and has escaped many researchers in this field. The possible deviation from these patterns results from the presence of constraints on the available production capacity.

Fortunately, solving the LP model of equations (14) through (16) usually provides an excellent approximation of the true optimum. Since $T + N$ constraints are in the model, there will be at most $T + N$ positive variables in the optimal LP solution. And at least one of these variables will be associated with each of the N constraints (16). Thus, there could be at most T instances for which more than one θ_{ij} is positive. Clearly, if only θ_{ij} is positive for a given item i, that value of θ_{ij} should be 1, because of constraints (16). Consequently, whenever N is much larger than T—almost always the case in practical applications—the θ_{ij} fractional values are relatively only a few and are rounded off in some arbitrary manner. The error thus introduced is usually insignificant.

As indicated before, this model can be expanded to include not only manpower availabilities but also any number K of limited resources. When this is the case, the split of production sequences is not significant whenever N (the number of items to be scheduled) is much greater that $K \times T$ (number of resources times number of time periods). This condition usually is satisfied in practice.

Regardless of the integrality problems posed by the variables θ_{ij}, the resulting LP is hard to solve by conventional methods. In some situations, there might be several thousand items to schedule, and a model with that many rows can be impossible to compute with regular simplex procedures. In addition, each item generates 2^{T-1} dominant production sequences. If $T = 12$, there will be $2^{12-1} = 2048$ variables for each item; if there are a thousand items to schedule, the model will have more than two million θ_{ij} variables.

To bypass these difficulties, Dzielinski and Gomory (1965) suggested a Dantzig-Wolfe (1960) decomposition approach in which the subproblem led to uncapacitated lot-size models of the Wagner-Whitin type. These subproblems, which can be computed simply, are used to generate attractive entering production sequences so that there is no need to specify all the θ_{ij} variables from the beginning.

The decomposition approach, however, has one severe limitation for this type of problem. As is well known, the decomposition technique finds a near-optimum solution relatively quickly, but a large number of iterations might be necessary in obtaining the optimum. In most applications, getting the final optimum is not critical. Lower bounds can be evaluated to determine how well the current solution approximates the optimum. Stopping rules can be designed accordingly. In our problem, however, it is important to obtain the optimum, since only then the integrality requirements for the production sequences are satisfied and a feasible solution to the original problem is found.

To resolve this limitation, Lasdon and Terjung (1971) maintained the column-generation procedure suggested by Dzielinski and Gomory (thus bypassing the computational problem introduced by the large number of columns); but instead of defining a decomposition master program, they solved the original LP formulation using generalized upper-bounding techniques (Dantzig and Van Slyke 1967), thereby taking advantage of the structure of the initial model.

In using the column-generation procedure, let π_t, t-1,2. . . , T be the set of dual variables associated with the constraints (15), and π_{T+i}, $i = 1, \ldots, N$ be the dual variables associated with the first set of constraints (16). The reduced costs corresponding to problems (14) and (16) are given by the expression:

$$\overline{t_{ij}} = t_{ij} - \sum_{t=1}^{T} \pi_t l_{ijt} - \pi_{T+i}.$$

To choose the entering variable, find

$$\min_{i} \; \min_{j} \; \overline{t_{ij}}.$$

With the introduction of the values of t_{ij} and l_{ijt}, given by their respective expressions and rearranging the terms, the inner minimization becomes

$$\underset{j}{\text{Minimize}} \left\{ \sum_{t=1}^{T} [(s_{it} - \pi_t a_i)\delta \, (X_{ijt}) + (v_{it} - \pi_t k_i)X_{ijt} + c_{it}I_{it}] \right\} . \tag{17}$$

Since $\pi_t \leq 0$, the coefficients are all positive. The problem then involves minimizing setup, variable manufacturing, and inventory carrying costs so that the production quantities X_{ijt} satisfy the demand requirements for item i over the multiperiod planning horizon. This is the uncapacitated lot-size problem that can be resolved by the DP approach of Wagner and Whitin (1958) and Wagner (1960). In practice, subindex j in expression (17) is somehow irrelevant, since its minimization does not require all the production sequences j to be enumerated. The application of the Wagner-Whitin approach will generate the optimum production schedule for item i at every time period t, which we called X_{ijt}.

To determine which column to enter in the basis, subtract π_{T+i} from the optimum value of expression (17) corresponding to each item i. The minimum of these quantities identifies the entering column. The LP problem thus generated is solved by the standard generalized upper-bounded techniques.

Gorenstein (1970) used a similar model to support long-range production decisions in a tire company. In addition, he linked the output of that model to a short-range scheduling plan and introduced precedence relationships in the production of finished and semifinished tires and their components. An alternative approach to the capacitated fixed-cost problem was developed by Kortanek, Sodaro, and Soyster (1968).

Since the Lasdon and Terjung approach constitutes a continuous approximation to an IP problem, it is applicable only when the number of items N is much greater than the number of time periods T. To eliminate this shortcoming, Newson (1971) suggested a heuristic procedure that is independent of column-generation techniques and treats the lot-size problem as a shortest-route problem.

In this model, the workforce size also becomes a decision variable. Using the notation defined previously, the model can be formulated as:

$$\text{Minimize } z = \sum_{i=1}^{N} \sum_{t=1}^{T} [s_{it}\delta(X_{it}) + v_{it}X_{it} + c_{it}I_{it}] + \sum_{t=1}^{T} (r_tW_t + o_tO_t + h_tH_t + f_tF_t)$$

subject to

$$X_{it} + I_{i,t-1} - I_{it} = d_{it}, \qquad i = 1, \ldots, N; t = 1, \ldots, T$$

$$\sum_{i=1}^{N} [a_i\delta(X_{it}) + k_iX_{it}] - W_t - O_t \leq 0, \quad t = 1, \ldots, T$$

$$W_t - W_{t-1} - H_t + F_t = 0, \qquad t = 1, \ldots, T$$

$$-pW_t + O_t \leq 0, \qquad t = 1, \ldots, T$$

$$X_{it}, I_{it} \geq 0, \qquad i = 1, \ldots, N; t = 1, \ldots, T$$

$$W_t, O_t, H_t, F_t \geq 0, \qquad t = 1, \ldots, T$$

where

$$\delta(X_{it}) = \begin{cases} 0 \text{ if } X_{it} > 0 \\ 1 \text{ if } X_{it} = 0. \end{cases}$$

The interpretation of the model should now be straightforward to the reader. One could easily add backorder costs following the procedure suggested in the linear-cost/variable-workforce model.

The solution procedures used to deal with this model are identical to those employed with the lot-size/fixed-workforce model; that is, a fixed-cost model is generated whenever the downtime incurred in manufacturing setup a_i is negligible. Otherwise, the LP approximations suggested by Dzielinski and Gomory (1965) or Lasdon and Terjung (1971) can be applied.

Newson (1971) proposed to attack the problem in two stages. The first stage deals with the detailed scheduling decision for each individual item over the multiperiod planning horizon, neglecting the manpower constraints. For a given product i, this stage can be formulated as:

$$\text{Minimize } z_i = \sum_{t=1}^{T} [s_{it}\delta(X_{it}) + v_{it}X_{it} + C_{it}I_{it}]$$

subject to

$$\begin{aligned} X_{it} + I_{i,t-1} - I_{it} &= d_{it}, & t = 1, \ldots, T \\ X_{it}, I_{it} &\geq 0, & t = 1, \ldots, T. \end{aligned}$$

After this model has been solved for each of the N items, the capacity required by the detailed schedule for each time period t is computed as:

$$\hat{P}_t = \sum_{i=1}^{N} [a_i\delta(X_{it}) + k_iX_{it}], \qquad t = 1, \ldots, T.$$

Then, the second-stage model dealing with the aggregate capacity decision is solved. The model is defined as:

$$\text{Minimize } z\,(\hat{P}) \;=\; \sum_{t=1}^{T} (r_t W_t \,+\, o_t\, O_t \,+\, h_t\, H_t \,+\, f_t\, F_t)$$

subject to

$$
\begin{aligned}
W_t + O_t - \hat{P}_t &\geqslant 0, & t &= 1, \dots, T \\
W_t - W_{t-1} - H_t + F_t &= 0, & t &= 1, \dots, T \\
-pW_t + O_t &\leqslant 0, & t &= 1, \dots, T \\
W_t, O_t, H_t, F_t &\geqslant 0, & t &= 1, \dots, T.
\end{aligned}
$$

Newson suggested a heuristic iterative process that relates two models sequentially until a terminal criterion is met.

Advantages and Disadvantages of Lot-Size Models

The primary advantage of these models is that they incorporate the scheduling issues associated with lot-size indivisabilities into the capacity planning decisions. This, however, creates the need for a great deal of detailed information throughout the planning horizon, information that is costly to gather and to process.

Another approach to coordinate the aggregate capacity planning and detailed scheduling decisions is represented by the construction of hierarchical planning systems (Hax and Meal 1975, Bitran and Hax 1977).

GENERAL-COST MODELS

The linear and lot-size models we have analyzed, although appropriate for a great number of applications, impose several restrictions on the nature of the cost functions to be used. Some authors have argued that realistic industrial situations tend to exhibit cost functions that are nonlinear and discontinuous and, therefore, cannot be treated by any of the methods outlined previously. Buffa and Taubert (1972) report the following factors as mainly responsible for this cost behavior: supply-and-demand interactions, manufacturing or purchasing economies of scale, learning-curve effects, quantum jumps in costs with addition of a new shift, technological and productivity changes, and labor slowdowns.

Several aggregate capacity planning methods that attempt to be more responsible to the complexities introduced by the specific decision environment have been suggested. Generally, these more realistic approaches do not guarantee that an optimum solution will be found. They can be classified roughly according to the following categories:

— Nonlinear analytical models, which provide a mathematical treatment of general nonlinear cost structures (Johnson and Montgomery 1974, Sobel 1970, Zangwill 1966, 1968, and 1969, Veinott 1964 and 1969, Kalymon 1972, Florian and Klein 1971, and Baker et al. 1978).
— Heuristic decision rules, which attempt to bring in the decision-maker's intuition of the problem under consideration by incorporating rules of thumb that contribute to the solution of the problem (Bowman 1956).
— Search decision rules, which consist of the application of hill-climbing techniques to the response surface defined by a nonlinear cost function and the problem constraints (Jones 1967, Taubert 1968, Wilde 1964, and Goodman 1973).

—Simulation decision rules, which represent the problem under consideration by a set of programmed instructions. The decision-maker is able to test various approaches in an iterative fashion, where the outcome of each run suggests what the subsequent run might be. Simulation is particularly suitable to treat the uncertainties that can be present in a decision (Vergin 1966).

Since these techniques have not been used extensively in practical settings, they will not be reviewed here; their strengths and weaknesses will be discussed briefly.

Advantages and Disadvantages of General-Cost Models

One of the greatest advantages of the general-cost models is the realism, including uncertainties and special cost structure and constraints, they are capable of introducing to reflect more accurately the production planning environment. In addition, they are more closely associated with the actual decision process, making them more acceptable to managers and easier to explain and justify.

However, these advantages have a price. Usually, the models are expensive to develop and run, and the computational procedures used to solve them seldom guarantee overall optimization. Some of the models require a high degree of aggregation, creating implementation problems when decisions need to be disaggregated at the lower levels. Moreover, general-cost models do not lend themselves to handling a large number of interactive constraints, a function easily managed by LP methods.

Analytical models are helpful in determining qualitative properties of the optimum solutions, but seldom generate algorithmic procedures.

INTEGRATING THE PRODUCTION PROCESS

Economists define production as the process by which goods and services are created. In more specific terms, production can be defined as the process of converting raw materials into finished products. Of course, the terms *raw materials* and *finished products* are relative, since what constitutes a finished product for one industry could be the raw material for another. Effective management of the production process should provide the finished products in appropriate quantities, at the desired times, or the required quality, and at reasonable cost.

A Framework for Production Decision-Making

Production management encompasses a large number of decisions that affect several organizational echelons. The role of OR in supporting those decisions is better understood by classifying them according to the taxonomy proposed by Anthony (1965) regarding strategic planning, tactical planning, and operations control (Hax 1976).

Strategic Planning: Facilities Design. Strategic planning is mostly concerned with establishing managerial policies and with developing the resources necessary for the enterprise to satisfy its external requirements in a manner consistent with its goals. In the area of production management, the most important strategic decisions deal with the design of the production facilities, involving major capital investments for the development of new capacity and the expansion of existing capacity. These decisions include determining the location and size for new plants, the acquisition of new equipment, and the design of work centers within each plant. Other decisions, which require strong coordination with marketing, are the selection of new products and the design of the logistics system (warehouse location and capacity, transportation means, etc.)

These decisions are extremely important because, to a great extent, they are responsible for maintaining the competitive capabilities of the company, determining its rate of growth, and, eventually, defining its success or failure. An essential characteristic of these strategic decisions is that they have long-lasting effects, thus forcing long planning horizons in their analysis. This, in turn, forces the recognition of the impact of uncertainties and risk attitudes in the decision-making process and imposes some problems in the proper use of mathematical-programming models, which, except for parametric analyses, do not allow for proper handling of uncertainties.

Moreover, investments in new facilities and expansions of existing capacities are resolved at fairly high managerial levels and are affected by information that is both external and internal to the company. Thus, any form of rational analysis of these decisions has, necessarily, a very broad scope, requiring that information be processed in a very aggregated form to allow for all the dimensions of the problem to be included and to prevent top managers from being distracted by unnecessary operational details.

Tactical Planning: Aggregate Production Planning. Once the physical facilities have been decided upon, the basic problem to be resolved is the effective allocation of resources (production, storage and distribution capacities, workforce availabilities, financial and managerial resources, etc.) to satisfy demand and technological requirements, taking into account the costs and revenues associated with the operation of the production and distribution process. When several plants, many distribution centers, regional and local warehouses, and products requiring complex multistage fabrication and assembly processes affected by strong randomness and seasonalities in their demand patterns are involved, these decisions are far from simple. They usually involve consideration of a medium-range time horizon, divided into several periods, and the aggregation of the production items into product families. Typical decisions to be made within this context are utilization of regular and overtime workforce allocation of aggregated capacity resources to product families, accumulation of seasonal inventories, definition of distribution channels, and selection of transportation and transshipment alternatives. This paper has dealt exclusively with model approaches to support aggregate planning.

Operations Control: Detailed Production Scheduling. After an aggregated allocation of capacity among product families has been made, the day-to-day operational and scheduling decisions that require the complete disaggregation of the information generated at higher levels into the details consistent with the managerial procedures followed in daily activities must be dealt with. Decisions at this level are assigning customer orders to individual machines, sequencing these orders in the work shop, inventory accounting and inventory control activities, dispatching, expediting and processing of orders, vehicular scheduling, etc.

The Need for a Hierarchical Decision-Making System

Dealing with these three distinct levels of decisions requires recognition of several complexities. First, the investment, location, allocation, and scheduling decisions cannot be made in isolation because they interact strongly with one another; therefore, an integrated approach is required to avoid the problems of suboptimization. Second, this approach, although essential, is impossible without decomposing the elements of the problem in some way, within the content of a hierarchical system in which higher-level decisions are effectively linked with lower-level ones and decisions made at higher levels provide constraints for lower-level decision-making. This hierarchical approach recognizes the distinct characteristics of the type of management participation, the scope of the decision, the level of aggregation of the required information, and the time framework in which the decision is to be made. In our opinion, attempting to deal with all these decisions at once, using a single mathematical model, would be a serious mistake. Even if the computer and methodological capabilities could allow solving a large, detailed, integrated production model—clearly not the case today—that approach is inappropriate because it is not responsive to management needs at each level of the organization and would prevent interactions between models and managers at each organization echelon.

Designing a system to support the overall production management decisions demands, therefore, identifying ways in which the decision process can be partitioned, to allow selecting adequate models to deal with the individual decisions at each hierarchical level, designing linking mechanisms for transferring higher-level results to the lower hierarchical levels (this includes means to disaggregate information), and providing quantitative measures to evaluate the resulting deviations from optimal performance at each level. Some suggestions on how to implement such an approach are provided by Hax (1974).

Several hierarchical systems that deal with production decisions have been reported in the literature. Particularly, Hax (1974) describes an application for a continuous manufacturing process. Hax and Meal (1975), Bitran and Hax (1977), and Bitran, Haas, and Hax (1980 and 1981) address the use of hierarchical systems in a batch-processing environment, and Armstrong and Hax (1974) and Shwimer (1972) analyze an application for a job-shop activity. The next section describes the hierarchical production planning system, as presented by Bitran and Hax (1977).

A HIERARCHICAL PRODUCTION PLANNING SYSTEM

Bitran and Hax (1977) have adopted the hierarchical structure recommended by Hax and Meal (1975), interpreted their heuristics in terms of optimization subproblems, suggested iterative procedures to optimize the subproblems, and discussed the linking mechanisms that relate the subproblems to one another.

Hierarchical Structure of the Production Planning Process

In a hierarchical planning system, decisions are made in sequence. Aggregate decisions are made first and impose constraints within which more detailed decisions are made. In turn, detailed decisions provide feedback to evaluate the quality of aggregate decision-making. Each hierarchical level has its own characteristics, including length of the planning horizon, level of detail of the required information and forecasts, scope of the planning activity, and type of manager in charge of executing the plan.

The basic design of a hierarchical planning system includes partitioning the overall planning problem and linking the resulting subproblems. An important input is the number of levels recognized in the product structure. Hax and Meal (1975) identify three levels:

1. *Items* are the final products to be delivered to the customers. They represent the highest degree of specificity regarding the manufactured products. A given product may generate a large number of items differing in characteristics such as color, packaging, labels, accessories, and size.
2. *Families* are groups of items that share a common manufacturing setup cost. Economies of scale are accomplished by jointly replenishing items belonging to the same family.
3. *Types* are groups of families whose production quantities are to be determined by an aggregate production plan. Families belonging to a type normally have similar costs per unit of production time and similar seasonal demand patterns.

These three levels are required to characterize the product structure in many batch-processing manufacturing environments. In practical applications, more or fewer levels might be needed. The authors propose a hierarchical planning system based on three levels of item aggregation. The system can be extended to different numbers of aggregation levels by defining adequate subproblems.

The first step in hierarchical planning is allocating production capacity among product types using an aggregate planning model. The planning horizon of this model normally covers a full year to allow for proper consideration of the fluctuation demand requirements for the products. The authors advocate the use of a linear-programming model at this level. The advantages of using such a model will be discussed in the following section, ''Aggregate Production Planning for Types.'' The major drawback is that a linear-programming model does not consider setup costs. The implications of this limitation will be examined later.

The second step is allocating the production quantities for each product type among the families belonging to that type by disaggregating the results of the aggregate planning model only for the first period of the planning horizon. Thus, the required amount of data collection and data processing is reduced substantially. The disaggregation assures consistency and feasibility among the type and family production decisions and, at the same time, attempts to minimize the total setup costs incurred in the production of families. It is only at this stage that setup costs explicitly are considered.

Finally, the family production allocation is divided among the items belonging to each family. The objective of this division is to maintain all items with inventory levels that maximize the time between family setups. Again, consistency and feasibility are the driving constraints of the disaggregation process.

An extensive justification of this approach is provided by Hax (1974 and 1976) and by Hax and Meal (1975). Figure 1 shows the overall conceptualization of the hierarchical planning effort. A computer-based system has been developed to facilitate its implementation. The details of such a system are reported elsewhere (Hax et al. 1976). This section will concentrate on the methodological issues associated with the system design.

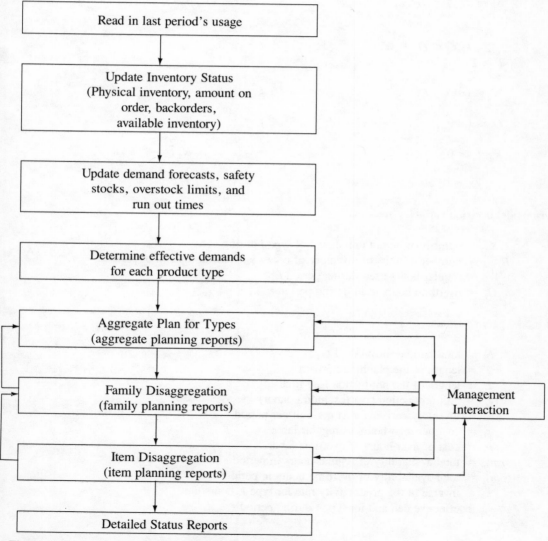

Figure 1. Conceptual overview of hierarchical planning system

Aggregate Production Planning for Types

Aggregate production planning is the highest level of planning in the production system, addressed to the product-type level. Any aggregate production planning model discussed previously can be used as long as it adequately represents the practical problem under consideration. Consider the following simplified linear program at this level:

Problem P

$$\text{Minimize} \quad \sum_{i=1}^{N} \sum_{t=1}^{T} (v_{it} X_{it} + c_{i,t+L} I_{i,t+L}) \; + \; \sum_{t=1}^{T} (r_t W_t + o_t O_t)$$

subject to

$$X_{it} - I_{i,t+L} + I_{i,t+L-1} = d_{i,t+L}, \qquad\qquad i = 1, \ldots, N; t = 1, \ldots, T,$$

$$\sum_{i=1}^{N} k_i X_{it} \le O_t + W_t, \qquad\qquad t = 1, \ldots, T,$$

$$W_t \le (rm)_t, \qquad\qquad t = 1, \ldots, T,$$

$$O_t \le (om)_t, \qquad\qquad t = 1, \ldots, T,$$

$$X_{it}, I_{it} \ge 0, \qquad\qquad i = 1, \ldots, N; t = 1, \ldots, T,$$

$$W_t, O_t \ge 0, \qquad\qquad t = 1, \ldots, T.$$

where model decision variables are

$\quad X_{it}$ = number of units to produced of type i during t
$\quad I_{i,t+L}$ = number of units of inventory of type i left over at the end of period $t + L$
$\quad W_t$ = regular hours used during period t
$\quad O_t$ = overtime hours used during period t

and model parameters are

$\quad N$ = total number of product types
$\quad T$ = length of the planning horizon
$\quad L$ = length of the production lead time
$\quad v_{it}$ = unit production cost (excluding labor)
$\quad c_{it}$ = inventory carrying cost per unit per period
$\quad r_t$ = cost per man-hours of regular labor
$\quad o_t$ = cost of man-hours of overtime labor
$\quad (rm)_t$ = total availability of regular hours in period t
$\quad (om)_t$ = total availability of overtime hours in period t
$\quad k_i$ = inverse of the productivity rate for type i, hours/unit
$\quad d_{i,t+L}$ = effective demand for type i during period $t + L$.

When seasonal variations are present in the demand pattern of product types, the planning horizon must cover a full seasonal cycle. Normally, aggregate planning models have planning horizons of one year, divided into equally spaced intervals. If there is significant production lead time, there should be a frozen planning horizon equal to the production lead time. Changes in production schedules normally cannot be made during the length of the frozen horizon, since it takes a full production lead time to implement the changes. Thus, the decision regarding the amount to be produced during period t, X_{it} has as primary input the effective demand during period $t + L$, $d_{i,t+L}$. Figure 2 illustrates the timing implications.

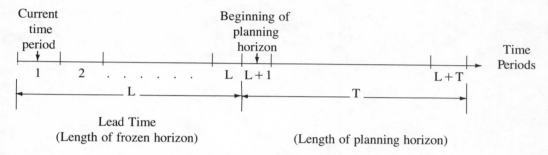

Figure 2. Timing implications in aggregate planning

When production costs v_{it} are invariable with time and the payroll of regular workforce is a fixed commitment, terms $v_{it}X_{it}$ and r_tW_t are deleted from the objective function. The model simply seeks an optimum aggregate plan that considers inventory holding costs and overtime costs as the basic trade-offs. Other cost factors—hiring and firing, backorders, subcontracting, lost sales, etc.—can easily be included in the model. And the constraints can represent any number of technological, financial, marketing, and other considerations.

Linear programming is a convenient type of model to use at this aggregate level because of its computational efficiency and the wide availability of linear-programming codes. Linear programming also permits sensitivity and parametric analysis to be performed easily. The shadow price information that becomes available when solving linear-programming models can help to identify opportunities for capacity expansions, market penetrations, introduction of new products, etc.

An aggregate approach has some advantages over a detailed approach. First, aggregate demands can be forecast more accurately than their disaggregate components. Second, there is a reduction in computational and data-gathering time because at a given period it is not necessary to forecast detailed demand for the complete seasonal cycle.

Notice that manufacturing setup costs purposely are ignored in this aggregate model formulation. Normally, setup costs have a secondary impact on determining the total production cost. Moreover, the inclusion of setup costs would force the model to be defined at a family level and would imply a high level of detail that would invalidate all the advantages of aggregate planning by generating high computational costs, forecast inaccuracies, and difficult managerial interactions. Consequently, setup costs are considered only at the second level of the hierarchical planning process.

Because of the uncertainties in the planning process, only the first time period results of the aggregate model are implemented. At the end of every time period, new information, used to update the model with a rolling planning horizon of length T, becomes available. Therefore, the data transmitted from the type level to the family level are the production and inventory quantities for the first period of the aggregate model. These quantities will be disaggregated among the families belonging to each type.

The Family Disaggregation Model

The central condition to be satisfied at this level for a coherent disaggregation is the equality between the sum of the productions of the families in a product type and the amount dictated by the higher level for this type. This equality will assure consistency between the aggregate production plan and the family disaggregation process. This consistency is achieved by determining run quantities for each family that minimize the total setup cost among families.

The authors propose the following model for family disaggregation, that must be solved for every product type i:

Problem P_i

$$\text{Minimize} \quad \sum_{j \in J^\circ} \frac{s_j d_j}{Y_j}$$

subject to

$$\sum_{j \in J^\circ} Y_j = X_i^*$$

$$lb_j \leq Y_j \leq ub_j, \qquad j \in J^\circ, \tag{18}$$

where

$$
\begin{aligned}
Y_j &= \text{number of units of family } j \text{ to be produced} \\
s_j &= \text{setup cost for family } j \\
d_j &= \text{forecast demand (usually annual) for family } j \\
lb_j &= \text{lower bounds for quantity } Y_j \\
ub_j &= \text{upper bounds for quantity } Y_j \\
X_i^* &= \text{total amount to be allocated among all the families belonging to type } i.
\end{aligned}
$$

X_i^* has been determined by the aggregate planning model and corresponds to the optimum value of the variable X_{i1} since only the first-period result of the aggregate model is implemented.

The lower bound lb_j, which defines the minimum production quantity for family j, is given by:

$$lb_j = \max \, [0, (d_{j,1} + d_{j,2} + \ldots + d_{j,L+1}) - AI_j + SS_j]$$

where

$$
\begin{aligned}
d_{j,1} + \ldots + d_{j,L+1} &= \text{total forecast demand for family } j \text{ during the production lead time plus} \\
&\quad \text{the review period (assumed to equal 1)} \\
AI_j &= \text{current available inventory for family } j \text{ (equal to the sum of the physical} \\
&\quad \text{inventory and the amount on order minus the backorders)} \\
SS_j &= \text{required safety stock.}
\end{aligned}
$$

The lower bound lb_j guarantees that any backorders will be caused by forecast errors beyond those absorbed by the safety stock SS_j.

The upper bound ub_j is given by

$$ub_j = OS_j - AI_j$$

where

$$OS_j = \text{overstock limit of family } j.$$

When family j has a terminal demand at the end of its season, OS_j can be calculated by means of a newsboy model (Zimmerman and Sovereign 1974, p. 370).

The objective function of problem P_i assumes that the family run quantities are proportional to the setup cost and the annual demand for a given family. This assumption (which is the basis of the economic order quantity formulation) tends to minimize the average annual setup cost. Notice that the total inventory carrying cost already has been established in the aggregate planning model; therefore, it does not enter in this formulation.

The first constraint of problem P_i

$$\sum_{j \in J^\circ} Y_j = X_i^*$$

assures the equality between the aggregate model input X_i^* and the sum of the family run quantities. It can be shown (Bitran and Hax 1981) that this condition can be substituted by

$$\sum_{j \in J^\circ} Y_j \leqslant X_i^* \tag{19}$$

without changing the optimum solution to problem P_i. In what follows, the equality constraint will be relaxed into inequality.

Initially, J° contains only those families that trigger during the current planning period. A family is said to trigger whenever its current available inventory cannot absorb the expected demand for the family during the production lead time plus the review period—that is, those families whose current available inventory is such that

$$AI_j < (d_{j,1} + d_{j,2} + \ldots + d_{j,L+1}) + SS_j.$$

Equivalently, J° can be defined as containing all those families whose run-out times are less than one time period:

$$ROT_j = \frac{AI_j - SS_j}{\displaystyle\sum_{t=1}^{L+1} d_{j,t}} < 1.$$

It is necessary to start production for these families to avoid future backorders. All other families are put on a secondary list and will be scheduled only if extra capacity is available.

The authors (Bitran and Hax 1981) present an efficient algorithm to solve problem P_i through a relaxation procedure. The algorithm consists of initially ignoring the bounding constraints (18) and of solving the objective function subject to the knapsack restriction (19). Then, a check is made to verify that the optimum values Y_j^* satisfy the bounds (18). If they do satisfy the bounds, the Y_j^*'s constitute the optimal solution for problem P_i. If they do not satisfy the bounds, at least some of the Y_j^*'s are shown to be optimal and a new iteration takes place.

The Item Disaggregation Model

For the period in consideration, all the costs have been determined in the previous two levels, and any feasible disaggregation of a family run quantity has the same total cost. However, the feasible solution chosen will establish initial conditions for the next period and will affect future costs. To save setups in future periods, the family run quantity could be distributed among its items in such a way that the run-out times of the items coincide with the run-out time of the family. A direct consequence is that all items of a family will trigger simultaneously. To attain this objective, the authors propose the following strictly convex knapsack problem for each family j:

Problem P_j

$$\text{Minimize} \quad \frac{1}{2} \sum_{k \in K^\circ} \left[\frac{Y_j^* + \sum\limits_{k \in K^\circ} (AI_k - SS_k)}{(L+1) \sum\limits_{k \in K^\circ} \sum\limits_{t=1} d_{k,t}} - \frac{Z_k + AI_k - SS_k}{(L+1) \sum\limits_{t=1} d_{k,t}} \right]^2$$

subject to

$$\sum_{k \in K^\circ} Z_k = Y_j^*$$

$$Z_k \leq OS_k - AI_k, \qquad k \in K$$

$$Z_k \geq \max \left[0, \sum_{t=1}^{L+1} d_{k,t} - AI_k + SS_k \right], \qquad k \in K^\circ$$

where

$$
\begin{aligned}
Z_k &= \text{number of units to be produced of item } k \\
AI_k &= \text{available inventory of item } k \\
SS_k &= \text{safety stock of item } k \\
OS_k &= \text{overstock limit of item } k \\
d_{k,t} &= \text{forecast demand for item } k \text{ in period } t \\
K^\circ = \{1,2, \ldots\} &= \text{set of indices of all items belonging to family } j \\
Y_j^* &= \text{total amount to be allocated for all items belonging to family } j.
\end{aligned}
$$

Y_j^* was determined by the family disaggregation model.

The first constraint of problem P_j requires consistency in the disaggregation from family to items. The last two constraints are the upper and lower bounds for the item run quantities. These bounds are similar to those previously defined for the family disaggregation model.

The two terms inside the square bracket of the objective function represent, respectively, the run-out time for family j and the run-out time for an item k belonging to family j (assuming perfect forecast). The minimization of the square of the differences of the run-out times will make those quantities as close as possible. (The term 1/2 in front of the objective function is just a computational convenience.) An efficient algorithm to solve this problem optimally is given by Bitran and Hax (1981).

Issues of Infeasibility and Demand Forecasts

Combining the rolling-horizon aggregate planning procedure with disaggregation may lead to infeasibilities. This section will illustrate how the infeasibilities can occur and will suggest a way to eliminate them. The explanation may be simplified by assuming that a perfect forecast exists and that every family is composed of a unique item—that is, the disaggregation consists as passing directly from the aggregate solution to detail schedules.

A simple problem consisting of one product type ($i = 1$), two items ($k = 1, 2$), a planning horizon of three time periods ($t = 1, 2, 3$), and zero production lead time will be considered.

The aggregate constraints are

$$I_0 + X_1 - I_1 = d_1,$$

$$I_1 + X_2 - I_2 = d_2,$$

$$I_2 + X_3 - I_3 = d_3.$$

(Nonnegativity constraints)

The detailed constraints are

$$I_{k,0} + Z_{k,1} - I_{k,1} = d_{k,1}, \qquad k = 1, 2,$$

$$I_{k,1} + Z_{k,2} - I_{k,2} = d_{k,2}, \qquad k = 1, 2,$$

$$I_{k,2} + Z_{k,3} - I_{k,3} = d_{k,3}, \qquad k = 1, 2.$$

(Nonnegativity constraints)

Feasibility conditions require that these two constraint sets are satisfied and that

$$\sum_{k=1}^{2} Z_{k,t} = X_t \qquad t = 1, 2, 3.$$

Assume the demand and inventory conditions in table 3.

TABLE 3

DEMAND AND INVENTORY CONDITIONS

Item	Demand			Initial Inventory
	Period $t = 1$	Period $t = 2$	Period $t = 3$	
$k = 1$	$d_{11} = 5$	$d_{12} = 17$	$d_{13} = 30$	$I_{10} = 9$
$k = 2$	$d_{21} = 3$	$d_{22} = 12$	$d_{23} = 30$	$I_{20} = 20$
Total	$d_1 = 8$	$d_2 = 29$	$d_3 = 60$	$I_0 = 29$

47

The reader can verify that although

$$X_1 = 8, X_2 = 0, X_3 = 60, I_1 = 29, I_2 = 0, I_3 = 0$$

is a feasible solution to the aggregate problem, it does not have a corresponding feasible disaggregation. The reason for this infeasibility is that the aggregate model ignores that inventory for item 2 cannot be used to satisfy demand for item 1.

This type of infeasibility can be avoided by working with *effective demands*. If the initial inventory of an item is not zero, subtract it from the demand requirements in the first period to obtain the effective demand for that period. If the initial inventory exceeds the first-period demand, continue with this adjustment process until the inventory has been used up. Table 4 shows the effective demands of the example.

TABLE 4

EFFECTIVE DEMAND

Item	Effective Demand			Initial Inventory
	Period $t = 1$	Period $t = 2$	Period $t = 3$	
$k = 1$	$d_{11} = 0$	$d_{12} = 13$	$d_{13} = 30$	0
$k = 2$	$d_{21} = 0$	$d_{22} = 0$	$d_{23} = 25$	0
Total	$d_1 = 0$	$d_2 = 13$	$d_3 = 55$	0

It can be shown (Gabbay 1979) that if one works with effective demands any feasible solution to the aggregate model generates a feasible solution to the disaggregate model.

In general, if the forecast demand for item k in period t is $d_{k,t}$, its corresponding available inventory is AI_k, and its safety stock is SS_k, the effective demand $\bar{d}_{k,t}$ of item i for period t is given by:

$$\bar{d}_{k,t} = \begin{cases} max\left[0, \sum_{l=1}^{t} d_{k,l} - AI_k + SS_k\right], & t = 1, \ldots, T, \text{ if } \bar{d}_{k,t-1} = 0 \\ d_{kt} \text{ otherwise.} \end{cases} \tag{20}$$

The effective demand for a type i is given by the sum of the effective demands of all items belonging to a given type:

$$\bar{d}_{i,t} = \sum_{k \in K} \bar{d}_{k,t}. \tag{21}$$

The hierarchical planning system operates as follows:

1. An aggregate forecast is generated for each product type for each time period in the planning horizon. Since the number of types normally is reasonably small, these forecasts can be produced by using fairly sophisticated forecasting models (such as regression analysis) that would be prohibitively expensive at the item level because of the extensive number of items in most manufacturing environments. In addition, these forecasts can be reviewed by experienced managers to introduce judgmental inputs that the models cannot capture.

48

2. The type forecasts are disaggregated into item forecasts by forecasting the proportion of the total type demand corresponding to each item. These proportions can be updated by using exponential smoothing techniques appropriate to apply at a detailed level. Item and family forecasts only are required for a single time period in the models presented.
3. After the available inventory for each item has been updated, the effective item demand is obtained by applying expression (20). When the initial inventory exceeds the first-period demand, expression (20) requires item forecasts for successive periods in the planning horizon. Exponential smoothing techniques can be used to obtain these by making trend and/or seasonality adjustments to the initial period forecast.
4. The effective demand for types is obtained from expression (21). Computer programs that carry out the necessary calculations are discussed by Hax, et al. (1976).

Computational Results

The authors conducted a series of experiments to examine the performance of the hierarchical system and determine the size of forecast errors, capacity availability, magnitude of setup costs, and nature of the planning horizon.

The data used for these tests were taken from a manufacturer of rubber tires. The product structure characteristics and other information are given in figure 3. Figure 4 exhibits the demand pattern for both product types. Product type 1 has a terminal demand season (corresponding to the requirements of snow tires) and consists of two families and five items. Demand for product type 2 fluctuates greatly throughout the year. Product type 2 has three families and six items. Families are groups of items sharing the same molds in the curing presses and, therefore, a common setup cost. The items are, for instance, white-wall and regular-wall tires of a given class. Families and items have the same cost characteristic and the same productivity rates as their corresponding types.

The experiments consisted of applying the production planning system to a full year of simulated plant operations. Production decisions were made every four weeks, at which time a report identifying aggregate as well as detailed decisions was generated. The model was then updated using, normally, a one-year rolling planning horizon. The process was repeated thirteen times. At the end of the simulation, total setup costs, inventory holding costs, overtime costs, and backorders were accounted for. A summary of eleven simulation runs is provided in figure 5. The simulations were implemented in the Computer Based Operations Management System (COMS) developed at MIT (Hax et al. 1976).

Run 1 can be regarded as the *base case*. It has no forecast errors, a planning horizon of one year divided into thirteen periods of four-week durations each, a normal capacity (defined as 2000 hours of regular time and 1200 hours of overtime per period), on a normal setup cost ($90 per family belonging to product type 1 and $120 per family belonging to product type 2). All other runs include some variation of the characteristics of run 1.

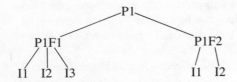
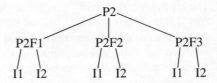

Family setup cost = $90
Holding cost = $0.31/unit/month
Overtime cost = $9.5/hour
Productivity factor = 0.1 hr/unit
Production lead time = 1 month

Family setup cost = $120
Holding cost = $0.40/unit/month
Overtime cost = $9.5/hour
Productivity factor = 0.2 hr/unit
Production lead time = 1 month

Regular workforce costs and unit production costs are considered fixed costs.

Total regular workforce = 2000 hr/month
Total overtime workforce = 1200 hr/month

Figure 3. Product structure and other relevant information

Time Period	Product Type 1	Product Type 2
t	P1	P2
1	12,736	6,174
2	7,813	2,855
3	0	4,023
4	0	4,860
5	0	7,131
6	0	9,665
7	1,545	17,603
8	7,895	14,276
9	10,982	11,706
10	15,782	15,056
11	16,870	8,232
12	15,870	7,880
13	9,878	10,762
Total	99,371	120,223

Figure 4. Demand patterns of product types

	1	2	3	4	5	6
Run Cost Components	Base case— no forecast errors	10 percent forecast errors	30 percent forecast errors	High setup cost		Tight capacity 1600 regular hours (no forecast error)
				Case I P1: 5000,50 P2: 400,400,1000 (no forecast error)	Case II P1: 6000,4500 P2: 400,5000,3000 (no forecast error)	
Setup	5,360	5,360	5,250	67,050	104,800	4,480
Holding	72,510	73,611	76,577	72,374	72,597	115,072
Overtime	81,111	81,425	82,365	81,111	81,102	117,439
Total cost	158,981	160,396	164,192	220,535	258,499	236,991
Backorders	2	1,513	6,243	10	4	144

	7	8	9	10	11
Run Cost Components	Loose capacity, 2500 regular hours (no forecast error)	6-month planning horizon, normal capacity (no forecast error)	6-month planning horizon, tight capacity (no forecast error)	6-month planning horizon normal capacity (10% forecast error)	1-1-1-1-3-6 planning horizon, normal capacity (no forecast error)
Setup	5,910	5,690	5,030	5,690	5,250
Holding	56,002	67,212	83,983	64,971	78,052
Overtime	48,507	88,597	103,332	90,773	75,440
Total cost	110,419	161,499	192,345	161,434	158,742
Backorders	0	0	16,658	2,951	73

Figure 5. Summary of computational results with proposed hierarchical planning system

Sensitivity to Forecast Errors. Runs 1, 2, and 3 show the impact of forecast errors in production planning decisions. Forecast errors are uniformly distributed in intervals of the type $[^-a, {}^+a]$ and are introduced in all three levels. Moreover, the demands of families in a same product type and the demands of items in a family add to the demand of the product type and the demands of items in a family add to the demand of the product type and of the family. Increasing forecast errors causes deterioration of the quality of the decisions. Both cost and size of backorders increase when forecast errors begin to escalate. However, the system performs reasonably well even under forecast errors of up to 30 percent. (The 6243 units backordered in run 3 represent a 97 percent service level.) These results show that aggregate forecasts can be more accurate than detailed forecasts and, thus, provide an important justification for the hierarchical approach.

Sensitivity to Changes in Setup Costs. The value input to the setup costs in the base case (run 1) were realistic measures of setup costs incurred in normal manufacturing operations. They included direct setup costs (manpower and materials) as well as opportunity costs for having the machines idle while changeover is performed. To test the system's performance under extreme setup-cost conditions, runs 4 and 5 were made with the setup cost characteristics shown in table 5.

TABLE 5

SETUP COSTS FOR RUNS 1, 4, AND 5

	Type 1		Type 2		
	Family 1	Family 2	Family 1	Family 2	Family 3
Run 4	5000	50	400	400	1000
Run 5	6000	4500	400	5000	3000
Base case — run 1	90	90	120	120	120

Naturally, the total cost associated with runs 4 and 5 increases significantly. Runs 1, 4, and 5 have almost identical inventory holding costs and overtime costs and, thus, indicate that the overall production strategies for these runs do not change much. This situation suggests a limitation of the hierarchical approach when applied to situations with extremely high setup costs, for a high inventory accumulation might be expected to obtain a better balance between inventory and setup costs.

Sensitivity to Capacity Availability. Runs 6 and 7 evaluate the performance of the system under different capacity conditions. Run 6 uses only 1600 hours of regular capacity per period; run 7 expands the regular capacity to 2500 hours. As indicated in the results in figure 5, the system's performance is quite sensitive to capacity changes. Under tight capacity, both costs and backorders increase significantly; the opposite is true under loose capacity. Clearly, the system can be useful in evaluating proposals for capacity expansion.

Sensitivity to Changes in Planning Horizon Characteristics. Runs 8, 9, 10, and 11 experiment with various lengths of the planning horizon under different conditions. Shortening the planning horizon from 13 periods to six periods does not affect the system's performance under normal capacity conditions. (Compare runs 1 and 8 and runs 2 and 10.) However, the size of backorders begins to increase significantly when the planning horizon is shorter and under tight capacity conditions (run 9).

Run 11 deals with an aggregation of time periods in the planning horizon. The length of the planning horizon is a full year divided into six time periods of uneven lengths. Each of the first four periods has a four-week duration; the fifth period covers twelve weeks (an aggregation of three four-week periods); the sixth period covers twenty-four weeks (an aggregation of six four-week periods). Run 11's performance is similar to that of the base case. This result indicates that this type of aggregation of the planning horizon could be useful in many situations, since it improves the forecasting accuracy in more distant time periods and reduces the computational effort of processing the system without experiencing a decline in performance.

Degree of Suboptimization. Although the proposed hierarchical planning system provides optimum solutions to the subproblems that deal with individual decisions at each level, it is not an overall optimum procedure. Setup costs are ignored at the aggregate level and, thus, suboptimization possibilities are introduced. To determine how serious this suboptimization problem can be, the authors developed a detailed mixed-integer programming (MIP) model at a detailed item level to identify the true optimal solution to the test problem. The MIP model was implemented by means of IBM's MPSX/MIP code, a general-purpose branch-and-bound algorithm.

Because of the expensive computational cost of solving MIP models, the authors limited the comparisons between the hierarchical planning system and the MIP model to situations that contained no forecast errors and for which the optimum yearly cost could be obtained by solving the MIP model only once. (If forecast errors had been introduced, each run would have required solving the MIP model 13 times.)

MIP solutions were computed for three of the previous runs: the base case (run 1'), the first high-setup-cost run (run 4'), and the tight-capacity run (run 6'). The MIP results are given in figure 6. The existing limits on the node tables of the branch-and-bound code used did not allow determination of the true optimum in the MIP runs. Therefore, the solutions reported in figure 6 might be improved. Figure 6 also provides the continuous lower bounds obtained when the computations were interrupted. For all practical purposes, the solutions corresponding to runs 1' and 6' could be considered optimal. Run 4' possibly could be improved.

Comparing the total costs of the three runs shows that the hierarchical planning system is extremely efficient. Only under abnormally high setup costs might the system's performance begin to depart significantly from the overall optimal solution.

TABLE 6

TOTAL COSTS OF THREE RUNS

	Hierarchical System	Best known MIP solution
Base case	158,981	158,339
High setup cost	220,535	203,360
Tight capacity	236,733	237,232

Run Cost Components	1′ Base case (no forecast error)	4′ High setup cost Case I P1: 5000,50 P2: 400,400,1000	6′ Tight capacity 1600 regular hours
Setup Holding Overtime	4,590 75,953 77,796	48,050 79,880 75,430	3,930 115,872 117,430
Total cost (best-known solution)	158,339	203,360	237,232
Lower bound	153,926	162,783	233,665

Figure 6. Summary of computational results with mixed-integer programming models

In summary, the proposed hierarchical system seems to perform near the optimum when setup costs are moderate. The base-case cost, which reflected the operating data of the tire industry, is only 0.4 percent higher than the best-known optimum solution obtained by the MIP formulation. However, each run of the hierarchical system costs about $5, compared to MIP run costs of about $50. The MIP approach would be computationally impossible to carry out for large problems. Moreover, the hierarchical system appears to offer coherent solutions for reasonable changes in forecast errors, for capacity availabilities, and for planning horizon lengths.

Extremely high setup costs could affect the performance of the system. In practice, families with very high setup costs are candidates for continuous (as opposed to batch) production if they have a high level of demand. In such cases, families can be handled independently of the prescribed system. In situations in which there are few high-setup families with low demand, special constraints can be imposed on the family disaggregation model to produce those families in large enough quantities by setting the lower bound of the family to its unconstrained economic order quantity. When all families in the product structure have high setup costs and low demand levels, eliminating setup costs at the aggregate level may not be desirable. In such a situation, one could eliminate the aggregate planning model for product types, allocate production quantities at the family level by using an approach similar to that proposed by Lasdon and Terjung (1971), and apply the item disaggregation model to allocate the family production quantities among them.

REFERENCES

Anthony, R.N. 1965. *Planning and control systems: A framework for analysis*. Boston: Harvard University, Graduate School of Business.

Antosiewicz, H., and A. J. Hoffman. 1954. A remark on the smoothing problem. *Management Science* 1:92-95.

Armstrong, R. J., and A. C. Hax. 1974. *A hierarchical approach for a naval tender job shop design*. Cambridge: Operations Research Center, MIT.

Baker, K. R., P. S. Dixon, M. J. Magazine, and E. A. Silver. 1978. An algorithm for the dynamic lot-size problem with time-varying production capacity constraints. *Management Science* 24:1710-1720.

Balinski, M. L. 1961. Fixed cost transportation problem. *Naval Research Logistics Quarterly* 8:41-54.

Bitran, G. R., E. A. Haas, and A. C. Hax. 1982. Hierarchical production planning: A single stage system. *Operations Research* 29:717-743.

————. 1982. Hierarchical production planning: A two stage system. *Operations Research* 30:232-251.

Bitran, G. R., and A. C. Hax. 1977. On the design of hierarchical production planning systems. *Decision Sciences* 8:28-54.

————. 1981. Disaggregation and resource allocation using convex knapsack problems with bounded variables. *Management Science* 27:431-441.

Bowman, E. H. 1956. Production scheduling by the transportation method of linear programming. *Operations Research* 4:100-103.

————. 1963. Consistency and optimality in managerial decision making. *Management Science* 9:310-321.

Brown, R. G. 1967. *Decision rules for inventory management*. New York: Holt, Rinehart and Winston.

Buffa, E. S., and W. H. Taubert. 1972. *Production-inventory systems: Planning and control*. Homewood, Ill.: Richard D. Irwin, Inc.

Cooper, L., and C. Drebes. 1967. An approximate solution method for the fixed charge problem. *Naval Research Logistics Quarterly* 14:101-113.

Dantzig, G. B., and R. M. Van Slyke. 1967. Generalized upper bounding techniques. *J. Computer and System Science* 1:213-226.

Dantzig, G. B., and P. Wolfe. 1960. Decomposition principle for linear programs. *Operations Research* 8:101-111.

Denzler, D. R. 1969. An approximate algorithm for the fixed charge problem. *Naval Research Logistics Quarterly* 16:411-416.

Dzielinski, B. P., C. T. Baker, and A. S. Manne. 1963. Simulation tests of lot size programming. *Management Science* 9:229-258.

Dzielinski, B. P., and R. E. Gomory. 1965. Optimal programming of lot sizes, inventory and labor allocations. *Management Science* 11:874-890.

Elmaghraby, S. E., and V. Y. Bawle. 1972. Optimization of batch ordering under a deterministic variable demand. *Management Science* 18:508-517.

Eppen, G. D., F. J. Gould, and B. P. Pashigian. 1969. Extensions of the planning horizon theorem in the dynamic lot size model. *Management Science* 15:268-277.

Florian, M., and M. Klein. 1971. Deterministic production planning with concave costs and capacity constraints. *Management Science* 18:12-20.

Gabbay, H. 1979. Optimal aggregation and disaggregation in hierarchical planning. *Disaggregation: Problems in manufacturing and service organizations.* Edited by P. Ritzman et al. Boston: Martinus Nijhoff Publishing: 95-106.

Goodman, D. A. 1973. A new approach to scheduling aggregate production and work force. *AIIE Transactions* 5:135-141.

Gorenstein, S. 1970. Planning tire production. *Management Science* 17:B72-B81.

Gray, P. 1971. Exact solution of the fixed-charge transportation problem. *Operations Research* 19:1529-1537.

Haussmann, F., and S. W. Hess. 1960. A linear programming approach to production and employment scheduling. *Management Technology* 1:46-51.

Hax, A. C. 1974. A comment on the distribution system simulator. *Management Science* 21:223-236.

————. 1976. Chapter 6: The design of large scale logistics systems: A survey and an approach. *Modern trends in logistics research.* Edited by W. H. Marlow. Cambridge: MIT Press.

Hax, A. C., and H. C. Meal. 1975. Hierarchical integration of production planning and scheduling. *TIMS Studies in Management Science.* Vol. 1, Logistics. Edited by Murray Geisler. New York: North Holland-American Elszier.

Hax, A. C., J. J. Golovin, M. Bosyj, and T. Victor. 1976. COMS: A computer-based operations management system. Technical report no. 121. Operations Research Center, MIT (January).

Hoffman, A. J., and W. Jacobs. 1954. Smooth patterns of production. *Management Science* 1:86-91.

Holt, C. C., F. Modigliani, J. F. Muth, and H. A. Simon. 1960. *Planning production inventories and work force.* Englewood Cliffs, N.J.: Prentice Hall, Inc.

Johnson, L. A., and D. C. Montgomery. 1974. *Operations research in production planning, scheduling, and inventory control.* New York: Wiley.

Johnson, S. M., and G. B. Dantzig. 1955. A production smoothing problem. *Proceedings of second symposium in linear programming.* Washington, D.C.: (January).

Jones, A. P., and R. M. Soland. 1969. A branch-and-bound algorithm for multi-level fixed-charge problems. *Management Science* 16:67-76.

Jones, C. H. 1967. Parametric production planning. *Management Science* 13:843-866.

Kalymon, B. A. 1972. A decomposition algorithm for arborescence inventory systems. *Operations Research* 20:860-874.

Kortanek, K. O., D. Sodaro, and A. L. Soyster. 1968. Multi-product production scheduling via extreme point properties of linear programming. *Naval Research Logistics Quarterly* 15:287-300.

Lasdon, L. S., and R. C. Terjung. 1971. An efficient algorithm for multi-item scheduling. *Operations Research* 19:946-969.

Lippman, S. A., A. J. Rolfe, and H. M. Wagner. Algorithm for optimal production scheduling and employment smoothing. *Operations Research* 15:1011-1029.

Lippman, S. A., A. J. Rolfe, H. M. Wagner, and J. S. C. Yuan. 1967. Optimal production scheduling and employment smoothing with deterministic demands. *Management Science* 14:127-158.

Magee, J. F., and D. H. Boodman. 1967. *Production planning and inventory control.* New York: McGraw-Hill.

Manne, A. S. 1958. Programming of economic lot sizes. *Management Science* 4:115-135.

McGarrah, R. E. 1963. *Production and logistics management.* New York: Wiley.

Murty, K. G. 1968. Solving the fixed charge problem by routing extreme points. *Operations Research* 16:268-279.

Newson, E. F. P. 1971. Lot size scheduling to finite capacity. Ph.D. dissertation. Cambridge: Sloan School of Management, MIT.

O'Malley, R. L., S. E. Elmaghraby, and J. W. Jeske. 1966. An operational system for smoothing batch-type production. *Management Science* 12:B433-449.

Rousseau, J. M. 1973. A cutting plane method for the fixed cost problem. Ph.D. dissertation. Cambridge: Sloan School of Management, MIT.

Shwimer, J. 1972. Interaction between aggregate and detailed scheduling in a job shop. Ph.D. dissertation. Cambridge: Sloan School of Management, MIT.

Sobel, M. J. 1970. Smoothing start-up and shut-down costs: Concave case. *Management Science* 17:78-91.

Steinberg, D. I. 1970. The fixed charge problem. *Naval Research Logistics Quarterly* 17:217-237.

Taubert, W. H. 1968. A search decision rule for the aggregate scheduling pattern. *Management Science* 14:B343-B359.

Veinott, A. F. 1964. Production planning with convex costs: A parametric study. *Management Science* 10:441-460.

————— 1969. Minimum concave-cost solution of Leontieff substitution models of multi-facility inventory systems. *Operations Research* 17:262-291.

Vergin, R. C. 1966. Production scheduling under seasonal demand. *Journal of Industrial Engineering* 7:260-266.

Von Lanzenauer, C. H. 1970. Production and employment and scheduling in multistage production systems. *Naval Research Logistics Quarterly* 17:193-198.

Wagner, H. M. 1960. A postscript to dynamic problems in the theory of the firm. *Naval Research Logistics Quarterly* 7:7-12.

Wilde, D. J. 1964. Optimum seeking methods. Englewood Cliffs, N.J.: Prentice Hall, Inc.

Yuan, S. C. 1967. Algorithms for multi-product model in production scheduling and employment smoothing. Technical report no. 22, NSF GS-552. Stanford: Stanford University.

Zabel, E. 1964. Some generalizations of an inventory planning horizon theorem. *Management Science* 10:465-471.

Zangwill, W. I. 1966. Production smoothing of economic lot sizes with non-decreasing requirements. *Management Science* 13:191-209.

—————. 1968. Minimum concave cost flows in certain networks. *Management Science* 14:429-450.

—————. 1969. A backlogging model and multiechelon model of a dynamic economic lot size production system—A network approach. *Management Science* 15:506-527.

Zimmerman, H. J., and M. G. Soverign. 1974. *Quantitative models for production management.* Englewood Cliffs, N.J.: Prentice Hall.

Reprinted, by permission, from Operational Research Quarterly, *Vol. 28, No. 4, 1977,*
reproduced by permission of The Operational Research Society — UK.

Effective Shift Allocation in Multiproduct Lines: a Mixed Integer Programming Approach

STELIOS H. ZANAKIS

Industrial Engineering & Systems Analysis Program, W.V. College of Graduate Studies, Institute,
WV 25112, U.S.A.

and

KENNETH D. LAWRENCE

Management Information Services Dept., Hoffmann–LaRoche, Inc., Nutley, NJ 07110, U.S.A.

This paper examines the problem of effectively allocating production shifts to a set
of production lines and assigning a product to each line under various resource restrictions. This is the kind of allocation problem encountered when the profit motive
is (partially, temporarily or totally) removed from the decision-making process (e.g.
aggressive marketing or military operations). The system effectiveness is measured
by the percent satisfaction of demands (readiness ratios). Two mixed integer programming models are developed and illustrated by means of an example. The first maximizes the smallest readiness ratio for a product, while the second minimizes the total
deviation from the goal of perfect satisfaction of all demands. Extensions of these
models are also suggested.

INTRODUCTION

THE OBJECTIVE of a resource allocation problem may not necessarily be profit
maximization or cost minimization. A company could have a short-term
goal to penetrate the market and dominate its competitors, at any reasonable
cost. A marketing department may sometimes aim at satisfying all customer
demands "as much as possible". Military operations, especially during war times,
may place particular emphasis on maximizing the effectiveness of a system,
at almost any cost.

This paper has been motivated by a military problem, involving the allocation of scarce resources (manpower, material and money) to several production lines. Each product (ammunition) can be made in several lines at different
production rates. When switching from one product to another, a line
requires some adjustment before actual production can begin. This loss in
productive time depends on the line and the new item produced; it is little
influenced by the type of the item previously produced. Since, also, we are
dealing with an (aggregate) planning and not a (detailed) scheduling problem,
these changeover (or setup) time losses are considered sequence independent.

The length of the planning horizon may vary from 1 to 6 months, consisting of a certain number of manpower shifts available to work on each line. The shift was chosen as the basic time unit because it was the inherent measurement in this planning process (e.g. production rates per shift, costs per shift, etc.). Moreover, a smaller time unit, such as an hour, would have made this planning process more detailed than needed. The modelling approach presented in this paper can, of course, accept any time unit.

The basic scenario assumes that demand for each product is known in advance of the planning period; for example, when production orders are contracted in advance (e.g. job shop work or some types of military manufacturing). In general, the nature of business and the degree of co-operation between the production–marketing–sales activities will influence the firm's production planning–modelling process.

An aggregate production plan is needed for a certain period, that will assure a maximum level of system effectiveness in fulfilling given requirements. The measure of system effectiveness used is the satisfaction of as large a percentage of demand as possible, given the existing level of available production resources. For each product, this per cent satisfaction may be expressed as the ratio of the number of units available (excess inventory + net production) to the number of units required, i.e.

$$RR_i = \left\{(a_i - l_i) + \sum_{j=1}^{n} d_{ij}[x_{ij} - y_{ij}\, p_{ij}]\right\}\Big/ r_i. \tag{1}$$

(All notation used in this paper is explained in the Appendix.) This relationship has been called the readiness ratio,[1] and provides an explicit measure of the degree to which given requirements for each product have been satisfied by the allocation process.

To arrive at an overall measure of system effectiveness, the relative importance of each product should be established. This may be an extremely difficult task, perhaps of limited value, in many practical situations. First, the construction of a series of value or ranking functions relating the various items[2] would be a considerable undertaking, requiring a great deal of time and effort and possibly a fair amount of fortuitous insight. Second, the development of new situations of use for the various items or the addition or modification of other items could alter their inter-relationships significantly. From a computational point of view, a series of such value functions relating hundreds of items would make the allocation process a difficult endeavor, especially if the value functions are quite complex in nature. Finally, most if not all of the items may be inherent to the performance of the system. Therefore, a serious shortage of one item may severely limit the effectiveness of the system. This may be somehow prevented by considering some *a priori* minimum readiness ratios for a few key items (identified in advance or after some initial model runs). Sometimes an upper bound (<1) for some readiness ratios may be necessary to prevent large production of small-value items on special (expensive) lines at the expense of other items.

TWO MILP MODELS FOR EFFECTIVE PLANNING

To avoid these difficulties, we will assume that all types of products have the same importance from a system effectiveness viewpoint. Model extensions to avoid this assumption—when needed—are discussed at the end of this paper.

Model 1—maximize the minimum readiness ratio

Max X^* (2)

$$\text{s.t. } X^* \leq \left\{ (a_i - l_i) + \sum_{j=1}^{n} d_{ij}[x_{ij} - p_{ij}y_{ij}] \right\} \bigg/ r_i \leq 1 \quad i = 1, 2, \ldots, m \text{ items}$$ (3)

$$\sum_{i=1}^{m} x_{ij} \leq N_j \quad j = 1, 2, \ldots, n \text{ production lines}$$ (4)

$$\sum_{i=1}^{m} \sum_{j=1}^{n} b_{ijk} d_{ij} x_{ij} \leq B_k \quad k = 1, 2, \ldots, s \text{ resources}$$ (5)

$$\sum_{i=1}^{m} \sum_{j=1}^{n} \{ c_{ij} d_{ij} (x_{ij} - p_{ij}y_{ij}) + u_{ij} p_{ij} y_{ij} \} \leq B_0$$ (6)

$$x_{ij} - M y_{ij} \leq 0 \quad \text{for all} \quad i, j$$ (7)

$$-x_{ij} + y_{ij} \leq 0 \quad \text{for all} \quad i, j$$ (8)

$$x_{ij} : \text{non-negative integers for all } i \text{ and } j$$ (9)

$$y_{ij} = 0, 1 \quad \text{for all } i \text{ and } j$$ (10)

$$X^* \geq 0.$$ (11)

Constraint set (3) restricts the readiness ratio RR_i of the ith product in (X^*, 1), while the objective function (2) maximizes the minimum readiness ratio X^*. Constraint set (4) ensures that the number of shifts allocated for setup and actual production of all items on the jth production line does not exceed the available number of shifts (N_j). The constraint set (5) on resource availability assumes that setup runs consume practically the same amount of resources as regular production runs. If not, it will be easy to change this constraint set accordingly. The budget restriction is expressed by constraint (6), where the two terms inside the brackets represent the regular production and setup costs, respectively.

Finally, constraint sets (7) and (8) ensure that, when $y_{ij} = 0$, there is no production shift allocation (i.e. $x_{ij} = 0$); and when $y_{ij} = 1$, constraint set (8) requires some production, while constraint set (7) imposes the trivial restriction $x_{ij} \leq M$, where M is a large pre-specified constant that exceeds all feasible values that any x_{ij} can take on. Thus, these two constraint sets ensure that a setup time is present in (3) and (6) only for those lines j, for which a nonzero allocation of x_{ij} shifts to produce the ith item has been made.

Model 2—maximize the total system readiness

$$\text{Min} \sum_{i=1}^{m} (R_i^- + R_i^+) \tag{12}$$

$$\text{s.t.} \frac{1}{r_i} \left\{ (a_i - l_i) + \sum_{j=1}^{n} d_{ij}(x_{ij} - p_{ij} y_{ij}) \right\} + R_i^- - R_i^+ = 1 \quad i = 1, 2, \ldots, m \text{ items} \tag{13}$$

plus constraints (4) to (10) of model 1 and

$$R_i^-, R_i^+ \geq 0 \quad i = 1, 2, \ldots, m \text{ items.} \tag{14}$$

This objective function minimizes the total deviation from the exact satisfaction of each demand. Oversatisfaction R_i^+ for each item is assumed to be allowable and equally important as undersatisfaction R_i^-. (This may be the case when uncertainties in the demands r_i make them goals rather than facts.) Thus, if resources are not very binding, this model may yield over satisfaction of some demands ($RR_i > 1$) yet undersatisfaction of some others ($RR_i < 1$). Nevertheless, these deviations will be small ($RR_i \simeq 1$). If oversatisfaction of some demands is not allowed, then this model may still be used by simply dropping the corresponding variables (i.e. set $R_i^+ = 0$).

AN EXAMPLE

The data for an illustrative example are shown in Tables 1–3.
The following results for the example problem were obtained using a mixed integer programming code (MINT).[3] Each problem required approxi-

TABLE 1. PRODUCTION FLOW DATA

Line j:	1	2	3	1	2	3			
Item i		d_{ij}			p_{ij}		a_i	l_i	r_i
1	10	12	8	1	2	1	35	10	380
2	8	10	14	2	1	3	70	20	440
3	10	8	12	1	1	1	95	0	160
N_j	20	60	40						

TABLE 2. COST DATA

Line j:	1	2	3	1	2	3
Item i		c_{ij}			u_{ij}	
1	5	7	6	60	80	70
2	4	6	3	50	60	40
3	6	7	9	70	70	100

TABLE 3. RESOURCE REQUIREMENTS (b_{ijk})

Material:	1			2			3		
Line j:	1	2	3	1	2	3	1	2	3
Item i									
1	200	210	215	300	320	315	150	170	165
2	175	190	185	210	215	225	275	280	300
3	400	425	415	170	180	190	170	190	200
B_j		150,000			200,000			170,000	

Total budget available $b_0 = 4500$.

TABLE 4. RESULTS OF MODEL 1

Line j:	1	2	3	1	2	3			
Item i		x_{ij}			y_{ij}		RR_i	R_i^-	R_i^+
1	0	0	40	0	0	1	0.887	0.113	0
2	0	32	0	0	1	0	0.818	0.182	0
3	0	6	0	0	1	0	0.844	0.156	0
Setup	0	2	1			$RR_{\min} = X^* = 0.818$		Tot. = 0.451	0
Unused	20	22	0	$\Rightarrow 42 = $ Tot.					
Total	20	60	40			Total cost 4272			

The y_{ij}s are directly implied by the x_{ij}s, since $x_{ij} = 0 \Rightarrow y_{ij} = 0$ and $x_{ij} \neq 0 \Rightarrow y_{ij} = 1$.

TABLE 5. RESULTS OF MODEL 2

Line j:	1	2	3	1	2	3			
Item i		x_{ij}			y_{ij}		RR_i	R_i^-	R_i^+
1	20	0	13	1	0	1	0.818	0.182	0
2	0	30	0	0	1	0	0.773	0.227	0
3	0	9	0	0	1	0	0.994	0.006	0
Setup	1	2	1			$RR_{\min} = X^* = 0.773$		Tot. = 0.415	0
Unused	0	21	27	$\Rightarrow 48 = $ Tot.					
Total	20	60	40			Total cost 3964			

mately 5 min on a H6080 computer, but a commercial MIP code on a bigger computer (e.g. MPSX/IBM) would have been considerably faster.

Since in the model 2 solution, all R_i^+ are equal to zero, the same solution would have been obtained here had the objective function been replaced by Min $\Sigma_{i=1}^3 R_i^-$ or all R_i^+ set to zero. Note that the second model achieved a higher total effectiveness (smaller $\Sigma_i R_i^-$) at the expense of a smaller RR_{min} and larger deviations between the readiness ratios. Both examples (especially the second) proved to be rather difficult to solve computationally.

SUMMARY AND EXTENSIONS

The choice between the two mixed integer programming models presented in this paper depends on management's objectives. The first model avoids a perhaps seriously low readiness ratio and tends to satisfy demands more uniformly, while the second model maximizes the total satisfaction of demands. When the number of product types is not too large, it could be desirable or even necessary to assign different importance to each product type. This may be the case of a business organization attempting a "market domination" for a few products or emergency military production which can be easily accommodated in the second model by simply changing the objective function [equation (12)] to

$$\text{Minimize} \sum_{i=1}^m P_i(R_i^- + R_i^+). \tag{15}$$

where P_i is the priority or weight of the ith product.

The previous models are effective in meeting given demands, but may not be cost effective. The conflicting objectives and priorities may be simultaneously considered via a goal mixed integer programming formulation. An objective function for such a model may be

$$\text{Min } P_0 \sum_{i=1}^m P_i R_i^- + Q \sum_{j=1}^n v_j S_j^- - Q_0 \cdot B_0^- \tag{16}$$

where P_0, Q_0, Q are goal priorities (omit P_0 if the P_is denote priorities); P_i is weight or priority of the goal $RR_i = 1$ (if these are difficult to determine, substitute the first term in the above objective function with $-P_0 X^*$); B_0^- is the unused budget [slack in equation (6)]; S_j^- is the unused capacity of the jth production line [slack in equation (4)]; v_j is per shift cost of idleness in the jth production line.

If the right-hand sides of the various restrictions are goals rather than quantities rigidly fixed, then for each constraint two variables should be introduced for over- and under-attainment of these targets in the usual goal programming formulation.[4] Such models to be solved would require powerful codes implementing goal mixed integer programming algorithms, that are now in their early stages of development.[5,6] In the absence of such a code, two attempts were made using MINT to reallocate any unused resources in order to minimize production costs without worsening the previously obtained solutions; i.e. Max B_0^- s.t. the additional restriction $X^* \geq 0.818$ or $\Sigma_{i=1}^3 \, (R_i^- + R_i^+) \leq 0.416$, respectively. These attempts failed to produce an equally effective but less costly solution.

A special branch-and-bound algorithm could probably be designed to solve the present problems more efficiently by taking into account their special structure, but was not attempted here. Good heuristic techniques making use of the various problem characteristics seem to be a more attractive alternative for solving large problems of this type encountered often in practice. A heuristic algorithm MAXMINRR has been developed earlier[7] for effectively solving a large-size problem of this type having a simplified structure of model 1 with no cost or material restrictions.

The optimization models presented in this paper may be (1) useful to other researchers having similar production resource allocation problems, (2) helpful in designing good heuristic techniques for solving large-size problems of this type, and (3) used as a vehicle in evaluating the performance of heuristic algorithms on similar small-size problems.

APPENDIX: NOTATION

a_i:
number of units of the ith item in inventory at the beginning of the allocation period minus desired ending inventory

B_0:
total budget available

B_k:
total availability of the kth resource (e.g. material)

b_{ijk}:
amount of kth resource needed to produce the ith item on the jth production line

c_{ij}:
cost to produce one unit of the ith item on the jth production line (excluding set-up costs)

d_{ij}:
number of units of the ith item that can be produced per production shift on the jth production line

l_i:
number of units of the ith item that are required for the maintenance of commitments not directly applicable to the central objective (i.e. transferred out of the system)

N_j:
number of available production shifts on the jth production line

p_{ij}:
number of production shifts required for setup time if the ith item is produced at the jth production line (assumed sequence independent)

r_i:
number of units of the ith item that are required

RR_i: readiness ratio of the ith item [equation (1)]
R_i^-:   under-attainment of the goal $RR_i = 1$
R_i^+:   over-attainment of the goal $RR_i = 1$
u_{ij}:   setup cost per shift to prepare the jth production line to produce the ith item (assumed sequence independent)
X^*:   smallest readiness ratio, i.e. $X^* = \min_i RR_i$
x_{ij}:   number of production shifts to be allocated to the ith item on the jth production line (this includes shifts required for setup)
y_{ij}: $= 1$ if the jth production line is used to produce the ith item, $= 0$ otherwise

$i = 1, 2, \ldots, m$ product types (items)
$j = 1, 2, \ldots, n$ production lines
$k = 1, 2, \ldots, s$ resource types.

EXAMPLE FOR MODEL 1

Max X^*
s.t.

$$380X^* \le \ 25 + 10x_{11} + 12x_{12} + 8x_{13} - 10y_{11} - 24y_{12} - 8y_{13} \quad \le 380$$
$$440X^* \le \ 50 + 8x_{21} + 10x_{22} + 14x_{23} - 16y_{21} - 10y_{22} - 42y_{23} \quad \le 440$$
$$160X^* \le \ 95 + 10x_{31} + 8x_{32} + 12x_{33} - 10y_{31} - 8y_{32} - 12y_{33} \quad \le 160$$

$$x_{11} + x_{21} + x_{31} \quad \le 20$$
$$x_{12} + x_{22} + x_{32} \quad \le 60$$
$$x_{13} + x_{23} + x_{33} \quad \le 40$$

$2000x_{11} + 2520x_{12} + 1720x_{13} + 1400x_{21} + 1900x_{22} + 2590x_{23} + 4000x_{31}$
$+ 3400x_{32} + 4980x_{33} \le 150{,}000$
$3000x_{11} + 3840x_{12} + 2520x_{13} + 1680x_{21} + 2150x_{22} + 3150x_{23} + 1700x_{31}$
$+ 1440x_{32} + 2280x_{33} \le 200{,}000$
$1500x_{11} + 2040x_{12} + 1320x_{13} + 2200x_{21} + 2800x_{22} + 4200x_{23} + 1700x_{31}$
$+ 1520x_{32} + 2400x_{33} \le 170{,}000$
$50x_{11} + 84x_{12} + 48x_{13} + 32x_{21} + 60x_{22} + 42x_{23} + 60x_{31} + 56x_{32} + 108x_{33}$
$+ 10y_{11} - 8y_{12} + 22y_{13} + 36y_{21} + 0.y_{22} - 6y_{23} + 10y_{31} + 14y_{32} - 8y_{33}$
$\le 4{,}500$

$x_{11} - 100y_{11} \le 0$	$-x_{11} + y_{11} \le 0$
$x_{12} - 100y_{12} \le 0$	$-x_{12} + y_{12} \le 0$
$x_{13} - 100y_{13} \le 0$	$-x_{13} + y_{13} \le 0$
$x_{21} - 100y_{21} \le 0$	$-x_{21} + y_{21} \le 0$
$x_{22} - 100y_{22} \le 0$	$-x_{22} + y_{22} \le 0$
$x_{23} - 100y_{23} \le 0$	$-x_{23} + y_{23} \le 0$
$x_{31} - 100y_{31} \le 0$	$-x_{31} + y_{31} \le 0$

$$x_{32} - 100y_{32} \leq 0 \qquad\qquad -x_{32} + y_{32} \leq 0$$
$$x_{33} - 100y_{33} \leq 0 \qquad\qquad -x_{33} + y_{33} \leq 0$$

$x_{ij} \geq 0[i = 1, 2, 3; j = 1, 2, 3]$ and all integer
$y_{ij} = 0$ or 1
$X^* \geq 0$.

EXAMPLE FOR MODEL 2

Min $\quad (R_1^- + R_1^+) + (R_2^- + R_2^+) + (R_3^- + R_3^+)$

s.t. $\quad \{25 + 10x_{11} + 12x_{12} + 8x_{13} - 10y_{11} - 24y_{12} - 8y_{13}\}/380 + R_1^-$
$\qquad - R_1^+ = 1$
$\qquad \{50 + 8x_{21} + 10x_{22} + 14x_{23} - 16y_{21} - 10y_{22} - 42y_{23}\}/440$
$\qquad + R_2^- - R_2^+ = 1$
$\qquad \{95 + 10x_{31} + 8x_{32} + 12x_{33} - 10y_{31} - 8y_{32} - 12y_{33}\}/160 + R_3^-$
$\qquad - R_3^+ = 1$
$\qquad R_i^-, R_i^+ \geq 0 \ i = 1, 2, 3$

plus all constraints of model 1 except the first three [equation (3)] and the last one [equation (11)].

REFERENCES

[1] C. S. MATHENY (1964) A budget model for procurement. DDPC Tech. Rep. PR-64-13.
[2] J. C. GILBERT (1964) A method of resource allocation using demand preference. *Nav. Res. Logist. Q.* **2**, 217.
[3] J. L. KUESTER and J. H. MIZE (1973) *Optimization Techniques with Fortran* p. 66. McGraw-Hill, New York.
[4] S. M. LEE (1972) *Goal Programming for Decision Analysis.* Auerbach, Philadelphia.
[5] S. M. LEE (1975) Integer goal programming algorithms. Paper presented at the S.E. AIDS Conf., Columbia, S.C.
[6] S. ZIONTS (1975) Integer linear programming with multiple objectives. Paper presented at the Workshop in Integer Programming, Bonn.
[7] K. D. LAWRENCE (1973) A sequential decision algorithm for resource allocation of production time. An invited paper presented at the 43rd National Meeting of the Operations Research Society of America, Milwaukee, WI.

Reprinted, by permission, from Decision Sciences, *Vol. 8, 1977, published by the American Institute for Decision Sciences.*

THE ASSIGNMENT OF MEN TO MACHINES: AN APPLICATION OF BRANCH AND BOUND

Jeffrey G. Miller, *Harvard University*

William L. Berry, *Indiana University*

ABSTRACT

This paper presents a branch and bound algorithm for assigning men to machines in a production system. The labor assignment problem of concern in this paper occurs when 1) a single operator can service several semi-automatic machines simultaneously, 2) the service and machine processing times are different among the machines and are deterministic, 3) a strict cyclic service discipline is assumed, and 4) the combined costs of idle labor and machine time are to be minimized. The paper includes a formal definition of the labor assignment problem, a description of the branch and bound algorithm, and a discussion of the computational experience with the algorithm.

Many production managers are routinely faced with the problem of assigning men to machines in scheduling plant operations. A manager's ability to solve these labor assignment problems often determines a plant's productivity and customer service. One labor assignment problem which has received attention in the operations research literature is that of determining labor assignments in situations in which a single man simultaneously operates several semi-automatic machines. These labor assignment decisions, referred to as the multi-machine labor assignment problem, are made in the shop at the time of actual production. They serve to establish both the number of operators required during a given work shift and the machines to which individual operators are assigned. Such decisions are to be distinguished from the long range, less detailed, aggregate employment level planning decisions covering several months or more for a plant [7]. The shop level labor assignments considered in this paper are made for short periods of time, *e.g.,* for several hours or for a single work shift.

Previous research on developing formal techniques for determining multi-machine labor assignments has proceeded along two lines. Queueing models have been applied in production systems for which very little detailed information is available regarding the jobs to be processed at individual machines [1] [6]. In this case the operator service and machine processing times are assumed to be stochastic with an identical pattern of variation at all machines. Other research has been concerned with the problem of preparing work assignments for plant personnel after individual jobs (orders) have been assigned to machines for processing [4] [5] [8] [9] [11]. Once jobs have been dispatched to machines, the operator service time and the machine processing time at each machine is known and can often be assumed to be deterministic because of the repetitive nature of the work. The branch and bound procedure presented in this paper provides optimal labor assignment solutions to the latter problem when the objective is to minimize the combined costs of idle labor and machine time and when a strict cyclic service discipline is employed. This algorithm is important for two reasons. First, it produces optimal solutions to small scale problems which may involve as many as 15 machines. Second, it provides a means of evaluating the solution quality of heuristic scheduling methods [11]. The discussion begins by providing an illustration and a formal statement of the labor assignment problem. Next, the branch and bound algorithm is presented, including a description of the bound setting procedures and the branching decision rules. Finally, a discussion of the authors' computational experience with the algorithm is presented.

THE MULTI-MACHINE LABOR ASSIGNMENT PROBLEM

Multi-machine labor assignment problems are common in machine shops, textile mills, rubber curing shops, and molding shops in which semi-automatic equipment is used. One example of the labor assignment problem described here was reported by Bakshi at the Acushnet Company [2]. In this case, the press operators in the Industrial Rubber Products Division need only be in attendance at a machine at certain times, *e.g.*, when a machine is to be unloaded and loaded. The balance of the operator's time can be spent working at other machines or can be applied to related activities such as inspection and material handling. Acushnet has applied the Labor Saved heuristic (reported earlier by Miller and Berry [11]) to determine daily operator work schedules. The problem assumptions for the branch and bound procedure described here are identical to those required in using the Labor Saved heuristic.

A simplified example of the multi-machine labor assignment problem is shown in Table 1. Here, an *active job set*, consisting of the jobs currently assigned to the four machines in the shop, is described in terms of the operator service and machine

TABLE 1

Example Problem

Machine Number	Service Time per unit (u_i)*	Processing Time per unit (p_i)*	Theoretical Production Rate Per Shift (in units)**
1	4	2	80
2	6	3	53
3	2	2	120
4	2	8	48

*In minutes

**The theoretical maximum number of units produced per shift $= \dfrac{t}{u_i + p_i}$ where t = 480 minutes per shift.

processing times.[1] These times measure the length of time required for an operator to load and unload a machine (u_i) and the machine time necessary to process a given unit (p_i). Because of the repetitive nature of the work and the fixed length of the machine processing cycle, the time values are assumed to be deterministic. The times may vary, however, among the machines (jobs) as is the case in Table 1.

Several additional assumptions serve to further define the particular multi-machine labor assignment problem of interest in this paper.

1. The machine operators are assumed to be equally productive at all machines. Furthermore, no restrictions are placed on either the number of the location of the machines that each man can operate.

2. The transportation time between machines is assumed to be negligible.

3. A minimum production rate (r_i) may be stated for each job (machine) so that scheduled delivery dates can be met.

4. The idle labor cost (C_1) is identical for all men and is nominally set at the average hourly wage rate for the shop.

5. The idle machine time cost (C_2) is identical for all machines and may reflect the overtime wage rate for the machine operators or other opportunity costs associated with idle machines.

6. The machine service times can not be segmented (interrupted).

These assumptions are not overly restrictive, and they do permit an analytic procedure to be developed for determining optimal multi-machine labor assignment solutions. In addition, they indicate useful topics for further work in generalizing the branch and bound algorithm presented in this paper.

Developing Alternative Solutions

Any solution to the multi-machine labor assignment problem must specify 1) the number of men required (N) and 2) their assignment to the M individual machines.[2] When the employment level is permitted to vary from 1 to M men, there are M^M possible solutions. However, if the men are assumed to be equally productive at all machines, the number of different solutions can be reduced to M!. In the four machine example shown in Table 1, this qualification means that the total number of solutions can be reduced from 256 to 24. This value (M!) should, however, be considered as an upper limit on the total number of distinct solutions because some functionally identical machine assignments, called isomorphs [13], are still included in the solutions to be enumerated. As an example, when a two man workforce is specified in the example

---

[1] Inactive jobs are those which have been accepted by the plant for manufacture, but which have not yet been assigned to a machine for processing. Another problem which is not included in the scope of this paper is that of determining the assignment of jobs to machines, *i.e.*, job dispatching.

[2] A special case exists when the size of the work force (N) is pre-specified. The branch and bound algorithm described in this paper is also applicable to this problem.

shown in Table 1, there are seven distinct solutions to be investigated. These solutions are listed in Table 2. Three additional functionally equivalent solutions may be enumerated. These three solutions are indicated in Figure 2. A procedure for identifying and eliminating isomorphs is presented in the discussion of the branch and bound algorithm in the latter part of the paper.

TABLE 2
Alternative Machine Assignments For N = 2

Assignment Number	Machines Assigned to Man 1	Machines Assigned to Man 2
1	1	2,3,4
2	2	1,3,4
3	3	1,2,4
4	4	1,2,3
5	1,2	3,4
6	1,3	2,4
7	1,4	2,3

A statement regarding the number of men and their respective machine assignments is not sufficient to define a solution for the multi-machine labor assignment problem. The sequence (or routing) to be followed by the operator in servicing the machines assigned to him during his work shift remains to be specified. The solution involving the assignment of a single operator to all four machines in Table 1 illustrates this point. A large number of distinct machine routings can be constructed to cover the entire shift in this case. One such routing would be: 1-2-3-4-3-4-1-2-3-4. However, in this paper only *strict cyclic machine routings* are considered, *i.e.*, a strict cyclic service discipline is applied [5]. The machines are serviced one after another in strict rotation until the last machine is serviced; then, the machine routing begins with the first machine again. Therefore in the single operator solution the machine routing would be: 1-2-3-4, 1-2-3-4, etc. Although other service disciplines exist, such as the first-come, first-served discipline, the strict cyclic service discipline is applied because it facilitates the evaluation of alternative solutions to the multi-machine labor assignment problem. Moreover, the strict cyclic service discipline is advantageous in actual operating situations because an operator can develop a regular motion pattern [3].

Evaluating Labor Assignment Solutions

Since the objective is to minimize the combined costs of idle labor and machine time, an expression is needed for determining idle labor and machine times for alternative labor assignment solutions. This expression follows directly from the assumption of a strict cyclic service discipline and represents an extension of the work reported by

Conway, *et.al.* [5]. It will be developed in two steps: 1) by determining the effective production rate for a labor assignment solution and 2) by expressing the idle labor and machine time per cycle as a function of the effective production rate for the man-machine assignments in a given solution.

Earlier in Table 1, the theoretical production rate was listed for each machine in the example. This production rate represents the maximum number of units that can be produced each shift at a machine if the machine is never idle. If a machine must wait for the operator to service it, however, the theoretical production rate cannot be achieved. Thus, the *effective production rate* is defined to be the output actually obtained from a machine during a work shift. This production rate is a function of the length of time (T_j) between successive visits by the jth operator in servicing each of the machines to which he is assigned. This time (T_j) is called the *effective machine cycle time* and is computed as follows:

$$T_j = Max \left[\sum_{i \in s_j} u_i, \ Max_{i \in s_j} \ (u_i + p_i) \right], \tag{1}$$

where: s_j = the set of machines assigned to operator j;

u_i = the time required to unload and load the ith machine;

p_i = the processing time for the ith machine.

The use of equation (1) can be illustrated by considering one and two man solutions to the example problem. In the case of the single operator solution, s_j contains all four machines listed in Table 1. Thus, the total service time $(\sum_{i \in s_j} u_i = 14$ minutes) exceeds the processing cycle $(u_i + p_i)$ for each of the four machines in s_j, and the machines must wait their turn for the operator to service them. The operator arrives at each machine once every 14 minutes (the effective machine cycle time, T_1, in this case). The effective production rate for each of the machines is 34 units per shift instead of the theoretical production rates listed in Table 1.[3] When two men are assigned to operate the four machines, one serving machines (2,4) and the other serving machines (1,3, *i.e.*, $s_1 = \{2,4\}$ and $s_2 = \{1,3\}$, the effective production rates for the machines change substantially. The man-machine activity chart presented in Figure 1 shows that idle time exists for machine 2 and operator number 1. In this case, operator number 1 visits each machine assigned to him (machines 2 and 4) once every ten minutes, and the length of the longest machine cycle $(u_i + p_i = 10$ minutes at machine 4) controls the effective machine cycle time (T_1). Therefore, while the effective production rate equals the theoretical production rate at machine 4, the effective production rate is smaller than the theoretical value for machine 2 (48 versus 53 units per shift).

---

[3] The effective production rate $= \dfrac{t}{14} = 34$ units per shift when t = 480 minutes per shift.

FIGURE 1

Two Man Solution Man-Machine Chart

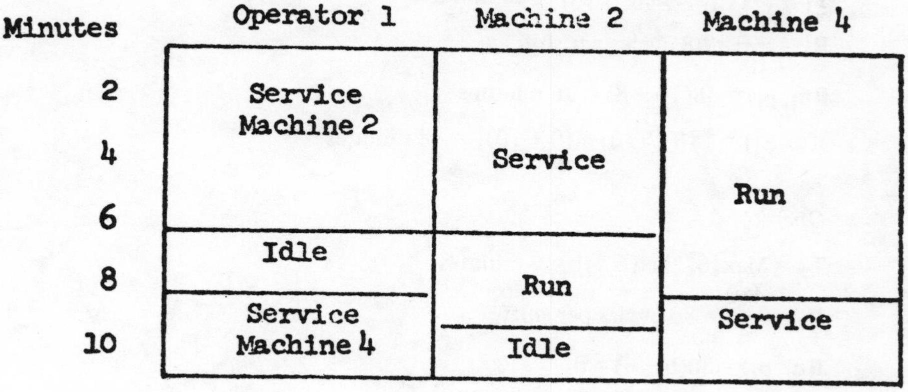

Minutes	Operator 1	Machine 2	Machine 4
2	Service Machine 2	Service	
4			Run
6			
8	Idle	Run	
10	Service Machine 4	Idle	Service

Having developed an expression for the effective machine cycle time associated with the jth man's assignment (T_j) and for the effective production rate $(R_j = \frac{t}{T_j}$, where t = 480 minutes per work shift or some other convenient unit of time), the idle man and machine time per shift for each man's assignment can be determined using equations (2) and (3) (these expressions follow from the work of Conway, *et.al.* [5] and Jones [8].

Idle Man Time: $\quad f(u_i,p_i) = R_j(T_j - \sum_{i \in s_j} u_i)$ $\qquad\qquad\qquad$ (2)

Idle Machine Time: $\quad g(u_i,p_i) = R_j[mT_j - \sum_{i \in s_j} (u_i + p_i)],$ $\qquad\qquad$ (3)

where m = the number of machines in the set s_j.

The one and two operator machine assignments mentioned above provide an illustration of the use of equations (2) and (3) in evaluating the amount of idle man and machine time for a particular solution. For the single operator solution where $s_1 = \{1,2,3,4\}$:

$T_1 = \text{Max } [14, \text{Max}(6,9,4,10)] = 14 \text{ minutes}$

$R_1 = \frac{480}{14} = 34 \text{ cycles per shift}$[4]

$f(u_i, p_i) = 34 \,(14-14) = 0$

$g(u_i, p_i) = 34 \,[(4)\,(14) - (6 + 9 + 4 + 10)] = 926 \text{ minutes per shift.}$

---

[4]Note that the number of cycles per shift and the effective production rate for a machine are identical.

For the two operator solution where $s_1 = \{2,4\}$ and $s_2 = \{1,3\}$:

Operator 1

$T_1 = \text{Max } [8, \text{Max}(9,10)] = 10$ minutes

$R_1 = \dfrac{480}{10} = 48$ cycles per shift

$f(u_i, p_i) = 48(10 - 8) = 96$ minutes

$g(u_i, p_i) = 48[(2)(10) - (9 + 10)] = 48$ minutes

Operator 2

$T_2 = \text{Max } [6, \text{Max}(6,4)] = 6$ minutes

$R_2 = \dfrac{480}{6} = 80$ cycles per shift

$f(u_i, p_i) = 80(6 - 6) = 0$

$g(u_i, p_i) = 80[(2)(6) - (6 + 4)] = 160$ minutes

Thus, when equation (3) is applied in this example, a major reduction in machine idle time occurs when the single operator solution is changed to this particular two man labor assignment, *i.e.*, 208 versus 926 minutes per shift.

A Formal Statement of the Problem

The multi-machine labor assignment problem can now be stated in general terms, using equations (2) and (3) to express the amount of idle man and machine time associated with each operator and summing the idle man and machine times for all operators.

$$\text{Minimize } \left[C_1 \sum_{j=1}^{M} \gamma_j f(\delta_{ij}, u_i, p_i) + C_2 \sum_{j=1}^{M} \gamma_j g(\delta_{ij}, u_i, p_i) \right] \tag{4a}$$

Subject to the following constraints:

$$\sum_{j=1}^{M} \delta_{1j} = 1 \tag{4b}$$

$$\sum_{j=1}^{M} \delta_{2j} = 1 \tag{4c}$$

$$\vdots$$

$$\sum_{j=1}^{M} \delta_{Mj} = 1 \tag{4d}$$

$$h(\delta_{ij}, u_i, p_i) \geqslant r_i \text{ for all } i \tag{4e}$$

$$\sum_{i=1}^{M} \delta_{ij} \leq M\gamma_j, \text{ for all } j \tag{4f}$$

where:

$TIC =$ the total idle labor and machine cost per unit of time (t) for a given labor assignment.

$\delta_{ij} =$ 1 if machine i, i = 1, . . ., M, is assigned to man j, j = 1, . . ., N $\leq$ M and O otherwise.

$\gamma_j =$ 1 if any machines are assigned to man j and O otherwise. (This variable is required since the f and g functions are undefined when machines are not assigned to the ith man.)

$C_1 =$ the cost of idle labor per time unit t.

$C_2 =$ the cost of idle machines per time unit t.

$u_i =$ the service time for machine i, i = 1, . . ., M, where M is the number of machines.

$p_i =$ the processing time for machine i.

$r_i =$ the minimum acceptable production rate for product i.

$$f(\delta_{ij}, u_i, p_i) = \frac{t}{T_j} (T_j - \sum_{i=1}^{M} \delta_{ij} u_i)$$

$$g(\delta_{ij}, u_i, p_i) = \frac{t}{T_j} [T_j \sum_{i=1}^{M} \delta_{ij} - \sum_{i=1}^{M} \delta_{ij}(u_i + p_i)]$$

$$h(\delta_{ij}, u_i, p_i) = R_j = \frac{t}{T_j}$$

$$T_j = \text{Max} \left[\sum_{i=1}^{M} \delta_{ij} u_i, \text{Max}_i [\delta_{ij}(u_i + p_i)] \right]$$

$t =$ a convenient time period, e.g. a single work shift where t = 480 minutes, that is expressed in the same time units as u_i and p_i.

The objective function defined in equation (4a), in conjunction with the constraint equations (4b) through (4f), comprise the complete formulation of the multi-machine labor assignment problem when a strict cyclic service discipline is assumed. The δ_{ij} variable has been introduced as a means of determining which of the machines (i) are included in the set (s_j) assigned to each of the men. Also, the γ_j variable has been used to specify the number of men to be employed in a given solution. Finally, this objective function assumes that the cost of idle time is identical for all men, and similarly the cost of idle time is the same for all machines.

The constraint set includes several types of restrictions. The first type of constraint, equations (4b) through (4d), specifies that each machine must be assigned to one and only one operator. The second type of constraint, equation (4e), ensures that each job is produced at a rate which is compatible with the scheduled delivery date for the work. This constraint also serves to establish a production volume limitation for the various products which the solution must satisfy. The last type of constraint, equation (4f), ensures that γ_j must be greater than zero if any machines are assigned to the jth man, *i.e.*, $\sum_{i=1}^{M} \delta_{ij} \geqslant 1$.

As formulated, this problem is a nonlinear, zero-one integer programming problem. This problem can not be solved by the use of well developed techniques such as integer linear programming methods. The combinatorial nature of the problem does, however, suggest the use of one technique which has a history of successful applications in integer linear programming problems—the method of branch and bound [12].

THE BRANCH AND BOUND ALGORITHM

Branch and bound provides a systematic method for searching a solution space to find the optimal solution. This method relies on the implicit enumeration of all the points in a solution space to partition it into two complementary subsets, one containing the optimum solution and one that does not. The partitioning is accomplished by comparing an *upper bound* on the optimum solution cost with a *lower bound* cost. The lower bound provides an optimistic estimate of the minimum cost that is likely to be obtained by pursuing a given *partial solution* to a *complete solution*. As is shown in the following sections, upper and lower bounds can be used to reduce the magnitude of the search by eliminating large numbers of partial solutions from further consideration. Four elements are necessary in constructing a branch and bound algorithm: 1) a method for enumerating partial solutions, 2) bound setting procedures, 3) a branching decision rule, and 4) feasibility checking procedures.

Enumerating Partial Solutions

Earlier it was noted that when the men are assumed to be equally productive at all machines and when the employment level (N) is permitted to vary from 1 to M men, the number of distinct solutions can be effectively reduced from M^M to at most M!. The branch and bound algorithm presented in this paper takes advantage of this reduction. In addition, the total number of solutions is further reduced by restricting the employment level to a smaller interval than $1 \leqslant N \leqslant M$., *i.e.*, to $N_1 \leqslant N \leqslant N_2$ where $N_1 \leqslant 1$ and $N_2 \leqslant M$. The procedure used to determine the range for the work force level is described in the following section which presents the bounding procedures.[5] When the range for N is narrowed, an upper limit on the number of distinct

---

[5] Alternately, one might choose to pre-specify the N_1 and N_2 values, *e.g.*, $N_1 = N_2 = 2$ when a fixed work force level is desired.

solutions can be determined by evaluating the expressions $(N_2)! (N_2)^{M-N_2} - (N_1-1)! (N_1-1)^{M-N_1+1}$.

The method used to enumerate partial and complete solutions in the branch and bound algorithm is illustrated by the tree diagram shown in Figure 2. This diagram shows all of the partial and complete solutions when $1 \leqslant N \leqslant 3$ for the four machine problem in Table 1. Partial solutions are indicated in the diagram at nodes b through j, and complete solutions occur at nodes k through ab. A partial assignment involving the assignment of machines 1 and 2 to operator number 1 is designated by the first two branches where δ_{11} and δ_{21} are set equal to 1. All solutions containing this partial assignment follow directly from these two branches, beginning at node d.

Two rules are used at each node in the tree to limit the enumeration of branches to the employment level range specified (N_1, N_2). These rules are: 1) the number of men in a solution must not exceed N_2 (the upper limit) and 2) an optimistic estimate of the total number of men in a complete solution $(j + M - i)$ must exceed N_1 (the lower limit). These rules may be verified by using the tree diagram in Figure 2 to isolate the eleven complete solutions that result when $1 \leqslant N \leqslant 2$ and the seven complete solutions that result when $N = 3$. A third rule is used to prevent enumerating solutions in which the number of men exceeds the number of machines, *i.e.*, when $j > i$.

Four redundant solutions are noted by the dashed lines in the tree diagram. Three of these solutions occur when $N = 2$, and one solution occurs for $N = 3$. These solutions, called isomorphs, are functionally equivalent to other solutions since the men are assumed to be equally productive at all machines. The isomorphs occur when the algorithm skips to a higher numbered man in making an assignment than the next man in consecutive order. At node h, for example, an assignment involving man number 3 is made before man number 2 has been assigned to a machine. Isomorphs can be discovered and eliminated by using an isomorphic rejection test. In this algorithm isomorphs are found when the new value for the j (man) index exceeds the highest previous value of j plus one. In the example shown in Figure 2, the solution developed at node q is not an isomorph since man number 2 has been assigned to a machine previously at node c. When the isomorphic solutions are eliminated by this test, the number of distinct solutions falls short of the number that would otherwise be estimated for the solution interval (N_1, N_2) using the formula

$$(N_2)! (N_2)^{M-N_2} - (N_1 - 1)! (N_1 - 1)^{M-N_1+1}.$$

Thus, in the example shown in Figure 2, eighteen solutions would be anticipated for the solution interval $(N_1 = 1, N_2 = 3)$, but only fourteen distinct solutions exist.

The Bound Setting Procedures

Three bound setting procedures are applied in the algorithm to evaluate and eliminate poor solutions from further consideration as partial and complete solutions are investigated in the branch and bound tree. These procedures include: 1) an *upper bound* on the total cost of a complete labor assignment solution which is provided

FIGURE 2

Tree Diagram For N = 1, 2, and 3 Man Solutions

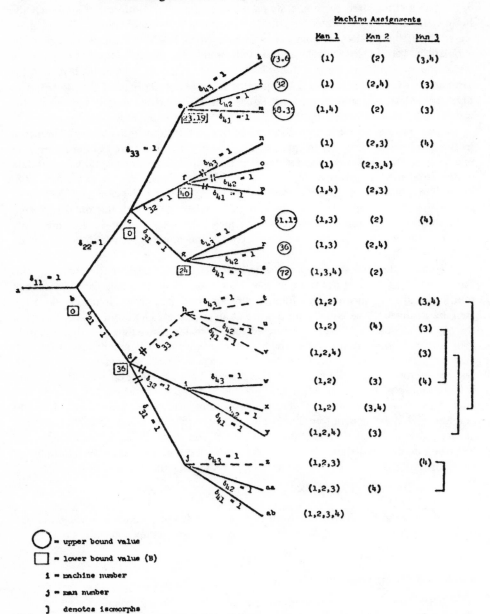

	Machine Assignments		
	Man 1	Man 2	Man 3
k (73.6)	(1)	(2)	(3,4)
l (32)	(1)	(2,4)	(3)
m (58.3)	(1,4)	(2)	(3)
n	(1)	(2,3)	(4)
o	(1)	(2,3,4)	
p	(1,4)	(2,3)	
q (51.1)	(1,3)	(2)	(4)
r (36)	(1,3)	(2,4)	
s (72)	(1,3,4)	(2)	
t	(1,2)		(3,4)
u	(1,2)	(4)	(3)
v	(1,2,4)		(3)
w	(1,2)	(3)	(4)
x	(1,2)	(3,4)	
y	(1,2,4)	(3)	
z	(1,2,3)		(4)
aa	(1,2,3)	(4)	
ab	(1,2,3,4)		

- ○ = upper bound value
- □ = lower bound value (B)
- i = machine number
- j = man number
-] denotes isomorphs
- ‖ the calculation is terminated because the lower bound ≥ the upper bound.

initially by a heuristic procedure, 2) a *pre-bound* that is computed to determine the work force level range to be investigated (N_1, N_2), and 3) a *lower bound* which is an optimistic cost estimate that is used to evaluate partial solutions in the branch and bound tree.

Upper Bound: An upper bound can be computed from any complete solution, but the total cost of this solution should be as small as possible to reduce the magnitude of the search for the optimal solution. In this algorithm a heuristic procedure, called the *man-loading heuristic,* has been used to set the initial upper bound value. Subsequent upper bounds are obtained from complete solutions which have a lower total cost. The man-loading heuristic ranks the machines in the active job set according to their $(u_i + p_i)$ values. The machine having the largest $(u_i + p_i)$ value receives the highest ranking. The $(u_i + p_i)$ value for the first item in the list establishes the effective machine cycle time (T_1) for the first man. Machines are added to his assignment so long as the $(\sum_{i \in s_1} u_i)$ value is less than T_1. When T_1 is exceeded, another man is added and the procedure is repeated, continuing until the active job set is exhausted. This heuristic has the advantage of finding solutions with low idle time costs. When the man-loading heuristic is applied to the example in Table 1, the two man labor assignment mentioned above results (1,3), (2,4). If the labor idle time cost (C_1) equals \$3 per hour and if the machine idle time cost (C_2) is \$9 per hour the initial upper bound value is \$36 per shift.

Pre-Bound: The initial upper bound is used to establish the range of work force levels to be evaluated (N_1, N_2). The entire range of values to be considered in setting N_1 and N_2 is, of course, $1 \leqslant N \leqslant 2$. A *pre-bound cost* is an optimistic cost estimate for each work force level (N). This value is compared with the initial upper bound, and those values of N for which the pre-bound cost exceeds the initial upper bound are eliminated from further consideration. The expression for the pre-bound cost is

$$PB(N) = \begin{cases} C_1 \ [Nt - X] \ \text{for} \ X < Nt \\ C_2 \ [X - Nt] \ \text{for} \ Nt \leqslant X \end{cases}, \tag{5}$$

where: X = the maximum amount of time per time unit (t) that could be spent by N operators in servicing all M machines.

$$X = t \sum_{i=1}^{M} \frac{u_i}{u_i + p_i} . \tag{6}$$

Two points should be noted regarding the pre-bound value. First, since the denominators in the ratios used to compute X do not include idle machine time, a minimum effective machine cycle time (equal to the theoretical machine cycle time) is assumed. Thus, each ratio used in determining X is computed at its maximum value, and X is a maximum value. As an example, in Table 1 (when t=8 hours per shift) X equals 16.27 hours. Therefore, if the four machines are operated at their theoretical production rates with no idle machine time, 16.27 hours of operator service time must be performed during a work shift. The 16.27 hours of operator service time represents the maximum amount of service work that can be performed under "ideal conditions" in this case.

Second, the estimate of the maximum service time that can be performed per shift (X) is used to estimate the pre-bound cost of idle labor and machine time for an N man work force, PB(N). If X exceeds the amount of operator time available during a shift (Nt), a minimum amount of idle machine time (X−Nt) must occur at a cost of C_2. However, if the available operator time (Nt) exceeds the maximum amount of service time per shift (X), a minimum amount of idle labor time (Nt−X) occurs at a cost of C_1 per time unit. If the pre-bound values, PB(N), for any work force level is *at least* as costly as the initial upper bound, that work force level can be eliminated from further consideration. When this procedure is applied to the example in Table 1, the pre-bound values for $1 \leqslant N \leqslant 4$ are: PB(1) = \$69.75, PB(2) = \$2.25, PB(3) = \$23.25, and PB(4) = \$47.25. Since the initial upper bound is \$36, the work force range (N_1, N_2) is narrowed to N = 2 and 3.

Lower Bound: The last bounding procedure, called the *lower bound,* is used to evaluate nodes in the branch and bound tree when searching for the optimal solution. Prior to starting the branch and bound algorithm, two important items of information exist: 1) the objective function value for a low cost complete solution (the initial upper bound) and 2) the range of work force levels to be investigated (N_1, N_2). It now is possible to proceed through the tree, evaluate partial solutions, and determine the optimum solution. The value of the lower bound to be computed at each node ideally should represent the value of the objective function for the lowest cost complete solution which is in the set of solutions defined by the partial solution currently under consideration. At node b in Figure 2, for example, the lower bound should reflect the lowest cost complete solution that includes the assignment of machine 1 to man 1 ($\delta_{11} = 1$). The computational efficiency of the algorithm may be improved by using a lower bound procedure that produces values which are as large as possible, *i.e.,* as close as possible to the lowest cost complete solution that is in the set of solutions which can be derived from the current partial solution.

Lower bound values (B) are determined by considering the combined costs of idle labor and machine time (B = L + E). The lower bound for the cost of idle labor (L) is computed using the number of men assigned in the partial solution currently being evaluated (n). This value is calculated much like the pre-bound, *i.e.,* by comparing the maximum amount of operator service time that can be performed per shift under ideal conditions (X) with the total amount of operator time available (nt). When $X < nt$, the difference between these two values is an estimate of the minimum amount of idle labor time per shift.

$$ L = \begin{cases} C_1 \ (nt - X) \text{ if } X < nt \\ 0 \text{ otherwise} \end{cases}, \qquad (7) $$

where X is computed using equation (6).

The lower bound value at node e in Figure 2 provides an illustration of this calculation. Since three men are assigned at this point and since the available labor per shift in this partial solution exceeds the amount of operator service time required under ideal conditions (nt = 24 > 16.27), the lower bound for the idle labor cost is \$23.19. At node b, however, the lower bound on the idle labor cost is zero since the maximum service time per shift exceeds the amount of labor time available (nt = 8 < 16.27). Idle labor time may or may not result in some solutions in the subset presently under consideration.

To complete the lower bound calculation at each node, a lower bound must also be computed for the idle machine cost (E) using equation (8). (This function is similar to the g function defined previously in the general statement of the problem, and is summed over $n \leqslant M$ men.)

$$E = C_2 \sum_{j=1}^{n} \frac{t}{T_j} [T_j \sum_{i=1}^{M} \delta_{ij} - \sum_{i=1}^{M} \delta_{ij} (u_i + p_i)]. \tag{8}$$

This expression derives from the fact that idle machine time cannot decrease as more machines are added to a man's assignment. This result occurs because idle machine time is a function of either the largest machine processing cycle ($u_i + p_i$) or the sum of the operator service times ($\sum_{i \in s_j} u_i$) in an operator's assignment. Thus, the effective machine cycle time (T_j) can never decrease as machines are added to an operator's assignment.

Node g in Figure 2 provides an illustration of the idle machine time lower bound. The partial solution at this point in the tree consists of the assignment of machines 1 and 3 to operator 1, and of machine 2 to operator 2. Since machine 1 has a longer processing cycle than machine 3 (6 versus 4 minutes), machine 3 accumulates 2 minutes of idle time during each of the 80 processing cycles in a work shift for a total idle machine cost of \$24 per shift. If the combined service times ($\sum_{i \in s_1} u_i$) had exceeded 6 minutes for operator 1, idle machine time would have been a function of the operator service times. However, the idle machine time for operator 1 clearly cannot decrease as machines are added to his assignment.

The Branching Decision Rule

The branching decision rule in conjunction with the enumeration and bounding procedures provides a method for moving through the tree to find the optimum solution. The branching rule employed is called "branch from the newest active branch" [10]. This rule moves the algorithm through the tree along a continuous path, indexing first on the machine number (i) until the branch is either terminated at a complete solution or is eliminated from further consideration. In the latter case, the rule moves the algorithm back to the immediately preceding node and starts down the next branch by indexing the man number (j). For example, the path taken by the algorithm in Figure 2 begins at node b and ends at node k by way of b-d-c-g-s-r-q-g-c-f-c-e-m-l-k. This branching rule was selected because it requires less computer storage than other rules; nevertheless, it may not lead directly to improved upper bound solutions.

The Feasibility Checking Procedures

The production rate constraint, equation (4e), forms the basis for an additional check on the acceptability of a partial solution enumerated in the tree. As the algorithm compares the upper bound to the lower bound at each node, it also checks to determine whether the effective production rate (R_j) of the machines in the partial assignment exceeds the minimum acceptable production rate (r_j). This procedure extends the ability of the algorithm to prune branches in the tree when due dates are important. (In the example problem due dates were set artificially long so that this check was never invoked.)

COMPUTATIONAL EXPERIENCE

The branch and bound algorithm was programmed in FORTRAN IV and executed on a CDC 6500 computer. Randomly generated problems were solved to gain computational experience with the algorithm. These problems ranged in size from 5 to 20 machines with a minimum acceptable production rate (r_j) of zero for each machine. The average computing time for each problem size is shown in Table 3. Fifteen problems were solved with the number of machines ranging from 5 to 15. One 20 machine problem was attempted, but the run was terminated at 3000 seconds at which time a final solution had not yet been reached. Thus, the computational requirements of the algorithm clearly restrict its use to problems with less than 20 machines.

TABLE 3

Average Computing Times

Number of Machines	Computer Time*
5	.073
7	.181
9	1.69
10	6.25
15	23.18
20	3000.00[+]

*Seconds per problem measured on a CDC 6500 computer.

CONCLUSIONS

While considerable work has been reported on solution methods for multi-machine labor assignment problems, few methods exist which are applicable in situations in which the operator service and machine processing times are different among the machines and for which the objective is to minimize the combined costs of idle labor and machine time. This paper demonstrates a method for obtaining an optimum solution to this problem for small problems when a strict cyclic service discipline is used. The branch and bound method exploits the special structure of this labor assignment problem in enumerating solutions and in setting bounds on the objective function to facilitate the search for the optimum solution.

Further work remains to be done in developing solution methods for this labor assignment problem. First, improvements may be made on the procedure for determining the lower bound values. Higher lower bound values would reduce the computational requirements for this algorithm. In addition, other branching rules, such as the "branch from the lowest lower bound" rule, may aid in reducing the search time. Second, the branch and bound algorithm may be extended to cover additional service disciplines for this problem. By allowing machines to be serviced several times per cycle rather than once per cycle with a strict cyclic service discipline, further reductions in the final solution cost might be obtained. The major problem in using other service disciplines is that of developing analytic expressions to evaluate the idle labor and machine time. Finally, the search time for the optimum solution might be reduced by the use of other heuristics that obtain low initial upper bounds. The criteria for developing such heuristics include both their computational efficiency and the proximity of their solutions to the optimum solution cost. The branch and bound algorithm presented in this paper provides optimum solutions against which to measure the effectiveness of heuristic solution methods.

REFERENCES

[1] Ashcroft, H. "The Productivity of Several Machines Under the Care of One Operator." *Royal Statistical Society Journal,* Vol. 12 (1950), pp. 145–151.

[2] Bakshi, M.S., "Development of An On-Line Dynamic Production Scheduling System for Efficient Multi-Machine Assignments In a Job Shop," Presented at the Joint ORSA/TIMS Conference, San Juan, Puerto Rico, November 1974.

[3] Berry, K.R. "Work Measurement in Multiple Machine Assignments." *Journal of Industrial Engineering,* Vol. 19, No. 8 (August, 1968), pp. xvii–xix.

[4] Burgess, A.R. "Comments on Simulation in the Application of Wage Incentives to Multiple Machines." *Journal of Industrial Engineering,* Vol. 13, No. 4 (July-August, 1962), p. 264.

[5] Conway, R.W., W.L. Maxwell, and H.W. Sampson. "On the Cyclic Servicing of Semi-automatic Machines." *Journal of Industrial Engineering,* Vol. 13, No. 2 (March-April, 1962), pp. 105–108.

[6] Fetter, R.N. "The Assignment of Operators to Service Semi-Automatic Machines." *Journal of Industrial Engineering,* Vol. 6, No. 5 (September-October, 1955), pp. 22–30.

[7] Holt, C.C., J.C. Muth, F. Modigliani, and H.A. Simon. *Planning Production, Inventories and Work Force.* Englewood Cliffs, N.J.: Prentice Hall, 1960.

[8] Jones, Dale. "Graphical Determination of Work Loads for Multiple Machine Assignments." *Journal of Industrial Engineering,* Vol. 4, No. 2 (May, 1953), pp. 16–25.

[9]   Killingback, J. "Cyclic Interference Between Two Machines on Different Work." *International Journal of Production Research*, Vol. 3, No. 2 (1964), pp. 115–120.

[10] Lawler, E.L. and P.E. Wood. "Branch and Bound Methods, A Survey." *Operations Research*, Vol. 14 (July-August, 1966), pp. 619–719.

[11] Miller, J.G. and W.L. Berry. "Heuristic Methods for Assigning Men to Machines: An Experimental Analysis." *AIIE Transactions* (June, 1974), pp. 97–104.

[12] Mitten, L.G. "Branch and Bound Methods: General Formulation and Properties." *Operations Research*, Vol. 18, No. 1 (January-February, 1970), pp. 24–34.

[13] Wells, M.B. *Elements of Combinatorial Programming*. London: Pergammon Press, 1971.

Reprinted, by permission, from Management Science, *Vol. 27, No. 3, 1981. Copyright 1981 by The Institute of Management Sciences.*

PRODUCTION AND SALES PLANNING WITH LIMITED SHARED TOOLING AT THE KEY OPERATION*

GERALD G. BROWN,† ARTHUR M. GEOFFRION‡ AND GORDON H. BRADLEY†

The focus of this paper is multiperiod production and sales planning when there is a single dominant production operation for which tooling (dies, molds, etc.) can be shared among parts and is limited in availability. Our interest in such problems grew out of management issues confronting an injection molding manufacturer of plastic pipes and fittings for the building and chemical industries, but similar problems abound in the manufacture of many other cast, extruded, molded, pressed, or stamped products. We describe the development and successful application of a planning model and an associated computational approach for this class of problems.

The problem is modeled as a mixed integer linear program. Lagrangean relaxation is applied so as to exploit the availability of highly efficient techniques for minimum cost network flow problems and for single-item dynamic lot-sizing type problems. For the practical application at hand, provably good solutions are routinely being obtained in modest computing time to problems far beyond the capabilities of available mathematical programming systems.

(INVENTORY/PRODUCTION APPLICATIONS; PRODUCTION—FLOW SHOP; INTEGER PROGRAMMING APPLICATIONS)

1. Introduction

This paper addresses production and sales planning in a seasonal industry with a single principal production operation for which tooling can be shared among parts and is limited in availability.

The specific context of our experience is the production of injection molded plastic pipes and fittings for the building and chemical industries. The principal production operation is injection molding and the tooling consists of mold bases used to adapt the injection molding machines to the molds proper. Mold bases typically require 4-6 calendar months to obtain at a cost which can approach the cost of the molding machine itself, so their availability is limited and good utilization is important.

Other possible domains of application include production facilities based on casting, molding, stamping, extrusion, or pressing of finished or nearly finished products. Dies and molds and associated adaptive tooling are usually expensive and often designed for use with more than one end product. Machine tooling with elaborate jigs and fixtures constitutes another large area of potential application. Although there can be just one principal operation to be modeled, there may also be preparatory and final finishing operations.

An informal statement of the problem treated is as follows. A facility produces many different parts (products), each by a principal operation calling for a specific type of tool and any one of a number of machines compatible with the tool. Machines

*Accepted by Martin K. Starr, Special Editor; received March 24, 1980. This paper has been with the authors 2 months for 1 revision.

†Naval Postgraduate School.

‡University of California, Los Angeles.

are aggregated into machine groups and tools into tool types. Production and sales are to be planned for each part over a multiperiod horizon (typically monthly for a full year):

Determine
  * how much of each part to produce in each time period
  * how much of each part to sell in each time period
  * how much of each part to carry forward as inventory from each time period into the next
  * a tool/machine assignment schedule specifying, for each time period, the number of days of production of each tool type in conjunction with each compatible machine group

so as to satisfy all necessary constraints
  * limited availability of tools in each time period
  * limited availability of machines in each time period
  * tool/machine compatibility restrictions
  * for each part in each time period, sales cannot exceed forecast demand

and so as to satisfy desired managerial policy constraints
  * for each part in each time period, sales must exceed a certain fraction of demand stipulated by management
  * for each part, the ending inventory at the conclusion of the planning horizon must take on a stipulated value
  * no planned backlogging (unfilled demand is lost)

in such a manner as to maximize total profits over all parts for the duration of the planning horizon, calculated according to
  * incremental net profit contribution per unit sold
  * less variable operating costs associated with production (by tool type and machine group)
  * less fixed costs associated with production (by part, for each period with positive production)
  * less part-specific inventory holding costs.

The problem as stated has elements in common with many familiar dynamic planning and resource allocation problems. It is more detailed than most seasonal planning problems in that discrete fixed costs are included and no aggregation is necessary over parts, yet it stops short of encompassing detailed scheduling because other aggregations are employed (tools → tool types, machines → machine groups, time → time periods). Related production planning and scheduling problems in the molding industry can be found in [3], [7], [9].

A proper mathematical formulation as a mixed integer linear program is given in §2. The next section presents a solution approach based on a particularly attractive Lagrangean relaxation and sketches our full scale computational implementation. §4 describes computational experience with the injection molding application mentioned earlier. For this application, solutions well within 2% of optimum are routinely produced in about 3 minutes of IBM 370/168 time for mixed integer linear programs on the order of 12,000 binary variables, 40,000 continuous variables, and 26,000 constraints.

2. Problem Formulation

This section formally defines and discusses the problem as a mixed integer linear program.

We adopt the following notation. Essential use is made of the concept of a *standard day*, which is a part-specific measure of quantity. It is, for a given part, the quantity that would be produced in one calendar day if a tool of the required type were operating normally on any compatible machine.

Indices

i indexes parts
j indexes tool types
k indexes machine groups
t indexes time periods, $t = 1, \ldots, T$
$\mathcal{I}(j)$ index set of the parts requiring tool type j (these index sets must be mutually exclusive and exhaustive)
$\mathcal{K}(j)$ index set of the machine groups compatible with tool type j

Given Data

a_{jt} days of availability of type j tools during period t
b_{kt} days of availability of machine group k during period t
c_{jkt} variable daily operating cost during period t of tool type j on machine group k, for compatible combinations of j and k
d_{it} demand forecast for part i in period t, in standard days
f_{it} fixed cost associated with the production of part i in period t
h_{it} cost of holding one standard day of part i for the duration of period t
I_0 initial inventory in period 1 of part i, in standard days (must be $\geqslant 0$)
I_{iT} terminal inventory desired for part i, in standard days, at the conclusion of the last period (must be $\geqslant 0$)
m_{it} maximum possible production of part i in period t, in standard days
p_{it} profit contribution associated with selling one standard day's worth of part i in period t, exclusive of the other costs included in the model
α_{it} minimum fraction of d_{it} which must be satisfied as a matter of marketing policy $(0 \leqslant \alpha_{it} \leqslant 1)$

Decision Variables

I_{it} planned inventory of part i at the end of period t, in standard days $(1 \leqslant t < T)$
S_{it} planned sales of part i in period t, in standard days
V_{jt} planned production days for tool type j in period t
W_{jkt} planned production days for tool type j on machine group k during period t, for compatible combinations of j and k
X_{it} planned production of part i during period t, in standard days
Y_{it} a binary variable indicating whether or not part i is produced during period t
Using this notation, the problem can be posed as the following mixed integer linear program.

$$\underset{I, S, V, W, X, Y}{\text{MINIMIZE}} - \sum_i \sum_t p_{it} S_{it} + \sum_j \sum_k \sum_t c_{jkt} W_{jkt}$$
$$+ \sum_i \sum_t h_{it} (I_{i,t-1} + I_{i,t})/2 + \sum_i \sum_t f_{it} Y_{it} \qquad (1)$$

subject to

$$\sum_{k \in \mathcal{K}(j)} W_{jkt} = V_{jt}, \qquad \text{all} \quad jt, \qquad (2)$$

$$V_{jt} = \sum_{i \in \mathcal{I}(j)} X_{it}, \qquad \text{all} \quad jt, \qquad (3)$$

$$\sum_{j} W_{jkt} \leqslant b_{kt}, \qquad \text{all} \quad kt, \qquad (4)$$

$$I_{it} = I_{i,t-1} + X_{it} - S_{it}, \qquad \text{all} \quad it, \qquad (5)$$

$$\alpha_{it} d_{it} \leqslant S_{it} \leqslant d_{it}, \qquad \text{all} \quad it, \qquad (6)$$

$$0 \leqslant X_{it} \leqslant m_{it} Y_{it}, \qquad \text{all} \quad it, \qquad (7)$$

$$0 \leqslant V_{jt} \leqslant a_{jt}, \qquad \text{all} \quad jt, \qquad (8)$$

$$I_{it} \geqslant 0, \qquad \text{all} \quad it \, (1 \leqslant t < T), \qquad (9)$$

$$W_{jkt} \geqslant 0, \qquad \text{all} \quad jkt, \qquad (10)$$

$$Y_{it} = 0 \text{ or } 1, \qquad \text{all} \quad it. \qquad (11)$$

It is understood that any summations or constraint enumerations involving j and k together will run only over compatible combinations of j and k.

The objective function is the negative of total profit over the duration of the planning horizon. It is the negative of profit contribution associated with sales over the planning horizon, plus: machine operating costs, inventory holding costs (applied to a simple 2-point estimate of the average inventory level of each part in each period), and fixed costs.

Constraints (2) and (3) serve to interrelate machines, tools, and parts. Constraints (4) and (8) respectively enforce the availability limitations on machines and tools. Constraint (5) defines ending inventories in the standard way. Constraint (6) requires the planned sales to be between forecast demand and some specified fraction thereof. Constraint (7) keeps production within possible limits and also forces Y_{it} to be 1 when X_{it} is positive. Constraint (9) specifies that there be no planned backlogging. Constraints (10) and (11) require no comment.

Some additional comments are appropriate.

1. There can be more than one tool (resp. machine) available of a given type (resp. group). Such census information, along with downtime estimates, determines the a_{jt} (resp. b_{kt}) coefficients.

2. The index sets $\mathcal{I}(\cdot)$ specify a unique tool type for each part. Typically these index sets will not be singletons, so that a number of parts compete for the same tooling.

3. The fixed cost coefficients f_{it} are perhaps best interpreted as surrogates for detailed setup costs; f_{it} is incurred in the model when part i is produced in period t irrespective of whether this requires a tool changeover (part i's tool type may be common to the part run previously), and irrespective of whether more than one machine must simultaneously make part i in order to achieve the planned production X_{it}. To specify setup costs at a greater level of detail would require a major revision of the model that would transport it from the realm of planning to the realm of detailed scheduling. Yet setup costs cannot be ignored entirely because this tends to cause some of every part to be produced during every period, a situation clearly unacceptable from the production viewpoint. Our solution is to take the f_{it}'s as empirically weighted average setup costs.

4. The terminal inventory level is the only significant terminal condition of the model. It is known from studies of related models (e.g., [8]) that I_{iT} can have a significant effect on solution quality, and hence that it should be set at some estimate of what the optimal inventory would be for part i at the end of period T in a similar model with many more periods. In practice, this means drawing on historical operating experience, insights obtained previously with the help of the model, and managerial judgment.

5. The maximum possible production m_{it} is the smaller of two limits: the physical limit imposed by full utilization of all available tooling and machines, and the limit on the amount of production that could be absorbed considering demand over the planning horizon, specified terminal inventory, and initial inventory. The second limit is redundant in view of (5) and (6); it is incorporated only to tighten the standard *LP* relaxation to be discussed later. The first limit, however, may well be binding (as it was in our application owing to part-specific limitations not subsumed by (4) and (8)).

6. The policy parameters α_{it} can be used, for instance, to maintain desired product line breadth when profit considerations alone would tend to narrow excessively the range of products produced.

7. There are several alternative problem representations which are equivalent to (1)–(11) and just as natural. Some of these are more compact; for example, the V_{jt} variables can be eliminated. The representation given is designed, principally through the introduction of the V_{jt} variables and the use of the standard day concept, to render the algorithmic manipulations of the next section as transparent as possible.

Before turning to the question of solving (1)–(11), we pause to define

$$h'_{it} = \tfrac{1}{2}(h_{it} + h_{i,t+1}) \quad \text{for all} \quad i \quad \text{and} \quad 1 \leqslant t < T,$$

$$H = \tfrac{1}{2} \sum_i (h_{i1} I_{i0} + h_{iT} I_{iT})$$

so that the third term of (1) can be expressed equivalently as

$$\sum_i \sum_{t=1}^{T-1} h'_{it} I_{it} + H.$$

3. Solution Via Lagrangean Relaxation

For the practical application at hand, there are approximately 1000 parts, 90 tool types, 15 machine groups, 12 time periods, and 480 compatible combinations of tool types and machine groups. This leads to dimensions of approximately

40,000   continuous variables (I, S, V, W, X)

12,000   integer variables (Y)

26,000   constraints of type   (2), (3), (4), (5), (7).

Problems of this magnitude are generally considered to be far beyond the current state-of-the-art of general mixed integer linear programming. Consequently, we sought a way to exploit the special structure of the problem.

The key was to recognize that (1)–(11) is a network flow problem with fixed charges for certain arcs, and that Lagrangean relaxation [4] [5] [10] with respect to (3) is an attractive way to generate lower bounds on the optimal value of (1)–(11). The resulting

Lagrangean subproblem separates into as many independent simple transportation problems in the W variables as there are time periods, and as many independent dynamic single-item lot-size problems as there are parts. The original monolith is thereby decomposed into manageable fragments.

It is easy to see that (1)–(11) is a fixed charge minimum cost network flow problem. See Figure 1 for an example with 3 parts, 2 tool types, 3 machine groups, 3 time periods, $\mathcal{I}(1) = \{1\}$, $\mathcal{I}(2) = \{2,3\}$, $\mathcal{K}(1) = \{1,2\}$, and $\mathcal{K}(2) = \{2,3\}$. The *notational conventions* followed in Figure 1 and subsequent figures are: the minimand term corresponding to each arc is written *over* the arc, the upper capacity limit of each arc is written *under* it (omission implies infinite capacity), the constraint on the net outflow of each node is written under it (omission implies $= 0$, or strict conservation), and a fixed cost arc is drawn as a dashed line, with the amount of the fixed charge incurred for its use given as the first of the two annotations written over it. The curved arcs between the part nodes are not annotated for lack of room; the typical arc is:

Now consider the Lagrangean relaxation of (1)–(11) using multipliers λ_{jt} for (3): drop (3) and replace the objective function (1) by

$$\underset{I,\,S,\,V,\,W,\,X,\,Y}{\text{MINIMIZE}} \; -\sum_i \sum_t p_{it} S_{it} + \sum_j \sum_k \sum_t c_{jkt} W_{jkt} + \sum_i \sum_{t=1}^{T-1} h'_{it} I_{it}$$

$$+ \sum_i \sum_t f_{it} Y_{it} + \sum_j \sum_t \lambda_{jt} \left(\sum_{i \in \mathcal{I}(j)} X_{it} - V_{jt} \right) + H. \qquad (1 - \lambda)$$

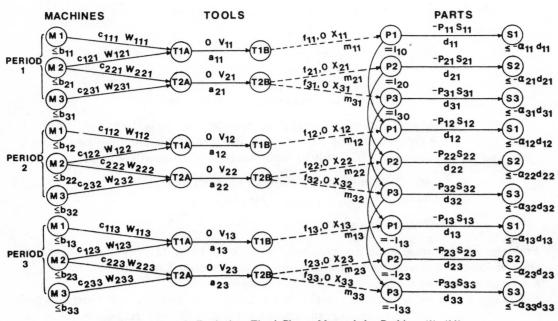

FIGURE 1. Sample Equivalent Fixed-Charge Network for Problem (1)–(11).

Dropping (3) causes the variables $\{V, W\}$ to become completely decoupled from the variables $\{I, S, X, Y\}$. In fact, the decoupling extends even farther: the first set of variables is decoupled over t and the second set over i. Thus the indicated Lagrangean relaxation of (1)–(11) yields the following independent problems: for each t,

$$\underset{V, W}{\text{MINIMIZE}} \sum_j \sum_k \sum_t c_{jkt} W_{jkt} - \sum_j \sum_t \lambda_{jt} V_{jt}$$

$$\text{subject to} \quad (2), (4), (8), (10) \quad \text{for fixed} \quad t \qquad\qquad (R')$$

and for each i,

$$\underset{I, S, X, Y}{\text{MINIMIZE}} - \sum_t p_{it} S_{it} + \sum_{t=1}^{T-1} h'_{it} I_{it} + \sum_t f_{it} Y_{it} + \sum_t \lambda_{j(i)t} X_{it}$$

$$\text{subject to} \quad (5), (6), (7), (9), (11) \quad \text{for fixed} \quad i \qquad\qquad (R_i)$$

where $j(i)$ is the index of the tool type required by part i.

Using $v(\cdot)$ to stand for the optimal value of problem $(\cdot)$, the optimal value of the full Lagrangean relaxation can be expressed as

$$\sum_t v(R') + \sum_i v(R_i) + H. \qquad\qquad (12)$$

This quantity is a lower bound on the optimal value of (1)–(11) for any choice of λ.

Figures 2 and 3 portray (R') and (R_i) for the example illustrated in Figure 1. The same notational conventions apply. Observe that the network for (R') has been simplified by using (2) to eliminate the V-variables, and that the network for (R_i) has been simplified by tying the pure source nodes together. Notice that Lagrangean relaxation amounts to "scissoring" the B-type tool nodes in Figure 1 and placing a penalty or premium on the incident arc flows.

How good a bound is (12)? The answer depends on the choice of λ. It is known that a good choice is the optimal dual vector associated with (3) in the standard LP relaxation of (1)–(11), in which (11) is relaxed to $0 \leqslant Y_{it} \leqslant 1$ for all it. This choice of λ yields a value for (12) that is at least as high as the optimal value of the standard LP relaxation itself. Moreover, strict improvement is likely because the Integrality Property defined in [5] does not hold. Superior choices of λ may well exist, and might be

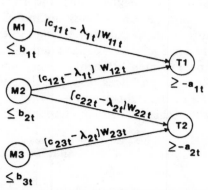

FIGURE 2. Sample Equivalent Network for (R').

89

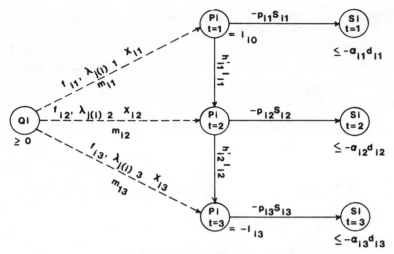

FIGURE 3. Sample Equivalent Fixed Charge Network for (R_i).

found by auxiliary calculations other than the standard *LP* relaxation, but we do not pursue such possibilities here.[1]

One can build a branch-and-bound procedure around this Lagrangean relaxation. For the industrial application which stimulated this work, however, it has proven sufficient to generate a feasible solution to (1)–(11) based on the Lagrangean solution. The objective value of this solution has consistently been sufficiently close to the lower bound from Lagrangean relaxation that no further refinement has been needed.

A formal description of the solution procedure is now presented.

Step 1. Solve the standard *LP* relaxation of (1)–(11) via an equivalent capacitated network formulation. Denote the associated dual variables for (3) by $\bar{\lambda}_{jt}$.

Step 2. Form the Lagrangean relaxation of (1)–(11) with respect to (3) using the values of $\bar{\lambda}_{jt}$ from Step 1. Solve it via the independent subproblems (R') and (R_i). Denote the combined optimal solution to the full Lagrangean relaxation by $(I^0, S^0, V^0, W^0, X^0, Y^0)$ and its optimal objective value by *LB*.

Step 3. Form the standard *LP* relaxation of (1)–(11) with f_{it} revised to 0 if $Y_{it}^0 = 1$ and augmented by a large positive constant if $Y_{it}^0 = 0$. Solve for an optimal solution (I', S', V', W', X', Y') via an equivalent capacitated network formulation. Let Y'' be Y' with all fractional components rounded up to unity. Form the revised solution with Y' replaced by Y'' and denote its objective value under (1) by *UB*. This solution is feasible in (1)–(11) and is within *UB-LB* of being optimal. Stop.

We comment on the nature of the problems needing to be solved at each step.

Steps 1 and 3 each yield an equivalent capacitated minimum cost network flow problem, and hence can be executed efficiently using one of the modern primal simplex codes developed for such problems (e.g., [2]). It is evident that, when (11) is relaxed to $0 \leqslant Y_{it} \leqslant 1$ for all *it*, the right-hand inequality of (7) must hold with strict equality for all *it* at optimality. This permits elimination of Y, whereupon (7) and (11) can be replaced by

$$0 \leqslant X_{it} \leqslant m_{it}, \quad \text{all } it \tag{11}'$$

---

[1]See [4], [5], [10], and the new convergent procedure in [6].

and the $\sum_i\sum_t f_{it}Y_{it}$ term of (1) is replaced by

$$\sum_i \sum_t \frac{f_{it}}{m_{it}} X_{it}.$$

In other words, the standard *LP* relaxation of (1)–(11) has no fixed cost feature.

Problem (R') can be converted easily to a simple transportation problem. However, using *LP* duality theory it can be shown that the values of W_{jkt} found at Step 1 are also optimal in (R') for all t. Thus no work at all need be performed in connection with these subproblems.

Problem (R_i) is a mixed integer linear program with T equations, $3T - 1$ continuous variables and T binary variables. Tying the S_i nodes of Figure 3 together with the Q_i node and performing a change of variables $S_{it} = S'_{it} + \alpha_{it}d_{it}$ to eliminate the lower bounds on the sales variables yields an equivalent capacitated transshipment problem with fixed charges on T of the arcs. The transshipment problem has $T + 1$ nodes, T capacitated sales arcs (S'_{it}), $T - 1$ inventory arcs (I_{it}) and T capacitated production arcs (X_{it}) with fixed charges. Because only the minimum sales demand must be satisfied, this problem has T more variables than the closely related dynamic lot-size problem presented in [1]. This feature of our model allows "lost sales," which is an important aspect of the planning problem for the application at hand.

4. Application and Computational Results

The model and computational procedure just described have been under development and application since 1977 at plants of R & G Sloane Manufacturing Company of Sun Valley, California. The following identifications and specializations are appropriate.

General Model	Molding Application (main plant)
parts (i)	the top 1000 injection molded fittings (about 92% of all sales volume)
tool types (j)	about 90 types of interchangeable mold bases (total mold base census about 130)
machine groups (k)	about 15 groups of interchangeable injection molding machines (total machine census about 60)
tool/machine compatibility	about 480 jk combinations permissible
time periods (t)	typically the next 12 months
$c_{jkt}, f_{it}, \alpha_{it}, p_{it}$	taken as independent of t

The problem faced by R & G Sloane is a strongly seasonal one. Since the bulk of the company's business involves residential plumbing products, demand peaks along with residential construction in the summer months. Since the peak season demand rate exceeds the available capacity of mold bases and machines, constraints (4) and (8) tend to be binding at that time of year (typically, about 40% of the mold base constraints and 80% of the machine constraints are binding 5-8 months of the year). Typical relative magnitudes of the major cost categories associated with an optimal solution are:

fixed costs	14.3
inventory carrying	16.9
variable operating	68.8
	100.0

Unfilled demand typically occurs for well under 10% of all parts.

Computational Implementation

A full scale computational implementation has been carried out for this application. The computer programs are in three modules:

1. data extraction and data base definition
2. problem preprocessing and diagnosis
3. optimization and report writing.

Data extraction primarily involves conversion of current production, marketing, and inventory control operating data to the form required by the model. The data base is organized and generated in sections:

· problem parameters and conditions
· machine group descriptions
· mold bases and their machine compatibility
· part descriptions and demand forecasts.

Preprocessing identifies structural and mathematical inconsistencies in the problem posed, and assists in preliminary diagnosis of critical shortages in equipment availability.

The optimization module solves the capacitated pure networks presented in Steps 1 and 3 with a GNET variant (XNET/Depth) [2]; an advanced starting solution is used which assumes high equipment utilization.

The fixed charge problems (R_i) are addressed with an enumeration algorithm that also employs GNET [2]. The overall algorithm applies implicit enumeration using a standard backtrack method to specify the binary variables. For each setting of the binary variables (or "case"), a capacitated transshipment problem is solved with a highly specialized version of GNET/DEPTH. The algorithm has several external parameters that permit tuning for high performance.

Extensive pre-solution analysis is performed to identify periods where production is mandatory (e.g., first period minimum demand greater than initial inventory) or precluded (e.g., large initial inventory). Additional dominance tests reduce the number of cases to be examined (a particularly effective technique involves keeping a running bound on the number of periods that can have positive production in an optimal solution).

Early analysis of this algorithm showed that a small number of problems ($\sim$10%) consumed a large fraction ($\sim$75%) of the total computer time in Step 2. Further analysis of the time-consuming problems showed that solution trajectories were characterized by frequent incumbent improvements in the initial cases followed by large numbers of cases with little or no improvement. This suggested a modification to construct very good (but not necessarily optimal) solutions in significantly less time. A single parameter, JUMP, directs the enumeration to skip over a number of cases when the number of cases since the last improvement increases; the enumeration skips the integer part of the number of cases since last improvement divided by JUMP.

Solving Step 2 with the modified algorithm actually yields final solutions at Step 3 that are better than those from the exact algorithm. Although the exact and estimated bounds in Step 2 are nearly equal, the modified algorithm produces solutions with more setups than the exact algorithm. Up to a point, more setups improve the value of the final solution in Step 3. Since the final solution from Step 3 always has more setups than the optimal solutions from Step 2, it is better to allow Step 2 to construct good, but not necessarily optimal, solutions with more setups than to require Step 3 to insert the setups.

The parameter JUMP is a very effective control on the number of setups. As JUMP decreases from the value that yields an exact algorithm (2^T), the number of setups tends to increase. Experimentally, JUMP = 3 has been shown to produce superior final solution values from Step 3 for a wide variety of problems.

The bound produced from Step 2 is a valid lower bound only if the optimal solution is obtained for each (R_i) problem. However, the estimated bound has been repeatedly verified to be very close (less than 1%) to the correct bound. It would be possible to use the modified algorithm to construct solutions for Step 3 and the exact algorithm to construct a valid lower bound; however, we have chosen to utilize routinely just the modified algorithm, with occasional use of the exact algorithm to verify the quality of the estimated bound.

After Step 3, solution reports are presented at several levels of aggregation so as to facilitate managerial interpretation. They display all detailed solution features, estimated opportunity costs for critical mold bases and machines, and an overall analysis of profitability, turnover, and customer service.

Computational Results

Approximately 30 runs per year are carried out. Computational performance has exhibited a high degree of run-to-run stability in terms of solution quality and computer resources consumed.

Table 1 summarizes several aspects of performance for a recent typical run. The main storage requirement was about one megabyte. Notice that the bound produced

TABLE 1

Typical Computational Performance: A Problem with 953 Parts, 92 Tool Types, 16 Machine Groups

	IBM 370/168 CPU Seconds	Normalized Objective Value [a]	Pivots
Preprocessing	10.0		
Optimization			
Step 1 (*LP* Relaxation)	55.0	103.2	37,933
Step 2 (Lagrangean Relaxation)	25.7	101.6	376,241
Step 3 (Generate Feasible Solution)	54.2	100.0	36,954
Report Writing	30.6		
	175.7		

[a]Normalization is relative to the value of the feasible solution obtained at Step 3. The Step 2 value is an estimated bound.

93

by the Lagrangean relaxation is significantly better than the standard linear programming relaxation bound. Notice also that the time in Step 2 is smaller than what one might expect; the 12-period fixed charge problems were processed in an average of only .027 seconds each (for comparison, the typical time quoted in [1] for exact solution of a proper subclass of these problems of the same size was 0.25 seconds on an IBM 370/158). For this run, 142 (resp. 10) of the 11,436 binary Y variables changed from value 0 (resp. 1) in Step 2 to value 1 (resp. 0) in Step 3. This shows that the solution to the Lagrangean relaxation of Step 2 required but minor adjustment with respect to the fixed charge arcs in order to yield the good feasible solution of Step 3.

More generally, our experience has been that optimization CPU time for similar-sized problems seldom varies more than $\pm 10\%$. Computing time is very nearly proportional to the total number of parts. The final estimated optimality tolerance (which was 1.6% in the Table 1 run) tends to become smaller the more tightly capacitated tool and machine availability is; tolerances in the vicinity of 2/10 of 1% are commonly observed in the most tightly constrained situations. In no case has the tolerance ever exceeded 2%.

5. Conclusion

This paper has demonstrated the practical applicability of a procedure based on Lagrangean relaxation to a significant class of integrated production and sales planning models. The particular way in which this procedure is designed thoroughly exploits the recent major advances made for minimum cost network flow problems. Provably good solutions are routinely being obtained in modest computing time to mixed integer linear programs of a size far beyond the capabilities of generally available mathematical programming systems.

The system is used regularly at R & G Sloane Manufacturing Company. Day-to-day production scheduling is still performed manually, but with the benefit of the system's guidance and predictions of bottlenecks in the future. The integrated nature of the model has made the system valuable as a focal point for coordinating planning activities among the key functional areas of the firm: inventory control, finance, marketing, and production operations. Two specific illustrations are the evaluation of major capital expenditure and interplant equipment transfer opportunities. A recent *Business Week* article [11] featured this application, with the Vice President of Operations quoted as crediting the new system for an increase in total operating profits during a recent year of $500,000.[2]

[2] Partially supported by the National Science Foundation and by the Office of Naval Research. This work could not have been completed without the abiding cooperation and support of R & G Sloane Manufacturing Company. Special thanks are due to Mr. Ralph G. Schmitt, Vice President of Operations. Valuable comments from the referees and from Jay Brennan are also gratefully acknowledged.

References

1. BAKER, K. R., DIXON, P., MAGAZINE, M. J. AND SILVER, E. A., "An Algorithm for the Dynamic Lot-Size Problem with Time-Varying Production Capacity Constraints," *Management Sci.* Vol. 24, No. 16 (1978).
2. BRADLEY, G. H., BROWN, G. G. AND GRAVES, G. W., "Design and Implementation of Large Scale Primal Transshipment Algorithms," *Management Sci.*, Vol. 24, No. 1 (1977).

3. CAIE, J., LINDEN, J. AND MAXWELL, W., "Solution of a Single Stage Machine Load Planning Problem," *OMEGA*, Vol. 8, No. 3 (1980).

4. FISHER, M. L., "Lagrangean Relaxation Method for Solving Integer Programming Problems," *Management Sci.*, Vol. 27, No. 1 (1981).

5. GEOFFRION, A. M., "Lagrangean Relaxation for Integer Programming," *Mathematical Programming Study 2*, North-Holland Publishing Co., Amsterdam, 1974.

6. GRAVES, G. W. AND VAN ROY, T. J., "Decomposition for Large-Scale Linear and Mixed Integer Linear Programing," Working Paper, Graduate School of Management, UCLA, November 1979, *Mathematical Programming* (to appear).

7. LOVE, R. R. AND VEMUGANTI, R. R., "The Single-Plant Mold Allocation Problem with Capacity and Changeover Restrictions," *Operations Res.*, Vol. 26, No. 1 (1978).

8. McCLAIN, J. O. AND THOMAS, J., "Horizon Effects in Aggregate Production Planning with Seasonal Demand," *Management Sci.*, Vol. 23, No. 7 (1977).

9. SALKIN, H. M. AND MORITO, S., "A Search Enumeration Algorithm for a Multiplant, Multiproduct Scheduling Problem," *Proceedings of the Bicentennial Conference on Mathematical Programming*, NBS, Gaithersburg, Maryland, December 1976.

10. SHAPIRO, J. F., "A Survey of Lagrangean Techniques for Discrete Optimization," in *Annals of Discrete Mathematics 5: Discrete Optimization*, P. L. Hammer, E. L. Johnson, and B. H. Korte (eds.), North Holland, Amsterdam, 1979.

11. " 'What if' Help for Management," *Business Week*, 21 January 1980, pp. 73–74.

Reprinted, by permission, from International Journal of
Production Research, *Vol. 9, No. 3, 1971.*

A linear programming model for integrating the annual planning of production and marketing

T. A. J. NICHOLSON and R. D. PULLEN*

The expansion and contraction of product lines in a company is a decision which affects marketing, production, and distribution staff collectively. This paper establishes a model for a multi-factory company which markets a variety of products in different market sectors with different distribution costs. The problem is to determine how much of each product to manufacture at each factory, whether overtime should be used, how much expenditure to put into selling the product, and how it should be priced. Linear programming has already been used to tackle the product mix problem and this model extends it to include the marketing variables and the possible use of extra capacity. The objective is to make the annual product line plans to maximize total variable profit. The model is illustrated on a simple example. It is organized into a computer programme for accepting files of typical accounting data and providing a variety of management reports.

Annual product planning

Decisions on the expansion and contraction of product lines form a major component of a company's forward strategy. It is a focal point at which policy on production, marketing, and distribution must be jointly coordinated. Typically, this type of planning is undertaken on a yearly basis and is linked to the annual budget proposals. The procedures for deciding product plans may vary from an exact objective approach using forward estimates to schemes for coping with current difficulties and alleviating the immediate pressures on marketing production or financial staff. However, as quantitative techniques become more common in management and more detailed data becomes available, it is possible to employ formal computational models to assist with the forward planning task. This is the aim of the system which we have designed and called MAPLE for Marketing and Product Line Evaluation. Its aim is to provide a simple means for a company to enter data into a computer, to perform an optimizing calculation and to point out typical planning and accounting information. The intention of the model is not just to indicate the best plan which could be adopted, but also to indicate the feasibility of proposed plans, to suggest the direction in which promising changes could be made and to point out areas where further investigations should be carried out. Perhaps the most powerful role of the programme is the commitment it provides to organize and analyse the company's data to be used for planning and to provide a central but neutral point of reference for functional management who may tend to operate independently.

* London Graduate School of Business Studies, Sussex Place, Regent's Park, London NW1 4SA, England.

Presented at the International Conference on Production Research, Birmingham, England, April 1970.

Published by Taylor & Francis Ltd., 10–14 Macklin Street, London WC2B 5NF.

The scope of the system

The system is planned on the basis of case investigations into what is needed in practice. Company control often extends across a number of production sites and a number of marketing zones, and the system therefore envisages a multi-factory and multi-market environment. The primary planning problem which a company faces is to decide how much of each product line should be manufactured at each production centre for each market sector. These decisions involve much more than finding the best product mix at a factory for given sales requirements, which is the traditional way in which linear programming has been used on this problem (Eisemann and Young 1960). Given the production process capacities we need to employ the resources efficiently, it is also necessary to plan how much to sell. The sales of the products can be influenced and controlled through the advertising and pricing policies. Further profit may depend not on production capacities but on an ability to generate extra sales. On the other hand, if sales can be increased beyond base production capacities the question of employing extra, more costly capacity such as overtime or sub-contracting, must be examined. Moreover, with each of these possibilities the distribution costs must be considered. The MAPLE system, therefore, sets out to consider the policy decisions on production, marketing and distribution collectively. The planning or control variables in the system are therefore as follows :

(i) The quantity of each product line to make at each factory for sale in each market sector.

(ii) The extent to which extra higher cost capacity should be used at each factory.

(iii) The advertising effort to spend on each product line.

(iv) The price levels which should be chosen.

The first two types of variables are primarily production decisions and the latter two types are marketing decisions. (The composite first type of variable implies the distribution policy.) The scope of the system is illustrated diagrammatically in the figure for two factories and three market sectors.

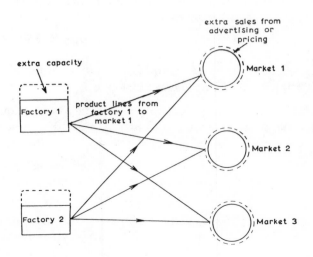

The linear programming formulation

For the system to be practicable it is important that the user should not have to formulate the company's planning problem in mathematical terms. The data input to the system is therefore arranged in a set of files of data items which are directly related to this planning problem. In order to apply the system it is only necessary to select the data items from the production, marketing and accounting records and fit them into the required slots. The principle data items contained in the six files are outlined below.

(i) Product line data—for each product line : material and processing requirements ; limits on total production.

(ii) Factory processing data—at each factory ; materials supplies and costs ; process base capacities, extra capacities and costs ; upper and lower limits on production levels for product lines.

(iii) Market data—for each market sector : product lines to be marketed ; upper and lower limits on demand ; costs of selling.

(iv) Distribution data—for each link between a factory and market : cost of transportation and upper limit on quantity.

(v) Financial data—upper limit on working capital available ; upper limit on advertising expenditure.

(iv) Demand and price data—for each set of prices : base demand in each market sector ; increase in demand through advertising ; limits on advertising expenditure on any given product line.

All this data is now organized automatically inside the programme into a linear programming form, and the linear programming problem is solved by a standard calculation. It is not possible to build prices into the formulation in a linear form ; instead, the various possible price combinations are studied individually by taking each set of prices and obtaining a solution to the problem in terms of the product quantities, extra capacities and advertising. The search over the possible price combinations can be guided by the successive solutions to the linear programming problem.

To indicate the way in which the linear programming problem takes shape we first define the problem variables as

x_{ijk} = quantity of product line i made at factory j and sold at market sector k.

y_{jm} = quantity of extra capacity required at factory j for process m.

z_i = advertising expenditure on product line i.

Next the objective expression is created which consists of a sum of terms in x_{ijk}, y_{jm} and z_i each variable being multiplied by a number or coefficient which is drawn from the data. For example, the coefficient for x_{ijk} is expressed as

(price per unit of product i) − (material and processing costs per unit of product i) − (cost of transportation between factory j and market sector k) − (cost of selling in market sector k).

This expression for total variable profit is to be maximized subject to a variety of constraints. The constraints are typically represented as inequalities. For instance, the total amount produced of product line i at all factories and distributed to market sector k must be less than the upper limit on demand at market sector k. The range of constraints include :

(i) Production levels for each product line at each factory and in total must lie between upper and lower limits.

(ii) Material supplies, process base and extra capacities must not be exceeded.

(iii) Sales of each product line at each market sector must lie between upper and lower limits. Also, sales cannot exceed the base demand augmented by any effects of advertising expenditure.

(iv) Distribution of product line i along a factory to market sector link must not exceed the link capacity.

(v) The advertising expenditures must not exceed the budgeted limits. Also, the cash required for advertising and for extra capacity must not exceed the upper limit on working capital available.

All these expressions specify the linear programming problem, and this can now be solved internally in the computer to give the values for the problem variables.

An illustrative example

It is useful at this point to illustrate the procedure with a small example in which there is one factory and one market. It is easy to tackle this problem by visual inspection and some simple judgments, but its simplicity assists the understanding of the procedure. It should be stressed, however, that the MAPLE system applies to the much wider context of many factories and many markets.

Suppose a factory is making four products A, B, C, D at a single factory for the national market. Each of the products are made by compounding some materials and then passing the material through one of two possible manufacturing processes. The output of the products is measured in tons. Products A and B go through process 1 and products C and D go through process 2. The costs of the materials and the variable costs of the processes are shown in the tables. The material costs are given in table 1.

Table 1

Product	A	B	C	D
Material cost £/ton	32	42	36	14

The variables production costs and capacities on the two processes are distinguished by regular time and overtime as shown in table 2. The variable production costs would not normally include machine depreciation, but could well include power and other variable inputs and possibly also labour as it may well be possible to plan the size of the required labour force with the planning horizon set at one year.

Table 2

| | Regular time | | Overtime | |
Process	Cost £/ton	Capacity tons p.a.	Cost £/ton	Capacity tons p.a.
1	8·0	100000	9·2	30000
2	6·0	90000	7·0	20000

Products A, B and C are currently all priced at £60 per ton and product D is priced at £35. The market demands have been assessed for these prices. It is also considered that the prices of products B and D might be raised by £5 and the sales under these alternative prices have also been estimated as shown in table 3.

Table 3. Price and demand alternatives

Product	Selling price £	Estimated sales tons p.a.
A	60	64000
B	60	18000
	65	11000
C	60	30000
D	35	60000
	40	45000

The demand can also be influenced by advertising expenditure. The response to advertising varies, depending on the product. The estimated percentage increase on the base demand for £10000 of advertising is shown in table 4.

Table 4. Advertising response

Product	A	B	C	D
Percentage increase in demand for £10000	1·0	7·0	0·4	8·0

There is a limit to the amount of money which can be spent on advertising. £70000 is the total advertising budget and there is a limit of £10000 to be spent on advertising on product C.

This data can be expressed in the linear programming formulation described in the previous section. As there is only one factory and one market, the production and advertising levels for the four product lines A, B, C, D can be denoted by x_1, x_2, x_3, x_4 ('000 tons) and z_1, z_2, z_3, z_4 ('000 £), and the extra capacity requirements for processes 1 and 2 can be denoted by y_1 and y_2 ('000 tons).

Taking the price £60 for products A, B and C and a price of £35 for product D, the objective function is expressed for any given values of the problem variables as

$$20x_1 + 10x_2 + 18x_3 + 15x_4 - 1 \cdot 2y_1 - 1 \cdot 0y_2 - z_1 - z_2 - z_3 - z_4$$

where the coefficient 20 for x_1 is the price (60) − materials cost (32) − processing cost (8).

The base capacity constraint on process 1 expresses the fact that the total production of products A and B, less the amount produced in overtime, must not be greater than 100000 tons. This is expressed by the inequality

$$x_1 + x_2 - y_1 \leqslant 100.$$

The extra capacity constraint on process 1 is

$$y_1 \leqslant 30$$

with similar constraints for process 2. The sales constraint for product 1 requires that

(sales of product A) $\leqslant$ (Base demand at price 60) $\times (1 + $ increase through advertising)

$$x_1 \leqslant 64 \left(1 + \frac{0 \cdot 1}{100} z_1\right),$$

and similarly for the other three products. Finally the advertising constraints require that

$$z_1 + z_2 + z_3 + z_4 \leqslant 70,$$

and

$$z_3 \leqslant 10.$$

This linear programming problem can now be solved to give the solution shown in table 5.

Table 5

Product	A	B	C	D
Production level	65·8	18·0	30·0	80·0
Advertising level	28·3	0·0	0·0	41·7

Process		1	2	
Overtime level		0·0	20·0	

| Profit | 3146000 | | | |

It shows that it is not worth while to use overtime on the first process, and that it is not worth advertising on products B and C. Most of process 2 is employed on product D and the demand on both A and D is stimulated by advertising. In fact, the total advertising of expenditure is taken up to the full limit. But the limit on advertising for product C seems to be irrelevant.

The problem can now be solved with the alternative price levels for products B and D to give the profit for alternative prices with different demands. For example, with the price of B set to £65 and the price of D set to £40 the total profit rises to £3463000.

This illustrative problem is very simple and it does not indicate the proper scope of the system. However, the system has also been applied to two much larger case studies with over a hundred product lines and with two factories and three market sectors. The documentation of these studies provides much stronger evidence of how the system can be used.

Output and sensitivity analyses

The output from the system provides classified reports on the plans and a sensitivity analysis to indicate the effects of making changes on the constraints.

The basic output includes detailed reports on the following topics :

  (i) Product line production levels.

  (ii) Factory production levels and cost allocations on product lines.

 (iii) Factory material and process costs total costs and variable profit.

  (iv) Distribution plans and costs.

  (v) Marketing plans, prices and profitability.

  (vi) Advertising allocations.

 (vii) Total company profitability measures.

The linear programming solution also provides a valuable sensitivity analysis. Besides the basic results on the problem variables of production, distribution and marketing the solution contains some quantities called simplex multipliers or shadow prices which give the change in profits that would result from altering any of the constraining values such as production capacities or market demands. The simplex multiplier for each constraint gives the marginal increase in profit for a unit change in the constraint. This is exactly the kind of information which is needed for a sensitivity analysis, and it is automatically provided without doing repeated runs on the programme.

The application of these simplex multipliers is achieved by matching the effect on profit against the cost of changing the constraint. This is sometimes a complex assessment. It can be illustrated on the previous example. The simplex multiplier associated with the constraint on base capacity on process 2 is 12·3 indicating that the total profit would increase £12300 if the capacity was increased by 1000 tons. Although base capacity cost is only £6/ton the cost of acquiring extra capacity may be much more, and the figure of £12·3 must be matched against the total extra cost. Similarly, the simplex multiplier associated the sales constraint on products B and C are £10·0 and £5·7 indicating a £10000 and £5700 return on a further 1000 tons of sales of products B and C. However, in order to increase demand the price may have to be reduced, and this will affect the profitability of the original demand. Therefore, the cost of increasing demand by 1000 tons is the cost profit on the original output and the profit from the extra demand is not as represented by the simplex multiplier but is smaller as the price has to be reduced. Therefore, in order to assess whether it is worth while to stimulate demand by a price reduction, it is necessary to examine the estimated elasticity of demand given by the price variation data. This information is valuable for conducting an efficient search over the possible price combinations.

The sensitivity analysis can also be helpful for assessing the effects of uncertainties in some of the data items. As the simplex multipliers indicate the rate of change of profit with change in a constraining value, it is clearly the quantities connected with the large simplex multipliers which need to be checked for accuracy and reliability. The further uncertainties in the data may be examined directly by running the programme with upper and lower limits on the data to check the sensitivity of the results in different circumstances.

Application of the system

The MAPLE system has been designed to provide a simple means for a company to consider applying quantitative methods to assist with their decisions on product planning. The data files of input which are planned specifically for this management area provide a scheme for the manager to recognize the scope of the system and enter data into the calculation to use the linear programming calculation. It means that once the data have been assembled the system can be run without any further time and money being spent on setting up a special computing project to solve the problem.

The file system envisages a general model for a multi-factory and multi-market situation and features within the programme can readily be altered to suit the special requirements of individual companies once it appears that the scheme is relevant for their planning problems. Sometimes these extensions simply involve a re-interpretation of a data item. For instance, a factory may wish to distinguish its contracting out from its use of overtime as a source of extra capacity. This can be done by renaming the contracting out facility as a separate factory on the same site. Equally, if it is required to price a product differently in two distinct market sectors, the product can be differentiated on two separate products with the same production characteristics.

It is important for management to recognize the flexibility of the system. It should not be seen simply as a single linear programming calculation, but a general decision making model which can be used to explore numerous possible opportunities to the company. The output from the programme does not dictate the annual plan which must be adopted but rather provides the basis for judgment across the three fields of production, marketing and distribution. The computation should be run regularly as a check on performance and as forecasts on sales and costs turn out to be inaccurate, to ensure that plans are monitored and updated in the light of changing circumstances.

Le développement et la réduction d'une série de produits est une décision qui affecte collectivement le personnel du marketing, de la production et de la distribution Cet article établit un modèle pour une compagnie à manufactures multiples qui vend une variété de produits dans des secteurs différents du marché à des frais de distribution différents. Le problème qui se pose est de déterminer quelle quantité de chaque produit doit être manufacturée dans chaque usine, si l'on devrait demander aux ouvriers de faire des heures supplémentaires, combien de capitaux à investir dans la vente du produit et comment le prix devrait en être fixé.

La programmation linéaire a déjà été utilisée pour aborder le problemè de la combinaison de la production des produits, et ce modèle prolonge cette programmation de façon à comprendre les variables du marketing et l'utilisation possible d'un accroissement de la capacité de production. On a pour objectif d'établir les plans annuels d'une série de produits, de façon à rendre maximal le bénéfice total variable. Ce modèle est illustré par un exemple simple. Il est arrangé en un programme d'ordinateur pour recevoir des dossiers de données de comptabilité typiques et pour fournir une variété de rapports de gestion.

Die Entscheidung über Ertweiterung und Verminderung von Erzeugnisserien in einer Gesellschaft wirkt sich gleichermaßen auf Marketing-, Produktions-jund Vertriebs- personal aus. In der vorliegenden Abhandlung wird ein Modell ausgearbeitet, das sich auf einen Mehr–Fabrik–Betrieb bezieht, der mit dem Marketing von verschiedenartigen Erzeugnissen auf mehreren Marktsektoren mit unterschiedlichen Vertriebskosten befaßt ist. Das Problem liegt in der Entscheidung (a) über die Anzahl jedes der zu produzierenden Erzeugnisse in jeder der Fabriken, (b) ob Überstunden gemacht werden sollten, (c) wie hoch die Ausgaben für den Verkauf des Produktes angesetzt werden sollten und (d) wie die Ware ausgezeichnet werden sollte. Lineare Programmierung ist in der Vergangenheit bereits zur Lösung des bei einem Produktegemisch entstehenden Problems eingesetzt worden, und das hier beschriebene, erweiterte Modell schließt die Marketing-Variablen ein und die mögliche Nutzung zusätzlich zur Verfügung stehender Kapazität. Angestrebt wird die Erstellung des jährlichen Planes über die Erzeugnisserien, ausgerichtet auf die Maximalisierung des veränderlichen Gewinnes als Gesamtheit. Das Modell wird anhand eines einfachen Beispieles veranschaulicht. Es ist in ein Datenverarbeitungsprogramm eingeschlossen. Zweck des Programmes ist das Aufnehmen von Akten mit typischen Buchhaltungs- daten und die Ausgabe einer Vielzahl von Management-Berichten.

REFERENCE

EISEMANN, K., and YOUNG, W. M., 1960, Study of a textile mill with the aid of linear programming, *Mgt Techn.*, p. 52.

Reprinted, by permission, from Management Science, *Vol. 24, No. 13, 1978. Copyright 1978 by The Institute of Management Sciences.*

THE APPLICATION OF A PRODUCT MIX LINEAR PROGRAMMING MODEL IN CORPORATE POLICY MAKING*

JACK BYRD, JR.† AND L. TED MOORE†

This paper reports a real-life application of linear programming to corporate policy making. The model used in the study was designed to analyze the company's marketing and production policies. The model structure is unique, incorporating features of product mix, sequencing and blending models. The model's structure is described as well as typical results it produced. The recommendations for corporate actions arising from the model are also explained. Recommendations were made to alter the existing corporate policies on brand proliferation and limited inventory levels. The product line has been reduced as a result of the study, and a policy decision to expand the inventory has been made. The process of implementation is sketched to provide a feeling for the difficulties involved in corporate policy making.
(PLANNING–CORPORATE; PRODUCTION/SCHEDULING; PROGRAMMING–LINEAR, APPLICATIONS)

Introduction

While there have been many applications of linear programming cited in the literature in the past years, few papers have discussed the application of linear programming at the highest level of corporate policy making. There are perhaps two reasons for this. First, there probably have been few instances of "trust" in linear programming at the highest corporate level; OR/MS techniques do not seem to have the support of top management necessary for their application at the highest levels of decision making. Second, successful application of linear programming at the highest corporate levels usually involves sensitive issues which these organizations do not wish to reveal in the literature.

This paper discusses an OR study which resulted in an application of linear programming in policy decision making for a medium size American corporation (identified as ABC Company in the paper). An evaluation of the impact of the model will be given to show those areas where the model has been successful as well as those areas where the study has not yet been implemented completely. Since the issues are sensitive, the nature of the company and its products are generalized. The results, however are actual findings of the study and are presented in a case study format, since this seems to be the best vehicle to describe the effort. The particular type of linear programming (LP) model used in this study was a product mix model; so before discussing the details of the study, an overview of conventional product mix models will be presented.

Conventional Product Mix Models

Product mix linear programming models are common OR/MS tools. In general these models take the form:

$$\text{Maximize Profit} = \sum_i P_i x_i \tag{1}$$

such that:

Capacity Restrictions Are Satisfied

$$\sum_i t_{ij} x_i \leqslant C_j \quad \text{for all } j \tag{2}$$

* Accepted by David G. Dannenbring; received October 22, 1977. This paper has been with the authors 1 month for 1 revision.
† West Virginia University.

Demand Restrictions Are Satisfied

$$L_i \leqslant x_i \leqslant U_i \quad \text{for all } i \tag{3}$$

Raw Materials Are Available

$$\sum_i r_{ik} x_i \leqslant R_k \quad \text{for all } k \tag{4}$$

where:
  x_i = the number of units of product i to be manufactured,
  P_i = the profit per unit of product i,
  t_{ij} = the time required per unit of product i on machine j,
  C_j = the capacity of machine j,
  L_i = the lower demand limit for product i,
  U_i = the upper demand limit for product i,
  r_{ik} = the material requirements per unit of product i for raw material type k,
  R_k = the availability of raw material type k.

The conventional model must undergo considerable revision before it is applicable to a particular industry; the ABC LP model required additional features characteristic of sequencing models and features common to blending models. These features will be described as a later step in the development of the model. The first step was to obtain a tenable problem definition.

Initial Problem Definition

The authors served as consultants to ABC Company and reported to a task force appointed by the company president to study a particular phase of the company's operations. The task force consisted of representatives, including two vice-presidents, from both the marketing and production departments of the company.

The task force had prepared a set of objectives in response to the president's charge. These were:
  –Define maximum manufacturing capabilities and capacity.
  –Define maximum physical volume and profit contribution.
  –Determine ways and costs to round out production capacity in existing and optimum product mix.
  –Perform design and cost studies of the low cost production facility that achieves maximum machine-rate contribution.
  –Perform plant location cost studies.
  –Perform analysis of overall ROI and cash flow on capacity expansion designs.
  –Establish standard costs of products.
  –Examine margins, capacity cost, and total contribution by product of possible product mixes.

Given such a broad list of objectives, the first task in the modeling effort was to develop a more limited statement of the problem. After considerable discussion with the management of ABC, it was decided that one specific plant would be studied. For this plant, a model would be developed which would optimize product mix, since management's prime interest was in how much profit could be achieved by adjusting the product mix.

The next problem confronted was the selection of the products to be included in the model. The plant produced 134 products in 1976 and maintained a list of over 200 products for customers to choose from. As is common, a small number of products accounted for most of the volume and a list of 29 products which had contributed 75% of the 1976 total volume was chosen for modeling.

106

To help decide how production stages would be modeled, a process flow sheet (based upon literature about the industry) was prepared as shown in Figure 1.

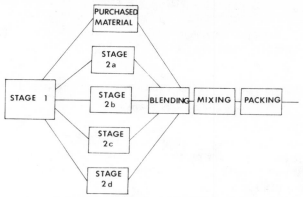

FIGURE 1. Outline of the Production Flow.

Stage 1 prepared raw materials for futher processing. The raw materials from this stage went to one of four second stage processing machines. In most cases, each raw material had to be processed on a specific second stage machine. After second stage processing, various combinations of materials were blended together. Each product included its own peculiar proportion of materials, and purchased material could also be included in the blending. Mixing and packaging were the last stages in processing products.

After the flow chart was developed, the next step was to select a modeling technique. Linear programming was chosen, since it has the flexibility to model the flow of products through the plant and to optimize product mix.

Development of a Prototype Model

A prototype model of a hypothetical five-product plant operating for a five-day week was developed. The reason for building this model was to provide a vehicle for discussing the eventual plant model's structure, its data requirements, and the types of information the model could provide.

The decision to develop this prototype model was fortuitous. As a communications vehicle it gave management something tangible to discuss. Since the model was developed early in the project, it gave management some assurance that the final output of the effort would correspond to their expectations. Thus, the prototype model "whetted management's appetite" for the project.

Apart from its public relations/communication mission, the prototype model expedited the development of the final model. Since raw materials were never in short supply a decision was made to eliminate stage 1 from the final model. Futhermore, raw materials were grouped into five broad categories, stage 2 finished products plus purchased materials. This eliminated the need to keep track of every individual raw material and subsequently reduced the size of the final model substantially.

The prototype model clarified data requirements. ABC personnel responsible for data collection were given a clearer idea of the data needed for the model, and a plant tour by the consultants completed their plans for transforming the prototype into the full scale model.

The Full Scale Model

Development of the full scale model was the project's next goal. While ABC obtained the required data, the consultants restructured the model.

A summary of the model is as follows.

The product mix problem is:

$$\text{maximize} \quad \sum_j P_j x_j \tag{5}$$

subject to demand constraints, capacity constraints and the remaining constraints which take two forms: (1) sequencing; and (2) blending.

Sequencing

In sequencing materials and products, variables change names as follows:

$$r_{ik} \to g_{ik} \to h_{ikj} \to y_{ij} \to m_{ij} \to P_{ij} \to x_j$$

where:

r_{ik} is the raw material of species k required on day i.

g_{ik} is the processed material (or purchased material) stored for use on day i.

h_{ikj} is the quantity of material k on day i used in making product j.

y_{ij} is the amount of product j produced on day i.

P_{ij} is the amount of product j packaged on day i.

x_j is the total of product j demanded during the week.

Raw materials (r_{ik}) are converted into intermediate products (g_{ik}) as they pass through stage 2 and are stored. Stored material (h_{ikj}) is then removed from storage and blended to make product (y_{ij}) which is then packaged (P_{ij}) and shipped (x_j) during the week.

The sequencing equations read as follows:

TABLE 1

Sequencing Equations and Their Descriptions

Purpose	Equations		
storage	$r_{ik} = g_{ik}$	for all i and k	(6)
materials supplies for products	$\sum_j h_{ikj} = g_{ik}$	for all i and k	(7)
blending	$\sum_k a_{km_j} h_{ikj} = 0$	for each m_j	(8)
materials used for products	$\sum_k h_{ikj} = y_{ij}$	for all k and j	(9)
mixing	$y_{ij} = m_{ij}$	for all i and j	(10)
packaging	$m_{ij} = P_{ij}$	for all i and j	(11)
final demand	$\sum_i P_{ij} = x_j$	for all i and j	(12)

Equations (8) are fairly complicated and are discussed below.

Blending

The blending equations,

$$\sum_k a_{km_j} h_{ikj} = 0 \quad \text{for each } m_j,$$

fix the ratios between raw materials. For example, say that product 4 requires 60% processed material 1, 30% processed material 3, and 10% material 5 (purchased product). Then two equations for each day i would be required for product 4 (i.e. $m_4 = 1, 2$). These blending equations would be:

$$h_{i14} - 2h_{i34} = 0 \quad \text{and} \quad h_{i34} - 3h_{i54} = 0.$$

Thus

$$
\begin{array}{ll}
a_{114} = 1, & a_{124} = 0, \\
a_{214} = 0, & a_{224} = 0, \\
a_{314} = -2, & a_{324} = 1, \\
a_{414} = 0, & a_{424} = 0, \\
a_{514} = 0, & a_{524} = -3.
\end{array}
$$

Demand and Processing Constraints

The demand constraints are as shown in (3),

$$L_i \leqslant x_i \leqslant U_i.$$

The raw material availabilities were assumed not to constrain plant operations; so no material constraints were modeled. The constraints that were modeled were:

Processing machine availability,
Processed material storage capacity,
Blending machine availability,
Mixing machine availability,
Packaging line availabilities.

The corresponding inequalities were:

processing machine

$$b_k r_{ik} \leqslant Q_k \quad \text{for all } i \text{ and } k, \tag{13}$$

materials storage

$$\sum_k c_k g_{ik} \leqslant G_i \quad \text{for all } i, \tag{14}$$

blending machine

$$\sum_j \sum_k d_{kj} h_{ikj} \leqslant B_i \quad \text{for all } i, \tag{15}$$

mixing

$$\sum_j f_j m_{ij} \leqslant M_i \quad \text{for all } i, \tag{16}$$

packaging

$$\sum_j z_j P_{ij} \leqslant S_i \quad \text{for all } i. \tag{17}$$

Running the Model

Once the model was running, a series of case studies outlined below were analyzed. Their statements were:

Case A: Fix the demand at 1976 levels and see what profits and machine utilization values are calculated. This case served as a benchmark for later cases.

Case B: Allow the demand for any product to vary from 0 to 2 × 1976 levels. This case examined what could have been done if the optimum product mix were sold.

Case C: Run the model to reflect an adjustment in stage 2a and 2b capacities. Allow the demand for any product to vary from 0 to 2 × 1976 levels. This case reflected a plant adjustment which was to be completed in 1977.

Case D: Allow the demand for any product to vary from 0 to 6 × 1976 levels. This case investigated the strategy of product line consolidation.

Case E: Investigate the stategy of producing for inventory rather than for specific job orders.

Results from these five cases were obtained and written up in a preliminary report, and a meeting between consultants and task force was arranged. The results showed that packaging capacity was the factor limiting production. Upon reviewing these results, the manufacturing side of the task force was aghast. Of all the production stages, they believed that the final stage was the least problematic.

It turned out that the modeled packaging capacity was only the capacity for one of three similar packaging lines. Therefore, the model had to be revised and run again to reflect this fact. This error in the model was accidentally helpful. First, it led the task force to take a serious look at the data provided. A few additional data errors were identified as a result of this new scrutiny. Second, the error gave some credence to the model. The model in essence showed that the plant could not run with only one packaging line. To the manufacturing side of the task force this was a meaningful indication that the model was running as it should.

The same cases were rerun and the new results showed a bottleneck at stage 2c as expected. However, a new problem was encountered in Case B. The model indicated that over 1000 tons of material would be moved from storage to stage 2. Production people pointed out that this was not possible, and suggested a way to model this materials handling limitation. Case B was run again after inclusion of an additional constraint on materials handling capacity.

Results of the Model

The results of the model for the corrected Cases A, B, and C are outlined in Table 2.

TABLE 2

Comparison of Cases A, B, and C

	Case A 1976 Fixed Production Requirements	Case B 1976 Optimum Product Mix	Case C 1978 Optimum Product Mix
Profit Margin	$60,369/week	$109,388/week	$129,324/week
29 Product Tons/week	544	834	1,053
Estimated Total Tons/week	725	1,112	1,404
% of Tonnage which is purchased material	31.0	40.0	30.9

Processing Hours Required/Hours Available*

Stage 2a	9.7/45.0	18.9/45.0	19.4/45.0
Stage 2b	17.2/50.0	1.9/50.0	34.5/75.0
Stage 2c	20.5/20.0	20.0/20.0	38.3/75.0
Stage 2d	6.3/18.75	8.7/18.75	9.8/18.75
Blending	36.2/150	46.0/150.0	67.5/150.0
Mixing	33.2/150	45.9/150.0	67.5/150.0
Packaging			
Line 1	39.6/67.5	66.8/67.5	67.5/67.5
Line 2	12.0/67.5	1.7/67.5	25.0/67.5
Line 3	3.3/67.5	4.0/67.5	6.5/67.5
Raw Materials Handling Capability	Fully utilized	Fully utilized	Not a Factor

* Hours available are 75% of estimated total hours available during regular operating times, allowing the remaining capacity to produce the products not modeled.

As described by a member of the management of ABC, the results were "dynamite." The model showed that, with the same capacity, the plant could have improved its profit margin markedly. The comparison of Cases A and B illustrated the importance of product mix to the company. In 1976, ABC's marketing section had contracted for a large number of orders that had to be processed by stage 2c. At the same time, the other stage 2 operations had significant amounts of processing time available, and the actual 1976 operations did not make full use of purchased materials which bypass stage 2 entirely. These points were well illustrated by model results.

The expansion already planned took on new importance. ABC had been planning to build an entire new plant in the future to alleviate overloads at the existing plants. The model showed that this would probably not be necessary; since overloads could be accommodated at the modeled plant with its new capacity.

Perhaps the most significant implication of the study was the possibility of producing to inventory rather than merely to satisfy immediate orders. Case E analyzed whether the plant would be able to produce enough inventory to maintain stocks for a one month demand cycle. The model indicated that this was indeed feasible.

Shifting to an inventory policy would create significant advantages for the company. First, it would allow ABC to implement marketing strategies giving it an edge on its competitors, since it could guarantee customers short lead times for their orders. Second, production scheduling could be greatly improved by increasing efficiencies of product changeovers, increasing stability, and improving control over production as a result of repetitive scheduling.

Case D was run to determine the effect of market concentration. The demands were free to vary up to 6×1976 levels, investigating how ABC could specialize in a restricted product line if this were profitable. The model results indicated that the profit margin would increase to $228,232 in this case. While this is a substantial increase in profit over Case C results, the attendant strategy is risky, and many factors need to be considered in assessing it.

Implementation of the Model

In any modeling effort, the important part is what happens after the results are presented. The task force for which the model was developed was impressed with the results. The highest level marketing and production representatives were readily receptive to the suggestions of reducing the product line and of building inventory. A lower level marketing manager was worried about losing low volume items he considered important inducements to some high volume customers; these products were specially made for clients in order to maintain sales of higher volume products. The consultants explained that these lower volume products could still be made, since time was allocated for their production in the model. Another lower level marketing manager was concerned about the validity of the model. He asked if the model couldn't be used to reproduce an actual week's production. Unfortunately, this couldn't be done, since the plant did not have the data collection capabilities necessary to make comparisons with model results. Production representatives on the task force tried to answer the question of model validity by saying the model looked "right" to them. Following this discussion, the task force agreed to release the study and send it to the corporation's president.

A cover letter was written to accompany the report. Recommendations made in the letter included:

A. Producing inventories as opposed to merely filling orders.

B. Eliminating certain low volume products.

C. Postponing additional expansion until further studies could be made.

The president was very interested in the profit margins in the different cases and felt that the letter submitted with the report could have been even stronger in stressing the recommendations. The president called an executive level meeting of all vice-presidents along with the marketing and production directors. As a result of the study two general recommendations were presented to this group.

1. Reduce the product line and specialize on high-profit items as indicated by the model.
2. Build inventories of the highest volume products in order to give shorter lead times.

The meeting became an extensive and heated discussion about these recommendations since they were counter to existing corporate policies. The vice-president for marketing and the brand managers opposed recommendation number one, since it restricted sales options. On the other hand the production representatives favored both recommendations since they would make their jobs easier. The president, after listening to the discussion, asked the marketing director and brand managers to prepare a plan to implement recommendation number one. The second recommendation was deferred until the company could assess the impact of the first recommendation. The president felt that the first recommendation might alleviate the long lead time problem.

Subsequent to the meeting, the active product list at the modeled plant was narrowed to 85 products. Orders for other products were to be filled only with the understanding that they would be delayed. For each product removed from the list, a substitute product was to be offered to the company's customers. The product list was to be studied by a task force with the objective of reducing the product line further.

The annual profit planning session of the company offered another opportunity to integrate the model into the policy decision making process. In this planning session, the company made profit projections for the next year based upon demand trends in various segments of the market. Members of the task force hoped that the model would become an important element in the profit plan since this would key the entire company to a change in marketing and production strategy. However, there were problems to be overcome before this could be accomplished. For instance, members of the profit planning committee did not understand the opportunity cost concept illustrated by the model. In essence, this concept is that producing a low-profit-margin item results in the lost opportunity to make higher profits from a higher-profit-margin

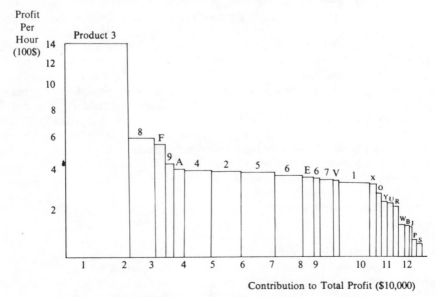

FIGURE 2. Contribution of Products to Total Profit vs. Profit Margin per Machine Hour.

112

item. Since some low-profit items require long production times, the opportunity costs are often large.

Executives on the planning committee still viewed the profit for a product as being independent of other products; so an attempt was made to illustrate the error of that view via a graph (Figure 2). The y-axis (\$/hour of machine capacity) values were derived by taking the total production hours required for a product and dividing this into the supposed profit margin per ton of product. The x-axis is the profit contribution of different products. As shown in Figure 2, hourly profit varied from as low as \$81 to as high as \$1,376. If a profit plan were developed which emphasized the marketing of products with higher \$/machine-hour values, significant improvements in the plant's profitability could be achieved. There is a limit to the volume of high profit items that can be sold, but the company's market share is low enough to make significant increases a reasonable goal.

The most substantial result of the project was the cancelling of plans to build an entirely new production facility, since model results showed that existing capacity would be sufficient if a better marketing strategy were adopted. At latest report the manager of Marketing Development reported that the model results had convinced the marketing department to limit its sales emphasis to the top 21 brands and to begin educating the customers to a new policy of upgrading, i.e., substituting for a product with a higher grade product. The net result of these moves is to reduce the number of small volume products made and the number of short production runs. In addition it was reported that a policy of stocking high volume products in inventory had been adopted.

As an extension of this project the consultants were asked to prepare a scheduling model for the modeled plant, which they have done. The scheduling model is interactive and is run from a terminal in the plant itself. An additional effort the company has asked for is a more complete LP product mix model. Company personnel are currently tracking down the requisite data.

It is apparent that the model is educating management and helping to shape corporate policy, since the company has continued to explore additional options with the model. In addition to the model extension described above, discussion has begun on the development of a similar model for another plant. The LP model gives ABC a way to study options for improving the company's future position, and many of the ideas suggested by the model have become integral parts of the company's thinking about production and marketing strategy.

This experience of trying to effect changes in corporate policy has pointed out two general principles pertaining to large companies. One is: "Competing objectives are inherent in corporate policy." As a result, OR/MS consultants can expect that a considerable fraction of their recommendations will meet with automatic opposition from some of the company's management personnel. It is, therefore, unlikely that all of a consultant's recommendations will be accepted no matter how well conceived and conveyed.

A second principle is:

"Acceptance and implementation of policy changes suggested by corporate models is an evolutionary process with success measured in stages." The model described in this paper has passed the initial stages of acceptance. Total acceptance of the model as a part of corporate policy making is a goal yet to be achieved.

APPLICATIONS OF PRODUCTION PLANNING AND SCHEDULING
Overview of Articles

This section contains papers that discuss six applications of mathematical programming to the planning and scheduling of operations in industrial and service organizations.

"Coordinating Decisions for Increased Profits," by R. H. King and R. R. Love Jr., discusses Kelly-Springfield Tire Company's 1970 implementation and 1976 extension of a coordinated total system of sales forecasting, inventory control, and production/distribution planning. The results—annual savings of $0.5 million with the old and $8.4 million with the new total system—coupled with the innovative and technically advanced use of management science techniques earned the authors the 1980 Management Science Achievement Award. A major reason for this success is the extensive involvement of the user in the design, operation, and refinement of the system.

A top-down sales-forecasting system employs intrinsic methods at each level, adjusted by managers at each level according to anticipated market changes and previous forecast errors. An inventory-control system determines order points and weekly production lot sizes for each product. These are adjusted by using a network flow algorithm if mold capacity is exceeded and by the production department if necessary.

The production planning system determines the number of molds needed daily for each product at each factory to balance customer service and manufacturing efficiency while satisfying manpower, process and physical restrictions, and interdependencies for the nearly 8,000 different finished tires. The vast number of columns and the special structure of the resulting linear-programming model are solved iteratively using a dynamic-programming decomposition technique*.

Finally, a heuristic assignment/distribution system determines (1) planned production shipments from four factories to nine major warehouses to minimize transportation costs and equalize customer service, and (2) transfer stock between warehouses at minimum freight cost in the case of great inventory imbalance.

No details regarding the structure of the mathematical models and solution approaches are included in this account of a successfully integrated production/inventory/distribution planning and control system.

"Production-Distribution Planning in a Large-Scale Commodity Processing Network," by Robert E. Markland and Robert J. Newett, discusses the methodology and application of a large-scale mathematical-programming model of a multiplant commodity, production-distribution network of a soybean company. It considers the production and distribution of soybean products with a multiplant soybean-processing complex. The model structure integrates the classical time-horizon linear-programming approach for production planning with the transportation method for distribution planning. Moreover, the model allows consideration of both internal and external demands while incorporating the unique milling-to-transit features associated with the distribution of soybean meals.

The model structure was tested and evaluated for an existing seven-plant soybean-processing network. Each plant has three soybean origins, and each can ship its end product to any of 10 regional destinations. Then, using a representative set of supply-and-demand conditions, the model was tested for a four-week planning horizon. The authors developed solutions to the model structure using the IBM mathematical programming package MPS. The size of the problem was approximately 900 rows by 3000 columns and the output produced was voluminous. Results of the problem solution are summarized in a series of tables. However, the report format severely limited the operational usage of the model as an actual planning device. Thus, the development of an output report writer was considered to summarize results for the following areas:

*Also refer to an earlier LP model by S. Gorenstein, "Planning Tire Production," *Management Science*, October 1970.

1. Purchasing volume requirements by origins and plants
2. Crushing reports by plants for both aggregate and detailed production
3. Distribution reports by plants, products, and destinations
4. Milling-in-transit reports by plants, products, and destinations.

"Experiments in Mixed-Integer Linear-Programming in a Manufacturing System," by Patrick G. Falk, discusses the design and development of a hierarchical planning system using mixed-integer programming. This system involved one of the smaller divisions of the Proctor & Gamble Co. The division is a typical large-scale, continuous-flow manufacturing operation. The general configuration of the division included

1. Multiple raw material supplies
2. Multiple plant manufacturing facilities
3. Multiple product output
4. Multiple warehouse distribution network
5. Multiple transportation modes
6. Multiple market zones.

The hierarchical planning system consists of a fully integrated four-module system designed to address the problems of strategic, tactical, and operational planning. The system consists of four modules in a descending hierarchical order:

1. Transportation model
2. Production planning model
3. Production scheduling model
4. Distribution simulation model.

The hierarchy was part of a program to promote the effective use of logistical resources. Part of this effort was directed toward re-evaluating the following items:

1. Raw materials purchasing strategies
2. Plant and warehouse sites and facilities
3. Production, distribution, and inventory schemes.

The issues at hand involved long-term strategic, mid-term tactical, and short-term operational planning decisions and various levels of management, serving different functions and concerned with details of varying degrees. Therefore, the authors decided that only a hierarchical approach would be suitable. Such a hierarchical process permits decisions to be made in a sequence. Furthermore, because of the complexity, size, and diversity of the topics involved, no single analytical approach would optimize the entire manufacturing operation in a single step.

This paper shows the direct application of the concept of the manufacturing hierarchy to a real-life situation and presents a detailed discussion of the flow process of the manufacturing operation and the system helping to manage the operation.

"Development of Integrated Production Scheduling System for Iron and Steel Works," by S. Sato, T. Yamaoka, Y. Aoki, and T. Ueda, discusses aggregating and then sequencing the many small-lot orders in multiplant steel works in a way that best uses the features of each plant while keeping delivery dates. This article presents an integrated system used by Nippon Steel Corporation to schedule about 25,000 orders through 25 main processes yielding 6 million tons of output annually.

An additional complication is that both the structure and strictness of optimization requirements vary with the content of orders and the type of process. About 1000 restrictions cover production-period, lot-sizing, and delivery-date constraints, whose degrees of freedom depend on order content. Order and process characteristics determine, for each case, which of the following conflicting objective functions to consider: (1) expediting urgent products, (2) leveling workload, (3) reducing production setup time by increasing lot quantities and changing dimensions within a lot, (4) smoothing the number of operating plants, and (5) reducing in-process inventory and material-handling costs through process changes.

A simulator model heuristically determines system parameters, production lot-size regrouping, and scheduling (considering both optimal and forced allocations). New orders are added to the existing information files and policy parameters are reviewed and entered by a production coordinating committee.

This integrated system evolved in three stages, spanning a ten-year period. Undoubtedly, the company encountered many implementation difficulties and resistance to computerization changes that are not covered in the paper.

"Improving Fuel Utilization in Steel Mill Operations Using Linear Programming," by Robert E. Markland, discusses the use of a linear-programming model to maximize fuel utilization at a steel mill of the National Steel Co. With the marketed competition from foreign imports, the problem of increasing operating costs are of major concern to the steel industry. A major operating cost for a steel mill is the cost associated with fuels used in the production of steel. As the cost of typical fuels such as natural gas and fuel oil have skyrocketed, ways of more effectively utilizing various fuels (including by-product gases produced during the steel making process) have been sought. The approach of this paper is to specify a fuel allocation plan that will reduce total fuel costs.

The objective function of this fuel-distribution linear-programming model was designed to minimize the total cost of fuel utilization. The four types of fuels considered are

1. Natural gas
2. Fuel oil
3. Coke gas
4. Blast furnace gas.

The constraints set of the model are:

1. Production fuel requirements
2. Base fuel requirement per month
3. By-product fuel availability based on production
4. External fuel sources supply constraints.

Numerous test runs of the fuel utilization linear-programming model are described using a monthly time horizon. These test runs view various times of operating conditions, as well as different production levels. The remaining results of the model show that considerable savings can be gained by using a fuel-allocation plan based on the effective utilization of product gases from the steel-making process. A number of potential extensions of the model could vary the costs of fuels to test for the sensitivity of fuel replacement, adding other energy sources to investigate the problems associated with curtailment of fuel oil or natural gas.

"A Case Study of Encoder Shift Scheduling Under Uncertainty," by Vincent A. Mabert, discusses a problem common to all banks—scheduling the time and number of workers needed to meet projected hourly requirements of magnetic-ink encoding of checks using a limited number of machines in a way that minimizes wage and opportunity costs. Investment opportunities for large float of unprocessed checks results.

A chance-constraint integer-programming model is developed to cope with this problem in the face of uncertainties in the total daily check volume and the within-day arrival rate.

An experimental application to Chemical Bank operations illustrates model performance under different shortage probabilities, workload levels, forecast errors, and opportunity costs. For a wide range of operating conditions, the model results compare favorably to current performance.

COORDINATING DECISIONS FOR INCREASED PROFITS

R.H. King and R.R. Love, Jr.

The Kelly-Springfield Tire Company, Cumberland, Maryland, 21502

ABSTRACT. This paper describes how a major tire manufacturer has attained an increase in productivity through the application of Management Science. Like most manufacturers, The Kelly-Springfield Tire Company has long recognized the difficulty and importance of coordinating sales forecasting, inventory control, production planning, and distribution decisions. The evolution of an integrated "Total System" approach is traced, with emphasis on the ability of the latest Management Science system to adapt to the constantly changing tire business. The original Total System, implemented in 1970, reduced production lead time to generate estimated annual savings of $500,000; benefits totaling over $5 million during the past decade.

Since the implementation of the latest system in 1976, Kelly-Springfield's share of the auto and truck tire replacement market has increased about 1% in an industry recently characterized by significant losses, excess productive capacity, and intense price competition. Average unit inventory decreased by 19% while customer service improved, productivity increased, and additional savings totaling $7.9 million annually resulted.

Numerous data support facilities were developed to attain the desired flexibility. The resulting capability to supply information quickly and accurately has been employed to obtain improved estimates of profit and loss and return on investment, to plan future sales strategies and advertising campaigns more effectively, to purchase production equipment, to analyze market share and product offerings, and to make and satisfy commitments to customers regarding availability of new products.

EARLY HISTORY

Kelly-Springfield, one of the oldest companies in the American tire industry, was founded in 1894 in Springfield, Ohio, by Edwin S. Kelly. The management of the company, having moved the main plant from Springfield to Akron, Ohio, decided about the time of World War I to move to Cumberland, Maryland — a site on the Potomac River, the National Highway, and the Western Maryland and B&O Railroads, located in the center of the nation's principal soft coal fields. However, the trauma of this major move crippled the company to the extent that by 1935, after a long decline, Kelly-Springfield went into receivership and was sold to Goodyear. Until 1962, when a new plant opened in Tyler, Texas, Cumberland was the only manufacturing facility; the company's policy was to produce a good quality tire and be satisfied with a small percentage of the passenger tire market.

With the opening of the Tyler plant, a decade of rapid growth and product diversification began. The company entered the custom brand tire market and rapidly became one of the leading manufacturers of tires for petroleum companies, department stores, discount chains, and tire merchandisers, while continuing to market its own house brands. The year after the Tyler plant opened, Kelly-Springfield built another plant in Freeport, Illinois, and seven years later the fourth plant, one of the largest tire factories in the world, went into production in Fayetteville, North Carolina.

THE 1960'S; AN EXPLOSION

The tire market increased tremendously during the 1960's and producers found it difficult to keep up with the demand, even though capacity rose by 30%. Revolutionary changes occurred in sales patterns, and independent tire dealers, who once controlled the market, found their sales slipping away to the private labels of department stores, discount chains, and petroleum companies. Private label or "custom" brands were now claiming 40% of all replacement sales, and Kelly-Springfield was in on the ground floor.

Even more dramatic than the changes in volume and sales patterns was the proliferation of product offerings that occurred. Traditional bias construction was augmented first by bias-belted construction and later by radial construction. These breakthroughs in design were accompanied by the development of new raw materials, particularly fabrics such as polyester and fiberglass. These innovations, and the quest of every company for market share, caused the product mix to explode, with the industry producing thousands of different pneumatic tires. As a leading custom brand producer, Kelly-Springfield found its product mix extremely complicated and becoming virtually unmanageable.

Growth during the decade was enormous; annual auto tire sales rose 307%, truck tire sales rose by 204%. In 1960, Kelly-Springfield had an inventory of one million tires stored primarily at the Cumberland factory; by 1970, the company had an inventory of 3.9 million tires in nine modern distribution centers located throughout the United States. The number of decisions related to manufacturing and distribution rose astronomically, and management recognized the magnitude of the problem by establishing the Operating Division in 1964. This Division was charged with balancing customer service objectives of the Sales Division and factory efficiency objectives of the Manufacturing Division, a concept unique to the rubber industry. It was given the authority to determine sales forecasts, to establish raw material and finished goods inventory levels, to specify daily factory production plans to be executed by the Manufacturing Division, and to plan the distribution of production as well as manage the distribution centers. The Operating Division was required to satisfy simultaneously goals for customer service, production capacity and efficiency, inventory levels, and return on investment.

As the number of products approached 5,000 and stockkeeping units approached 20,000 it became clear that, despite a large increase in work force, manual techniques were inadequate to maintain the performance level of the Operating Division. In the face of anticipated further product proliferation, a decision was made in 1967 to explore the possibilities of using the tools of Management Science, including computer technology, to assist the Division in meeting its charge.

A REVERSAL

The 1970's brought a reversal to the exploding tire market. Specific influences effected several general business slowdowns: inflation, energy shortages, cutbacks in consumer spending, record interest rates, soaring petroleum prices, and spiraling operating costs. Industry replacement auto tire sales fell from 149 million in 1978 to 136 million in 1979; original equipment auto tire sales dropped from 57 to 50 million units; and total large truck tire sales declined from 45 to 43 million units. Thus the industry reversed from a shortage to an excess in capacity. Eight tire plant closings were announced within 12 months. One company closed its last tire plant and filed for bankruptcy, and several others reported losses or reduced dividends during 1979.

Amid this turmoil, Kelly-Springfield continued to operate its four factories, served some 20 private-label customers (department store chains, petroleum companies, auto supply chains, and tire wholesalers) in addition to marketing its own house brands, and gained market share. With the implementation of its latest Management Science system, Kelly's share of the 140-million-unit replacement auto tire industry rose nearly 1% from 1976 to 1979, and rose a full 1% for the 32-million-unit truck tire replacement market.

OPERATING DIVISION SYSTEM

The principal activities related to the Operating Division's charge that needed to be addressed by Management Science techniques were sales forecasting, inventory control, production planning, and distribution. Kelly-Springfield, recognizing the interrelated nature of these activities, pioneered in the development of an integrated total system approach (illustrated in Figure 1):

- The Sales Forecasting section was to provide sales estimates by product at each warehouse by week.
- The Inventory Control section was to specify when, and how much, production was required for each tire.
- The Production Planning section was to determine where and how to produce each product.
- The Distribution section was to indicate where each factory should ship the finished tires.

FIGURE 1. TOTAL SYSTEM APPROACH.

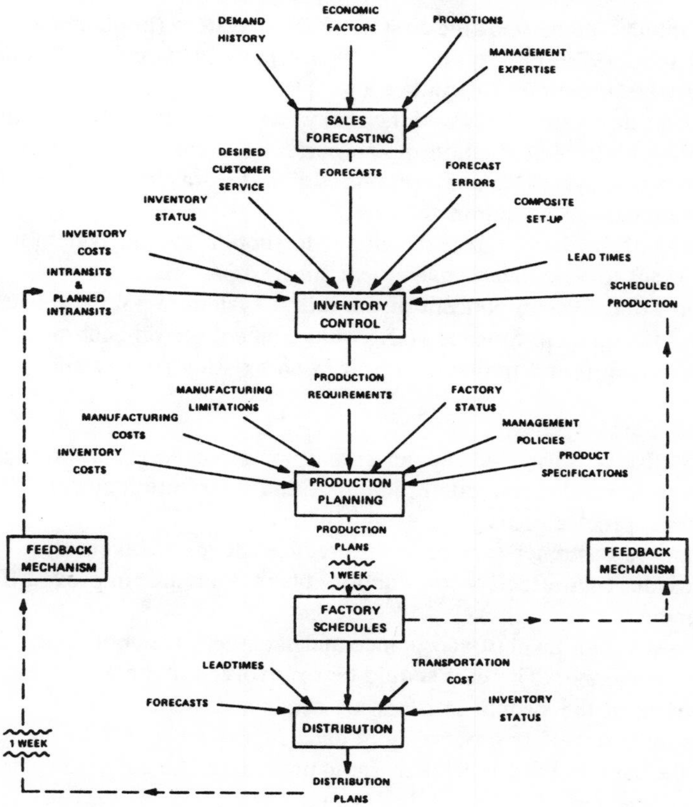

The integrated nature of this system is demonstrated by the presence of two dynamic feedback loops. The detailed factory schedule and the Distribution intransits (tires in shipment) and planned intransits (tires waiting for shipment) are both used as input to the Inventory Control System in the following week's processing.

The First Total System

The first attempt to develop an integrated system was proposed in 1967. Implementation began in the fall of 1970 and continued into 1971. This system was designed for the product mix, manufacturing equipment, Management Science technology, and computer capabilities of the late 1960's. During the early 1970's, dramatic changes occurred in each of these areas:

1. Kelly-Springfield's product mix became even more diversified; "green tires transgressing mold groups" meant that a particular green tire could be cured in more than type mold. This situation, unforeseen in the late 1960's, was catastrophic to the Production Planning System; acceptable product plans frequently could not be derived from the mold group plans developed earlier in the hierarchical solution technique (with Long, Intermediate, and Short Term Production Planning), resulting in more than 50% user overrides.
2. The manufacturing equipment became more varied and complex, generating a need for additional limitations in the planning system.
3. The technology for applying Management Science techniques (e.g., network algorithms and compacting of linear programs) increased, as well as computer speed and memory, making a system capable of handling the increased complexities feasible.

As problems intensified, the first automated system (implemented in 1970 and operational until 1976) rapidly lost its effectiveness. Although it declined in value, its legacies were important to another attempt:

1. The initial system "plowed the rocky field" of automation for the Operating Division. Implementation of the current system was a transition from one automated system to another, rather than the drastic adjustment from a manual process to an automated one.
2. Many of the data sources developed to support the old system would be used as input to new data management files.
3. The Total System concept of the initial system remained intact. Therefore, the Management Science staff could concentrate on each major subsystem, improving it and implementing it in an existing framework.

The Second Total System

In 1974, Kelly-Springfield began developing a second generation sales forecasting, inventory control, production planning, and distribution system. Based on the initial attempt, precise goals were established:

1. Improve customer service with a reduced level of inventory.
2. Provide cost-effective production plans yielding improved factory efficiency.
3. Attain a high level of acceptance and satisfaction among Operating Division user personnel. The user should be so involved in the design phase that he is convinced the system satisfies his needs and wants.
4. Insure that weekly processing of each subsystem would be the responsibility of the user, not the developer. Input procedures for each subsystem should be user-oriented.

5. Achieve a longer life expectancy through the development of generalized input and output capabilities and selection of flexible solution techniques.
6. Establish a modular design for ease of updating and modification to insure responsiveness to the user's changing needs.

A self-imposed requirement was to maintain the existing system, implement minor improvements as they became available, develop major subsystems to be run in a parallel mode until proved, and wind up with one total system that performed to all expectations. Although the integrated approach was to be preserved, the decision-making techniques for each operating activity would differ in basic philosophy:

- The existing Sales Forecasting System used the bottom-up approach beginning with product-warehouse forecasts. The new system was to employ a constrained top-down approach starting with total company estimates.
- The existing Inventory Control System used an order-point lot-size formula for each product and warehouse. The new system was to develop a corporate formula for each product, accept at any time management-specified inventory levels, and consider mold capacities, to derive production requirements by tire.
- The existing Production Planning System determined a production plan for each facility separately (e.g., Cumberland radial passenger). This implied that any product which could be produced in more than one facility had to have its production requirements assigned to facilities before processing the planning system. The new Production Planning System would determine a corporate production plan.
- The existing planning system used a hierarchical approach where higher level decisions imposed constraints on lower level actions, the new System was to employ a direct optimization approach. The existing system planned by mold group; the fundamental planning unit in the new System, the "thread set" (explained under "Production Planning"), was to consider green tires as well as molds.
- The existing Distribution System only considered the distribution of planned production for a product, and only specified the total quantity to be shipped from a factory to each warehouse during the succeeding week. The new Distribution System was to consider transfers of stock between warehouses and was to specify the destination for each pallet of scheduled production.
- Such a large-scale integrated system requires extreme data integrity on an ongoing basis for a vast amount of detailed information. Much of the success of the system must be attributed to the development of the basic data support facilities which are described in the Appendix.

DECISION SYSTEMS

To assist the Operating Division, there is a decision-making system for each of the four principal functions.

Sales Forecasting

The objective is to develop accurate sales estimates for 26,000 stocking units by week for up to 23 months.

The forecasting environment can best be described by a pyramidal structure, with the *national economy* at the top. Kelly-Springfield total sales potential is a share

121

of the projected *replacement market,* which is dependent on the *national economy.* Total corporate sales can be divided into *divisions,* such as Kelly's own brand, associated brands (subsidiary divisions), and retailers' private brands. Each division may sell tires to more than one *customer;* e.g., Kelly brand is sold to Kelly-Springfield dealers, Kelly's retail stores, and Sunmark Industries. Customers seldom purchase only one *line* of tires; they may need snow, radial, and bias belted tires. These tire lines consist of various *product* sizes and types (e.g., the A70-13 Whitewall) that are normally sold from several *distribution centers.*

The Sales Forecasting System uses a "top-down" approach as illustrated in Figure 2. Mathematical forecasts are developed using intrinsic methods for each level of the structure. At the corporate level, the forecast is adjusted to reflect industry estimates and changes in the economy. The forecasts at each level (below corporate) are adjusted to conform totally with the next higher level, considering relative forecast errors at the lower level. Each level allows for review by knowledgable individuals and overrides to reflect anticipated changes in market conditions. Final estimates at the stockkeeping level are the "company numbers" and are used for inventory control, production planning, distribution, estimated profit and loss, and other company applications.

FIGURE 2. SALES FORECASTING.

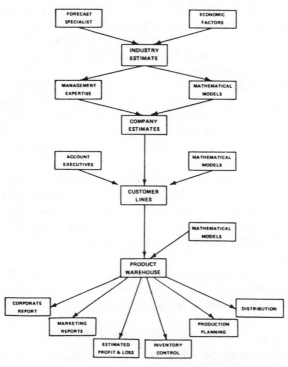

This approach was chosen after simulation and parallel testing demonstrated improved accuracy. The basis for selection of a forecasting technique is how well it performs in a live, ongoing environment. The forecast errors at the stockkeeping level that determine inventory safety stock requirements have continuously improved, from 84% in 1975 to 69% in 1979. Computerized monitoring of various forecasts versus actual activity is performed at all levels. Analysis of the errors leads to refinements of the forecasts, both automatically and manually.

Since 1975, forecasting reports, including automated versus manual revisions, have been delivered to the President, Vice Presidents, and Managers involved in sales forecasting. Some of these reports are daily, some weekly, some monthly, and some annual. General acceptance of the forecasts by Kelly's management strongly implies system integrity.

Inventory Control

The Inventory Control System has the responsibility to determine for each product:

- When to replenish inventory?
- How much to produce?

The answer for when to replenish inventory is given by an order point, and the answer for how much by a production lot size. The derivation of the order-point lot-size formula considers customer service, production lead time, shipping time, and an extra quantity of tires for "safety stock" (inventory required to avoid a stockout due to forecast error). The resulting formula minimizes the total cost to carry inventory and to set up the product in the factory. The production setup cost is a composite of the costs associated with introducing the components of the particular tire.

The Production Planning Department can override the mathematically derived inventory formulas by specifying the order point and lot size for any group of products. This department can also specify the production requirements by week or by month for any product.

The Inventory Control System determines production requirements by week for each product for 40 weeks, and sums the requirements to the mold level. If mold capacity is exceeded for any week, a network flow algorithm equitably adjusts the weekly production requirements for each product using that mold (see Figure 3). Approximately 300,000 production requirements for the Production Planning System are generated using only about 250 of the parameters supplied in the Command Compiler Subsystem described in the Appendix. This 1,200 to 1 automatic expansion ratio dramatically reduces input preparation and errors.

FIGURE 3. MOLD CAPACITY ALLOCATION NETWORK FORMULATION.

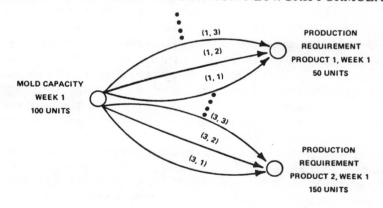

ARC LEGEND: (CAPACITY, COST)

SOLUTION: PRODUCT 1, WEEK 1 — 25 UNITS OF CAPACITY
PRODUCT 2, WEEK 1 — 75 UNITS OF CAPACITY

Production Planning

The Production Planning System can be more fully understood knowing the four basic steps in manufacturing a tire:

- *Preparation of Components.* In several parallel processes, raw materials are transformed into the components required to build a tire.
- *Tire Building.* The components are assembled at the tire building machine to form a barrel-shaped intermediate product called a "green tire." The green tire determines whether the finished product will be radial or conventional, whitewall or blackwall, 13-inch or 14-inch, etc.
- *Vulcanization.* The green or unvulcanized tire is placed in a curing press where heat and pressure are applied to obtain a finished tire. The mold placed in the press prior to vulcanization or "curing" determines the tire's tread pattern and sidewall markings.
- *Final Finish.* The tires are buffed if necessary (whitewall), inspected, and sorted for shipment to the warehouses.

The production planning problem is to determine the number of molds needed to cure each product at each factory during each day of the planning period, normally one week. The product mold-by-day plans should effectively balance customer service and manufacturing efficiency objectives, and the plans must satisfy factory restrictions established by physical, personnel, and process limitations.

The several thousand different finished tires cannot be scheduled independently since:

- More than one product may cure in the same type mold.
- More than one product may require the same type green tire.
- Groups of products share factory resources, such as production capacity, mold setups, and green tire setups.

The magnitude of the production planning problem indicated that a decomposition technique was required. One of the first problems in formulating a planning model was to determine a fundamental planning unit; i.e., how should the 7,400-plus products be divided into subsets for planning purposes? Any two products using the same type mold should be planned together to consider mold capacity and mold setups. Similarly, any two products requiring the same type green tire should be planned together to consider green tire setups and green tire types in process. Kelly-Springfield's Management Science staff developed the concept of a "thread set" as its fundamental planning unit. Each thread set begins with a single product and is successively expanded to include any product that shares a mold or green tire with the initial or subsequently added products. By planning a thread set as a fundamental unit, interrelationships between products, molds, and green tires can be considered. Given a plan for a thread set, the usage of shared resources that are product related (e.g., production capacity), mold related (mold setups), and green tire related (green tire types in process) can be determined. Moreover, the requirements for these shared resources are additive from thread set to thread set. An example of a thread set would be the following five products: (1) Mold A green tire X, (2) Mold B green tire X, (3) Mold A green tire Y, (4) Mold B green tire Y, (5) Mold C green tire Y. (This implies that no other product uses molds A, B, or C, or green tires X or Y.)

The factory restrictions that must be considered can be divided into two classes:

1. Restrictions that apply to individual thread set plans, such as mold capacity, minimum product, mold group, and green tire run sizes, and scheduling heuristics (rules of thumb). (An example of a scheduling heuristic would be

that a green tire cannot be torn down and subsequently set up within a two-week period.)

2. Restrictions that span thread sets, such as daily restrictions by factory by product group (e.g., Fayetteville radial) regarding production capacity, mold setups, green tire setups, number of green tire types in process, and number of different products curing.

The solution procedure in the Production Planning System uses a *linear programming (LP)/dynamic programming (DP) decomposition technique.* * This technique was first developed by Manne [1958] and later adapted to tire scheduling by Lasdon and Terjung [1968]. Lasdon and Terjung were associated with "The First Total System" and the application cited in their paper is the initial Planning System. The LP formulation in the current system has the structure described by Lasdon and Terjung and has approximately 1000 thread sets (items) and 300 thread-set spanning (shared resource) restrictions. The vast number of columns in the LP is handled by column generation using the DP Thread Set Planner.

The solution technique begins by having the Thread Set Planner generate independently for each thread set a minimum cost product mold-by-day plan that adheres to intra-thread-set restrictions. Since many of Kelly-Springfield's products can be manufactured in more than one factory, the Thread Set Planner is corporate in nature, and the resulting thread set plan specifies product mold-by-day plans for all factories. The total cost of a thread set plan consists of manufacturing costs plus inventory costs incurred if production requirements are not satisfied when requested from the Inventory Control System.

This initial collection of thread set plans is called the Unconstrained Solution, since these plans are generated without regard to the factory restrictions that span thread sets. The DP/LP Interface computes the usage of shared resources by each thread set plan for restrictions that span thread sets. The linear programming "Plans Coordinator" totals the shared resource usage, and derives a "rental cost" for each factory restriction depending upon whether the shared resource is being underutilized, utilized to capacity, or overutilized. Since many of Kelly's products can be manufactured in more than one factory, the linear programming problem is corporate in nature. The LP/DP Interface communicates the rental costs to the Thread Set Planner to generate independently for each thread set a new plan that satisfies intra-thread-set restrictions and minimizes total manufacturing, inventory, and rental costs. The Plans Coordinator determines the "best composite set" of thread set plans, updates the rental costs based on the shared resource usage of this composite set, and calls the Thread Set Planner to regenerate the thread set plans with the new rental costs. Iterating through this cycle (DP Thread Set Planner-DP/LP Interface, Shared Resource Usage-LP Plans Coordinator-LP/DP Interface, Rental Costs) continually improves the composite set of plans. This scheme is repeated until no further improvement in the current set of plans is possible, or until the process satisfies termination criteria established by empirical analysis of convergence and by the availability of computer time.

The magnitude of the production planning problem and the role of the Planning System in the scheduling function require numerous program features to reduce processing time, to use computer storage capabilities efficiently, to safeguard against machine failure, and to insure that the resulting production plans will be available when required.

---

*Technical notes describing this in greater detail are available from the authors.

Distribution

Kelly-Springfield has four factories and nine major distribution centers strategically located throughout the United States. Many products can be manufactured in more than one factory, and most products are stored in several distribution centers. The distribution problem has two aspects:

1. Consider where the planned production for each product should be sent to equalize customer service by warehouse. If the product is being manufactured in more than one factory, the factory-to-warehouse shipments should obtain minimum transportation costs subject to equalizing customer service by warehouse.

2. If a critical imbalance of inventory exists among the warehouses that cannot be corrected by the distribution of planned production, then transfers of stock between warehouses should be initiated to alleviate the imbalance. The transfers should be coordinated to obtain reduced freight costs through volume shipments.

The distribution problem for a product can be viewed as a problem of assigning the supplies to the demands to achieve minimum transportation costs. Supplies take the form of planned production at the factories and excess stock at some of the warehouses. Demands take the form of back orders, orders placed by the customer for future delivery, and forecasted demands at the warehouses. The Distribution System uses a set of rules, or heuristics, based on an efficient mathematical technique (the transportation algorithm) for solving the assignment problem. The heuristic, or rule-of-thumb, approach has several advantages:

- The user identifies with and more fully understands the Distribution System rules.
- Rules can be changed more rapidly and more predictably than could a mathematical technique.
- This approach provides flexibility that would have been difficult to achieve with a mathematical technique.

The Distribution System generates a Distribution Lineup Report directing each factory where to send each pallet of production to equalize customer service by warehouse at minimum transportation cost.

The Suggested Transfer Report advises the distribution analysts of transfers between warehouses considered necessary to correct critical imbalances of inventory. These suggested transfers are coordinated to satisfy management-specified minimum weights for each warehouse-to-warehouse route.

C. H. Wagner, Mananger of Sales Forecasting, Merchandise Distribution, and Inventory Control, states:

> Better execution of the Lineups in the factories resulting from specifying the destination for each pallet of planned production has achieved better allocation of production from factory to warehouse with reduced transportation costs. The improvement in sales forecasting allows me to place substantial reliability in the Suggested Transfer Report. The flexibility to change rules for the Lineups and the Transfer Report gives me the ability to react almost instantaneously to potential work stoppages, warehouse overflow situations, and warehouse reassignment of customers.

REASONS FOR SUCCESS

A discussion of the reasons for success of the second generation system yields lessons of transferable value that are relevant to most Management Science applications.

One reason for the success of the current system was the degree of user involvement in its development, and the continued user involvement in its control and maintenance. Evaluation Committees consisting of Operating Division management worked closely with the Management Science staff from initial design through final implementation of each decision-making system.

The result is a system controlled by the user. The Production Planning Department specifies the factory restrictions, inventory policies, and the values for all other planning parameters via the Command Compiler Subsystem of the Data Support Facility. The Merchandise Distribution Department submits predistribution information for any product whose planned production should not be distributed according to the Distribution System Rules. This degree of user control eliminates the "user decision" versus "system decision" problems.

Users and the Management Science staff discuss any potential problems informally. These discussions have spawned modifications to improve the resulting decisions and to reflect changes in the manufacturing and operating environments. This user involvement in maintaining the system has fostered a feeling that it is "his system."

Another reason for success is that from a user's viewpoint, this system was an extension of the previous system. The familiarity of the user with input requirements and output of automated systems and implementation of his recommendations for upgrading these aspects in the new system eased the transition and enhanced its acceptability.

The ability of the system to adapt to technological and management policy changes is a significant reason for its success. This flexibility stems from the generalized input and output capabilities and the selection of solution techniques.

The final reason for success is the continuity of the Management Science staff, which has enhanced user confidence and trust. The current manager of the staff has been associated with the integrated system since its infancy in the late 1960's. Moreover, the second generation system developers, who are most familiar with its capabilities and limitations, are maintaining the system. Modifications and enhancements requested by the user can be accomplished more rapidly and predictably than by strictly maintenance personnel.

DIRECT BENEFITS

How did Kelly-Springfield manage to increase its market share in an industry characterized by overcapacity resulting in intense price competition? The answer is by providing better customer service. Measured in terms of units shipped within 24 hours of receipt of an order, customer service for passenger tires has increased steadily from 78.9% in 1975 to 85.3% in 1979. How did Kelly-Springfield achieve this improvement in customer service? An essential ingredient was the decision in 1974 to develop the second generation Integrated Total System.

The original Operating Division system achieved an inventory reduction when production lead time was shortened one week by going from a manual to an automated planning process. This inventory reduction due to the data processing aspects of the original system was estimated in 1970 to generate annual savings of $500,000. Thus, Kelly-Springfield has derived benefits totaling over $5 million during the last decade from both the first and second systems.

The current system was implemented in late 1976 and 1977. Two principal objectives were to obtain increased customer service for a reduced level of inventory and to improve factory efficiency. Comparing 1975 to 1978, customer service increased from 78.9% to 81.3% for passenger tires, while average inventory expressed in days' supply decreased from 94.7 days to 78.8 days. This inventory reduction of 15.9 days represents an investment of $11.3 million (using 1978 product costs). Customer service remained static (69.8% in 1975, 69.3% in 1978) for truck tires, but average inventory decreased from 76.0 days to 52.2 days. This inventory reduction represents an investment of $3.2 million. Assuming a 15% prime rate, the total inventory investment reduction of $14.5 million generates annual savings of $2.2 million.

The improved production plans generated by the current system have resulted in increased productivity and reduced scrap levels in the factories. Two statistics that measure machine downtime due to changeovers, tires produced per building machine setup, and tires produced per mold setup, have improved by 10% percent and 33%, respectively, for passenger tires. The planning system used for passenger tires from 1970 to 1976 considered mold changes, but could not consider green tires. For truck tires, where the planning process had been a totally manual effort prior to 1977, these two statistics have improved by 13% and 79%, respectively. The Methods and Planning Department of Kelly-Springfield's Manufacturing Division estimates that the increased productivity in the factories resulting from this improvement in production plans generates annual savings of $4.2 million. The reduced scrap levels yield additional estimated annual savings of $860,000.

The system has proved valuable as a simulation tool to measure the impact of proposed modifications to manufacturing restrictions and management policies. A simulation study in early 1978 concluded that the number of different green tires being built per week in Cumberland's heavy-truck facility could be reduced by 15% without a decrease in customer service. When implemented, this reduction in green tires resulted in an increase in output of 200 tires per day with annual savings of $970,000. This is included in the $4.2 million savings resulting from increased productivity. A simulation study in early 1979 measured the impact on transfer tonnage of various transfer policies. Implementation of the recommendations from this study reduced transfer tonnage by 33%, or 7 million pounds, from 1978 to 1979, with recurring savings of $500,000.

Implementation of the current system has yielded additional benefits. A 30% reduction in the user staffs has been achieved from 1976 to 1979 despite a 25% increase in production levels. This reduction in personnel represents an annual savings of $175,000. The number of sizes and types planned weekly has more than doubled since the implementation of the original Production Planning System.

Another objective of the current system was to attain a high level of user satisfaction and acceptance. The gap between mathematical forecasting guidelines and final forecasts has narrowed dramatically, user overrides to the automated production plans have declined by 50%, and changes to the distribution lineups have become negligible.

Thus, the current system satisfies the development objectives and provides direct benefits totaling $8.4 million annually. Kelly-Springfield does not publish sales and earnings information. However, stated in broad terms, the impact of the direct benefits is in the range of 7% to 18% of Kelly's pretax profits.

No dollar benefits are claimed for the increased market share that Kelly-Springfield has experienced since implementation of the current system. Inclusion of the pretax earnings from these additional sales would make a substantial increase in the $8.4 million savings.

The cost of each computer run is automatically calculated. For the mathematical programming and other scientific algorithms in the current Management Science system, the calculated annual cost is $10,260. The data processing portions of the System would be required for any approach to the Operating Division functions and are not included.

INDIRECT BENEFITS

The direct benefits are only a portion of the total gains derived from the current system. The data-support facilities required by the system provide the capability to supply information quickly and accurately and have been used to assist many other divisions.

Financial Division. Improved sales forecasts give Kelly's Financial Division the ability to project more accurately profit and loss and return on investment. Since the short-term forecasts are revised weekly based on changes in the market place, current month financial estimates continuously improve.

Sales Division. Reports are generated by tire line for each account containing sales history, forecasts, inventory, production, and current month order position. Account executives review these reports with each customer to plan future strategies.

Development. In order for the Operating Division to make and satisfy commitments to customers regarding availability of new products, an automated system now tracks and reports the status of mold budgets, drawings, equipment purchases, and factory testing. This information is vital to the Development Division — the tire engineering group that is kept extremely busy by the proliferation of new products.

Marketing Division. Marketing uses Sales Forecasts to analyze market share and product offerings. Monthly reports indicating shortages and excesses of mold capacity are used to purchase additional molds and to seek additional sales. The vast amount of specification data is correlated and reported for Marketing to propose consolidation of products.

Advertising. Kelly-Springfield is a national advertiser, and Kelly brand tires are sold in all 50 states. However, sales are limited in certain markets. Using reports containing market share and potential by type of tire, the advertising thrust has become one of saturation campaigns in specific markets, with much improved results. Marketing and advertising staff have the information available to make judgments on what products should be featured, which markets should be covered, and the weight of advertising needed by market.

CONCLUSION

The President of the United States, in his speech to Congress on March 27, 1979, cited declining productivity in American industry as a prime contributor to inflation. He strongly urged Congress to declare the increase in productivity of American workers a very high national priority. Kelly-Springfield, through its innovative use of the tools of Management Science, has improved its sales forecasting, inventory control, production planning, and distribution functions and has increased productivity in its factories. These improvements have helped the tire company gain market share in an industry recently characterized by excess capacity, ferocious price competition, and the quest of each company for increased market share. This success has developed an awareness in Kelly-Springfield of the potential benefits to be derived from increased use of Management Science in the management decision process. Flexibility of the system gives the potential for application in many companies.

REFERENCES

Dantzig, G. B., 1968, "Large Scale Linear Programming," in Dantzig, G. B., and Veinott, A. F., Jr. eds., *Mathematics of the Decision Sciences*, Part 1, American Mathematical Society, Providence, Rhode Island.

Ford, L. R., Jr., and Fulkerson, D. R., 1962, *Flows in Networks*, Princeton University Press, Princeton, New Jersey.

Glover, F., Hultz, J., and Klingman, D., 1979, "Improved Computer-Based Planning Techniques, Part 1," *Interfaces* Vol. 8, No. 4, pp. 16–25.

Glover, F., Hultz, J., and Klingman, D., 1979, "Improved Computer-Based Planning Techniques, Part 2," *Interfaces* Vol. 9, No. 4, pp. 12–20.

Glover, F., Jones G., Karney, D., Klingman, D., and Mote, J., 1979, "An Integrated Production, Distribution, and Inventory Planning System," *Interfaces* Vol. 9, No. 5, pp. 21–35.

Lasdon, L. S. and Terjung, R. C., 1971, "An Efficient Algorithm for Multi-Item Scheduling," *Operations Research* Vol. 19, pp. 946–969.

Manne, A. S., 1958, "Programming of Economic Lot Sizes," *Management Science* Vol. 4, No. 2, pp. 115–135.

Mulligan, W., 1967, "Kelly-Springfield Uses On-Line Computer To Control, Schedule Tire Output," *Rubber World*, December.

Newell, R. H., 1971, "Use of Computers in Manufacturing," *Industrial Engineers Handbook*, 3rd Edition, McGraw Hill Book Company, New York.

(See Appendix next page.)

APPENDIX: DATA SUPPORT FACILITIES

Such a system requires a vast amount of detail information: much of the success of the current system must be attributed to the development of the basic data support facilities. The developers realized that the integrity of the data must be maintained on an on-going basis if the large-scale mathematical programming effort were to succeed.

Command Compiler Subsystem

One of the primary innovations toward the goal of flexibility was the development of the *Command Compiler Subsystem*. This subsystem permits the various system users to submit commands in normal English and translates these commands into the machine-readable form required by the many application programs.

Using the Command Compiler, the Production Planner can communicate to the Planning System scheduled workdays, inventory policies, factory restrictions, and values for planning parameters for any group of products. He can specify, "For heavy-truck limit mold-change minutes Cumb Mon-Wkl Maximum 660" and restrict the resulting plans to no more than 660 minutes of mold changes for heavy-truck tires in Cumberland on Monday of the first planning week. Production Planning specifies values for approximately 1,000 entries through the Command Compiler Subsystem. These numbers can be updated on a weekly basis; however, there is only occasional need to update most of the parameters (i.e., production capacities, minimum run sizes, desired customer service levels).

The Sales Forecasting user may desire specific information at a specific time. Instead of a general report of forecasts, he may require information on radial, or maybe steel radial, or any of approximately 130 product groups. Through the Command Compiler, he can specify the product group and even control his report formats.

Thus, through a specially designed command language, each system user can order just what he needs.

Factory Status Subsystem

Knowledge of which tires are being produced is necessary to plan a smooth transition in the factory from week to week. To supply this information, Kelly's four factories have a computerized communications network that automatically receives a continuous stream of information from the various work stations and storage locations. This Production Control System was a pioneering effort for Kelly-Springfield [Mulligan, 1967]. From this information, the *Factory Status Subsystem* once each week determines the current production schedule, thereby obtaining the product, mold, and green tire status at the beginning of the planning horizon.

Inventory Status Subsystem

A vital link in all operating functions is knowing the precise inventory of each product, including tires in the distribution centers, tires in transit, and finished tires still at the factories. Kelly-Springfield has an on-line order entry system that automatically notifies the central computer of any orders, shipments, or receipts at the various warehouses and factories. This information is used for financial recordkeeping and customer billing. The *Inventory Status Subsystem* modifies each product's inventory position by future production already scheduled to become the *effective available inventory*.

Master Information Subsystem

Kelly-Springfield, like most companies, has many data files designed for specific departments. For example, a Development Department maintains a file of the general specifications of each tire, and each factory has a file indicating the materials and production specifications for the tires it produces. However, the Operating Division requires information from many of these files. Knowledge of product components, mold inventory, and vulcanizing time is required to plan production. To schedule shipments, tire weight is required; and to communicate forecasts, customer names and tire lines are necessary. The *Master Information Subsystem* was developed to collect, edit, and relate data from many different sources, and create a file for use in many Operating Division applications. As the system processes each week, reports are generated for use throughout the company.

Reprinted, by permission, from Decision Sciences, *October 1976, published by the American Institute for Decision Sciences.*

SPECIAL SECTION—OPERATIONS MANAGEMENT

PRODUCTION-DISTRIBUTION PLANNING IN A LARGE SCALE COMMODITY PROCESSING NETWORK

Robert E. Markland, *University of Missouri, St. Louis*

Robert J. Newett, *Ralston Purina Company*

This paper describes a methodology for production-distribution planning in a large scale commodity processing network. Based on earlier research efforts dealing with single-commodity and multi-commodity distribution system modeling and on production planning for a single-plant commodity processing facility, a mathematical programming methodology is developed for a multiplant soybean processing network. Application of the model leads to the specification of a production plan for a multi-period time horizon, while at the same time indicating the quantities of soybean meal and soybean oil to be supplied to various customers in various locales. Both sets of decisions are made under the general criterion of maximizing the net income produced by the soybean processing complex, subject to various production, inventory, capacity, supply and demand constraints. Test results from application of the model are presented and discussed.

INTRODUCTION

This paper describes the development and testing of a large-scale mathematical programming model of a multi-plant commodity production-distribution network. This modeling effort is evolutionary and is based on several previous research efforts which were conducted within the production-distribution environment of a major American agri-business company. The earliest of these efforts was the work of Meyer [13] which dealt with the construction of a transportation model for a single commodity milling-in-transit distribution network. Meyer's work was later extended to an analysis of multi-commodity networks having milling-in-transit features by Markland [8] [9] and then to a large scale simulation model of a company's Consumer Products distribution system [7] [11] [12]. In addition, production planning over a multi-period time horizon for a single soybean processing plant was investigated by Markland and Newett [10]. Collectively, these previous efforts provide the foundation for the present investigation.

THE INTEGRATED SOYBEAN PROCESSING COMPLEX

The soybean was one of the first crops grown by man. Reference to it was made in Chinese records almost 5,000 years ago. It has been used for many centuries by people in Asiatic countries in the preparation of numerous fresh, fermented, and dried food products. Soybeans were introduced in this country in 1804, but remained a mere botanical curiosity for nearly a century. Recently, rapid expansion in the cultivation and use of soybeans has occurred. In the last 50 years, production has increased from 5 million bushels to over 1.1 billion bushels. Soybeans now rank second in total value among United States agricultural products, and are this country's leading export commodity [3] [14].

This paper considers the production and distribution of soybean products within a multi-plant soybean processing complex. Soybean processing occurs with a two-fold objective:

1. The production of high grade soybean meals (49 % protein content and 44 % protein content), soybean oil, and soybean hulls which are sold *externally* by the company;
2. The production of high grade soybean meals, oil, and hulls which are used *internally* in production by other operating units within the company.

Soybean processing begins with the purchase of soybeans from soybean growers in widely scattered locales. These soybeans are transported to soybean processing plants where they are "crushed" to produce soybean meal, soybean oil, and soybean hulls. One bushel (60 pounds) of soybean yields approximately

11 pounds of soybean oil,
48 pounds of soybean meal,
1 pound of soybean hulls.

Computation of the "gross crushing margin" (GCM) for the soybean processor requires valuation of the oil and soybean meal obtained from a given quantity of soybeans, and comparison of this value with the cost of the beans. When production units (bushels of soybeans, tons of soybean meal, and pounds of soybean oil) are considered, the resulting equation for computing the gross crushing margin can be written as

$$\text{GCM} = 11.0 \text{ pounds of oil (oil price/pound)} +$$
$$\frac{48 \text{ pounds of meal}}{2000 \text{ pounds/ton}} \text{ (meal price/ton)} - \text{(bean cost/bushel).} \tag{1}$$

From this gross crushing margin the cost of plant operation must be subtracted, and a decision must be made as to whether or not processing is economically warranted. The hulls produced by the crushing process are not considered in the computation of the gross crushing margin because soybean hulls are not actively traded and are a relatively low unit value "by product" of the crushing process. The soybean meal produced by the crushing process is generally of the 49 % protein content variety.

If crushing is profitable, some or all of the original end products may be sold externally. Alternatively, these original end products may be consumed internally in the production of other products. Additionally, some or all of the 49 % protein meal and hulls produced by crushing may be blended to produce 44 % protein meal. The following is the approximate blending equation:

$$1 \text{ Ton } 44\% \text{ Meal} = 0.89 \text{ Tons of } 49\% \text{ Meal} + 0.11 \text{ Tons of Hulls.} \tag{2}$$

The 44 % meal may then be sold externally or consumed internally in the production of other products. Finally, any or all of these products may be "outside purchased" and shipped directly to the end destination customers.

Distribution costs within this production-distribution complex are also an important consideration. The freight charges associated with the movement of soybeans from the origins to the plants are initially considered as a distribution

FIGURE 1.

Milling-in-transit network.

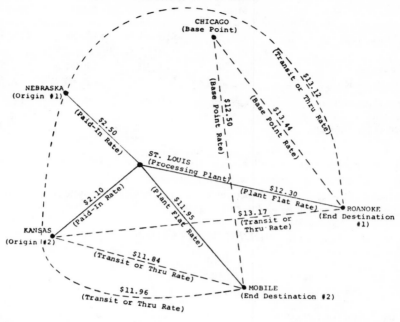

cost. However, the outbound movements of soybean meal (49% and 44%) are subject to milling-in-transit privileges. Under the milling-in-transit privilege, the soybean processor is allowed to ship soybeans from the origins to the plants, crush the soybeans to produce soybean meals (49% and 44%), and then ship these meals to final destinations. He is charged freight for the entire movement as if he had shipped only soybeans from the origins to the destinations. Figure 1 illustrates milling-in-transit.

As can be seen in Figure 1, the soybean processor pays the "transit" or "thru" freight rate to the common carrier. He then absorbs the "paid-in" rate associated with the origin to plant movement of soybeans. At this juncture, a set of "transit balance" rates can be computed simply as the "transit" rates minus the "paid-in" rates. These "transit balance" rates are a cost of distribution to the processor. Now, the soybean meals are sold to the end destination customer at a price which includes the freight charge (the "base point rate") associated with the end destination and the base point (Chicago, Illinois). As a result, the processor actually collects a "balance rate pickup" (computed as the "base point" rate minus the previously determined "transit balance" rate) from the end destination customer. These balance rate pickups are computed as shown in Table 1.

As can be seen in Table 1, in order to maximize the freight associated profit, the soybean meal demands in both Mobile and Roanoke should be satisfied by using soybeans grown in Nebraska. Depending upon the spatial aspects of a particular movement, the balance rate pickup may be positive, zero, or nega-

TABLE 1
Computation of Balance Rate Pickups

Type of Freight Rate	Nebraska→ Mobile	Nebraska→ Roanoke	Kansas→ Mobile	Kansas→ Roanoke
Base Point Rate	$12.50	$13.44	$12.50	$13.44
Transit Rate	11.96	13.12	11.84	13.17
Less: Paid in Rate	−2.50	−2.50	−2.10	−2.10
Transit Balance Rate	9.46	10.62	9.74	11.07
Balance Rate Pickup	3.04	2.82	2.76	2.37

tive. A soybean processor will always try to maximize the sum of the transit balance rate pickups associated with all movements of soybean meals to the end destinations. Milling-in-transit privileges do not apply to soybean oil and hulls since these products are priced F.O.B.-plant.

MODEL DERIVATION

Indices

Assume a fixed time period T, such as a month, which can be partitioned into production periods such that $t = 1, 2, \cdots, T$. Let

i be the index for the commodity, soybeans, and its products, and let I = max i.

Soybeans and their products, then, are indexed $i = 1, 2, \cdots, I_0, I_0 + 1, I_0 + 2, \cdots, I$, such that $i = 1$ is soybeans, $i = 2, \cdots, I_0$ are the indices of the transitable products ($i = 2$ is 49% protein soybean meal, $i = 3$ is 44% protein soybean meal), and $I_0 + 1, \cdots, I$ are the indices of the non-transitable products ($i = 4$ is soybean oil; $i = 5$ is soybean hulls).
Let

    j be the index for the origins and J = max j;
    k be the index for the processing plants and K = max k;
    l be the index for the customer demand zones and L = max l;
    t be the index for the time periods and T = max t.

Variables and Parameters

The variables and parameters for the model are:

D_{il}^t — demand for product i, i > 1, in customer demand zone l, period t;
Q_j^t — soybeans purchased at origin j, period t;
S_{ik}^t — supply availability for product i, i > 1, at plant k, period t;
$S_j'^t$ — soybean supply availability, origin j, period t;
b_{ikl}^t — balance rate pickup, transit products ($i = 2, \cdots, I_0$), from plant k to demand zone l, period t;
c_{1j}^t — unit cost of soybeans, origin j, period t;

$c_{il}^{\prime t}$ — unit cost of "outside purchased" product i, i > 1, for demand zone l, period t;

f_{jk}^{t} — unit inbound freight cost on soybeans from origin j to plant k, period t;

g_{k}^{t} — 49 % protein meal used in blending of 44 % protein meal, plant k, period t;

h_{k}^{t} — hulls used in blending of 44 % protein meal, plant k, period t;

p_{il}^{t} — unit selling price of product i, i > 1, at demand zone l, period t;

q_{k}^{t} — unit "crushing" cost, plant k, period t;

r_{ik}^{t} — unit inventory carrying cost, product i, plant k, period t;

$r_{1j}^{\prime t}$ — unit inventory carrying cost, soybeans, origin j, period t;

w_{ik}^{t} — amount of product i, i > 1, produced at plant k, period t;

x_{1jk}^{t} — amount of soybeans purchased and shipped from origin j to plant k, period t;

x_{ikl}^{t} — amount of product i, i > 1, shipped from plant k to demand zone l, period t;

$x_{il}^{\prime t}$ — amount of product i, i > 1, "outside purchased" for demand zone l, period t;

y_{1j}^{t} — inventory of soybeans associated with origin j at end of period t;

y_{ik}^{t} — inventory of commodity i, i > 1, plant k, at end of period t;

z_{k}^{t} — amount of soybeans crushed at plant k, period t;

α_{k}^{t} — 49 % protein meal production coefficient, plant k, period t;

β_{k}^{t} — oil production coefficient, plant k, period t;

γ_{k}^{t} — hull production coefficient, plant k, period t;

δ_{k}^{t} — 49 % protein soybean meal blending rate for 44 % protein soybean meal production at plant k, period t $(0.00 < \delta_{k}^{t} < 1.00)$;

$(1 - \delta_{k}^{t})$ — hull blending rate for 44 % protein meal production at plant k, period t.

Mathematical Formulation of the Model

For any production planning time horizon T, the model can be formulated as follows:

$$
\text{Max } Z = \sum_{t=1}^{T} \left[\sum_{i=2}^{I_0} \sum_{k=1}^{K} \sum_{l=1}^{L} (p_{il}^{t} \pm b_{ikl}^{t}) x_{ikl}^{t} + \sum_{i=I_0+1}^{I} \sum_{k=1}^{K} \sum_{l=1}^{L} p_{il}^{t} x_{ikl}^{t} \right.
$$

$$
+ \sum_{i=2}^{I} \sum_{l=1}^{L} (p_{il}^{t} - c_{il}^{\prime t}) x_{il}^{\prime t} - \sum_{j=1}^{J} \sum_{k=1}^{K} (c_{1j}^{t} + f_{jk}^{t}) x_{1jk}^{t} \qquad (3)
$$

$$
\left. - \sum_{k=1}^{K} q_{k}^{t} z_{k}^{t} - \sum_{j=1}^{J} r_{1j}^{\prime t} y_{1j}^{t} - \sum_{i=2}^{I} \sum_{k=1}^{K} r_{ik}^{t} y_{ik}^{t} \right].
$$

An explanation of each of the terms in the objective function is provided in Table 2. The objective function given by Equation (3) is subject to the following sets of equations and constraints:

$$
y_{1j}^{t-1} + Q_{j}^{t} = S_{j}^{\prime t} \qquad \text{for each j and each t.} \qquad (4)
$$

The total soybean availability at each origin for each period is equal to the

TABLE 2
Objective Function

Term	Representation
$\sum\limits_{i=2}^{I_0} \sum\limits_{k=1}^{K} \sum\limits_{l=1}^{L} (p_{il}^t \pm b_{ikl}^t) x_{ikl}^t$	Total value, plant to destination shipments of transitable products (including balance rate pickups);
$\sum\limits_{i=I_0+1}^{I} \sum\limits_{k=1}^{K} \sum\limits_{l=1}^{L} p_{il}^t x_{ikl}^t$	Total value, plant to destination shipments of non-transitable products;
$\sum\limits_{i=2}^{I} \sum\limits_{l=1}^{L} (p_{il}^t - c_{1l}^{\prime t}) x_{il}^{\prime t}$	Total value, outside purchased products for destinations;
$\sum\limits_{j=1}^{J} \sum\limits_{k=1}^{K} (c_{1j}^t + f_{jk}^t) x_{1jk}^t$	Total purchase and inbound freight cost, soybeans;
$\sum\limits_{k=1}^{K} q_k^t z_k^t$	Soybean processing (crushing) cost;
$\sum\limits_{j=1}^{J} r_{1j}^{\prime t} y_{1j}^t$	Inventory carrying costs for soybeans at origins;
$\sum\limits_{i=2}^{I} \sum\limits_{k=1}^{K} r_{ik}^t y_{ik}^t$	Inventory carrying costs for products at plants.

sum of the previous period's "carryover" plus the current period's purchases. The soybean inventory is actually maintained at the plant, but is associated with the origins because of milling-in-transit considerations.

$$\sum_{j=1}^{J} x_{1jk}^t = z_k^t \qquad \text{for each k and each t.} \qquad (5)$$

The total soybeans crushed at each plant each period is equal to the sum of the origin(s) soybeans committed to crushing at each plant each period.

$$S_j^{\prime t} - \sum_{k=1}^{K} x_{1jk}^t = y_{1j}^t \qquad \text{for each j and each t.} \qquad (6)$$

The total soybean carryover for each origin for the current period is equal to the total soybean availability minus the soybeans committed to the crushing process.

$$z_k^t \epsilon = w_{ik}^t \qquad \text{for each k and each t, } i = 2, 4, 5. \qquad (7)$$

where

$$\epsilon = \alpha_k^t \quad \text{for} \quad i = 2 \quad (49\% \text{ protein meal});$$
$$= \beta_k^t \quad \text{for} \quad i = 4 \quad (\text{soybean oil});$$
$$= \gamma_k^t \quad \text{for} \quad i = 5 \quad (\text{soybean hulls}).$$

The total soybeans crushed at each plant each period initially results in 49% protein meal, oil, and hulls (internal production balance equations).

$$y_{ik}^{t-1} + w_{ik}^t = S_{ik}^t \qquad \text{for each k and each t, } i = 2, 3, 4. \qquad (8)$$

The total supply availabilities of 49% protein meal, 44% protein meal, and oil at each plant each period is equal to the carryover from the previous period plus the internal production.

$$y_{5k}^{t-1} + w_{5k}^{t} + x_{5l}^{\prime t} = S_{5k}^{t} \qquad \text{for each k and each t.} \qquad (9)$$

The total supply availability of hulls at each plant each period is equal to the carryover from the previous period plus the internal production plus the external purchases of hulls for 44% protein soybean meal production.

$$w_{2k}^{t} > g_{k}^{t} \qquad \text{for each k and each t.} \qquad (10)$$

The total 49% protein meal produced must be greater than or equal to the 49% protein meal used in the production of 44% protein meal in each plant each period.

$$S_{5k}^{t} > h_{k}^{t} \qquad \text{for each k and each t.} \qquad (11)$$

The total supply availability of hulls must be greater than or equal to the hulls used in the production of 44% protein meal in each plant each period.

$$w_{3k}^{t}(\delta_{k}^{t}) = g_{k}^{t} \qquad \text{for each k and each t (49\% protein soybean meal).} \qquad (12)$$

$$w_{3k}^{t}(1 - \delta_{k}^{t}) = h_{k}^{t} \qquad \text{for each k and each t (hulls).} \qquad (13)$$

The total 44% protein meal produced is obtained by blending 49% protein meal and hulls in each plant each period.

$$S_{2k}^{t} - y_{2k}^{t} - w_{3k}^{t}(\delta_{k}^{t}) = x_{2kl}^{t} \qquad \text{for each k, l, and t.} \qquad (14)$$

$$S_{ik}^{t} - y_{ik}^{t} = x_{ikl}^{t} \qquad \text{for each k, l, and t; i = 3, 4.} \qquad (15)$$

$$S_{5k}^{t} - y_{5k}^{t} - w_{3k}^{t}(1 - \delta_{k}^{t}) = x_{5kl}^{t} \qquad \text{for each k, l, and t.} \qquad (16)$$

The shipments of 49% protein meal, 44% protein meal, oil, and hulls from plant k to destination l in period t is equal to the total availability minus the carryover to the next period. For 49% protein meal and hulls, the respective quantities of each used for blending of 44% protein meal must also be subtracted.

$$\sum_{k=1}^{k} x_{ikl}^{t} + x_{il}^{\prime t} = D_{il}^{t} \qquad \text{for each l and t, i > 1.} \qquad (17)$$

The total demand for the products derived from soybeans for each demand zone and for each time period is equal to the sum of the products shipped from the various plants plus the amount of product "outside purchased." In actually applying the model, an exogenous demand forecast is used. This forecast is based on actual plant capacities and recent demand experience.

This model's uniqueness derives from its structure which facilitates both production and distribution planning. The structure of the present model integrates features of the classical time horizon linear programming approach for production planning [4] [2] with the transportation method for distribution planning [1] [6]. Additionally, this model allows consideration of both internal and external demands, while incorporating the unique milling-in-transit features associated with the distribution of soybean meals. The characteristics noted above and the model's multi-plant nature make it a comprehensive, rigorous, and useful planning tool.

MODEL TESTING

The model formulated above has been tested and evaluated for an existing seven plant soybean processing network. In this network each plant has three soybean origins, and each plant can ship its end products to any of ten regional destinations. The model, using a representative set of supply and demand conditions, has been tested for a four week production planning horizon. The problem size resulting from this set of conditions was approximately 900 rows by 3000 columns and had a constraint matrix with a density of approximately 0.21%.

Solution to this problem was obtained using IBM's Mathematical Programming System (MPS) software [5] on an IBM 370/165 configuration. Running time for the problem was 2 minutes, 24.3 seconds (CPU), with 2 minutes, 23.7 seconds (CPU) being required for the linear programming solution. A feasible solution was obtained in 601 iterations (21.1 seconds, CPU), and an optimal solution was obtained in an additional 1319 iterations (122.6 seconds, CPU).

ANALYSIS AND DISCUSSION OF TEST RESULTS

The output produced by MPS for a model of this size is voluminous. In an attempt to facilitate the interpretation of this output, the authors have prepared a number of summary tables.

Table 3 presents a summary of the crushing volumes (aggregate production plan) for each of the seven production facilities over the four weeks of the production planning horizon. The production facilities are not identified for pro-

TABLE 3
Summary of Crushing Volumes (Thousands of Bushels)
(Aggregate Production Plan)

Crushing Capacity (Thousands of bushels)	Plant	1	% of Crushing Capacity	2	% of Crushing Capacity	3	% of Crushing Capacity	4	% of Crushing Capacity
500	A	293	(59)	147	(29)	457	(91)	186	(37)
500	B	280	(56)	500	(100)	470	(94)	500	(100)
500	C	303	(61)	500	(100)	500	(100)	500	(100)
500	D	300	(60)	234	(47)	0*	—	292	(58)
500	E	500	(100)	500	(100)	500	(100)	67	(13)
1000	F	1000	(100)	1000	(100)	1000	(100)	850	(85)
750	G	750	(100)	750	(100)	750	(100)	750	(100)
4250		3426	(81)	3631	(85)	3677	(98)**	3145	(74)

* Upper bound set equal to 0 to evaluate plant closing for maintenance.

** Total crushing capacity for week #3 equal to 3,750,000 bushels because of closing of plant "D".

prietary reasons. Furthermore, upper bounds were placed on the crushing capacities of the various plants to reflect the actual crushing capacities of the respective facilities. In all weeks except the fourth, the actual total crushing volume exceeded 80% of the total crushing capacity. The actual crushing volumes required as a percent of crushing capacities varied considerably between plants. For example, plants "F" and "G" crushed at or near capacity in every week, while plant "D" crushed at 60% or less of capacity every week.

Table 4 presents a summary of the production output (detailed production plan) for each of the seven production facilities over the four weeks of the production planning horizon. This production output summary reflects the crushing volumes, and indicates the amounts of the various products that are available for shipment at the respective facilities. Observe the shift between the production of 44% protein meal and 49% protein meal at various plants over time. Observe further that in several instances 44% protein meal is produced without the production of hulls. This analysis indicates that large amounts of hull purchases are required in order to meet the 44% protein meal production requirements. Finally, observe that soybean oil production is quite heavy at both plants "F" and "G" over the time horizon, while of much smaller magnitude at plant "A" during the time period. This difference is a reflection of the geographical distribution of the demand for soybean oil.

Table 5 presents a distribution summary for 49% protein meal and 44% protein meal for the first week of the processing horizon. This table reflects the actual distribution by plant to each of the ten regional destinations of the first week's production volume (see Table 4) of these two products. The destinations are not identified for propriety reasons. Both lower and upper bounds are placed on the end product demand requirements at the destinations. The lower bounds represent the internal requirements of the corporation which must be met. The upper bounds are largely judgemental and constrain the total demand by destination to a level that reflects previous regional sales experience. Upper bounds on the outside purchases of each of the end products are also specified (not shown in Table 5), and are equated to the lower bounds set on the demands for the end products at the destinations. In this manner, real "make or buy" decisions are forced as a part of the solution. In Table 5 outside purchases of 44% protein meal were required to satisfy the lower limit of demand for destinations "8", "9", and "10". Actual shipments to most destinations exceeded their lower bounds. This fact suggests that the production from the various plants was in excess of that required for internal consumption. This finding was consistent with the generally favorable conditions in the soybean processing industry which existed for the period of time for which the model was tested. This solution of the model indicated that a level of production that satisfied both internal and external demands was needed.

Table 6 presents a detailed summary of a one-week section of the aggregate production-distribution plan for plant "A". Table 6 is divided into sections which detail one week's purchasing, production, inventory, and distribution decisions. Table 6 thus provides the detailed information which was summarized for plant "A" in Tables 3, 4, and 5. Detailed output for the other plants and other time

TABLE 4
Summary of Production Output
(Detailed Production Plan)

Plant	Week	44% Protein Meal (Tons)	49% Protein Meal (Tons)	Oil (Million Lbs.)	Hulls (Tons)
A	1	7910	0	3.2	0
B	1	0	6720	3.1	0
C	1	0	7280	3.3	0
D	1	8090	0	3.3	0
E	1	13483	0	5.5	0
F	1	0	24000	11.0	200
G	1	0	18000	8.2	175
Total-Week	1	29483	56000	37.6	375
A	2	584	3000	1.6	259
B	2	6000	6660	5.5	100
C	2	6000	6660	5.5	0
D	2	4416	1680	2.6	50
E	2	10000	3100	5.5	0
F	2	10000	15100	11.0	0
G	2	18202	1800	8.2	0
Total-Week	2	55202	38000	39.9	409
A	3	2000	9180	5.0	8
B	3	8000	4160	5.2	152
C	3	6000	6660	5.5	0
D	3	0	0	0	0
E	3	10000	3100	5.5	0
F	3	10000	15100	11.0	0
G	3	18202	1800	8.2	0
Total-Week	3	54202	40000	40.4	160
A	4	5016	0	2.0	0
B	4	13483	0	5.5	0
C	4	0	12000	5.5	250
D	4	0	7000	3.2	146
E	4	0	1600	.7	33
F	4	0	20400	9.3	425
G	4	0	18000	8.2	375
Total-Week	4	18499	59000	34.4	1229
Four Week Total		157386	193000	152.3	2173

TABLE 5
Distribution Summary—Soybean Meals

A) WEEK 1: 49% Protein Meal

Plant Source \ Destination	Distribution Volumes (Tons) 1	2	3	4	5	6	7	8	9	10	First-Week Total
A											0
B			3000	3000	720						6720
C	3000	3000			1280						7280
D											0
E											0
F					1000	1000		10000	10000	2000	24000
G							10000			8000	18000
Outside Purchase											0
Lower Bound	2000	2000	2000	2000	2000	0	7500	7500	7500	7500	40000
Actual	3000	3000	3000	3000	3000	1000	10000	10000	10000	10000	56000
Upper Bound	3000	3000	3000	3000	3000	1000	10000	10000	10000	10000	56000

B) WEEK 1: 44% Protein Meal

Plant Source \ Destination	Distribution Volumes (Tons) 1	2	3	4	5	6	7	8	9	10	First-Week Total
A	1910	3000	3000								7910
B											0
C											0
D	1090			3000	3000	1000					8090
E							10000	3483			13483
F											0
G											0
Outside Purchase								4017	7500	7500	19017
Lower Bound	2000	2000	2000	2000	2000	0	7500	7500	7500	7500	40000
Actual	3000	3000	3000	3000	3000	1000	10000	7500	7500	7500	48500
Upper Bound	3000	3000	3000	3000	3000	1000	10000	10000	10000	10000	56000

periods is quite similar to that presented in Table 6, and these data are thus omitted for the sake of brevity.

As evidenced in Table 6, the model is initiated with zero carryover of soybeans, hulls, oil, or meal. Purchases of soybeans at each origin are upper bounded in each period to reflect the economics of soybean supply. A plant's production (crushing) capacity is upper bounded in each period to reflect actual plant ca-

TABLE 6

Detailed Production-Distribution Plan, Plant "A"
(WEEK $t = 1$)

Soybean Purchasing (Bushels)

Origins	Carryover $0 \to 1$		Purchases^U		Total Availability		Crushing^U Commitment		Carryover $1 \to 2$
Origin 1	0	+	0	=	0	−	0	=	0
Origin 2	0	+	160,000	=	160,000	−	113,333	=	46,667
Origin 3	0	+	180,000*	=	180,000	−	180,000	=	0
	0	+	340,000	=	340,000	−	293,333	=	46,667

Internal Production (Crushing)

Hulls: 293,333 Bushels $\times \left(\dfrac{.0005 \text{ Tons of Hulls}}{\text{Bushel of Soybeans}} \right) = 146.67$ tons

Oil: 293,333 Bushels $\times \left(\dfrac{11 \text{ Pounds of Oil}}{\text{Bushel of Soybeans}} \right) = 3,226,663$ pounds

49% Meal: 293,333 Bushels $\times \left(\dfrac{.024 \text{ Tons of Meal}}{\text{Bushel of Soybeans}} \right) = 7,040$ tons

44% Meal: 7,040 Tons of 49% Meal (.89) + 870.11 Tons of Hulls (.11) = 7,910 tons

Inventory Summary

Hulls (Tons)

Carryover $0 \to 1$		Internal Production		Outside Purchase^U (for 44% Meal)		Total Availability		Used in 44% Meal		Carryover $1 \to 2^U$
0	+	146.67	+	973.44	=	1120.11	−	870.11	=	250

Oil (Pounds)

Carryover $0 \to 1$		Internal Production		Total Availability		Shipments		Carryover $1 \to 2^U$
0	+	3,226,663	=	3,226,663	−	3,226,663	=	0

49% Soybean Meal (Tons)

Carryover $0 \to 1$		Internal Production		Total Availability		Used in 44% Meal		Shipments		Carryover $1 \to 2$
0	+	7040	=	7040	−	7040	−	0	=	0

44% Soybean Meal (Tons)

Carryover $0 \to 1$		Internal Production		Total Availability		Shipments		Carryover $1 \to 2$
0	+	7910	=	7910	−	7910	=	0

TABLE 6—*Continued*

Distribution

Hulls (Tons)

No Distribution

Oil (Pounds)

Destinations	Shipments	Outside[U] Purchases		Total[L] Demand
1		+	=	
2	3,226,663	+	=	
3		+	=	
4		+	=	
5		+	=	
6		+	=	
7		+	=	
8		+	=	
9		+	=	
10		+	=	

Total   3,226,663

49% Meal (Tons)

No Distribution

44% Meal (Tons)

Destinations	Shipments	Outside[U] Purchases		Total[L] Demand
1	1,910	+	=	
2	3,000	+	=	
3	3,000	+	=	
4		+	=	
5		+	=	
6		+	=	
7		+	=	
8		+	=	
9		+	=	
10		+	=	

Total   7,910

Notes: 1. The symbol "U" designates an upper bounded variable.
2. The symbol "L" designates a lower bounded variable.
3. The symbol "*" designates that the variable is at its upper bound in the optimal solution.
4. The symbol "†" designates that the variable is at its lower bound in the optimal solution.

pacity. Outside purchases of hulls to be used in the production of 44% meal are upper bounded, again reflecting the economics of hulls supply. The hull carry-over and oil carryover for $t > 0$ are upper bounded at levels which correspond to the plants' inventory capacities for these two products. No carryover inventories of 49% protein meal and 44% protein meal are allowed. This bound is based upon the actual operation of the crushing facility. Upper bounds on the outside purchases of each of the end products are specified; and are equated to the lower bounds set on the demands for the end products at the destinations. In this fashion real "make or buy" decisions are forced as a part of the solution. The total demand at each destination is equal to the sum of the shipments and outside purchases for that destination. The "total demand" columns in Table 6 were left blank because the "total demand" must be determined by summing over all plants. Table 6 presents only a single plant's results.

Underlying the product mix economics which are indicated by the optimal solution are a number of interesting tradeoffs between the production and distribution constraints of the model. One such example is presented below.

Example—**Production-Distribution Tradeoffs** (Plant "D"—Week 3)

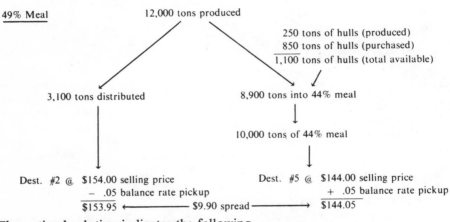

The optimal solution indicates the following.

Sell   3,100 tons 49% meal @ $153.95/ton = $ 477,245.00
Sell 10,000 tons 44% meal @ $144.05/ton = $1,440,500.00
   13,100 tons meal $1,917,745.00

Less: 850 tons of outside purchase hulls
     @ $76.00/ton   −   64,600.00
              Net Profit = $1,853,145.00
        Average Price/Ton = $ 141.46

Soybean costs can be ignored since they are the same, irrespective of whether 49% meal, 44% meal, or both are being produced.

If no 44% meal had been produced, the following alternative (non-optimal) solution would have resulted.

Sell 12,000 tons 49% meal @ $152.75/ton = $1,833,000.00
Sell   250 tons hulls   @ $ 76.00/ton = $ 19,500.00
Net Profit = $1,852,500.00
Average Price/Ton = $ 151.22

This alternative solution forces the distribution of the entire 12,000 tons of 49% soybean meal to four destinations at an average price of $152.75/ton. In the optimal solution the original 12,000 tons of 49% meal is blended with hulls to produce 3,100 tons of 44% meal, which are then distributed at an average price of $146.39/ton. After adjusting for the cost of the hulls in the optimal solution and for the profit for the hulls in the non-optimal solution, the average prices per unit of product distributed are $141.46/ton and $151.22, respectively. However, in the optimal solution 13,100 tons of product are being distributed, while in the alternative solution only 12,500 tons of product are being distributed. Thus, the optimal production mix of both 49% soybean meal and 44% soybean meal for this plant for this time period is dictated by both the production and distribution aspects of the model. Other similar production-distribution tradeoffs can be observed over the time horizon.

CONCLUSION

In this study a mathematical programming methodology has been applied to a production-distribution planning problem involving a large scale soybean processing network. Test results from application of the model indicate its general usefulness in the context of this complex problem environment.

Consideration is currently being given to the construction of a user-oriented input data matrix generator and output report writer. In particular, the output report writer will produce four major summaries:

1. Purchasing volume requirements by origins and plants;
2. Crushing (aggregate and detailed production plans) reports, by plants;
3. Distribution reports by plants, by products, and by destinations;
4. Milling-in-transit reports by plants, by products, and by destinations.

Other future work will involve extension of the model's time horizon, probably to a 12–15 week planning period. Finally, further research with the model involving different beginning "carryovers" will probably be required.

REFERENCES

[1] Hadley, G. *Linear Programming*. Reading, Massachusetts: Addison-Wesley Publishing Company, Inc., 1962.

[2] Hansmann, F. and S. W. Hess. "A Linear Programming Approach to Production and Employment Scheduling." *Management Technology*, Vol. 1, (January, 1960), pp. 46–51.

[3] Hieronymus, T. A. *Economics of Futures Trading*. New York: Commodity Research, Inc., 1971.

[4] Holt, C. C., F. Modigliani, and H. A. Simon. "A Linear Decision Rule for Production and Employment Scheduling." *Management Science*, (October, 1955), pp. 1–30.

[5] *IBM Mathematical Programming System/360, User's Manual*. White Plains, N. Y.: International Business Machines Corporation, 1973.

[6] McMillan, C. *Mathematical Programming*. New York: John Wiley & Sons, Inc., 1975.

[7] Markland, R. E. "Analyzing Geographically Discrete Warehousing Networks by Computer Simulation." *Decision Sciences*, Vol. 4, No. 2 (April, 1973), pp. 216–236.

[8] Markland, R. E. "Analyzing Multi-Commodity Networks Having Milling-in-Transit Features." *Management Science*, Vol. 21, No. 12 (August, 1975), pp. 1405–1416.

[9] Markland, R. E. "Logistics Planning Using Teleprocessing." *Journal of Systems Planning*, Vol. 24, No. 10 (October, 1973), pp. 32–36.

[10] Markland, R. E. and R. J. Newett. "An Application of Mathematical Programming to Soybean Processing." *OMEGA* (*The International Journal of Management Science*), Vol. 3, No. 3 (June, 1975), pp. 313–320.

[11] Markland, R. E. and R. J. Newett. "Optimizing Discrete Location Warehousing Networks by Computer Simulation." *Proceedings 1971 Summer Computer Simulation Conference*, pp. 1283–1290.

[12] Markland, R. E. and R. J. Newett. "Optimizing Food Product Distribution by Computer Simulation." *Proceedings-1970 Summer Computer Simulation Conference*, pp. 1103–1109.

[13] Meyer, C. F. "A Model For Production-Distribution Networks With Transit Billing." *Management Science*, Vol. 14, No. 4 (December, 1967), pp. B204–B218.

[14] Tewles, R. J., C. V. Harlow, and H. L. Stone. *The Commodity Futures Trading Guide*. St. Louis: McGraw-Hill, 1969.

Reprinted, by permission, from Omega, *Vol. 8, No. 4, 1980.*
Copyright 1980 by Pergamon Press Ltd.

Experiments in Mixed Integer Linear Programming in a Manufacturing System[1]

PATRICK G FALK

International Paper Company, New York, USA

(Received January 1979)

This paper reports on a Manufacturing System and two Mixed Integer Programming (MIP) applications concurrent to it. The System is made up of four integrated modules designed to address problems of Strategic, Tactical and Operational Planning. The MIP applications concern problems of plant site selection and production planning. Optimization is done via the IBM's MPSX/370 Mathematical Programming Software.

INTRODUCTION

THIS PAPER reports on a Manufacturing Hierarchy and two Mixed Integer Programming, MIP, applications concurrent to it.

The hierarchy is a fully integrated four-module affair designed to address problems of Strategic, Tactical and Operational Planning. The four modules are in a descending hierarchical order:

● A Transportation Model

● A Production Planning Model

● A Production Scheduling Model

● A Distribution Simulation Model

The MIP matrixes and solution reports are generated by PL/1 codes and optimization is done via the IBM's MPSX/370 Mathematical Programming Software. The distribution simulation is done via SIMPL/I, a Continuous Simulation Language.

We describe below the details concerning the hierarchy and the two MIP applications in particular. We discuss computational simplifications that made the use of MPSX/370 more efficient than a purely brutal use of the code.

The Transportation Model is utilized for the selection of Plant Sites over a 15 yr horizon. We use foundations of parametric optimization techniques for Integer Programming to construct P_θ-families. The outcome is a static representation of a dynamic problem whereby time-periods are handled individually instead of collectively. The interface between periods is provided by the P_θ-families and permits optimization by MPSX/370.

In the case of the Production Planning situation a pre-processing code to MPSX/370 eliminates 'trivial' binary variables that determine production activities in a given period. The resulting problem has 64 binary variables against 220 in the original formulation and is thus much more manageable.

1. THE MANUFACTURING HIERARCHY

The application at hand involves one of Procter & Gamble's smallest Divisions. It has a typical large scale, continuous flow manufacturing operation. The most important ingredients of its very general configuration are:

● Multiple-raw materials/suppliers

● Multiple-plant manufacturing facilities

● Multiple-product output

● Multiple-warehouse distribution network

[1] Paper presented at TIMS/ORSA Conference, May 1–3, 1978, New York, USA.

TABLE 1. GENERAL FUNCTIONAL AND INFORMATIONAL FLOW-CHART FOR A P & G DIVISION.

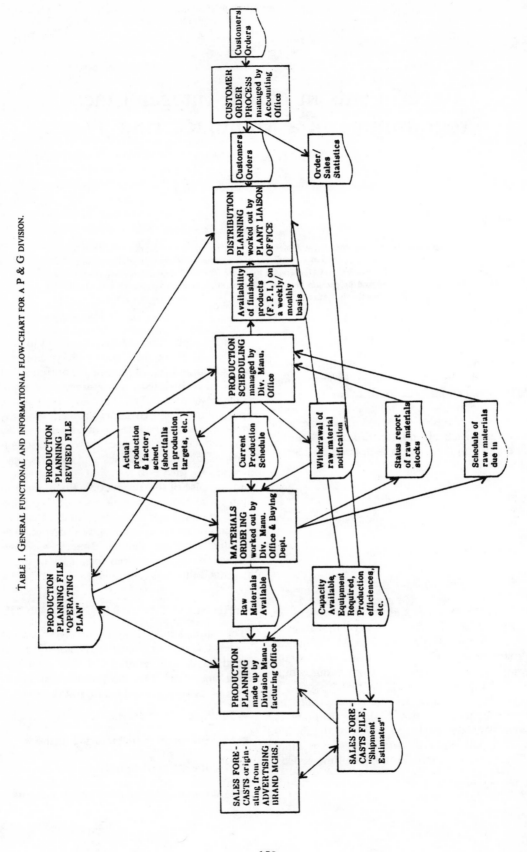

● Multiple-transportation modes

● Multiple-market zones.

The hierarchy was launched in part to promote the effective use of Logistics resources. A comprehensive effort was started to re-evaluate:

● Raw materials Purchasing strategies

● Plant/Warehouse sites and facilities

● Production, Distribution and Inventory schemes.

The issues at hand concerned long-term/Strategic, mid-term/Tactical and short-term/Operational Planning and related decisions. Various levels of Management serving different functions and concerned with details of varying degrees were implicated.

Because of these circumstances we decided very early into the project that only a hierarchical approach would be suitable, e.g. one that permits decisions to be made in sequence. This was done principally to preserve the functional and organizational Division mechanism and its managerial decision process, see Hax, [8], and Table 1.

We also felt that because of the complexity, size and diversity of the topics to be studied that no single analytical approach could optimize the entire manufacturing operation in one single step. We thus opted for a system integrating sets of sequential decisions. Each set of decisions providing new constraints within which at the next level of the hierarchy new, more detailed decisions have to be made.

The result of this philosophy is a fully integrated four-module hierarchy (see Fig. 1), consisting of:

● A Transportation Model

● A Production Planning Model

● A Production Scheduling Model

● A Distribution Simulation Model.

The Transportation and Production Planning models are classics in the MIP field.

Because of the continuous flow shop environment of this Company the Production Scheduling posed no problems. As a result, a simple manual heuristic was constructed. The Distribution Simulation was another classic in its own field.

Handling those models one at a time and providing the necessary mechanism between them enabled us to take advantage of the special structures that characterizes each of them.

Proceeding from the 'top' to the 'bottom' of the hierarchy, the planning horizon gets shorter, the level of management lower, the decision scope narrower and the data requirements more intricate.

1.1 The transportation model

The first module of the hierarchy concerns the classic Transportation model, see AM Geoffrion [6]. This module is employed for long-term, (1–15 yr-horizon), Strategic Planning for site selection and facilities planning. On a yearly basis the model is put to use for plant production allocation on the basis of minimum raw materials purchases, manufacturing and distribution costs. Input to the model are facilities characteristics and costs, distribution guidelines and tariffs, yearly demand forecast etc, (see Fig. 2).

Output from this module are suggestions for future facilities' site and design, shipping patterns, production/raw materials allocation etc. This information is far reaching and provides the basis for the decisions that will shape tomorrow's manufacturing operation and long term contractual agreements.

In terms of LP problem size a typical application of this module had 2000 rows and 9000 columns. Runs were made on a yearly basis with frequent re-runs during the year as business dictated.

1.2 The production planning model

The second module is another classic in the MIP field and is commonly referred to as the fixed cost or lot size model, see Buffa and Taubert [2], and Fig. 3.

It is applied for medium-term, (horizon of 12 months), Tactical Planning. Input to the model is brand allocation which produces facilities as provided by module 1, individual machine characteristics and requirements, inventory

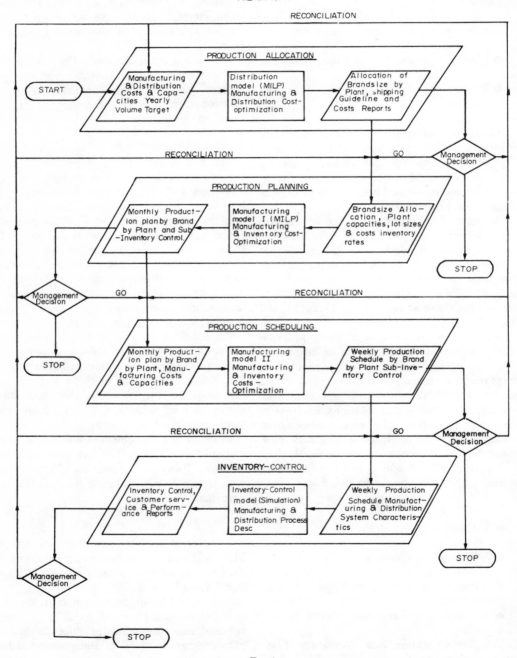

A PRODUCTION ALLOCATION PLANNING, SCHEDULING AND INVENTORY CONTROL HIERARCHY

FIG. 1.

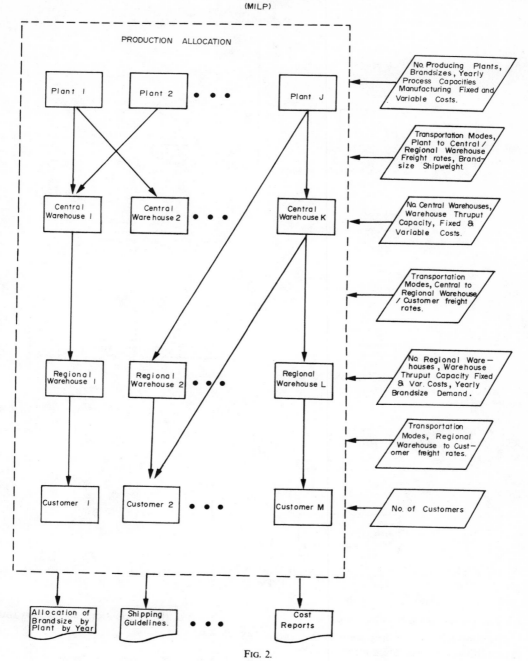

DISTRIBUTION MODEL

(MILP)

PRODUCTION ALLOCATION

Plant 1　Plant 2 ● ● ●　Plant J

No. Producing Plants, Brandsizes, Yearly Process Capacities Manufacturing Fixed and Variable Costs.

Transportation Modes, Plant to Central / Regional Warehouse Freight rates, Brand-size Shipweight.

Central Warehouse 1　Central Warehouse 2 ● ● ●　Central Warehouse K

No. Central Warehouses, Warehouse Thruput Capacity, Fixed & Variable Costs.

Transportation Modes, Central to Regional Warehouse / Customer freight rates.

Regional Warehouse 1　Regional Warehouse 2 ● ● ●　Regional Warehouse L

No. Regional Ware-houses, Warehouse Thruput Capacity Fixed & Var. Costs, Yearly Brandsize Demand.

Transportation Modes, Regional Warehouse to Cust-omer freight rates.

Customer 1　Customer 2 ● ● ●　Customer M

No. of Customers

Allocation of Brandsize by Plant by Year　Shipping Guidelines. ● ● ●　Cost Reports

FIG. 2.

guidelines and monthly plant brandsize demand.

Output from this model is a monthly production plan by facility, machine, and brandsize for the entire year. The plan is reviewed each month to account for the latest changes in business conditions.

A typical LP size for this module is 250 rows and 500 columns, 200 of which are binary variables.

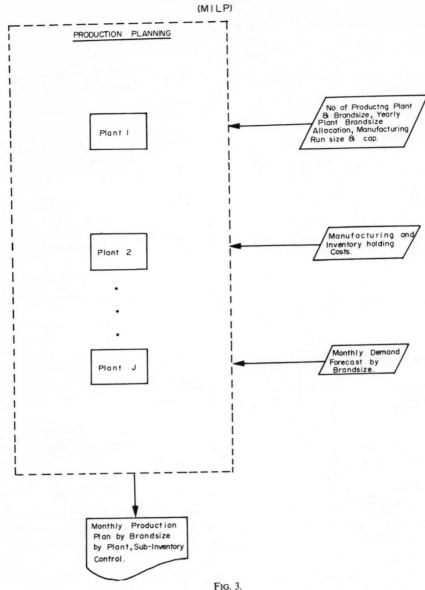

MANUFACTURING MODEL I
(MILP)

PRODUCTION PLANNING

Plant I

Plant 2

Plant J

No. of Productng Plant & Brandsize, Yearly Plant Brandsize Allocation, Manufacturing Run size & cap.

Manufacturing and Inventory holding Costs.

Monthly Demand Forecast by Brandsize.

Monthly Production Plan by Brandsize by Plant, Sub-Inventory Control.

FIG. 3.

1.3 The production scheduling model

The simplicity of the flow shop of this application did not necessitate the mechanization of this step. Rather, a manual heuristic was developed that took up each facility's monthly production plan as given by module 2 and translated it into a daily machine production schedule. This we found allowed all the necessary flexibility needed for the inevitable last minute changes of the operational circle.

Each run of the production plan would thus ready a new schedule.

1.4 The distribution simulation model

The last module is the result of SA Dastur and JD Weeks' work at Procter & Gamble. It is another classic in the simulation of finished goods flow through distribution pipelines, see Buffa and Taubert [2], and Fig. 4.

This model is fed by production schedules,

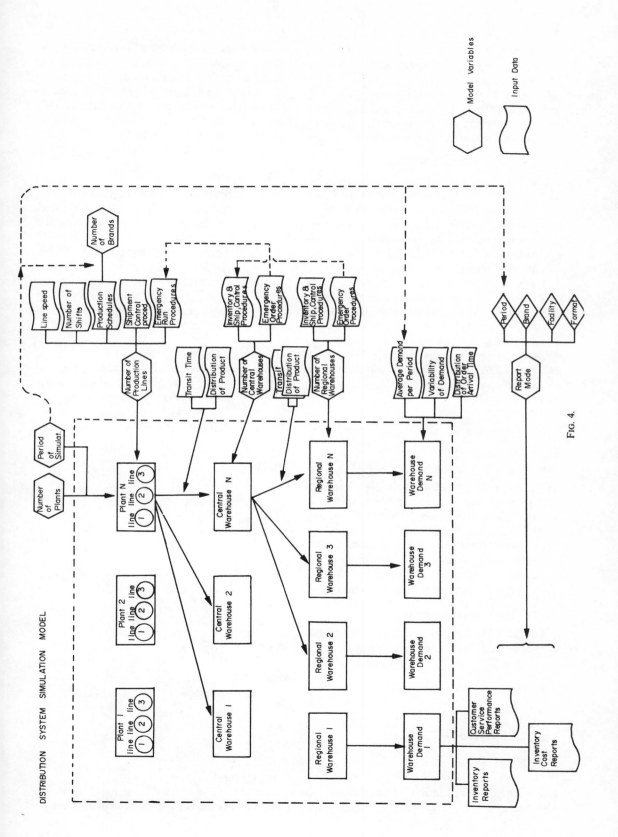

DISTRIBUTION SYSTEM SIMULATION MODEL

Fig. 4.

Model Variables

Input Data

155

distribution guidelines, lead times, inventory and reorder policies, customer level of service, brandsize demand etc.

From the model is obtained an impact statement of the effect of a given production schedule and shipping guidelines on the inventory patterns of the distribution operation.

1.5 *Applications of the hierarchy*

The hierarchy was responsible for realizing $2,400,000 in manufacturing and distribution cost during its first year of operation. Furthermore, it was useful in discouraging management from adopting new shipping guidelines for one small sector of the business. More specifically, module 1 identified savings of $140,000 with certain shipping patterns. However, module 2 showed that those patterns if they were to be implemented would increase inventories by 15%. Module 4 revealed that at equal customer service, inventories would rise throughout the distribution pipeline by an average of 52%. This obviously was enough to discourage management from exploring this matter any further.

2. EXPERIMENTS IN MIXED INTEGER PROGRAMMING

Now that we have discussed the application background of our Manufacturing Hierarchy let us review the approaches used to handle module 1/Transportation Model and module 2/Production Planning Model via MPSX/370. In both applications computational simplifications are made to make the use of MPSX/370 more resource effective. We first cover the subject of module 1 and next that of module 2.

2.1 *The transportation model*

The model at hand is the famed Transportation Model. It concerns four levels of operation, (Fig. 2):

● Manufacturing facilities/plants

● Central/plant warehouses

● Local warehouses/DC

● Market regions/customer zone

The particular application of this model we wish to discuss is that of plant and local ware-house site selection over a 10 yr horizon. A new plant is sought for a new manufacturing site among four possible candidates. The question of possible new local warehousing sites is momentarily set aside since they involve only minimal capital investments versus those of new plants which reach into the $100 millions and above. We make the following definitions:

(A) Coefficients:

c_{ijkl} = unit cost of producing and shipping commodity i from plant j through local warehouse k to market region l

CAP_{ij} = manufacturing capacity for brandsize i at plant j

D_{il} = forecasted yearly brandsize i demand at customer zone l

f_j = fixed portion of the annual ownership and operating costs of plant j

(B) Variables:

X_{ijkl} = units of brandsize i manufactured at plant j sent through local warehouse k and to customer zone l

$Y_j = \begin{cases} 1, \text{ if plant } j \text{ is opened} \\ 0, \text{ if plant } j \text{ is not opened} \end{cases}$

(C) Model Formulation:

Minimize

$$\sum_{i=1}^{I} \sum_{j=1}^{J} \sum_{k=1}^{K} \sum_{l=1}^{L} (c_{ijkl} \cdot X_{ijkl}) + \sum_{j=1}^{J} (f_j \cdot Y_j) \qquad (1)$$

subject to:

$$\sum_{k=1}^{K} \sum_{l=1}^{L} X_{ijkl} \leqslant CAP_{ij}, \quad \forall i, j \qquad (2)$$

$$\sum_{i=1}^{I} \sum_{k=1}^{K} \sum_{l=1}^{L} X_{ijkl} \leqslant \sum_{i=1}^{I} CAP_{ij} \cdot Y_j, \quad \forall j \qquad (3)$$

$$\sum_{j=1}^{J} \sum_{k=1}^{K} X_{ijkl} \geqslant D_{il}, \quad \forall i, l \qquad (4)$$

$$\sum_{j=1}^{J} Y_j = 1, \quad \forall j \qquad (5)$$

$$X \geqslant 0 \qquad (6)$$

Where

$$i = 1, \ldots, I; \quad j = 1, \ldots, J; \quad k = 1, \ldots, K;$$
$$l = 1, \ldots, L;$$

and

$$\sum_{i=1}^{I} CAP_{ij}$$

is plant j total capacity.

For the 10 yr horizon at hand a yearly demand forecast is supplied. Further, management assumes a fixed proportion over time of distribution to manufacturing costs. Cost data is fixed over time.

The difficulty with selecting a site over such a horizon arises because for most large scale applications which are commercially available Mathematical Programming Softwares, including MPSX/370, cannot handle this situation as a multi-period problem. Thus, an alternative must be found to address this type of problem in a fashion other than that of a tedious model re-run for every year of the horizon.

We are proposing such an option in constructing P_θ families. The outcome is a static representation of a dynamic problem whereby time-periods are handled individually instead of collectively. The inter-period interface is provided by the P_θ families and permits optimization via MPSX/370.

We define a P_θ family to be parametric in the right hand side such that:

(P_θ) Minimize cx subject to $Ax \geqslant b + \theta r$, x_j integer $\in I$, $0 \leqslant \theta \leqslant 1$.

where, c, x, A and b are given comformable vectors and I is an index set specifying which variables must be integers. By assumption due to our application $r \geqslant 0$ and so the P_θ family is monotone. Thus, the family members are nested restrictions of one another as θ increases from 0 to 1. In addition, as shown in (7), when $r \geqslant 0$, any optimal solution of $(P_{\theta'})$ remains optimal at all $\theta \geqslant \theta'$ for which it remains feasible. In terms of our multi-period plant selection it means that only a finite number of optimization runs need to be done if θ increases from 0 to 1. Hopefully, the runs necessary to survey the horizon are less than the number of years involved.

Our problem then becomes one of selecting a way of increasing θ by small increments starting with 0 and retain feasibility. That is we want to select θ^{k+1} such that it is slightly less than θ^k which leads to infeasibility.

To do just that we are employing the following method via MPSX/370:

Step 1—Solve P_θ to continuous and integer optimality with $\theta = 0$. Save the optimal continuous basis and the pseudo cost of the optimal integer variables.

Step 2—Make a step forward by increment-

ing θ by 0.1. Restore the continuous and optimal basis.

If feasibility is maintained then keep incrementing θ in successive steps of 0.1, till infeasibility occurs or $\theta = 1$.

If feasibility cannot be maintained then take a step backwards in increments of 0.01, starting with the θ^k first found infeasible. Until we get θ^{k+1} feasible. If $\theta = 1$ then STOP!

Step 3—Solve the continuous problem with the θ^{k+1} feasible to optimality using the previously saved optimal basis. Start the MIP/370 branch and bound using the pseudo cost and the branching priority of the previous run.

Step 4—Save the continuous optimum basis and the pseudo cost of the best integer solution. Go back to step 2!

This method can be automated with the MPSX/370 Extended Control Language, ECL-PL/1. The use of MPSX/370 MPS Control Language is somewhat more tedious. In any case, our smallest problem had the following statistics: 2000 rows, 9000 columns and four binary variables, density of 0.16. It took 7.23 CPU minutes on an IBM 370/168 to reach the first, $\theta = 0$, continuous solution. It took another 6.25 min to reach the best integer solution.

In the concurrent plant site selection four complete cycles of the above procedure were completed, a slight improvement over the eleven individual runs otherwise needed with a traditional approach. Figure 5 illustrates this and the P_θ family in the form of the marginal cost of selecting a site j against the optimal site j^+. Here the marginal costs only involve operational manufacturing and distribution expenses.

One can see from Fig. 5 that site 1 seems attractive at first but is soon to be replaced by site 2 and in the long run site 3. Sites 4 and 5 are never real contenders. This behaviour is of course the result of the inherent characteristics of the business but also the foreign government local policies. In this instance, the local author-

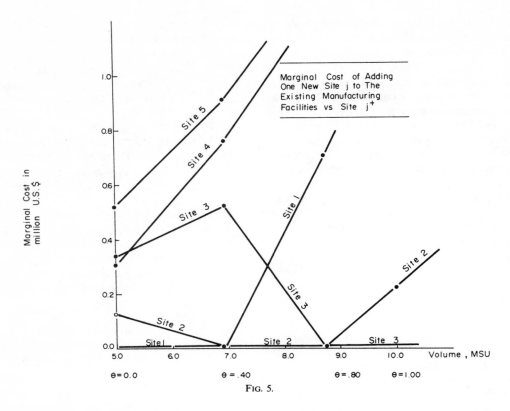

Fig. 5.

ities will only allow a limited start-up capacity at a new plant site. Gradually, and according to a government schedule, this initial capacity can be increased step by step over the years.

Also from Fig. 5, one can deduce the four complete cycles performed through the application of our method. They were executed at $\theta = 0.0$, 0.39, 0.77 and 1.0 respectively. Computation-wise, the average cycle of optimization took 1.35 and 3.45 CPU minutes to reach continuous and integer optimality respectively. This of course is savings versus the individual run statistics.

The cumulation of the four complete cycle times aggregated in one run added up to 41.88 CPU minutes. Comparatively, the 'brutal' approach of making individual runs for every year of the horizon (re-starting with a previously saved basis), came to 83.45 CPU minutes and an untold amount of time preparing each run.

Without any doubt the inter-period interface provided by the P_θ family in the process of site selection has merits. However, we feel that our method can be improved. More specifically, a dynamic stepping procedure could be experi-

mented with rather than our primitive method. This seems especially worthwhile since it took an average of 1.41 CPU minutes to perform step two per mini-cycle. This is 33% of total time.

2.2 *The production planning model /module* 2

This model is none other than the so called fixed cost or lot size model. Its name is owed to the fact that when production lines are set up for a batch a fixed cost is incurred (Fig. 3).

In our case we further assume that batches of given brandsizes can only be run above/below minimum/maximum runsizes. Also, because of Company policies a fixed workforce is hypothesized. The resulting model is non-linear but can be approximated by a Mixed Integer Program, MIP. Let us make the following definitions:

(A) Coefficients:

c_{it} = unit production cost for brandsize i in period t

D_{it} = forecasted monthly brandsize i demand in period t

e_i = unit engineering production coefficient for brandsize i

f_{it} = set-up cost for brandsize i in period t

i_{it} = unit inventory carrying cost for brandsize i in period t

I_{i0} = starting inventory level for brandsize i in period 0

L/U = lower/upper bound on brandsize production levels

M_t = total regular manpower time available in period t

N = total number of brandsizes i

o_t = labor overtime hourly cost in period t

r_t = labor regular hourly cost in period t

s_i = set-up time for brandsize i

SS_{it} = safety stock for brandsize i at the end of period t

T = total number of periods t

W_0 = starting regular time workforce level in period 0

% = percentage of overtime to regular time

(B) Variables:

I_{it} = units of brandsize i inventoried at the end of period t

O_t = overtime labor used in period t

W_t = regular labor time in period t

X_{it} = units of brandsize i produced in period t

Z_{it} = 1, if brandsize i is produced in period t

Z_{it} = 0, if brandsize i is not produced in period t

(C) Model Formulation:

Minimize

$$\sum_{i=1}^{N} \sum_{t=1}^{T} (f_{it} \cdot Z_{it} + c_{it} \cdot X_{it} + i_{it} \cdot I_{it}) + \sum_{t=1}^{T} (r_t \cdot W_t + o_t \cdot O_t) \quad (1)$$

subject to:

$$X_{it} + I_{it-1} - I_{it} = D_{it}, \quad \forall i, t \quad (2)$$

$$L \cdot Z_{it} \leq X_{it} \leq U \cdot Z_{it}, \quad \forall i, t \quad (3)$$

$$\sum_{i=1}^{N} (s_i \cdot Z_{it} + e_i \cdot X_{it}) - W_t - O_t \leq 0, \quad \forall i, t \quad (4)$$

$$O_t - \% \cdot W_t \leq 0, \quad \forall t \quad (5)$$

$$W_t \leq M_t, \quad \forall t \quad (6)$$

$$I_{it} \geq SS_{it}, \quad \forall i, t \quad (7)$$

$$Z = 0/1; \quad I, O, W, X \geq 0. \quad (8)$$

Note:

$\sum_{t=1}^{T} D_{it}$ = plant brandsize allocation provided by module 1.

In this particular situation management decides that regular time will have to be used up before any consideration will be given to overtime. This is not explicitly formulated here although $o_t = 2 \cdot r_t$. Also note that if it were not for equation (4) a decomposition approach could be used over the brandsizes i. This approach has been put to use in another setting by (6) and (3)–(4).

One limiting factor in terms of MPSX/370 branch and bound algorithmic speed is of course the number of decision variables Z_{it}. Thus, everything must be done to keep this number as small as possible. Although, Falk and Tumbusch, [3, 4], are reporting some encouraging results.

In our case, the combination of brandsizes i and period t yields 220 binary variables Z_{it}. To eliminate as many of them as possible the following procedure is applied:

Step 1—Solve quations (1) to (8) to continuous optimality relaxing the integrality constraint on the Z_{it}.

Step 2—Scan the optimal continuous solution for the basic X_{it}, (this can be done automatically with MPSX/370 Extended Control Language, ECL-PL/1).

Step 3—If all the basic X_{it} for a given i solve the LP and equation (3) with the integrality in force for all t then save the solution. It is integer optimal.

Step 4—If the basic X_{it} for a given i solves LP with (3) integral for a given t then fix Z_{it} to 1.

If the basic X_{it} for a given i gives a degenerate solution for a given t then fix Z_{it} to 0.

Otherwise let Z_{it} be free for the other basic and non-basic X_{it}.

Step 5—Start the MIP/370 branch and bound taking into account the modifications of step 4 and restoring the solution of step 3 with its basic X_{it}'s fixed at their optimal continuous value.

159

After the execution of this procedure our problem had the following statistics: 267 rows, 460 columns, 64 of which were free binary variables, see (3) and (4). Starting after the completion of the above procedure only 1.42 CPU minutes and 1203 iterations were needed to reach integer optimality on an IBM 370/168. As a comparison it took about 6 times as many CPU minutes for the full fledge problem with 220 binary variables to reach integer optimality and only achieve a 0.57% better solution.

This is not totally unexpected since a large proportion of the basic variables fell into the category of step 3 after a continuous optimum had been obtained. Clearly, this happens whenever D_{it} is greater or equal to L for a given i for all t. Our success has thus been due in this application to a very definite data pattern that we had recognized. Other utilization of this approach might not be as fruitful.

CONCLUSION

We have applied the concept of a Manufacturing Hierarchy to a real life application. It provides Divisional Managers the necessary mechanization to evaluate the impact of given Strategic, Tactical and Operational plans on their manufacturing and distribution operation. Yet it retains the necessary versatility for given managers to continue performing, as before but only faster, their operational duties.

In terms of MIP problems we have learned again that nothing can replace a sound 'tight' formulation. A computational approach that minimizes the number of integer variables and/or the effort to arrive at a solution in a given situation is also highly desirable. Also, nothing can substitute for the understanding of the behaviour of a given model and its continuous solution and log before going into the mixed integer phase. Finally, it is best to utilize first and understand well optimization macros before utilizing some of the more specialized features offered by large scale Mathematical Programming softwares including MPSX/370.

REFERENCES

1. BÉNICHOU M, GAUTHIER JM, GIRODET P, HENTGÈS G, RIBIÈRE G & VINCENT O (1971) Experiments in mixed integer linear programming. *Math. Programm.* **1**(1), 76–94.
2. BUFFA ES & TAUBERT WH (1972) Production-Inventory Systems: Planning and Control. Irving, Homewood, Illinois, USA.
3. FALK PG & TUMBUSCH JJ (1977) User evaluation of MPSX/370. SHARE 49, Washington, DC, USA.
4. FALK PG & TUMBUSCH JJ (1978) User evaluation of MPSX/370. SIGMAP Newsletter, **23**, 41–54.
5. GAUTHIER JM & RIBIÈRE G (1977) Experiments in mixed integer linear programming using pseudo-costs. *Math. Prog.* **12**(1), 26–47.
6. GEOFFRION AM & GRAVES GW (1974) Multicommodity distribution system design by benders decomposition. *Mgmt Sci.* **20**(5), 822–844.
7. GEOFFRION AM & NAUSS R (1977) Parametric and postoptimality analysis in integer linear programming. *Mgmt Sci.* **23**(5), 453–466.
8. HAX AC (1973) Hierarchical Integration of Production Planning and Scheduling. *TR No.* **88**, Operations Research Center, MIT, Massachusetts, USA.
9. MARSTEN RE & MORIN TL (1975) Parametric Integer Programming: The Right-Hand-Side Case. *Work. Pap.* **808**-75, Sloan School of Management, MIT, Massachusetts, USA.
10. MARSTEN RE & MORIN TL (1976) A Hybrid Approach to Discrete Mathematical Programming. *Work. Pap.* **838**-76, Sloan School of Management, MIT, Massachusetts, USA.
11. SHAPIRO JF (1976) Sensitivity Analysis in Integer Programming. *Ops Res. Pap. No.* **048**, Operations Research Center, MIT, Massachusetts, USA.
12. SLATE L & SPIELBERG K (1978) The extended control language of MPSX/370 and possible applications. *IBM Syst. Jl* **17**(1), 64–81.

ADDRESS FOR CORRESPONDENCE: *Patrick G Falk, Esq, Supervisor: Resource Allocation Systems, International Paper Company, 220 East 42nd Street, New York, NY 10017, USA.*

Reprinted, by permission, from International Journal of
Production Research, *Vol. 15, No. 6, 1977.*

Development of integrated production scheduling system for iron and steel works

SHUZO SATO†, TAKASHI YAMAOKA‡, YUTARO AOKI‡ and
TORU UEDA‡

The primary purpose of production scheduling at an integrated iron and steel works
is to establish and execute the optimum production schedule that can improve both
productivity and yield at each of the plants such as the steelmaking plants and rolling
mills, while giving first consideration to the keeping of the date of delivery.

However, it is by no means a simple matter to establish and control an integrated
or consistent production schedule covering about ten production processes for various
products with an annual output of 6 million tons or more, or about 25 000 orders
monthly.

In our system-development efforts, therefore, we made the system under study
simple and usable in practical applications, designed a scheduling simulator capable of
policy selection, and thereby successfully developed an integrated production scheduling system centring around the scheduling simulator.

Introduction

The iron and steel industry is one of the process industries, and is therefore
generally regarded as typical of the speculative ' small product mix and mass
production '. However, Nippon Steel Corporation conducts operations on a
perfect ' multi-kind and job-order production ' basis, satisfying the severe
requirements of users.

Nagoya Works, NSC, currently manufactures hot-rolled coils, cold-rolled
coils, tin plate, galvanized sheets, pipe and tubes, heavy plate, etc., attaining an
annual crude steel production of 6 million tons.

Under these circumstances, Nagoya Works has been introducing a large-
scale computer system since 1965 to develop a production scheduling system.
The development of this system has been made through the following three
main stages:

(1) Stage I (1965–1969):   where emphasis was placed on the introduction
of Electronic Date Processing (EDP).

(2) Stage II (1970–1972):   where emphasis was placed on the development of ' Individual Production Scheduling
Systems '.

(3) Stage III (1973–1976):   where emphasis was placed on total optimization for all processes.

Figure 1 diagramatically shows these three stages. The individual production scheduling systems (hereinafter sometimes referred to as individual

---

Presented at the 4th International Conference on Production Research (Tokyo),
August 1977.

† Production Control Department, Nippon Steel Co. Ltd., 2–6–3 Otemachi,
Chiyoda–Ku, Tokyo 100, Japan.

‡ Computer System Planning Office, Nippon Steel Co. Ltd., Nagoya Works,
3,5–chome, Tokai–cho, Tokai–shi 476, Japan.

Published by Taylor & Francis Ltd, 10–14 Macklin Street, London WC2B 5NF.

systems, for simplicity), separately developed for the respective plants as they were newly constructed, were able to achieve local or partial optimization. However, there inevitably arose the need for collective or total optimization of all kinds of products and all production processes with a 5 or 10 day period as a unit.

(1) Stage 1   (1965-1969)

Introduction of Electronic Data Processing

(2) Stage 2   (1970-1972)

Local Optimization in Individual Systems

(3) Stage 3   (1973-1976)

Total Optimization through Integrated System

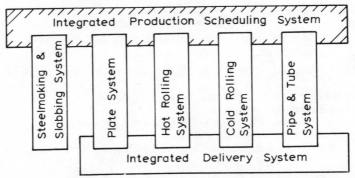

Figure 1.   Brief history of production scheduling system.

Features of production scheduling at steelworks

Nagoya Works produces 500 000 tons of crude steel a month while individual orders amount to about 20 tons each. Therefore, the number of orders that are fulfilled in a month reaches about 25 000. Meanwhile, each of the production plants is large-scale and of the mass production type, having production constraints.

Thus the role of integrated production scheduling system at the steelworks, where a number of such plants are connected to form integrated production processes, is to best re-form or rearrange small-lot orders into proper-sized and properly-sequenced lots for the above-mentioned integrated processes, while making the best use of the features of each plant, and thereby achieving improvements of overall productivity and efficiency.

The constraints and objective functions for production scheduling at our steelworks are enumerated as follows:

Constraints

There are about 25 main production processes, the production constraints of which amount to about 1000 in total. Moreover, some of these constraints may be definitely determined depending upon the contents of orders; however, most of them have degrees of freedom and therefore are more or less indefinite, resulting in greater complexity.

Constraints are broadly divided into three categories, i.e. production-period constraints, production-lot constraints and delivery-date constraints.

(i) *Production-period constraints and 10 day production period:* Since the processes involved vary with the kind of products, production or processing time at each process also varies therewith, even if delivery time is the same. This relationship can be expressed by the following equation (see Fig. 2):

$$t_{i1} = DT_i - \sum_{k=1}^{n} \delta_{ik} LT_{ik},$$

where DT_i is the delivery time of the kind i of products, t_{ik} the production starting time at the process k of the kind i of products, δ_{ik} a coefficient which assumes the value one if the material of the kind i of products involves the process k and assumes the value 0 if not, and LT_{ik} the standard production or processing period at the process k.

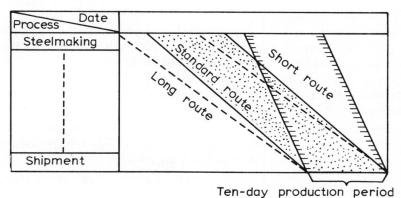

Figure 2. Lead-time constraints.

In order to establish the 10 day production schedule, it is necessary to make 10 day production periods for each process, which are usually determined on the basis of the production or processing periods of the typical kinds of products.

(ii) *Production-lot constraints:* These vary with production period and equipment, and may be broadly classified into production-lot-formation constraints, production-lot-sequence constraints and daily-allocation constraints

In the steelmaking process, for instance, production lots refer to heats; and, in the case of steels for ingotmaking, daily-allocation constraints may be expressed by the following relationships:

$$\sum_a \sum_b \sum_c X_{jabc} \leqslant L_j,$$

$$\sum_b \sum_c X_{jabc} \leqslant K_{ja},$$

$$\sum_a \sum_c X_{jabc} \leqslant M_{jb},$$

$$\sum_a \sum_b X_{jabc} \leqslant S_{jc},$$

where X_{jabc} is the number of heats on the jth day of the kind a of steels involving the ingot mould b and treatment c; L_j the upper limit of the number of heats on the jth day; K_{ja} the upper limit of the number of heats on the jth day classified by the kind a of steels; M_{jb} the upper limit of the number of heats on the jth day classified by the ingot mould b; and S_{jc} the upper limit of the number of heats on the jth day classified by the special treatment code c.

(iii) *Delivery-date constraints:* Let the date of shipment be DT, the 10 day period of shipment be the lth and the jth day of the lth 10 day period be D_{lj}, and delivery-date constraints will be expressed as follows:

(a) For products with a specified date of delivery, $DT = D_{ljs}$, where the subscript js represents a specified date.
(b) For products in urgent need, $DT \leqslant D_{l5}$, where subscript $j = 5$.
(c) For products to be delivered within the jth 10 day period, $D_{l1} \leqslant DT \leqslant D_{lj\max}$.
(d) For products the delivery date of which may be carried over to the next 10-day period, $D_{l1} \leqslant DT \leqslant D_{(l+1)j\max}$.

Objective functions

Objective functions used as the criteria of optimization may fall into two categories, one of them being associated with optimization concerning the production period of each order and the other being associated with optimization concerning the combinations of orders (for instance, production lots) at each process. The former will be hereinafter referred to as production-period objective functions and the latter as process-by-process objective functions.

(i) *Production-period objective functions:* In the designated processes, including production and shipping processes, production-period objective functions may be classified into the following two kinds:

(a) Reduction of the production period of products in urgent need,

$$\bar{t} = \sum_t t W(t) / \sum_t W(t) \to \min.$$

(*b*) Decrease of the dispersion of production times,

$$\sum_t (t - \bar{t})^2 W(t) / \sum_t W(t) \to \min.$$

In these expressions $W(t)$ is the quantity of a certain order lot allocated for production on the tth day.

(ii) *Process-by-process objective functions:* These vary with the process as a matter of course, and are broadly divided as following:

(*a*) Improvements in production capacity and yield and decrease in unit consumption, achieved by increase in production lot size. For example, the reduction of the roll-changing time achieved by the increase in rolling lot size,

$$\sum_e \sum_f (T_{ef} / R_{ef}) \to \min,$$

where T_{ef} is the roll-changing time for the fth rolling lot of the kind e, and R_{ef} is the tonnage of the rolling lot ef.

(*b*) Reduction of the set-changing time achieved by the change in size within the same production lot, for example, reduction of the set-changing time for the values of thickness and width within a hot-rolling lot may be substantially approximated to the decrease in the number of kinds of thickness and width within the same lot,

$$\sum_e \sum_f ((A_{ef} + B_{ef}) / R_{ef}) \to \min,$$

where A_{ef} is the number of kinds of thickness within the same lot, B_{ef} the number of kinds of width within the same lot, and R_{ef} is the tonnage of the rolling lot ef.

(*c*) Smoothing of the number of plants in operation.

(*d*) Decrease in materials-handling cost achieved by changing the process sequence.

(*e*) Reduction of the quantity of goods in process.

Generally speaking, however, the above-mentioned process-by-process objective functions and production-period objective functions are contrary in nature to each other. This relationship is schematically shown in Fig. 3 with the production lot size as variable.

Problems of the conventional scheduling system

(i) *Outline:* In the case of the conventional scheduling system, the 10-day production schedule is established by the procedure including the steps of optimizing each individual production scheduling system of a down-stream process with respect to the contents of orders supplied thereto as the input, giving the results of the above optimization to an adjacent up-stream process as the information input, optimizing each individual production scheduling system of the above up-stream process with respect to the above information input, and repeating the above sequence of steps as required.

Since the conventional scheduling system carries out partial optimization repeatedly as mentioned above, it inevitably has disadvantages from the

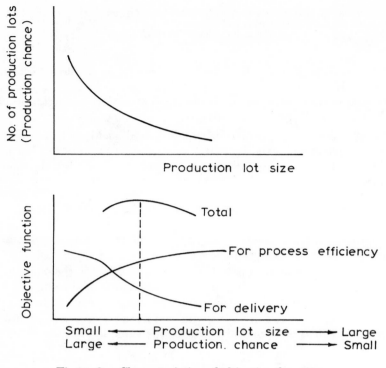

Figure 3. Characteristics of objective functions.

collective point of view in that it can hardly achieve scheduling from the start in some cases and therefore cannot accomplish collective or total optimization.

(ii) *Problems:* Thus the conventional scheduling system involves the following problems.

First, the division of the production lot causes decrease in yield, increase in material consumption, decrease in production efficiency, etc. In the case of the hot-rolling process, for instance, production lots refer to rolling lots, which are generally classified into the kinds L, S, T, D, etc. Among these lots, the lots L account for a relatively large proportion of orders, the quantity thereof reaching 20–30 lots per 10 day period. On the other hand, the lots D are infrequent lots, about one lot being put in process per 10 day period. Under these circumstances, no serious problems arise even if the materials of the lot L do not flow as scheduled; on the other hand, the lot D is often divided into two or three rolling lots in view of the date of delivery and, as a result, the divided small rolling lots or production lots incur deterioration of yield, material consumption, production efficiency, etc. Such requirements for the production lot are seen in every process.

Another problem is the increase of the inventory in process caused by the scattering of production periods. In cases where shipments are made to the Middle East or the Far East, which areas do not have a frequent shipping

Item	Integrated production scheduling system	Individual system
Function	Total optimization for all production processes	Partial optimization for each process according to the consistent production schedule
Scheduling process	All processes	Each process
Scheduling period	10 days	1 or 2 days
Execution time	2 days before the steelmaking time	1 day before production at each process
Scheduling cycle	Every 10 days	Every day
Input	1. Order file 2. 10-day plants operation file 3. Parameter file 4. Actual results of the last 10 days	1. Integrated production schedule file 2. Daily plants operation file 3. Daily actual production results
Output	1. Order analyses of new orders 2. Integrated production schedule file	1. Daily production instructions 2. Reports concerning the production results
Action for fluctuations	1. Re-schedule for major production fluctuations 2. Giving the ' priority for schedule change ' to each system	1. Scheduling for the daily fluctuations according to the proposed priority
Evaluation and analysis	Analysing about each control item and reporting its results	Analysing about the last day's production results at each process

Function and characteristics of each system.

service, it is indispensable to finish the assortment of the whole loads before shipment. If it takes much time to complete the production of all products of interest, products in process will inevitably increase. Meanwhile, there are some products which canot remain in intermediate processes for a long time because of quality problems such as rusting.

Design policies for the integrated production scheduling system

Since production scheduling involves very complicated and large-scale problems as mentioned above, it is necessary to functionally divide the whole system into the integrated production scheduling system and individual systems, to make it possible to handle each system independently to some extent, and to definitely provide for coordinating these systems. On the basis of such a concept, the integrated production scheduling system was designed according to the following policies:

(i) *Positioning of the integrated production scheduling system:* The role of integrated production scheduling system is to provide a consistent production schedule for all production processes. Therefore, it involves rescheduling for major variations such as fluctuations in the production status and those caused by large-scale facility troubles. To be specific, it is necessary to determine the process-by-process scheduled dates of completion of the processing of each order, to give instructions to the individual systems concerning the above scheduled dates and, in addition, to give instructions to the individual systems concerning the ' priority for schedule change ' in order to prevent from rescheduling when a partial change occurs to the production schedule in an ' execution phase ' due to production fluctuations. Meanwhile, the role of each individual system is to provide a detailed ' execution schedule ' according to the above-mentioned policies.

The functional division mentioned above enables coordination of total and partial optimizations.

(ii) *Configuration of the integrated production scheduling system:*

(*a*) Provision of a preparatory system for scheduling, by unifying various sorts of information inputs such as information on production instructions which have been hitherto classified according to the kinds of products and by conducting order analyses, etc.

(*b*) Provision of a scheduling simulator for establishing the integrated production schedule.

(*c*) Provision of a system for evaluating and analysing the results of scheduling and those of a comparison between the proposed schedule and its actual results.

(iii) *Perfection of simulator functions:*

(*a*) Introduction of an integrated scheduling system.

(*b*) To give the model a moderate ' roughness ' so that the influences of minor fluctuations thereon may be removed while preserving fundamental factors.

(*c*) Provision of many kinds of evaluation or value functions—to make it possible to select several evaluation functions, since requirements for optimization vary with the order and process.

(*d*) To enable many kinds of policy selections.

(*e*) To divide the simulator function into two parts, one for preparing production lots and the other for scheduling.

Simulator model

(i) *Model types:* We made various examinations of the model types of the simulator section, the heart of the integrated production scheduling system, according to the above-mentioned design policies. From these examinations, we determined the following:

Approximate solutions that can be regarded as practically optimum can be obtained by the procedure which heuristically seeks executable solutions though not optimum according to the ' priority rule '.

Besides, among the above-mentioned constraints, there are a relatively small number of constraints that must be strictly satisfied; many of them being those that should be satisfied to the utmost extent. Therefore, here is also room for the application of the ' priority rule '.

According to the above-mentioned findings, we determined the model type. The model is divided into three sub-models (for determining parameters, for

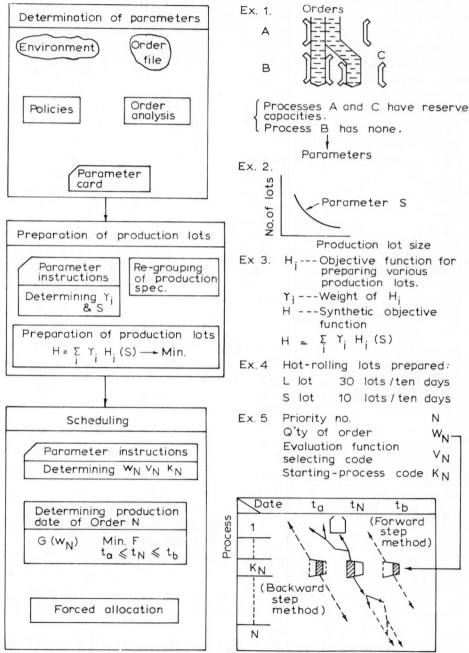

Figure 4. Simplified scheme of simulator model.

preparing production lots, and for scheduling). Figure 4 shows a simplified scheme of this model.

(ii) *Determination of parameters:* Various policies must be converted into parameters so that the system may be flexibly or elastically operated under the varying environment. The first sub-model is so formed that it can determine parameters in consideration of various policies and the results of order analysis concerning the order file supplied every 10 days as an input. Since it requires a prodigious amount of effort for workers to prepare groups of parameters one by one each time, this sub-model is made to have a ' hierarchy structure ' in which higher-ranking parameters can automatically change lower-ranking parameters and in which lower-ranking parameters can be individually changed as required. These parameters play important roles in the subsequent sub-models for ' preparing production lots ' and ' scheduling '.

(iii) *Preparation of production lots:* Preparation of production lots carried out as pre-processing for scheduling follows the procedure given below:

(*a*) Reductive regrouping of an enormous number of kinds of sizes, chemical composition ranges, shapes, and materials specified in the order specifications: For instance, the kinds of chemical composition ranges are regrouped, being reduced in number from 130 to 30; and, in the case of the kinds of hot-rolled coil widths, the kinds being reduced in number from 300 to 25. In a similar manner, other regrouping procedures are performed.

(*b*) Heuristic determination of the production lot to which each order belongs: The method of preparing production lots varies with the process, and therefore the production lot to which each order belongs is not determined unitarily in general, though there are some differences. Accordingly, this problem may be regarded as a combinatorial problem involving many constraints, which must be solved by heuristic techniques.

(*c*) Determination of the sizes and number of production lots: Production lot size is generally not constant and has degrees of freedom. The lot size and the number of lots are inversely proportional to each other, as shown in Fig. 4. In view of this relationship, the lot size and the number of lots are determined using parameters obtained from the results of order analysis.

Examples of the production lots prepared by the above procedure are as follows, and are also shown in Fig. 4:

For hot-rolling process:

L lot — 30 lots per 10 day period.
S lot — 10 lots per 10 day period.

(iv) *Scheduling:* This sub-model performs scheduling by the following procedure, as shown in Fig. 4.

(*a*) To determine the priority for scheduling, evaluation functions to be selected, and the starting process for scheduling, using parameters given to each order.

(*b*) To determine the proper time when a given order is processed in each process and the proper production lot to which it belongs:

The proper time when a given order is processed in each process and the proper production lot to which it belongs are determined by the 'overflow method with forward and backward steps'. The forward step method is to perform scheduling according to the branch-and-bound technique in which processing is carried out from the starting process to the up-stream processes. The backward step method is to perform scheduling in a similar manner in which however processing is carried out from the starting process to the down-stream processes. Incidentally the overflow method is so named from the fact that it additionally produces a new production lot when a given production lot to which each order can belong which may be regarded as a 'vessel' overflows.

Scheduling for the Nth order is performed by obtaining the minimum value of the following function under the complex constraints of each process:

$$G(W_N) = \text{Min } F(v_N \quad k_N \quad t_N \quad w_N)$$
$$t_a \leqslant t_N \leqslant t_b,$$

where

$G(W_N) = $ results of process-by-process schedules for the Nth order.

$F = $ decision function for scheduling.
$v_N = $ evaluation function selecting code.
$k_N = $ code of the starting process for scheduling.
$t_N = $ starting date at the starting process.
$W_N = $ quantity of the Nth order.
$t_a \sim t_b = $ period when production is allowed at the starting process.

In this manner the process-by-process scheduled dates of completion of the processing of each order and the preparation of daily production lots are determined.

(c) *Forced allocation:* If scheduling proceeds in the above-mentioned procedure the scheduling of about one-tenth of the orders low in priority will become impossible in view of various constraints in spite of the fact that each process still has a reserve of production capacity. In other words this condition may be regarded as similar to the condition where a vessel cannot be filled with materials though there is enough space left therein.

In order to cope with this problem frequently-appearing lots having much production chance are made low in allocation priority so that they may be used as 'filling material'. In addition only the constraints that must be strictly satisfied are adopted for use the rest being neglected. Forced allocation carried out in this manner can solve the above-mentioned problem of the non-feasibility of scheduling.

In this case the decision function for scheduling is basically similar to that shown in (b).

Operational organization

The operational flow of the integrated production scheduling system is shown in Fig. 5.

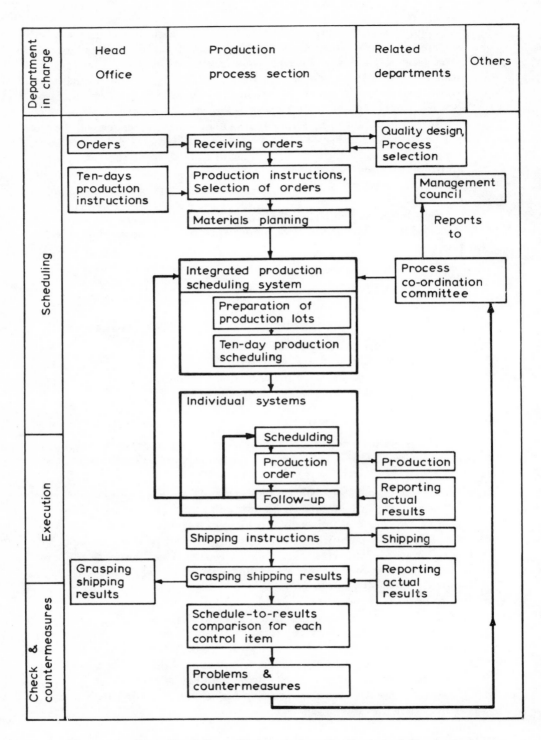

Figure 5.   Operational flow of integrated production scheduling system.

When the order file sent from head office is received the processing of orders such as quality designing and process selection is performed. According to the 10 day production instructions sent from head office the order of interest are then picked up from the order file while calculating the quantities of materials required thereby preparing information inputs for the integrated production scheduling system.

Policies for establishing the integrated production schedule are determined by the process coordination committee. This committee makes a collective examination of the results of the order analyses of new orders and the comparative data of the integrated production schedule and its actual results of the last two 10-day periods together with the present production conditions and operation schedule, while giving reconsideration to the past activities.

After these preparations each of the individual systems performs with ten proposed integrated production schedule as a guide the preparation execution and feedback of actual results, of the daily production orders or instructions. After each order lot has been passed through all the necessary processes, a comparison between the proposed schedule and its actual results is carried out concerning each control item, and its results are reported to the process coordination committee and management council.

The integrated production scheduling system has been in operation since July 1975, and as was expected it has accomplished various successful results such as an increase in yield, decrease in material consumption, and decrease in the quantity of products in process. In the last 10 day period of October 1975, for instance, the quantity of products in process and of product inventory could be reduced as much as about 20%.

ACKNOWLEDGMENTS

In conclusion, we would like to acknowledge the assistance of Professor Iri of Tokyo University and Professor Muramatsu of Waseda University, who both gave us useful advice on questions pertaining to the model for the integrated production scheduling system.

L'objectif primordial de la programmation de la production dans une fonderie de fer et d'acier, est d'établir et d'exécuter le programme de production optimum capable d'améliorer la productivité et le rendement de chacune des installations telles que l'aciérie et les laminoirs, tout en donnant la priorité à honorer la date de livraison.

Cependant, il n'est pas facile d'établir et de contrôler un programme de production intégré ou compatible couvrant environ dix procédés de production pour divers produits, avec une production annuelle de 6 millions de tonnes ou davantage, environ 25 000 commandes par mois.

Par conséquent, nous avons préparé le système en question pour qu'il soit simple et utilisable dans des applications pratiques. Nous avons conçu un simulateur de programmation capable de sélectionner une politique et par conséquent, nous avons réussi à mettre au point un système de programmation de production intégré établi sur le simulateur de programmation.

Der Hauptweck der Produktionsplanung in integrierten Eisen- und Stahlwerken besteht darin, einen optimalen Produktionszeitplan auszuarbeiten und durchzuführen, der einerseits für eine Verbesserung der Produktivität und des Ertrags der einzelenen Anlagen, wie z.B. der Stahlherstellungswerke und der Walzwerke, sorgt, der andererseits aber, und dies in erster Linie, die Einhaltung von Lieferfristen berücksichtigt.

Es ist jedoch keineswegs einfach, einen umfassenden, konsequenten Produktionsplan für etwa zehn Produktionsprozesse für die verschiedensten Produkte mit einer Jahresproduktion von 6 Millionen Tonnen oder mehr oder etwa 25 000 Aufträgen pro Monat aufzustellen und durchzuführen.

In unseren Bemühungen zur Entwicklung eines Zeitplansystems sind wir von einem einfachen, praktisch anwendbaren System ausgegangen, haben einen einen Plansimulator entwickelt, der in der Lage war, unter verschiedenen Maßnahmen zu wählen, und haben hiermit ein integriertes Produktionszeitplansystem entwickelt, in dessen Mittlepunkt der Plansimulator steht.

REFERENCES

BELLMAN, R., and DREYFUS, S., 1962, *Applied Dynamic Programming* (New Jersey: Princeton University Press).

CHOYAFAS, D. N., 1958, *Operations Research for Industrial Management* (New York: Reinhold Publishing Company).

CHURCHMAN, C. W., ACKOFF, R. L., and ARNOFF, E. L., 1960, *Introduction to Operations Research* (Tokyo: Charles E. Tuttle).

IRI, M., 1964, *Linear Programming—Decomposition Principle* (Tokyo: Union of Japanese Scientists and Engineers).

OPITZ, H., 1967, *Werkstucksystematik und Teilefamilienfertigung* (Essen: Verlag W. Girardet).

Reprinted, by permission, from Journal of Operations Management, *Journal of the American Production and Inventory Control Society, Inc., November 1980.*

Improving Fuel Utilization In Steel Mill Operations Using Linear Programming

Robert E. Markland*

ABSTRACT

This paper describes the use of linear programming to improve the fuel utilization at a major Midwestern steel mill. In particular, linear programming is used to determine an efficient fuel allocation plan for this steel mill, which reduces the total fuel costs for the steel mill operations. The efficient fuel allocation plan that is developed utilizes two externally purchased fuels: natural gas and fuel oil, and two gases: blast furnace gas and coke plant gas, which are internally generated as natural by-products of the production process. Test results from the application of the linear programming model are presented and discussed, and indicate that considerable cost savings can be achieved by utilizing a fuel allocation plan which more effectively utilizes the by-product gases which are produced within the steel making process.

INTRODUCTION

Many developments in the domestic steel industry in the last decade have posed difficult, continuing problems. Indeed, there has been much talk about a loss of world steelmaking leadership by the United States, reinforced by reports of more modern mills being constructed abroad and by loss of markets to foreign imports. As the United States steel industry moves into the decade of the 80's, it faces at least three major problems:

1. Possible further loss of markets to foreign imports if United States trade laws are not properly enforced.
2. Inadequate cash flows to meet capital needs for modernization and expansion.
3. Restrictions and inflationary pressures caused by various environmental regulations.

The United States steel industry, faced with these problems, has become acutely concerned with operating costs. A major operating cost for a typical steel mill is the cost associated with fuels used in the production of steel. Since the fuels used include natural gas and fuel oil, there has been tremendous upward pressure on overall fuel costs, as the energy costs associated with fossil fuels have skyrocketed.

As a result of soaring fuel costs, managers within the steel industry have begun to search for ways of more efficiently utilizing various fuels, including the by-product gases produced during the steelmaking process. This paper describes one such approach to energy utilization, that has been modeled and tested within the working environment of a major Midwestern steel mill. The approach developed utilizes linear programming to specify a fuel allocation plan which will reduce total fuel costs for the steel mill operations.

PHYSICAL ENVIRONMENT OF THE STUDY

This study was done for the Granite City Steel Division of the National Steel Corporation. The National Steel Corporation, with its subsidiaries and affiliates, makes iron, steel, and aluminum products. It is the fourth largest steel producer in the United States, and has two major steel markets: the automobile and container industries. In 1979, steel mill products accounted for 94% of the company's total sales and revenues, and the automobile and container industries encompassed about 27% and 18%, respectively, of total steel shipments by tonnage.

The principal steel products produced by the company are hot and cold rolled sheets and strip, tin plate, galvanized sheets, pig iron, nailable steel flooring, steel pipe and oil country goods, pre-engineered metal building systems and components, steel tubing, and highway and construction products. The Granite City Steel Division is a wholly owned subsidiary of the company, with its major production facility being located in Granite City, Illinois.

National Steel Corporation has maintained a strong record of production and cost reduction innovations. It introduced the first continuous hot-strip mill, the first big basic oxygen furnace,

---

*Professor— Management Science, University of South Carolina.

and the first 80-inch computerized hot strip mill in the United States. More recently it brought into operation what is still the only cold-reduction mill in the United States, and it is presently converting all of its steel furnaces to a "top-and-bottom-blown" design that will further reduce costs.

All of these technological innovations have been coupled with continuous cost-reduction programs which have advanced productivity and efficiency. In the early 1970's National Steel Corporation became very concerned about its rapidly increasing raw material and operating costs. One particularly important element of its operating cost was the cost associated with fuels used in the steelmaking process. An Industrial Engineering study completed in late 1975 at the Granite City steel mill indicated that considerable operating savings might be possible through the collection and use of two by-product gases, blast furnace gas and coke oven gas, throughout the steel making process. In this environment, it was desired to fully investigate the general problem of efficiently allocating fuels throughout the production process.

The Granite City steel mill used four types of fuels in eight locations throughout the blast furnace and steel works complex. The four fuels that were used and their associated costs at the time of the study (April, 1976) were:

1. Natural Gas (NG)—(Outside Purchase—$1.090/thousand cubic feet)
2. Fuel Oil (FO)—(Outside Purchase—$0.310/gallon)
3. Blast Furnace Gases (BG)—(By-Product-$0.450/thousand cubic feet)
4. Coke Plant Gases (CG)—(By-Product-$0.048/thousand cubic feet)

Note that the latter two gases were natural by-products of the production process and were available at a very low cost, in contrast to the first two fuels which had to be purchased externally, and were considerably higher in cost.

The eight production units which consumed these fuels, and the fuels that could be utilized were:

1. Blast Furnace [BF]—the first step in the conversion of iron ore into steel takes place in the blast furnace where iron ore, coke, and limestone are transformed into pig iron. Natural gas and blast furnace gas could be utilized in the blast furnace.
2. Basic Oxygen Furnaces [BOF]—pig iron and scrap are mixed together in the basic oxygen furnace and oxygen is injected into the bath of molten metal to produce steel. Natural gas is utilized to produce the necessary heat in the basic oxygen furnace.
3. Coke Plant [CP]—coal is introduced into coke plant ovens, where it burned in the absence of air, driving gases from the coal to produce coke. Natural gas and coke gas may be utilized as fuels in this process.
4. Blast Furnace Boilers [BFB]—used to produce great quantities of heated air which are blown up to the blast furnace to meet descending amounts of iron ore, coke, and flux stone. Natural gas, fuel oil, blast furnace gas, and coke gas may be utilized to fire the blast furnace boilers.
5. Sintering Plant [SP]—the sinter plant is used to agglomerate small or fine pieces of iron ores into larger "clinkers" of iron ore which can then be used as input to the blast furnace. Natural gas and coke gas can be used in the sintering plant.
6. Blooming Mill Soaking Pits [SOP]—in the blooming mill hot steel ingots are rolled into various semi-finished shapes (i.e., blooms, slabs or billets). The blooming mill soaking pits are used to keep the steel blooms hot so that they can be rolled. Natural gas and coke gas can be used in the blooming mill soaking pit.
7. Steelworks Boiler [SWB]—the steelworks boiler is used to produce steam and hot water which is then used in several parts of the steelmaking process. Natural gas, fuel oil, and coke gas can be utilized in the steelworks boiler.
8. Hot Strip Slab Furnaces [SF]—the hot strip slab furnaces are used to heat the slabs prior to their being rolled into plates or sheets. Natural gas or fuel oil can be used in the hot strip slab furnace.

A flow diagram of the steel mill fuel sources and uses is shown below in Figure 1.

Note that not all of the production units were equipped to use all four of the fuels available. However, the fuel requirements of each unit could be expressed in terms of millions of BTUs which provided a common denominator for the analysis of existing fuel utilization, and for consideration of alternative fuel utilization configurations. Various resources constraints existed in specific areas, such as a minimum level of natural gas usage in the steelworks boilers, a limitation on the availability of natural gas and fuel oil in certain time periods, and a limitation on the availability of the two by-product gases as a func-

FIGURE 1.
Flow Diagram-Steel Mill Fuel Sources and Uses

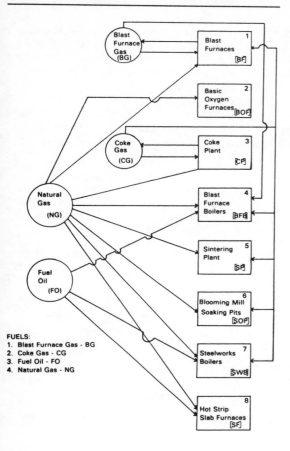

FUELS:
1. Blast Furnace Gas - BG
2. Coke Gas - CG
3. Fuel Oil - FO
4. Natural Gas - NG

tion of coke plant and blast furnace production levels.

MATHEMATICAL FORMULATION OF THE FUEL DISTRIBUTION LINEAR PROGRAMMING MODEL

The fuel distribution linear programming model was designed to minimize the total cost of fuel utilization:

Minimize Total Cost of Fuel = Σ
Utilization   all fuel types
        ($/unit of fuel × units of fuel used).

subject to four types of constraints:

1. Production fuel requirements in millions of BTUs (MMBTU) taking into consideration the interchangeability of fuels at particular producing units. For example, referring to

Figure 1, natural gas or coke plant gas may be used interchangeably to fuel the sintering plant.

2. Base requirements of fuels per month, including minimum amounts of specific type fuels to be used at various producing units. For example, the pilots for the steelworks boiler required at least 1,000 MCF per day, while the coke plant required at least 6,700 MCF of natural gas each month.

3. By-product fuel availability based on production. For example, each ton of coke produced each month resulted in the production of 16.61 MCF of coke gas as a by-product.

4. External fuel source supply constraints. For example, at the time of the study the monthly supply availability of natural gas was in the range of 35,000 MCF/day–50,000 MCF/day.

The mathematical formulation of the steel mill fuel utilization model encompassing the variables and relationships described above was constructed in the following manner.
First we define:

x_{ij}—number of units of fuel i; $1 = 1, 2, 3, 4$, used at production unit j; $j = 1, 2, 3, \ldots, 8$.

c_{ij}—cost ($/unit) of fuel is used at production unit j.

As noted previously, at the time of the study the base costs for the fuels were as follows:

Base Fuel Costs:
(i = 1) Natural Gas—
$1.090/thousand cubic feet
(i = 2) Fuel Oil—$0.310/gallon
(i = 3) Coke Gas—
$0.450/thousand cubic feet
(i = 4) Blast Furnace Gas—
$0.048/thousand cubic feet

The base fuel costs for the by-products, coke gas and blast furnace gas, reflected the costs associated with their extraction, storage, and utilization. The base fuel costs for the externally purchased fuels reflected their average purchase cost during the time of the study.

The objective function for the steel mill fuel utilization model was written as:

$$\text{Minimize COST} = \sum_{i=1}^{4} \sum_{j=1}^{N} c_{ij} \, x_{ij} = \$1.090 \sum_{j=1}^{N} x_{1j}$$

$$+ \; \$0.310 \sum_{j=1}^{N} x_{2j} + \$0.450 \sum_{j=1}^{N} x_{3j}$$

$$+ \; \$0.048 \sum_{j=1}^{N} z_{4j}$$

Data Conversion Factors:
Natural Gas—1.0363 MMBTU/MCF
Fuel Oil—0.1500 MMBTU/GAL
Coke Gas—0.5252 MMBTU/MCF
Blast Furnace Gas—0.0923 MMBTU/MCF

The constraints for the model were then written as follows:

1. Production Fuel Requirements and Interchangeability.

a.) *Coke Plant*
(MMBTU/# Tons Production = 4.176)
(0.5252 × Coke Gas Utilized) + (1.0363 × Natural Gas Utilized) =
4.176 × # Tons of Coke Production.

b.) *Blast Furnaces*
(MMBTU/# Tons Production = 3.314)
(0.0923 × Blast Furnace Gas Utilized) + (1.0363 × Natural Gas Utilized) = 3.314 × # Tons of Blast Furnace Production.

c.) *Sinter Plant*
(MMBTU/# Tons Production = 0.269)
(0.5250 × Coke Gas Utilized) + (1.0363 × Natural Gas Utilized) + 0.269 × # Tons of Sinter Production.

d.) *Blast Furnace Boilers*
(MMBTU/M # = 1.549)
—Steam Production (base) =
148,000 M #
—Steam Production (turbo blowers) =
0.895 × Wind Rate of Blast Furnaces
(0.5250 × Coke Gas Utilized) + (0.0923 × Blast Furnace Gas Utilized) + (1.0363 × Natural Gas Utilized) + (0.1500 × Fuel Oil Utilized) = 1.549
(148,000 + 0.895 (Wind Rate))

e.) *Basic Oxygen Furnace)*
—Natural Gas Utilization is a function of (4 MCF/Preheat) × (Average Minutes/Preheat) × (% preheats) × (Total Number of Heats Produced)
Natural Gas Utilized = 4 × Average Preheat Minutes × % Preheats × Heats Produced

f.) *Blooming Mill Soaking Pits* (MMBTU/# Ingot Tons Production = 0.601)
(0.5250 × Coke Gas Utilized) + (1.0363 × Natural Gas Utilized) =
0.601 × #Ingot Tons Produced

g.) *Steelworks Boilers* (MMBTU/M #−1.442)
—M # Production = 156,000 + 0.005
Fuel Oil Utilization
at Slab Furnaces
(0.5250 × Coke Gas Utilized) + (1.0363 × Natural Gas Utilized) + (0.15000 × Fuel Oil Utilized) = 1.442 (156,000 + 0.005 Fuel Oil Utilization at Slab Furnaces) = 224,952 + 0.007 Fuel Oil Utilization at Slab Furnaces

h.) *Slab Furnaces*
(MMBTU/# Tons Production = 3.690)
(1.0363 × Natural Gas Utilized) + (0.15000 × Fuel Oil Utilized = 3.690 × # Slab Tons Produced

2. Base requirements of Fuels (Per Month)
a.) *Natural Gas Availability (Externally)*
—Present Allocation—45,000 MCF/Day
Sum of Natural Gas Utilization at the Eight Production Facilities ≤ 45,000 × Days/Month
b.) *Natural Gas at Steelworkers Boiler*
—Present Requirement =
1,000 MCF/day for pilots
Natural Gas Utilization at Steelworkers Boiler ≤ 1,000 × Days/Month
c.) *Natural Gas at Blast Furnace Boiler*
—Present Requirement =
1,000 MCF/day for pilots
Natural Gas Utilization at Blast Furnace Boiler ≤ 1,000 × Days/Month
d.) *Natural Gas at Coke Plant*
—Present Requirement =
6,700 MCF/Month
Natural Gas Utilization at Coke Plant ≤ 6,700

3. By-Product Fuel Availability Based on Production
a) *Coke Gas By-Product Availability*
—Coke Gas Produced at a Rate of 16.61 MCF/# Ton of Coke Production
Sum of Coke Gas Utilization at Coke Plant, Sinter Plant, Blast Furnace Boiler, Blooming Mill Soaking Pits, and Steel Works Boiler ≤ 16.61 MCF × # Tons Coke Produced
b) *Blast Furnace Gas By-Product Availability*
—Blast Furnace Gas Produced at a Rate of 59.75 MCF/MCF Wind Rate
Sum of Blast Furnace Gas Utilization at Blast Furnace and Blast Furnace Boiler ≤ 59.75 MCF × Wind Rate

4. External Fuel Source Supply Constraints
The external fuel source supply constraints were varied for each run of the model. They were of very simple form, for example:
Monthly Natural Gas Supply Availability ≤ 40,000 MCF × (days/month).

TEST RESULTS AND DISCUSSION

Numerous test runs of the fuel utilization linear programming model described above have been made, using a monthly time horizon. However, it should be noted that no specific time frame is inherent in the model and it is readily adaptable to shorter or longer time periods. In these test runs, various types of operating conditions have been examined. Specific test results will now be presented for the following six operating conditions:

1. Baseline condition—current operating conditions for the steel mill.
2. No venting of coke oven gas—utilize coke oven gas which is presently vented.
3. Coke oven underfiring with blast furnace gas, coke oven gas used at the hot strip slab furnaces—use of both by-product gases in the production process.
4. Natural gas availability assumed to be 50,000 MCF/day.
5. Natural gas availability assumed to be 40,000 MCF/day.
6. Natural gas availability assumed to be 35,000 MCF/day.

In Table 1, test results for these six operating conditions are presented for input data reflecting existing production levels.

Referring to Table 1, it can be seen that by using the coke gas that is presently vented (Run

TABLE 1
Test Results—Existing Production Levels

RESULTS	Run #1– BASELINE CONDITIONS	Run #2– NO VENTING OF COKE GAS	Run #3 (CG) @ [SF] (BG @ [CP]	Run #4 NATURAL GAS AVAILABILITY = 50,000 MCF/DAY	Run #5 NATURAL GAS AVAILABILITY = 40,000 MCF/DAY	Run #6 NATURAL GAS AVAILABILITY = 35,000 MCF/DAY
VALUE OF OBJ. FCN. (Total Cost of Fuel Distribution)	$2,580,606	$2,562,886	$2,322,472	$2,440,116	$2,926,096	$3,098,840
FUEL DISTRIBUTION PLAN:						
Coke Gas (MCF)						
Coke Plant	464,032	464,032	—	430,432	464,032	464,032
Sinter Plant	35,577	37,577	—	—	35,577	35,577
Blast Fce Boilers	—	—	—	—	—	—
Soaking Pits	176,769	176,769	176,769	176,769	176,769	176,769
Steelworks Boilers	297,117	325,022	—	366,294	297,117	297,117
Slab Furnaces	—	—	796,726	—	—	—
Blast Furnace Gas (MCF)						
Coke Plant	—	—	2,639,402	—	—	—
Blast Furnace	4,354,085	4,354,085	4,111,531	4,354,085	4,354,085	4,354,085
Blast Fce Boilers	3,859,591	3,859,591	3,859,591	3,859,591	3,859,591	3,859,591
Natural Gas (MCF)						
Coke Plant	6,700	6,700	6,700	23,722	6,700	6,700
Blast Furnace	—	—	21,603	—	—	—
Sinter Plant	—	—	18,023	18,023	—	—
Blast Fce Boilers	31,504	31,504	31,504	31,504	31,504	31,504
BOF	25,403	25,403	25,403	25,403	25,403	25,403
Soaking Pits	—	—	—	—	—	—
Steelworks Boilers	31,504	31,504	217,072	31,504	31,504	31,504
Slab Furnaces	524,889	524,889	211,247	614,877	224,889	74,889
Fuel Oil (Gal.)						
Steelworks Boilers	271,132	173,465	—	—	367,854	416,214
Slab Furnaces	621,696	621,696	—	—	2,694,296	3,730,596

#2 a savings of $17,720/month from current operating conditions (Run #1) is possible. This cost savings results because a total of 97,667 gallons of fuel oil are replaced with 27,905 MCF of coke gas, at the steelworkers boiler. The marginal value of the coke gas is $0.635/MCF, and thus a savings of $0.635/MCF × 27,905 MCF = $17,720 results.

The test run involving use of blast furnace gas at the coke ovens, and coke oven gas at the hot strip slab furnaces (Run #3) indicates that a saving of $258,134/month from current operating conditions (Run #1) is possible. For this run, no fuel oil is required and an excess of approximately 88,500 MCF/month of natural gas exists. Also, due to the high cost of replacing fuel oil at the slab furnaces with coke gas, it becomes less expensive to use a small amount of natural gas at the sinter plant and blast furnaces, rather than either coke gas or blast furnace gas.

The final three test runs summarized in Table 1 (Run's #4, #5, and #6) involve varying the natural gas availability under the baseline operating conditions. As can be observed in the last three columns of Table 1, the greatest fuel distribution cost increase occurs as the natural gas availability drops from 50,000 MCF/day to 40,000 MCF/day, i.e., Δ = $485,980/10,000 MCF/day = $48.60/MCF/day.

In Table 2, test results for the same size operating conditions are presented for input data reflecting increased production levels. Again, consider-

TABLE 2
Test Results-Increased Production Levels

RESULTS	Run #1 BASELINE CONDITIONS	Run #2 NO VENTING OF COKE GAS	Run #3 (CG) @ [SF] (BG) @ [CP]	Run #4 NATURAL GAS AVAILABILITY = 50,000 MCF/DAY	Run #5 NATURAL GAS AVAILABILITY = 40,000 MCF/DAY	Run #6 NATURAL GAS AVAILABILITY = 35,000 MCF/DAY
VALUE OF OBJ. FCN. (Total Cost of Fuel Distribution)	$3,815,570	$3,797,528	$3,498,121	$3,642,825	$4,161,060	$4,333,804
Coke Gas (MCF)						
Coke Plant	470,394	470,395	—	470,395	470,395	470,395
Sinter Plant	35,149	35,149	35,149	35,149	35,149	35,149
Blast Fce Foilers	—	—	—	—	—	—
Soaking Pits	290,834	290,834	290,834	209,834	209,834	209,834
Steelworks Boilers	270,960	299,373	—	270,960	270,960	270,960
Slab Furnaces	—	—	741,355	—	—	—
Blast Furnace Gas (MCF)						
Coke Plant	—	—	2,675,597	—	—	—
Blast Furnace	5,385,707	5,385,707	5,385,707	5,385,707	5,385,707	5,385,707
Blast Fce Boilers	4,005,985	4,005,985	3,291,196	4,005,985	4,005,985	4,005,985
Natural Gas (MCF)						
Coke Plant	6,700	6,700	6,700	6,700	6,700	6,700
Blast Furnace	—	—	—	—	—	—
Sinter Plant	—	—	—	—	—	—
Blast Fce Boilers	31,504	31,504	31,504	31,504	31,504	31,504
BOF	10,190	10,190	10,190	10,190	10,190	10,190
Soaking Pits	—	—	—	—	—	—
Steelworks Boilers	31,504	31,504	31,504	31,504	31,504	31,504
Slab Furnaces	540,102	540,102	540,102	690,102	240,102	90,102
Fuel Oil (Gal.)						
Steelworks Boilers	977,523	878,078	1,804,795	929,163	1,074,245	1,122,605
Slab Furnaces	3,698,013	3,698,013	1,103,269	2,661,713	5,770,613	6,806,913
Blast Furnace Boilers	—	—	439,834	—	—	—

able cost reductions are possible by not venting coke oven gas, or by using blast furnace gas at the coke ovens and coke oven gas at the hot strip slab furnaces. However, at the increased production rates (Table 2— Run #3), natural gas demand exceeds supply and the amount of coke gas available is insufficient to replace all fuel oil requirements. Indeed, demands on the blast furnace boilers necessitate the use of fuel oil. The test runs involving varying the natural gas availability again indicate that the greatest fuel distribution cost increase occurs as the natural gas availability decreases from 50,000 MCF/day to 40,000 MCF/day.

CONCLUSION

The paper has presented a linear programming approach to fuel utilization within the production environment of a large Midwestern steel mill. Test results involving various operating conditions indicate that considerable cost savings can be achieved by using a fuel allocation plan which more effectively utilizes by-product gases which are produced in the steelmaking process.

Application of this model to other steel mill operations could be expected to produce similar results, since virtually all steelmaking requires coke production and uses blast furnaces. Thus, the by-product gases are naturally produced. The biggest obstacle to their utilization is the physical layout of the steel mill. First, it must be possible to capture and store the by-product gases. Second, a means of transporting the by-product gases to other production units (i.e., an adequate piping network) must be available. Third, the energy consuming production units must be capable of utilizing the by-product gases. These physical conditions were present in the steel mill which was analyzed in this study. If they were not present in a steel mill, the capital costs required to secure them might well outweigh the operating cost savings. It may also be possible to extend this work to other metal processing industries, although this has not been done to date. If this were done, it would need to be done for metal processing industries which produce by-product energy sources which could be alternatively used as fuel sources in the production process.

Obviously, since the time at which the study was conducted (i.e., early 1976), fuel costs have increased dramatically, and the availability of externally purchased fuels have become more restricted. One extension of this work would involve restructuring the model, using current operating conditions and current costs. Assuming that the current operating conditions, as reflected in the revised constraint set, were not markedly more restrictive than the original operating conditions, we would expect greater cost savings to occur, since each term in the model's objective function would be simply scaled upward as a result of fuel cost increases. A more dramatic cost savings might well suggest the desirability of making increased capital expenditures to more efficiently capture and allocate the by-product gases.

The transference of this methodology to other processing industries is also being considered. The author is currently working with a large Southeastern based textile manufacturer to reduce energy related production costs. However, in this operating environment alternative energy sources are not produced as natural by-products of the production process. Thus, the problem becomes one of the efficient allocation of existing energy sources. Also, some of the energy sources cannot be obtained in a continuous fashion. Thus, the problem has a mixed integer programming structure rather than a linear programming structure. Interestingly, in a recent article appearing in *Interfaces* [6], an entire steelmaking operation in Sweden was modeled, using a mixed integer programming framework. Unfortunately, the approach described in this article did not appear to explicitly consider the fuel costs associated with the steelmaking process.

There are a number of other extensions and refinements for this model which are currently being examined. These include varying the costs of the fuels to test for the sensitivity of fuel replacement, adding other energy sources, such as electricity, and investigating problems associated with curtailment of natural gas and fuel oil availability.

ACKNOWLEDGEMENT

The author would like to gratefully acknowledge the original work done on this project by Mr. David A. Page, a graduate student in the School of Business Administration at the University of Missouri—St. Louis.

REFERENCES

1. Daellenbach, H. G. and E. J. Bell, *User's Guide to Linear Programming*, (Englewood Cliffs, N.J.: Prentice-Hall, Inc., 1970).

2. Dalal, J. G., "Evaluation of a Cooling Temperature Control Procedure For A Hot Strip Mill," *Journal of Quality Technology,* Vol. 10, No. 1, (January, 1978), pp. 31–39.

3. Hadley, G., *Linear Programming,* (Reading, Massachusetts: Addison-Wesley Publishing Company, Inc., 1963).

4. Skinner, W. and D.C.D. Rogers, *Manufacturing Policy In The Steel Industry,* (Homewood, Illinois: Richard D. Irwin, Inc., 1970).

5. *The Making of Steel,* (New York, N.Y.: The American Iron and Steel Institute, 1964).

6. Westerberg, C. H., B. Bjorklund, and E. Hultman, "An Application of Mixed Integer Programming In A Swedish Steel Mill," *Interfaces,* Vol. 7, No. 2, (February, 1977), pp. 39–43.

Reprinted, by permission, from Management Science, *Vol. 25,
No. 7, 1979. Copyright 1979 by The Institute of
Management Sciences.*

A CASE STUDY OF ENCODER SHIFT SCHEDULING UNDER UNCERTAINTY*‡

VINCENT A. MABERT†

This paper illustrates a shift scheduling procedure for a commercial bank's encoder work force for check processing in the presence of daily work load uncertainty. The author presents a chance constraint model for determining the appropriate safety capacity, analogous to safety stock in inventory theory, to meet varying volume demands when forecast errors are present. A series of tests are conducted to evaluate the model's performance under different operating costs, forecast errors, and volume arrival rates, which are based on data collected at Chemical Bank. The results indicate this model provides low cost solutions.

This study provides two contributions to managers and management scientists. First, even though the paper illustrates the encoder work force shift scheduling decision, the methodology presented can be extended to other service oriented organizations. The main elements that need to be present are: varying between day work loads, varying within day work loads, uncertainty in estimating work loads, and critical deadlines at specific times during the day. And second, a classification scheme is developed which indicates how the general shift scheduling problem in service organizations can be viewed. This classification system helps to structure this complex problem and indicates how this proposed procedure contributes to this important area.

(FINANCIAL INSTITUTIONS—BANKS; MANPOWER SCHEDULING; PROGRAMMING—STOCHASTIC, CHANGE CONSTRAINED)

1. Introduction

The literature during the last few years has seen a number of researchers investigate the shift scheduling decision in service organizations. This service sector research can be characterized along two dimensions to assist in focusing upon what prior work has been done and how this study contributes to the body of knowledge for this shift scheduling problem. First, prior research can be viewed by the *degree of demand certainty* present, where certainty implies deterministic demand and uncertainty indicates the presence of forecast error.

And second, Chase [4] provides a concept called the *degree of customer contact* for service operations. This continuum for service organizations ranges from pure service to quasimanufacturing. Pure service has the customer and server interacting continuously, like a patient in a hospital. On the other hand, quasimanufacturing requires only limited contact between the customer and the server, where a surrogate item (check in a bank's back office or a lab sample in a hospital) actually receives the processing. In general, those organizations faced with a pure service system attempt to provide service when demanded. However, in a quasimanufacturing situation, the organization can usually inventory the service demanded for a short period of time and process later.

Based upon the two way classification scheme presented above, Figure 1 presents the prior literature dealing with the shift scheduling problem. One quickly sees that a number of researchers have investigated the certain/deterministic demand situation. In only one work [2], dealing with a pure service environment, was there any attempt to recognize the uncertainty present in demand estimation. Personnel requirements per period were estimated by determining the number of individuals needed to meet a specified service level given the forecast error present.

* Accepted by David G. Dannenbring; received February 23, 1978. This paper was with the author 2 months for 2 revisions.

† Indiana University.

‡ This paper recieved the "Stanley T. Hardy Best Paper Award" from Midwest AIDS, May 1979.

This study investigates the empty cell in Figure 1, the quasimanufacturing situation when forecast errors are present. The specific organization under investigation is the check processing operations of a commercial bank. The presence of positive and negative forecast errors in this type of organization has different cost implications that should be addressed. In fact, many firms plan on having some excess staff to handle the uncertainty in forecasting because opportunity (shortage) costs are present. This is similar to the classic safety stock concept in inventory theory. It is important that the decison maker take into account these costs when arriving at an appropriate shift schedule. Scheduling too few workers increases the chance of poor service and increases opportunity costs, while assigning extra capacity increases operating costs per unit processed.

Degree of Customer Contact

Degree of Demand Certainty	Pure Service	Quasi-Manufacturing
Certain/ Deterministic	Henderson and Berry [5] [6] Raedels and Mabert [9]	Showalter, Krajewski, and Ritzman [10] Mabert [7]
Uncertain/ Forecasted	Buffa, Cosgrove, and Luce [2]	

FIGURE 1.   Shift Scheduling Research Classification.

The balancing of wage and opportunity costs represents the specific problem bank management faces for the check processing function. The lack of processing capacity can increase opportunity costs, since the presence of a large float reduces the amount of available funds for investment. Check processing is a highly automated function at most banks, except for the encoding phase. Many large banks employ over a hundred people for this particular task. Even with Electronic Funds Transfer Systems (EFTS) on the horizon, the load levels on this paper oriented system are projected to increase well into the 1980's. Therefore, management must make appropriate staffing decisions to minimize costs.

In this paper a chance constraint model for encoder shift scheduling is presented to provide low cost decisions. The model determines the timing and number of workers needed to meet projected work loads. It uses the labor wage rate, opportunity cost of foregone interest and forecast error as a basis for determining the appropriate shift schedule. The design of an encoder shift scheduling system at Chemical Bank [8] provides the basis for this model and the data to test its performance.

This paper will initiate the shift scheduling analysis by reviewing the elements that comprise the encoding function at Chemical Bank. Then a deterministic mathematical program formulation of the shift scheduling model is presented. Next, uncertainty is characterized and included in the model using a chance constraint approach. The following section outlines a set of experiments when forecast errors, opportunity costs, and arrival rates are varied to test the feasibility of the chance constraint approach to provide low cost solutions. Finally, a statistical analysis of the results is conducted and conclusions are presented.

2. Encoder Operations

Like many of the major New York banks, the encoding function at Chemical Bank represents a very labor intensive operation. The main processing center at 55 Water Street contains 100 encoding machines for encoding checks with magnetic ink, so that these checks can be automatically sorted by appropriate destination. At the same moment the checks are being sorted, the information is being recorded on a transaction file that is being used to update the master records.

Work arrives from branches throughout the Manhattan Island area. Most of the volume arrives in the late afternoon and must be processed by early evening if the bank is to maximize funds availability. Figure 2 illustrates one week's arrival pattern

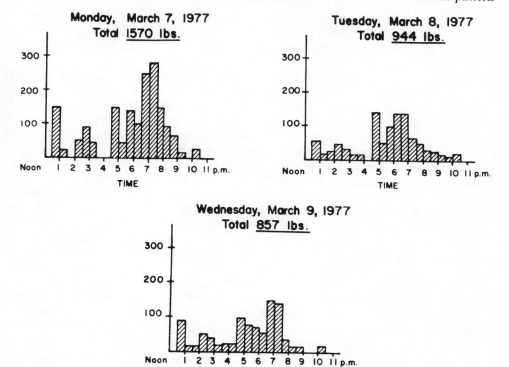

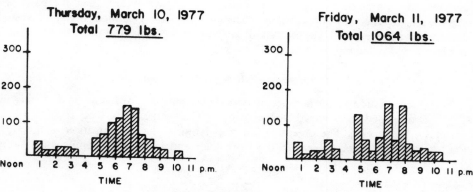

FIGURE 2. Check Volume Arrival at Water Street.

in half hour increments. One quickly sees that work starts to arrive just after the noon hour and peaks around 7:00 p.m. About 70 percent arrives between 4:30 p.m. and 8:00 p.m.

Chemical Bank utilizes a part-time work force for encoding. A few years ago the operators were all full-time employees, but management decided greater flexibility could be obtained with a part-time force. Two types of part-timers are employed: regulars and contract. Regulars are employees of the bank and are processed through Chemical's personnel office. Contract workers are actual employees of a service agency that the bank hires for short periods to help when work loads become heavy.

Workers are assigned to shifts of varying lengths from three to seven and a half hours. These shifts may overlap each other and vary in length. The operators are paid an hourly wage based on the number of hours worked. Those part-time workers scheduled to work on shifts to begin after 4:00 p.m. receive a 10 percent increase in wages to reflect a shift differential.

The processing rate of operators does vary, but productivity studies indicate it is small. The typical operator can encode 2.6 lbs. of items per hour. Operators also experience some fatigue on this repetitive task with a slight reduction in productivity during later hours of the shifts.

Management faces two major sources of uncertainty in making the shift scheduling decision: total daily check volume and the within day arrival rate. Chemical Bank experiences substantial variations in daily volume and a multivariable regression model [1] has been developed to predict daily volumes. It has proved to be a good procedure, providing forecasts with seven to ten percent forecast error. The model is updated monthly and has an R^2 that averages around 0.85.

The second source of uncertainty deals with the timing of work from the branches. As Figure 2 indicates, within day arrivals vary. For example, a comparison of Monday and Thursday arrival provides an interesting contrast. Monday's pattern contains a more spiked rate than Thursday. An analysis of historical data by half hour intervals for each day of the week indicated no statistical difference between daily arrival patterns at a 95% confidence level. The variations within days are due to weather storms and traffic congestion which affect the courier arrivals. An analysis of three months' arrivals provided a weighted period coefficient of variation of 0.24, which indicates substantial variation within the day.

Bank management also faces a time constraint. The encoding department is faced with a 10:30 p.m. deadline to get work done. Any checks not encoded by this time cannot be machine sorted and, therefore, Chemical cannot receive credit on those checks drawn against other banks throughout the country. On a typical day, Chemical will process $400 million in out-of-town or transit checks. Just a 1 percent holdover represents a substantial opportunity cost, which fluctuates with the interest rate. For example, if current short term money markets are at 8 percent, then the bank will experience a $222 loss (opportunity cost) per day for a million dollars invested. Therefore, management faces the task of keeping opportunity and operating costs at a minimum with adequate staff levels.

3. Deterministic Mathematical Formulation

The determination of the number of workers to employ at different times during the day can be stated as a mixed integer problem when the work load is known with certainty, Mabert [6]. The objective function requires the minimization of the wage and opportunity costs, subject to the work load and encoding machine availability. The model is:

$$\text{Min } Z = \sum_{jk} C_{jk} X_{jk} + \sum_{t} C_t' Y_t$$

subject to:

$$\sum_{jk} a_{tjk} X_{jk} + (Y_t - Y_{t-1}) \geq b_t, \qquad t = 1, 2, \ldots, T, \tag{2}$$

$$\sum_{jk} a'_{tjk} X_{jk} \leq M_t, \qquad t = 1, 2, \ldots, T, \tag{3}$$

$$X_{jk} = \text{integer}, \tag{4}$$

$$Y_t \geq 0, \tag{5}$$

where:

X_{jk} = the number of j type workers assigned to work shift k.
Y_t = the number of unprocessed items at the end of period t.
C_{jk} = the cost per worker j to work shift k.
C'_t = the opportunity cost of an unprocessed item missing its deadline at time t.
a_{tjk} = the process rate (in items/period) for worker j assigned to shift k for period t.
a'_{tjk} = a zero/one element in the matrix, indicating the absence (zero) or presence (one) in period t of worker j assigned to shift k.
b_t = the number of items arriving in period t and available for processing.
M_t = the number of available encoding machines in period t.
T = the number of periods in the work horizon.

Equation (1) represents the combined wage and opportunity cost to be minimized. Equation (2) is the traditional inventory identity function, where the greater than constraint allows for capacity to exceed available work in any period. Equation (3) represents the encoding machine limitations. An operator can not encode checks without a machine being available.

4. Chance Constraint Model

The major sources of uncertainty as indicated earlier were total daily volume and arrival rates within a given day. This makes b_t of equation (3) a random variable with a mean and distribution. Management would like to schedule the appropriate work force where the marginal additional of one more unit of operator capacity equals the marginal opportunity cost. Since we are dealing with a stochastic problem, equation (3) can be stated as a chance constraint [3], given by

$$P\left\{ \sum_{jk} a_{tjk} X_{jk} + (Y_t - Y_{t-1}) \geq E(b_t) \right\} \geq 1 - \alpha, \tag{6}$$

where α reflects the probability of not having enough capacity to meet expected work loads, $E(b_t)$. Since equation (6) can not be solved in its present form, it is converted to a deterministic equivalent [3].

$$\sum_{jk} a_{tjk} X_{jk} + (Y_t - Y_{t-1}) \geq B_t. \tag{7}$$

Now B_t represents the amount of work management should base the staffing decision upon. The determination of the appropriate B_t is a function of the expected volume, forecast error and costs.

Since close to 100% of all work arrives before 10:30 p.m., the deadline time, the uncertainty associated with daily volume is the major element. An analysis of historical arrival data indicated that 90% of all work arrives before 9:00 p.m., which Figure 2 confirms visually. Since an hour and a half exists before the deadline time and checks can be inventoried for short periods of time, the daily variations are more critical in work force timing and sizing considerations than within day variations.

Therefore, the daily forecast error is assumed to be the key element of uncertainty present in this study. The forecast model [1] provides the volume estimate ($\hat{V}$) and forecast error (s_v). The expected within day arrival proportion per period, $E(p_t)$, controls the rate that the work accumulates on a half hour basis. Knowing this information, B_t can be estimated as

$$B_t = (\hat{V} + Z_{1-\alpha} s_v) \cdot E(p_t), \tag{8}$$

where $Z_{1-\alpha}$ is the normal deviant reflecting the service level desired. The determinant of the appropriate service level can be obtained by equating the marginal cost of added capacity against holdover.

Let $v(x)$ represent the daily work load density function of items to be processed at the check processing department. Since the daily volume is a random variable, the probability of having V or fewer items arrive is given by

$$P(V) = \int_0^V v(x)dx. \tag{9}$$

Therefore, there is a $1 - P(V)$ chance that the daily load will exceed V items. To minimize processing costs, one equates the *expected* labor capacity cost to the *expected* opportunity cost of not having enough labor. The probability of daily volume exceeding V is given by

$$P'(V) = 1 - P(V) = 1 - \int_0^V v(x)dx = \int_V^\infty v(x)dx, \tag{10}$$

Let C_s represent the opportunity cost of a unit of capacity shortage and C_e the cost of a unit of extra capacity. Costs will be at a minimum where the expectations are equal.

$$C_s \cdot P'(V) = C_e \cdot P(V) = C_e \cdot (1 - P'(V)). \tag{11}$$

(This structure is similar to the well known *newsboy problem* of inventory control theory [11].) Therefore, based upon the economics of a unit of capacity and opportunity cost, we can obtain the appropriate breakeven probability for staffing. Solving equation (11), one obtains:

$$P'(V) = C_e/(C_e + C_s). \tag{12}$$

Assuming $v(x)$ to be normally distributed, $P'(V)$ can now be expressed using the normal deviate ($Z_{1-\alpha}$) and knowing the forecasted value ($\hat{V}$) and error standard deviation (s_v),

$$P'(V) = P[V \geqslant \hat{V} + Z_{1-\alpha} s_v] = \alpha. \tag{13}$$

5. Experimental Study

To test whether the preceeding model could adequately staff the encoder work force, a series of tests were conducted. The first test involved using the current data at the Water Street facility of Chemical Bank to develop parameter values to determine staffing decisions. Then using the chance constraint model with two levels of daily forecast errors (CV of 0.1 and 0.2), opportunity costs at 8%, a forecasted value at average and high levels–a series of shift scheduling decisions were generated using different values of $Z_{1-\alpha}$. The normal deviate was varied from zero to 2.25 in increments of 0.25.

The decisions were put into a computer model that simulated 500 hundred days, where daily loads changed and within day rates varied. Three replications were conducted using unique seeds. The results are summarized in Table 1 and indicate a minimum exists in the range of 0.75 to 1.25 for $Z_{1-\alpha}$. You can check these results

TABLE 1
Shift Schedule Cost Performance for Two Load Levels and Forecast Errors

Z^* $1 - \alpha$	Average Volume Level		High Volume Level	
	CV = 0.1**	CV = 0.2	CV = 0.1	CV = 0.2
0	$3360***	$3979	$4394	$4983
0.25	3223	3724	4272	4740
0.50	3139	3524	4178	4561
0.75	3100	3423	4114	4527
1.00	3031	3363	4070	4547
1.25	3009	3364	4060	4589
1.50	3014	3399	4092	4650
1.75	3040	3464	4128	4724
2.00	3055	3555	4170	4800
2.25	3101	3655	4216	4894

* The specified level of confidence desired.
** The coefficient of variation reflects the amount of forecast error present (assumed normally distributed).
*** The average daily cost (wage and opportunity) for three replications of 500 days each.

against equation (12) and (13). The average hourly wage is $5.75 and the opportunity cost of not having one hour of capacity is $31.45. Based on these costs, the breakeven probability is $P'(V) = 0.15$, which equates to a normal deviant value of 1.05. Thus, one sees that the estimated $Z_{1-\alpha}$ value for the minimum cost is approximately equal to the low costs for the simulation tests.

Table 1 also indicates the extent of improvement over just applying the deterministic formulation of the model. By setting $Z_{1-\alpha}$ to equal zero, the model determines a shift configuration excluding the presence of uncertainty. Applying this configuration in the 500 day simulator, one sees that costs range from $351, $615, $334, and $456 respectively above the minimum for the four test problems illustrated. This represents a 12%, 18%, 8%, and 10% difference between the deterministic and chance constraint approach.

A second evaluation of the model's performance was conducted with different work load levels, forecast errors, and opportunity costs. Expected (forecasted) volume levels were set at two levels for the Water Street facility. They were at a moderate (857 lbs.) and high (1428 lbs.) levels based upon historical loads. The forecast error, as measured by the coefficient of variation, was set at three levels (0.05, 0.15, and 0.25) of the forecasted volume. The opportunity cost was at three levels reflecting a 4.5%, 8%, and 20% investment market. Six test problems were developed that incorporated different random arrival rate patterns. Based upon the six test problems and factor levels settings, initial shift schedule decisions were developed which should provide low total cost solutions.

Each set of decisions was then put into a computer simulation model where 500 operating days were simulated, and three replications were conducted. The simulation model used the same settings that the shift schedule decisions were based upon. However, the daily volume and arrival rates were allowed to vary stochastically, using a normally distributed random number generator. Average daily total cost was collected for each replication and test problem within factor level setting.

Since the model does not guarantee an optimal solution, a systematic search was conducted to find the lowest cost known for the set factor levels and test problems investigated. Operators were systematically added and subtracted from different shifts. Then the 500 day simulation was executed to see if costs were reduced. The search continued until no improvement could be found. The lowest cost solution was divided into the model's average replication solution. The results are summarized in Table 2.

The results in Table 2 indicate a number of interesting facts. First, the model produces solution costs that are less than 2% above the known lowest cost. Second, the variations in solution costs are small, with 0.014 being the largest standard deviation. Third, at higher expected volume levels, performance is slightly better. Fourth, increasing cost factor levels are matched by increases in poorer performance by the model. And fifth, the level of forecast error does not affect performance. An ANOVA was conducted on the experimental factors of forecast error, volume, and cost. The test indicated that there was no difference in performance of the model due to forecast error levels at the 99% confidence level. However, there was a significant difference due to volume and cost.

TABLE 2

Average and Standard Deviation Results of Model Costs Divided by Lowest Known Cost

Forecast Error CV	Opp. Cost Rate	Forecasted Volume Level			
		Moderate		High	
		Mean*	Std. Dev.***	Mean	Std. Dev.
5%	4.5%	1.004	0.004	1.003	0.002
	8.0%	1.008	0.006	1.005	0.004
	20.0%	1.016	0.014	1.008	0.007
	Average	1.009	0.010	1.005	0.005
15%	4.5%	1.005	0.003	1.005	0.003
	8.0%	1.005	0.003	1.005	0.003
	20.0%	1.011	0.005	1.005	0.005
	Average	1.007	0.004	1.005	0.003
25%	4.5%	1.009	0.004	1.008	0.005
	8.0%	1.007	0.002	1.006	0.004
	20.0%	1.010	0.003	1.006	0.003
	Average	1.009	0.004	1.007	0.004

* The mean of 18 observations where the model cost was divided by the lowest known cost.
** The standard deviations of the 18 observations cost performance.

6. Conclusions

In the prior sections, a procedure for encoder operator shift scheduling was outlined based upon operating data from Chemical Bank. The technique utilizes the procedures of chance constraint programming and inventory theory to determine useful shift schedules when uncertainty exists in the daily volume levels and within day arrival rate. A series of tests were conducted with the model and compared against the lowest known costs. The results indicate good performance, with penalities being less than two percent for a wide range of operating conditions.

The approach outlined here could be extended to other service organizations with varying daily volumes, within day variations, and dispatch deadlines utilizing the quasimanufacturing approach to operations. For example, the U.S. Post Office and United Parcel Service are two organizations with similar problem structures. Although neither has an explicit opportunity cost like a commercial bank, their cost could be viewed as an implicit service level goal. This goal, such as 95% service, would specify the level of capacity in relationship to the uncertainty level. One would have to develop a forecasting model and error distribution to operationalize the level of coverage that is needed. If both daily and within day variations are critical to staffing, then a joint probability distribution could be developed to provide the appropriate level of coverage.

References

1. Boyd, K. and Mabert, V. A., "A Two State Forecasting Model at Chemical Bank for Check Processing," *J. Bank Res.*, Vol. 5, No. 1 (Summer, 1977), pp. 101–107.
2. Buffa, E. S., Cosgove, M. J. and Luce, B. J., "An Integrated Work Shift Scheduling System," *Decision Sci.*, Vol. 7, No. 4 (October, 1976), pp. 620–630.
3. Charnes, A. and Cooper, W. W., "Chance-Constrained Programming," *Management Sci.*, Vol. 6, No. 1 (October, 1959), pp. 349–355.
4. Chase, Richard, "Where Does a Customer Fit in a Service Operation?" *Harvard Business Rev.*, Vol. 56, No. 6 (November-December, 1978), pp. 137–143.
5. Henderson, W. and Berry, W. L., "Heuristic Methods for Telephone Operator Shift Scheduling: An Experimental Analysis," *Management Sci.*, Vol. 22 (August, 1976), pp. 1372–1380.
6. ———— and ————, "Determining Optimal Shift Schedules for Telephone Traffic Exchange Operations," *Decision Sci.*, Vol. 6, No. 8 (Janaury 1977), pp. 239–255.
7. Mabert, V. A., "Heuristic Work Force Scheduling with Variable Shift Lengths and Labor Productivity Differences: A Case Study of Encoder Staffing," *Proceeding of the Disaggregation Conference*, Ohio State University, Columbus, Ohio, March 1977.
8. Mabert, V. A., Fairhurst, R. and Kilpatrick, M. J., "An Encoder Daily Shift Scheduling System at Chemical Bank," *J. Bank Res.* (to appear).
9. Raedels, A. and Mabert, V. A., "A Comparison of Labor Shift Scheduling Techniques with Labor and Facility Constraints," Working Paper, School of Business, Indiana University, Bloomington, Indiana.
10. Showalter, M. J., Krajewski, L. J. and Ritzman, L. P., "Manpower Allocation in U. S. Postal Facilities: A Heuristic Approach," *Computers and Operations Res.*, Vol. 4 (1977), pp. 257–269.
11. Wagner, H., *Principles of Operations Research*, Prentice-Hall, Englewood Cliffs, N. J., 1969.

3. Production Planning Under Multiple Goals and Objectives

INTRODUCTION

This chapter focuses on the development and discussion of production planning models with multiple goals and objectives. Most work done in multiple-goal or objective mathematical models for production planning has concerned the aggregate output planning problem.

The goal-programming and multiple-objective linear-programming models discussed here deal with extensions of the conventional linear-programming models for aggregate production planning. These models are concerned not only with the conventional goals and objectives such as cost minimization or profit maximization but also with those that conform to the company's needs for aggregate production planning. Such goals and objectives can deal with varied considerations—maximizing resource utilization, minimizing overtime manpower, maximizing production of specific item types in given periods, etc. These goals and objectives are often conflicting. Such conflicts between management goals can be analyzed in terms of the trade-offs that result from attaining particular goals, as opposed to those resulting from attaining others.

The majority of the model structures presented in the series of papers in this section can be implemented by adopting commercially available linear-programming computer software. The models proposed here are adaptable to different actual aggregate production planning problems.

Goal Programming

Goal programming is an extension of linear programming. It can handle decision problems dealing with a single goal and multiple subgoals, as well as problems with multiple goals and subgoals. In addition, goal programming can provide an optimal solution to an objective function in which the goals are in multiple dimensions.

In the typical real-world situation, goals set by the decision-maker are achievable only at the expense of other goals, which are often incompatible. Thus, there is a need to establish a hierarchy of importance among these incompatible goals so that the most important are satisfied or reach the point beyond which no further improvements are desirable. If the decision-maker can provide an ordinal ranking of goals in terms of their contributions or importance to the organization, the problem can be solved using goal programming.

The basic concept of goal programming involves incorporating all goals into a single model. Instead of trying to maximize or minimize the objective criterion directly (as in linear programming), the deviations between goals and achievable limits dictated by the set of system constraints are minimized within the pre-emptive goal-priority structure. These deviational variables (known as slack variables in the linear-programming environment) have a slightly different meaning in the goal-programming environment. They are split into positive and negative deviations from each goal or subgoal. The objective function may also include real variables with ordinary pre-emptive weights.

Developing the goal-programming model is similar to developing models under linear programming. The first step is defining the decision variables X_1, X_2, ... Then, all managerial goals must be specified and ranked by priority. Even though it is generally not possible for management to relate the various goals on a cardinal scale, they can usually associate an ordinal ranking with each of their goals or objectives. The distinction of goal programming is that it provides for the solution of problems involving multiple (often conflicting) goals arranged according to a priority structure specified by management.

The linear goal-programming model can be mathematically expressed as:

$$\text{Minimize } Z = \left[\sum_{i \in I_1} (w_1^+ d_{1i}^+ + w_1^- d_i^-), \quad \ldots \quad \sum_{i \in I_k} (w_k^+ d_i^+ + w_k^- d_i^-) \right] \tag{1}$$

subject to

$$\sum_{i=1}^{n} a_{ij} x_j - d_i^+ + d_i^- = b_i \qquad i = 1, 2, \ldots, m$$

$$\text{All } x_j, \, d_i^+, \, d_i^- \geqslant 0$$

where $(b_1, b_2, \ldots, b_m)$ expresses m goals, a_{ij}'s express the relationship between goals, x_j's represent the decision variables, d_i^+ and d_i^- represent deviations from these goals grouped in k priorities with appropriate weights w_i^+, w_i^- in each. The form of general goal programming has been provided in the first chapter.

Management must analyze each goal in the model to determine if overachievement or underachievement is satisfactory. For example, if overachievement of the ith goal is acceptable, the overachievement deviation d_i^+ can be eliminated from the objective function; similarly, if underachievement is satisfactory, d_i^- can be eliminated from the objective function. If exact achievement of the goal is desired, both d_i^+ and d_i^- must be included in the objective function and ranked according to their pre-emptive priority weights. Observe that at least one of the two deviations for each goal will always equal zero (since overachievement and underachievement are not possible at the same time).

In goal programming, the most important goal is optimized to the extent possible before the second goal is considered. This procedure is followed within the given system constraints of the problem until all goals are fulfilled to the extent possible.

Multiple-Objective Linear Programming (MOLP)

Multiple-objective linear programming allows analyzing an optimization problem in terms of the separate and often-conflicting objectives inherent in many real-world decision problems. Moreover, the value of each effectiveness measure or criterion can be compared and contrasted for the candidate solutions, because of the explicit treatment given to each of the objectives in the analysis. Rather than seeking a single solution and thus imposing inflexibility on decision-makers, MOLP can be used to produce a set of alternative solutions for evaluation. These solutions can be evaluated with respect to any qualitative political, social, legal, moral, or other factors decision-makers might wish to consider.

An MOLP model with n decision variables, m constraints, and k maximization objectives can be formulated as

$$\text{Maximize } \sum_{j=1}^{n} c^1_j x_j = z_1,$$

$$\text{Maximize } \sum_{j=1}^{n} c^2_j x_j = z_2,$$

$$\vdots$$

$$\text{Maximize } \sum_{j=1}^{n} c^k_j x_j = z_k,$$

subject to

$$\sum_{j=1}^{n} a_{ij} x_j = b_i \quad i = 1, \ldots, m$$

$$x_j \geq 0 \qquad j = 1, \ldots, n$$

(2)

One extreme or limiting approach to solving (2) is to have the decision-maker specify the preferences in terms of fixed points

$$\lambda_l > 0 \ (1 \leq l \leq k), \quad \sum_{l=1}^{k} \lambda_l = 1$$

for each objective such that the solution to the single-objective linear-programming problem

$$\text{Maximize } \sum_{i=1}^{k} \lambda_l \sum_{j=1}^{n} c^l_j x_j$$

subject to

$$\sum_{j=1}^{n} a_{ij} x_j = b_i \qquad i = 1, \ldots, m$$

(3)

will be the decision-maker's most desired solution. A problem with this single-solution approach is that it requires a decision-maker to agree upon a single most desirable weighting vector λ. Decision-makers are often unwilling or unable to reduce multiple objectives to a single objective in this manner.

However, to allocate the problem of a-priori weights determination, a method referred to as multi-parametric programming has been developed. Instead of maximizing the objective function $z_1(x) \ldots z_k(x)$ as separate parallel entities, they can be combined in a linear case into a multi-parametric aggregate

$$z(\lambda, x) = \sum_{i=1}^{k} \lambda_i z_i(x) = \lambda z(x) \tag{4}$$

where $\lambda = (\lambda_1, \ldots, \lambda_k)$ is a vector of parameter weights such that $\lambda_i \geq 0$ and

$$\sum_{i=1}^{i} \lambda_i = 1$$

In linear cases, the *nondominated** set of X can be computed by maximizing $z(\lambda, x)$ for all possible combinations λ satisfying the above conditions.

When $z(\lambda, x) = \lambda_1 z_1(x) + \ldots + \lambda_k z_k(x)$ is maximized over a convex set X, each nondominated extreme point of X will be associated with a particular subset of λ's such that $z(\lambda, x)$ will reach its maximum at that point. That is, the set of all parameters can be decomposed into subsets associated with individual nondominated solutions. This methodology is not a method to approximate a decision-maker's utility function; it is simply a computational device to trace out the whole or part of the nondominated set.

In multiple-objective linear programming, the number of computed nondominated solutions is often too large for a decision-maker to intelligently identify the preferable one. Various approaches to prune or filter the size of the nondominated solution to a manageable size have been developed (Steuer and Hams 1980). As an extension of the multiparametric decomposition method, the decision-maker specifies some lower or upper bound l_i or u_i for each weight λ_i. The resulting set of nondominated solutions will be significantly smaller and more manageable. The decision-maker only obtains the cluster of nondominated solutions as specified by the bounds on the weights. From the solution set, the decision-maker selects the preferred solutions. To keep the number of nondominated solutions from going beyond a specified level and only representing a given portion of the nondominated set, a filtering process is applied. In this process of filtering, the redundant solutions are removed (Steuer and Hams 1980).

Multiple Goals and Objectives in Aggregate Production Planning and Scheduling

Among the earliest attempts at incorporating multiple goals and objectives into the modeling process for aggregate production planning is the work of Lee and Jaaskelainen (1971). This early work focused on the development of a simple goal-programming structure and how it incorporates various management goals into previously oversimplified linear-programming models for aggregate production planning. Other management goals than merely minimizing total cost were included in this early model structure—for example, minimizing the underutilization of production capacity, the underutilization of sales capacity, and overtime production. Although this model is small and relatively simplified, it does show the development of actual management goals and their trade-offs. Furthermore, this model structure included restrictions on demand, assemblies, inventory, and production capacity.

---

*A point within a set is nondominated in that there is no other feasible point at which the same or better performance could be achieved with respect to all criteria.

Another early use of a multiple-goal formulation on the aggregate production planning process was by Goodman (1974). Goodman's work attempts to approximate and reformulate the original quadratic cost model for aggregate production planning of Holt (1955). This model structure, however, did not provide production management with direct measures of the often-conflicting objectives in the aggregate production planning process and, thus, did not allow viewing the effects of variations in the objectives and goals directly and logically. It merely used goal programming as a method for linearization of Holt's original model's objective function. Deviational variables were also introduced earlier by Haussmann and Hess (1960) for the same purpose. (They did not call it goal programming, since the Holt term was coined by Charnes and Cooper a year later [see Welam 1976]).

An extension of Goodman's model, presented by Laurent (1976), is called range programming. Range programming relies on a satisficing range concept rather than on the optimal point concept of goal programming. In practice, the range programming formulation allows acceptable values for a variable to be restricted within a range derived by managers from their practical experiences. This concept offers the decision-maker the additional opportunity of minimizing and satisficing the objectives simultaneously. The model structure allows the use of multiple management goals to minimize regular payroll, hiring and layoff, overtime and idle time, and inventory holding. It provides direct insight for behavioral objectives, policy consideration, and directions by varying priority levels and goals.

Variations of the previous goal-programming models that consider more detailed objectives for aggregate output planning have been presented by Fisk (1974) and Hindelang and Hill (1978). These included minimizing capacity underutilization, excess queue level during lead time (Fisk 1974), goals on worker productivity (learning) and motivation (through job rotation), inventory investment, and subcontracting costs (Hindelang and Hill 1978). Such details increase the flexibility and adaptability of the basic goal-programming model for many aggregate production planning situations. On the other hand, they require additional analyst expertise, usually available only in larger companies, and may restrict management's willingness to employ such details when first confronted with the problem. A more realistic case is presented by Lockett and Muhlemann (1978) in developing an aggregate schedule to smooth factory workload and meet delivery dates. Finally, a comprehensive exposition on the subject is the article by Masud and Hwang in this chapter.

A summary and presentation of multiple-objective optimization applications to different production planning problems is provided in the remainder of this chapter.

REFERENCES

Fisk, J. C. 1974. A goal programming model for output planning. *Decision Sciences* 10:593-603.

Goodman, D. A. 1974. A goal programming approach to aggregate planning of production and work force. *Management Science* 20:1569-1575.

Haussmann, R., and S. W. Hess. 1960. A linear programming approach to production and employment scheduling. *Management Technology* (January):46-51.

Hindelang, T. J., and J. L. Hill. 1978. A new model for aggregate output planning. *OMEGA* 6:267-272.

Holt, C., F. Modigliani, and H. A. Simon. 1955. A linear decision rule for production employment scheduling. *Management Science* (October).

Laurent, G. 1976. A note on range programming: Introducing a satisficing range in a LP. *Management Science* 22(6):713-716.

Lee, S. M., and V. Jaaskelainen. 1971. Goal programming: Management's math model. *Industrial Engineering* (February): 30-35.

Lockett, A. G., and A. P. Muhlemann. 1978. A problem of aggregate scheduling—An application of goal programming. *International Journal of Production Research* 16:127-135.

Steuer, R. E., and F. U. Hams. 1980. Intra-set point generation and filtering in decision and criterion space. *Computers & Operations Research* 7(1-2):41-54.

Welam, U.P. 1976. Comments on goal programming for aggregate planning. *Management Science* 22(6):708-712.

APPLICATIONS OF PRODUCTION PLANNING
UNDER MULTIPLE GOALS AND OBJECTIVES

The six articles in this section discuss applications of production planning under multiple goals and objectives.

"A Practical Approach to Production Scheduling," by S. M. Lee and L. Moore, gives a simple, practical managerial aspect to the use of goal programming in the process of aggregate production scheduling. The authors stress management's need to consider a multitude of goals and objectives in the decision-making process rather than using the single-dimensional approach of previous linear-programming studies. They first review, in a qualitative manner, the basic nature of goal programming.

Discussion of the model begins with the development of a scenario surrounding a company's schedule for producing expensive electric transformers to meet nine deliveries for a U.S. government contract. To meet this schedule efficiently and effectively, the management of the company must be concerned with a number of goals:

1. Operating within the limits of productive capacity
2. Meeting the contracted delivery date
3. Operating at a minimum level of 80 percent of regular-time capacity
4. Keeping inventory below a certain level
5. Minimizing total production and inventory costs
6. Minimizing overtime production.

The goal-programming model of this formulation is then traced by discussions of: (1) various model constraints on production capacity, manpower and production requirements, (2) goal constraints, and (3) objective function. The discussion ends with the solution of the sample model and its managerial implications to the company.

Because this article provides the practitioner with a concise and easy-to-follow discussion, it is presented first in this section. However, it makes several simplifying assumptions that will restrict the model's use in several real situations—for example, the company maintains a fixed workforce whose learning is not influenced by the type and size of the contracts, and there is no allowance for costs associated with changes in production levels and capacity underutilization.

"An Aggregate Production Model and Application of Three Objective Decision Models," by Abu S. Masud and C. L. Hwang, develops a multiple-objective model formulation of a multiproduct, multiperiod aggregate production planning problem. The authors solve a small numerical example of the model structure using three multiple-objective decision-making methods—goal programming, step method, and sequential multiple-objective linear programming.

The solutions of these methods to the given aggregate planning model structure are highlighted, especially with regard to their implications and the practical problems of their usage.

A large section of the paper details the development of the mathematical programming model. The situation that serves as the basis of the model development refers to a multiperiod production planning problem of a multiproduct manufacturer. This manufacturer wishes to find, for each product and time period, the optimum levels of production, inventory, and the regular and overtime workforces. The model structure includes constraints for labor force balance, production balance, production capacity, and regular/overtime labor.

The objectives of the model are to

1. Maximize the contribution to profit and overhead
2. Minimize capital investment and inventory
3. Minimize backorders
4. Minimize changes in workforce levels.

The three solution methods of the model are thoroughly analyzed and compared. The practicality in solving actual planning problems with multiple goals is highlighted and an appendix summarizes the three multiple-objective programming methods.

"Multiple Criteria Optimization in Production Planning: An Application for Large Industrial Goods Manufacturers," by Lee Krajewski, presents the development of a realistic model of an aggregate production plan for two plants of a truck-axle component manufacturer. The company produces 12 product families and 90 finished-good items. A major complicating factor in developing an aggregate production plan is the major setups of machinery for the various families.

The management of the company considers four criteria in developing its aggregate production plan:

1. Maximizing utilization of plant #1
2. Maximizing utilization of plant #2
3. Maximizing customer service
4. Minimizing total production costs.

The model structure seeks to minimize the weighted deviations from the stated management goals, subject to a series of constraints on inventory, demand setups, and work levels. The complete model is a mixed-integer program consisting of 882 variables (120 binary setup variables) and 722 rows. Because of the size of the problem and the expense of running a commercial mathematical-programming system, a heuristic solution technique was used. The procedure is a quasi-utility approach in which the decision-maker supplies weights for the criteria in an iterative fashion until a satisfactory solution is found. This procedure includes the repeated use of a rounding procedure for determining optimal values of the binary variables.

"A Multiple-Goal Linear-Programming Model for Coordinated Production and Logistics Planning," by K. D. Lawrence and J. J. Burbridge, presents a model for coordinating a company's production and logistics planning in a multiple-goal environment. Several of the company's key objectives considered in developing its aggregate production and logistics planning are:

1. Maximizing total sales revenue for specific location and customer
2. Minimizing the total production and distribution cost
3. Maximizing the production of a particular item at a particular location.

Additionally, the model structure includes several economic and operational constraints:

1. Total demand for each item at each customer location
2. Available production capacity at each production location
3. Maximum shipping weights for all items from each production location
4. Total budget for production and transportation for all locations and for all items.

The paper also highlights the multiple-objective linear-programming structure and methodologies developed by Steuer for solving such problems. A small-scale example is solved using the computerized methodology of Steuer. This methodology produced a set of efficient extreme-point solutions in terms of both the number of items produced and the associated objective-function values. These solutions allow the decision-maker to evaluate the problem with respect to fulfilling the objectives of management and in terms of other qualitative factors that are not directly measured.

"Chemical Production Planning via Goal Programming," by S. H. Zanakis and J. S. Smith, develops a goal-programming model for planning production quantities of various intermediate and final chemical products in the presence of multiple and often-conflicting objectives. This article concentrates on production planning in a chemical plant area that has had little, if any, significant attention.

Chemical-plant production planning concerns itself with determining, for each product, production quantities that will maximize management's goal attainment while meeting forecasted demand, satisfying various economic and operational constraints. The model was developed around a simple industrial case in which cell liquor is produced in two production units and subsequently transformed into four final products in four chemical reactors.

The management goals in the model were

1. Operating within available production capacity
2. Satisfying material balances
3. Maintaining production and sales limits
4. Attaining outside company product sales goals
5. Attaining corporate production goals
6. Maximizing profits
7. Minimizing transfers of all liquor to reduce unproductive costs and environmental overflows
8. Maximizing sales
9. Minimizing underutilization of cell room capacities.

The authors analyzed various goal priorities and levels to evaluate different what-if scenarios to arrive at the most satisfying solution for management. The unusual feature of this article is that it applies goal programming to *continuous*-process production planning.

"Multiple Goal Operations Management Planning and Decision Making in a Quality Control Department," by K. D. Lawrence and J. I. Weindling, focuses on the development of an operations planning model for a quality-control department in a large-scale, multiproduct chemical company. The model served as a planning aid for the management in allocating its resources to the quality testing and control tasks to assure the quality of the numerous products.

The quality-control department of the company operates on a wide variety of management objectives. To allocate resources to the quality-control testing effectively, the following management objectives must be included in the allocation process:

1. Adhere to a budget level for total operational costs of sampling and testing
2. Minimize the amount of outside quality testing and storage
3. Minimize the amount of quality testing done beyond a short period after production, to reduce spoilage and delivery delays
4. Minimize the amount of testing during maintenance periods in internal facilities.

The model structure also contains operational constraints for:

1. Assuring the testing of produced items
2. Capacities on internal testing facilities.

Finally, the paper deals with two problems of goal programming:

1. Uncertainty of priority structure levels
2. Ranges of the management goal levels. This problem is examined by solving statistically sampled problem structures and then clustering the observed solutions into a suitable form for management review.

A PRACTICAL APPROACH TO PRODUCTION SCHEDULING

Sang M. Lee
Laurence J. Moore
Virginia Polytechnic Institute & State University
Blacksburg, Virginia

Introduction

Mathematical programming techniques have developed quite rapidly in the years since the simplex method for solving linear programming problems was devised by George Dantzig in 1947. New areas of mathematical programming such as nonlinear programming, quadratic programming, piece-wise linear programming, integer programming, and stochastic programming have all contributed toward advancing the power of analysis for managerial decision making. Also, in many cases, new algorithms have been developed to aid in the solution of problems formulated as mathematical programming models.

However, management's use of the solutions yielded by mathematical programming has very often been restricted due to one limitation common to all of the above-mentioned techniques. This limitation is the requirement that the decision maker formulate, for inclusion in the mathematical programming model, a unidimensional objective function. That is, all managerial or organizational objectives must be reduced to a single, measurable criterion. Reality would suggest that management must consider not one, but a multitude of objectives or goals when evaluating most decision problems. Experience has shown that the reduction of diverse objectives, often measured on different scales, to some sort of utility function is simply not a practical approach for most cases.

The Goal Programming Approach

The purpose of this paper is to present and illustrate an application to production scheduling of an important new technique for the analysis of problems involving multiple goals and linear relationships. The technique is called Goal Programming, which is closely related to linear programming[1]. Goal Programming (G.P.), however, does not include the limitation of linear programming requiring a unidimensional objective function. Also, in many cases where linear programming would yield an infeasible solution, goal programming will still yield a feasible solution.

The basic concept of goal programming involves incorporating all managerial goals into the constraints of the model. The objective function of the goal programming model then includes only the deviational variables of the various model constraints which measure the achievement of managerial goals. The objective function of goal programming is always of the minimization type. That is, the objective is to minimize the deviations from the goals which have been incorporated into the constraints of the model[2]. One of the advantages of goal programming is that it can be solved by a modified version of the familiar simplex method[3].

The approach to constructing the goal programming model is somewhat similar to linear programming. The decision variables are first defined, i.e., x_1, x_2, x_3. Following this step, all managerial goals are specified and ranked as to priority. The ranking process includes a fundamental difference from other mathematical programming techniques. Although management may know what goals they wish to achieve, it is not generally possible to relate the various goals to one another on a cardinal scale. They can, however, associate a priority, or ordinal ranking, with each of their goals or objectives.

The constraints of the goal programming model will generally include such operational constraints as are typical to linear programming. In addition, all managerial goals must be incorporated into constraints also. All constraints, operational or managerial goals, include both slack and surplus variables, generally referred to as deviational variables in goal programming.

The objective function of goal programming attempts to minimize the deviations (values of deviational variables) from the specified right hand side values of the goal constraints. This is done, in the objective function, by associating with each deviational variable the priority of each goal, as specified by management. Thus, goal programming involves an iterative process by which the highest goal is first considered. This is followed by an attempt to achieve the second goal, to the extent possible, given the higher order goal achievement already accomplished and the constraint relationships. This process continues until all goals have been considered in the order of the ranking specified by management.

As higher order goals are achieved or partially achieved, the feasible solution space is diminished for lower order goals. Since some goals may actually conflict, the feasible solution space may actually result in what would be an infeasible solution for an L.P. type problem. Goal programming, however, will simply achieve higher order goals at the expense of lower order goals, and indicate in the final solution the extent to which some goals have not been met, i.e., some constraints violated.

The following example of a multiperiod production sheduling problem will be solved by goal programming in order to illustrate the preceding discussion.

A Multiperiod Production Scheduling Problem

A manufacturing firm which produces large, expensive electric transformers, custom-built according to specifications, has just received word that they have been awarded a contract from the U.S. Government for 34 new units. The contract also specifies the required delivery schedule (Table 1) for the

Month	Quantity
1	3
2	8
3	10
4	13

TABLE 1. Quantities Contracted to Deliver

Month	Regular Time	Overtime
1	7	3
2	8	3
3	9	3
4	10	3

TABLE 2. Maximum Production Capacity by Month

finished products, to meet the government's planned installation dates.

The manufacturing firm is relatively small and can, therefore, only handle one production contract at a time. They do have some flexibility, however, in that they can operate on an overtime basis for short periods of time in order to produce at a level beyond normal capacity. They can also temporarily lay off some short-tenured regular production workers, down to about 80 percent of normal capacity.

The firm estimates that it can produce, immediately upon setup of the production facilities, a maximum of seven units per month on a regular time basis. It is also projected that an additional three units per month could be produced by operating on an overtime basis. However, the firm also feels, based on past experience, that a learning curve effect may be included such that regular time productive capacity will increase at a rate of about one unit per month. The resulting projected schedule of production capacity is given in Table 2.

The firm's accounting department has determined the expected variable cost per transformer which is primarily a function of labor costs, to be four thousand dollars, on a regular time basis. Since overtime is paid at the rate of one and a half times regular time, the variable cost would be six thousand dollars per unit on an overtime basis. However, two factors affect these costs over the time period in question. First, due to the learning curve effect, the variable cost for units produced on regular time decreases at a rate of approximately $100 per month. The learning curve effect is not included in overtime production since management has found from past experience that other factors tend to offset the effect of learning when operating on an overtime basis. The second factor to be considered is a new union contract which takes effect at the beginning of the third month. The result of the union-management negotiation was an increase in wages by 50 percent. Thus the expected variable cost per transformer, excluding the learning curve effect, for units produced on regular time would become six thousand dollars apiece. The resulting schedule of anticipated variable cost per unit produced, on regular time and overtime, over the four month period is given in Table 3.

Month	Regular Time	Overtime
1	4.0	6.0
2	3.9	6.0
3	5.8	9.0
4	5.7	9.0

TABLE 3. Variable Production Cost Per Unit (in thousands of dollars)

Since production requirements and productive capacity are considerably different over the four month period, and since production costs also vary from month to month, the problem of devising an optimal production schedule is not trivial. An additional factor which must be included, at this point, is the opportunity to produce for inventory. The government will take delivery of the contracted units only according to the prescribed schedule. Since the firm has no excess storage capacity, any excess units produced and held for delivery must be shipped to another firm's warehouse. Also, the units require special servicing immediately prior to delivery. Therefore, stored units must be shipped back to the plant for servicing and then delivered. Thus, inventory costs are relatively high at a rate of one thousand dollars per unit per month stored. The firm would like to avoid producing for inventory if at all possible.

Management would obviously like to minimize the total production and inventory costs in their determination of the multiperiod production schedule. That is one of their goals. However, other goals and operational constraints also come into play, which must be considered by management in their decision process.

First, management has determined, based on production equipment and other facilities available, that they cannot exceed the previously stated production limits. Thus, this is an operational constraint which, in the short space of four months, cannot be altered. Second, management feels that if they do not meet the specified delivery schedule contracted for, they will probably never be able to obtain another contract from the U.S. Government. Since they do the majority of their business with the government, they cannot accept that possibility. Thus, as far as management is concerned, the production requirements schedule is, for all practical purposes, another operational constraint.

Another goal of management, which is very high on their list of priorities, is to keep production at a level of at least 80 percent of normal productive capacity. Management has found that operation at a level of less than 80 percent of capacity introduces prohibitively high costs. Not only is it difficult to lay off employees below that level due to their seniority on the job, but also the costs associated with rehiring and training during a production run are very high. Labor problems, along with the fact that equipment idle for a period must be again started up, results in more increased costs. Thus, utilization of less than 80 percent of productive capacity is highly undesirable.

A fourth goal of management is to keep the level of inventory at a maximum level of three units. Again, management has found through experience that when the number of excess units in storage exceeds three, the associated costs become prohibitive.

Management has determined that the production capacity and production requirements constraints must obviously be met. They also place very high priorities on operating at a level of at least 80 percent of normal capacity and on keeping inventory to a maximum of three. Thus, the objective of minimizing the total production and inventory costs follows the above goals. A final goal of management is to keep overtime production to a minimum. Overtime operation involves not only additional labor costs but also taxes the equipment resulting in increased repair costs. They have also found that the quality of items produced drop off, and the frequency of accidents increase on overtime operation.

A summary of managerial goals, including both the meeting of operational constraints and striving to achieve other objectives, will now be presented. These goals will be presented in the order in which they are ranked by management, where P_1 equals the highest priority.

Management Goals

P_1: Operate within the limits of productive capacity
P_2: Meet the contracted delivery schedule
P_3: Operate at a minimum level of 80 percent of regular time capacity
P_4: Keep inventory to a maximum of three units
P_5: Minimize total production and inventory costs
P_6: Hold overtime production down to a minimum

Formulation of the Goal Programming Model

The Goal Programming model will be presented by first identifying the problem variables, followed by formulation of the model constraints required by either operational or managerial goals. Included with each goal constraint discussion will be a specification of the corresponding term of the objective function, including managerial priorities and appropriate constraint deviational variables. Lastly, the complete goal programming model will be presented.

A. Model Variables

x_1 = Quantity of product produced on regular time in period 1
x_2 = Quantity of product produced on regular time in period 2
x_3 = Quantity of product produced on regular time in period 3
x_4 = Quantity of product produced on regular time in period 4
x_5 = Quantity of product produced on overtime in period 1
x_6 = Quantity of product produced on overtime in period 2
x_7 = Quantity of product produced on overtime in period 3
x_8 = Quantity of product produced on overtime in period 4

B. Model Constraints and Objective Function Components

(1) The production restrictions must be formulated as operational constraints, based on available productive capacity, both on regular time
and on overtime. These constraints are given as follows:

Regular Time	Overtime
$x_1 \leq 7$	$x_5 \leq 3$
$x_2 \leq 8$	$x_6 \leq 3$
$x_3 \leq 9$	$x_7 \leq 3$
$x_4 \leq 10$	$x_8 \leq 3$

With the addition of the deviational variables, standard to goal programming, these constraints become:

$$x_1 + d_1^- - d_1^+ = 7 \qquad x_5 + d_5^- - d_5^+ = 3$$
$$x_2 + d_2^- - d_2^+ = 8 \qquad x_6 + d_6^- - d_6^+ = 3$$
$$x_3 + d_3^- - d_3^+ = 9 \qquad x_7 + d_7^- - d_7^+ = 3$$
$$x_4 + d_4^- - d_4^+ = 10 \qquad x_8 + d_8^- - d_8^+ = 3$$

Since the first goal (an operational constraint) requires that we not exceed
productive capacity, the objective function will attempt to minimize, with the
highest priority, any excess. Thus, the first term of the objective function will
be formulated as:

$$\text{Minimize } P_1 \cdot \sum_{i=1}^{8} d_i^+$$

(2) The production requirements, based on the contracted delivery
schedule, may also be viewed as quasi-operational constraints. These,

however, could also easily be viewed as goals of management. These constraints are given as follows:

$$x_1 + x_5 \geq 3 \qquad\qquad\qquad\qquad\qquad\qquad \text{(Period 1)}$$

$$x_1 + x_5 - 3 + x_2 + x_6 \geq 8 \qquad\qquad\qquad\qquad \text{(Period 2)}$$

$$x_1 + x_5 - 3 + x_2 + x_6 - 8 + x_3 + x_7 \geq 10 \qquad\quad \text{(Period 3)}$$

$$x_1 + x_5 - 3 + x_2 + x_6 - 8 + x_3 + x_7 - 10 + x_4 + x_8 \geq 13 \qquad \text{(Period 4)}$$

These constraints then reduce to:

$$x_1 + x_5 \geq 3$$

$$x_1 + x_2 + x_5 + x_6 \geq 11$$

$$x_1 + x_2 + x_3 + x_5 + x_6 + x_7 \geq 21$$

$$x_1 + x_2 + x_3 + x_4 + x_5 + x_6 + x_7 + x_8 \geq 34$$

The deviational variables of goal programming are next added to yield the following:

$$x_1 + x_5 + d_9^- - d_9^+ = 3$$

$$x_1 + x_2 + x_5 + x_6 + d_{10}^- - d_{10}^+ = 11$$

$$x_1 + x_2 + x_3 + x_5 + x_6 + x_7 + d_{11}^- - d_{11}^+ = 21$$

$$x_1 + x_2 + x_3 + x_4 + x_5 + x_6 + x_7 + x_8 + d_{12}^- - d_{12}^+ = 34$$

The second goal is to meet the delivery schedule prescribed by the contract. Therefore, the objective function will attempt to minimize any underachievement of that goal, as follows:

$$\text{Minimize } P_2 \cdot \sum_{i=9}^{12} d_i^-$$

(3) The goal to operate at a minimum level of 80 percent of regular time capacity is based on the fact that it is very difficult and costly to lay off production workers with high seniority on the job. Also, when equipment is shut down for a period of a month or longer, the start-up costs are quite high when the production level is later raised to require their use. This goal also requires the formulation of the appropriate model constraints, as follows:

$$x_1 \geq .8 \ (\ 7) \approx x_1 \geq 5$$

$$x_2 \geq .8 \ (\ 8) \approx x_2 \geq 6$$

$$x_3 \geq .8 \ (\ 9) \approx x_3 \geq 7$$

$$x_4 \geq .8 \ (10) \approx x_4 \geq 8$$

These constraints then reduce to the following goal programming equations, with the addition of deviational variables.

$$x_1 + d_{13}^- - d_{13}^+ = 5$$

$$x_2 + d_{14}^- - d_{14}^+ = 6$$

$$x_3 + d_{15}^- - d_{15}^+ = 7$$

$$x_4 + d_{16}^- - d_{16}^+ = 8$$

The third goal, to operate at a minimum level of 80 percent of regular time productive capacity, is included in the objective function as:

$$\text{Minimize } P_3 \cdot \sum_{i=13}^{16} d_i^-$$

(4) The inventory goal of three or less must also be formulated as a constraint. It is the surplus of product produced beyond the amount contracted for, in any given period, which will constitute the inventory. We can, therefore, construct the appropriate constraints by addign the maxmum allowable inventory level (3) to the right hand sides of the delivery requirements constraints and insert new deviational variables. These constraints are developed as follows:

$$x_1 + x_5 - 3 \leq 3$$

$$x_1 + x_2 + x_5 + x_6 - 11 \leq 3$$

$$x_1 + x_2 + x_3 + x_5 + x_6 + x_7 - 21 \leq 3$$

$$x_1 + x_2 + x_3 + x_4 + x_5 + x_6 + x_7 + x_8 - 34 \leq 3$$

Rearrangement of terms and addition of deviational variables yields the following:

$$x_1 + x_5 + d_{17}^- - d_{17}^+ = 6$$

$$x_1 + x_2 + x_5 + x_6 + d_{18}^- - d_{18}^+ = 14$$

$$x_1 + x_2 + x_3 + x_5 + x_6 + x_7 + d_{19}^- - d_{19}^+ = 24$$

$$x_1 + x_2 + x_3 + x_4 + x_5 + x_6 + x_7 + x_8 + d_{20}^- - d_{20}^+ = 37$$

The fourth goal, to keep inventory to no greater than three units, will be included in the objective function as follows:

$$\text{Minimize } P_4 \cdot \sum_{i=17}^{20} d_i^+$$

(5) The goal of management to minimize total production and inventory costs must also be included in the goal programming model as a constraint. This constraint simply sets total production and inventory costs equal to zero, and then attempts to minimize the positive deviation from this goal in the objective function. We recall that inventory holding cost was one thousand dollars per unit per month. The constraint is given as follows:

$$4.0x_1 + 3.9x_2 + 5.8x_3 + 5.7x_4 + 6.0 \, (x_5 + x_6) + 9.0$$
$$(x_7 + x_8) + (x_1 + x_5 - 3) + (x_1 + x_2 + x_5 + x_6 - 11) +$$
$$(x_1 + x_2 + x_3 + x_5 + x_6 + x_7 - 21) + (x_1 + x_2 + x_3 +$$
$$x_4 + x_5 + x_6 + x_7 + x_8 - 34) \geq 0$$

With consolidation of terms and insertion of a positive deviational variable, the constraint becomes:

$$8.0x_1 + 6.9x_2 + 7.8x_3 + 6.7x_4 + 10.0x_5 + 9.0x_6 +$$
$$11.0x_7 + 10.0x_8 - d_{21}^+ = 69$$

The fifth goal, to minimize total production and inventory costs, will be included in the objective function by minimizing the surplus beyond 69, as follows:

$$\text{Minimize } P_5 \cdot d_{21}^+$$

(6) The final goal of keeping overtime production to a minimum requires the following constraints:

$$x_5 \geq 0$$
$$x_6 \geq 0$$
$$x_7 \geq 0$$
$$x_8 \geq 0$$

Again, we must allow for the possibility that overtime production may occur. Thus, we introduce surplus deviational variables as follows:

$$x_5 - d_{22}^+ = 0$$

$$x_6 - d_{23}^+ = 0$$

$$x_7 - d_{24}^+ = 0$$

$$x_8 - d_{25}^+ = 0$$

The sixth goal, to keep overtime operation to a minimum, is reflected in the objective function by minimizing the positive deviations of the above constraints, as follows:

$$\text{Minimize } P_6 \cdot \sum_{i=22}^{25} d_i^+$$

C. The Complete Goal Programming Model

$$\text{Min } Z = P_1 \sum_{i=1}^{8} d_i^+ + P_2 \sum_{i=9}^{12} d_i^- + P_3 \sum_{i=13}^{16} d_i^- + P_4 \sum_{i=17}^{20} d_i^+ + P_5 d_{21}^+ + P_6 \sum_{i=22}^{25} d_i^+$$

Subject to:

$$x_1 \qquad\qquad\qquad\qquad + d_1^- - d_1^+ = 7$$

$$x_2 \qquad\qquad\qquad + d_2^- - d_2^+ = 8$$

$$x_3 \qquad\qquad\qquad + d_3^- - d_3^+ = 9$$

$$x_4 \qquad\qquad + d_4^- - d_4^+ = 10$$

$$x_5 \qquad\qquad + d_5^- - d_5^+ = 3$$

$$x_6 \qquad\qquad + d_6^- - d_6^+ = 3$$

$$x_7 \qquad + d_7^- - d_7^+ = 3$$

$$x_8 + d_8^- - d_8^+ = 3$$

$$x_1 \qquad + x_5 \qquad\qquad\qquad + d_9^- - d_9^+ = 3$$

$$x_1 + x_2 \qquad + x_5 + x_6 \qquad\qquad + d_{10}^- - d_{10}^+ = 11$$

$$x_1 + x_2 + x_3 \qquad + x_5 + x_6 + x_7 \qquad + d_{11}^- - d_{11}^+ = 21$$

$$x_1 + x_2 + x_3 + x_4 + x_5 + x_6 + x_7 + x_8 + d_{12}^- - d_{12}^+ = 34$$

$$x_1 \qquad\qquad\qquad\qquad + d_{13}^- - d_{13}^+ = 5$$

$$x_2 \qquad\qquad\qquad + d_{14}^- - d_{14}^+ = 6$$

$$x_3 \qquad\qquad\qquad + d_{15}^- - d_{15}^+ = 7$$

$$x_4 \qquad\qquad\qquad + d_{16}^- - d_{16}^+ = 8$$

$$x_1 \qquad\qquad + x_5 \qquad\qquad + d_{17}^- - d_{17}^+ = 6$$

$$x_1 + x_2 \qquad\quad + x_5 + x_6 \qquad\qquad + d_{18}^- - d_{18}^+ = 14$$

$$x_1 + x_2 + x_3 \qquad + x_5 + x_6 + x_7 \qquad + d_{19}^- - d_{19}^+ = 24$$

$$x_1 + x_2 + x_3 + x_4 + x_5 + x_6 + x_7 + x_8 \quad + d_{20}^- - d_{20}^+ = 37$$

$$8.0x_1 + 6.9x_2 + 7.8x_3 + 6.7x_4 + 10.0x_5 + 9.0x_6 + 11.0x_7 + 10.0x_8 \qquad - d_{21}^+ = 69$$

$$x_5 \qquad\qquad\qquad - d_{22}^+ = 0$$

$$x_6 \qquad\qquad\qquad - d_{23}^+ = 0$$

$$x_7 \qquad\qquad\qquad - d_{24}^+ = 0$$

$$x_8 \qquad\qquad\qquad - d_{25}^+ = 0$$

$$x_1, \ x_2, \ldots x_8, \ d_1^-, d_2^-, \ldots d_{20}^-, d_1^+, d_2^+, \ldots, d_{25}^+ \geq 0$$

Model Results and Discussion

The preceding described model was solved by a specially designed computer program modification of the simplex method. The results yielded were as follows:

Variables:

$x_1 = 6.0$ $\qquad\qquad\qquad\qquad\qquad x_5 = 0.0$

$x_2 = 8.0$ $\qquad\qquad\qquad\qquad\qquad x_6 = 0.0$

$x_3 = 9.0$ $\qquad\qquad\qquad\qquad\qquad x_7 = 0.0$

$x_4 = 10.0$ $\qquad\qquad\qquad\qquad\quad x_8 = 1.0$

From the above solution results the multiperiod production (and inventory) scheduling solution may be summarized in Table 4.

In addition, the production and inventory costs which resulted are given in Table 5.

Goal Attainment

The results of the solution, in terms of goal attainment, are given as follows:

Production Capacity (P_1)	Achieved
Product Delivery (P_2)	Achieved
Minimum Utilization of Production Capacity (P_3)	Achieved
Inventory Capacity (P_4)	Achieved
Minimization of Production and Inventory Cost (P_5)	Not Achieved
Minimization of Overtime Production (P_6)	Not Achieved

Month	Regular Time Production	Overtime Production	Production for Delivery	Surplus to Inventory
1	6	0	3	3
2	8	0	8	3
3	9	0	10	2
4	10	1	13	0

TABLE 4.   Production and Inventory Quantities

Period	Regular Time Production	Overtime Production	Inventory	Totals
1	24.0	0	3.0	27.0
2	31.2	0	3.0	34.0
3	52.2	0	2.0	54.2
4	57.0	9.0	0	66.0
Totals	164.4	9.0	8.0	181.4

TABLE 5.   Summary of Production and Inventory Costs (in thousands of dollars)

Thus, the results of the goal programming solution indicate that, given the goal priority structure and model constraints, production should be scheduled within normal operational capacity in the first three months. This does, of course, include a surplus of three units to be held in inventory in months one and two, and two units in month three. The total production of 23 units within the normal capacity was sufficient to meet the delivery requirements in the first three months. This did result in operating a less than 100 percent of regular time capacity in month one. Also, in the fourth month, overtime production of one unit was required to satisfy product delivery requirements of 13 units.

The results indicate that the first four most important goals specified by management were completely attained. The last two goals were only partially achieved. Of course, it was expected that the fifth goal, minimization of total production and inventory costs could never reach zero. As indicated previously, the total production and inventory cost was $181,400. This represents the minimum costs possible to attain the specified heirarchy of goals. The sixth goal, which was minimization of overtime production, was in direct conflict was the second, higher priority goal, for product delivery requirements. Hence, overtime production of one unit was yielded and violation of the overtime constraint for month four was allowed by the goal programming procedure.

Conclusion

A relatively new subset of mathematical programming, called goal programming, has been presented as a powerful aid to managerial decision making. The problem of multiperiod production scheduling was illustrated as an important area of application for goal programming. Numerous other real-world applications might also have been selected.

In general, goal programming performs three types of analysis: (1) identification of the input (resources) requirements to attain the desired goals; (2) the degree of goal attainment with the given inputs; and (3) the degree of goal attainments under various combinations and goal structures. The model illustrated provided the second type of analysis. The results of the model appear to be realistic and satisfactory for the problem. If the decision maker desired to pursue further analysis in terms of sensitivity of the solution, it could be easily accomodated by pursuing the first and third types of analysis.

It has been shown that problems involving multiple and even conflicting goals can be formulated and solved with goal programming. The primary requirement of goal programming, which is the same as linear programming, is that the model relationships be linear. Goal programming, however, allows the decision maker to include a heirarchy of goals or objectives without requiring their reduction to a single dimension criterion. Due to the popularity and general knowledge of linear programming, goal programming can be readily understood. Likewise, most practical applications of linear programming can be easily converted to goal programming problems in which the decision maker is allowed to incorporate all relevant managerial goals in their heirarchy of importance.

References

(1) For the classic work which introduced the original concept of goal programming see, A. Charnes and W.W. Cooper, *Management Models and Industrial Applications of Linear Programming*. (New York: John Wiley and Sons, Inc., 1961). The preceding is a highly theoretical presentation of goal programming. The technique of goal programming has, however, been developed extensively in the last several years along the lines of practical application by Professor Sang M. Lee and his associates. See for example, S.M. Lee and M.M. Bird, "A Goal Programming Model for Sales Effort Allocation," *Business Perspectives*, Vol. 7, No. 4, Summer 1970, pp. 17-21; S.M. Lee, "Goal Programming: Management's Math Model," *Industrial Engineering*, January 1971, pp. 30-35; S.M. Lee, "Decision Analysis Through Goal Programming," *Decision Sciences*, Vol. 2, No. 2, April 1971, pp. 172-180; S.M. Lee and E.R. Clayton, "A Goal Programming Model for Academic Resource Allocation," *Management Science*, Vol. 17, No. 8, April 1972.

(2) The general GP model can be expressed as:

$$\text{Minimize} \quad \sum_{i=1}^{m} (d_i^+ + d_i^-)$$

$$\text{subject to:} \quad AX - Id^+ + Id^- = b$$

$$x, d^+, d^- \geqslant 0$$

where m goals are expressed by an m component column vector $b(b_1, b_2, ..., b_m)$, A is an m by n matrix which expresses the relationship between goals and subgoals, $X(X_1, X_2, ..., X_n)$ represents variables involved in the subgoals, d^+ and d^- are m components column vectors for the variables representing deviations from goals, and I is an m by m identity matrix.

Now, each one of the m goals must be analyzed in terms of whether over- or underachievement of the goal is satisfactory. If overachievement is acceptable, d^+_i can be eliminated from the objective function. On the other hand, if underachievement is satisfactory, d^-_i should be left out of the objective function. If the goal must be achieved exactly as defined, both d^+_i and d^-_i must be in the objective function.

The deviational variables d_i^+ and d_i^- must be ranked according to their priorities, from the most important to the least important. If goals are classified in k ranks, the priority factor $P_j (j = 1,2,..., k)$ should be assigned to the deviational variables. The priority factors have the following relationship: $P_j \ggg k \cdot P_{j+1}$ $(j = 1,2,..., k-1)$, which implies that the multiplication of k, however large it may be, cannot make P_{j+1} greater than or equal to P_j.

(3) For a computer program of the modified simplex method solution to GP, see S.M. Lee, *Goal Programming for Decision Analysis*, Auerbach, 1972, pp. 126-160.

About the Authors—

DR. SANG M. LEE *is Associate Professor of Management at Virginia Polytechnic Institute and State University. Dr. Lee received his Ph.D. in Management Science at the University of Georgia in 1968. Dr. Lee has published numerous articles, including such journals as Industrial Engineering, Management Science, and Decision Sciences. He is a member of AIDS, TIMS, and Academy of Management.*

DR. LAURENCE J. MOORE *is Assistant Professor of Management at Virginia Polytechnic Institute and State University. Dr. Moore received his D.B.A. in Statistics at Arizona State University in 1970. Dr. Moore was previously head of quantitative studies at Continental Bank in Chicago, and Senior Analyst in Long Range and Capital Planning for American Oil Company. He is a member of AIIE, TIMS, and AIDS.*

Reprinted, by permission, from International Journal of
Production Research, *Vol. 18, No. 6, 1980.*

An aggregate production planning model and application of three multiple objective decision methods†

ABU S. M. MASUD‡ and C. L. HWANG§

This paper presents a multiple objective formulation of the multi-product, multi-period aggregate production planning problem. The proposed model provides for individual consideration of the conflicting multiple objectives without resorting to *a priori* trade-off decisions through subjective cost estimation. A numerical example is solved using three Multiple Objective Decision Making Methods.

Introduction

An aggregate production planning problem, like many other real life problems, involves multiple objectives which are, more often than not, conflicting. The conflict arises because improvement in one objective can only be made to the detriment of one or more of the rest of the objectives. In the context of a 'typical' aggregate production planning problem, the multiple objectives may be:

(i) Maximize contribution to profit and overhead (or, conversely, minimize cost),

(ii) Minimize amount of inventory,

(iii) Minimize backorders (or shortages),

(iv) Maintain a balanced labour force,

(v) Maximum use of existing production facilities,

(vi) Minimize use of overtime, etc.

Some examples of conflict in these objectives are: decrease in inventory level may necessitate increasing use of overtime or decreased customer service and hence less profit; less balanced work force leads to less favourable employee relations and more cost; increasing backorder or shortages may result in unfavourable customer service, lost sales and less profit.

In a traditional single objective aggregate production planning model, estimation of costs associated with each of the above objectives is made. A total cost function is then formed which includes all the individual cost elements in some suitable functional relationship (Silver 1967, Eilon 1975). However, the estimation of the intangible cost which constitutes an important segment of these costs is very difficult, if not impossible. In such situations, management is often required to make subjective estimates of these costs without having the opportunity to make an intelligent trade-off between the objectives. These estimates, notwithstanding their

---

Received 14 April 1980.

†An extended version of this article was presented at the joint TIMS/ORSA National Meeting, Los Angeles, California, November 1978.

‡ Department of Industrial Engineering, Wichita State University, Wichita, KS67208, U.S.A.

§ Department of Industrial Engineering, Kansas State University, Manhattan, KS. 66506, U.S.A.

subjectivity, affect the final solution critically. While a post-optimal parametric analysis of the cost estimates enables one to estimate some of the trade-offs made, the fundamental problems with the traditional approach are that it conceals the issue of conflicting objectives and the necessity of making informed trade-offs to arrive at an acceptable solution.

This paper proposes an aggregate production planning model for multiple-product, single-facility case where the conflicting multiple objectives are treated explicitly. A numerical example is next solved using three Multiple Objective Decision Making (MODM) methods. The methods used are: Goal Programming (GP), Step Method (STEM), and Sequential Multiple Objective Problem Solving (SEMOPS). Implications and practical problems associated with the use of the three MODM methods are also discussed.

Since most of the MODM methods are of relatively new origin, a very brief review of the three methods used in this paper will be presented in the Appendix. For a detailed and systematic review of all the MODM methods, readers may refer to Hwang and Masud (1979).

The next section contains the detailed description of the proposed model and is followed by details of results and their discussion. The final section contains the concluding remarks.

A multiple objective model

Problem definition

The situation of interest is the aggregate multi-period production planning problem of a multi-product manufacturer who wants to find, for each product and each of the planning periods, the 'best' production level, inventory level, and amount of overtime production. He also wants to find for each period the work-force level. The problem also involves an element of product-mix decision. The projected maximum demands of each product are not necessarily constant from period to period. In addition, a portion of the projected demand (which can also vary from period to period) must be satisfied in that particular period. The rest of the projected sales can either be backordered or not satisfied at all. However, all backorders must be fulfilled within the next period.

The decision variables are: regular time production, overtime production and sales of each product in each period, and workers hired (or fired) in each period. The state variables are: inventory (or backorder) of each product at the end of each period, and the work-force level in each period. Initial values about the inventory (or backorder) level of each product and the work-force level are assumed to be known.

Notation

Variables:

B_{it} = backorder of product i at the end of period t (units)
H_t = worker hired in period t (man-day)
I_{it} = inventory of product i at the end of period t (units)
L_t = worker lay-off in period t (man-day)
P_{it} = regular time production of product i in period t (units)
S_{it} = product i sold in period t (units)
W_t = work-force level in period t (man-day)
Y_{it} = overtime production of product i in period t (units)

Parameters and constants:

a_i = labour time for product i (man-hour/unit)

b_i = machine time for product i (machine-hour/unit)

c_{1i} = production cost (other than labour cost) for product i ($/unit)

c_{2t} = labour cost in period t ($/man-day)

c_{3t} = overtime labour cost in period t ($/man-hour)

c_{4i} = standard cost per unit of product i ($/unit)

M_t = regular time machining capacity in period t (machine-hour)

$\bar{M}_{t\,min}$ = lower bound on the utilization of machine capacity in period t (machine-hour)

r_i = per unit sales revenue of product i ($/unit)

$S_{it\,min}$ = minimum sales (which cannot be backordered) of product i in period t (units)

$S_{it\,max}$ = maximum forecasted sales of product i in period t (units)

$W_{t\,max}$ = maximum work force available in period t (man-day)

α_t = fraction of regular machine capacity available for use in overtime in period t

β_t = fraction of regular work force available for overtime use in period t

δ = regular time per worker (man-hour/man-day)

Initial values:

B_{i0} = outstanding backorder of product i at start of planning horizon (units)

I_{i0} = inventory of product i at the start of planning horizon (units)

W_0 = work-force at the start of planning horizon (man-day)

Constraints

For each period, there are three sets of balance equations for labour, product, and production capacity. Inventories (or backorders) and work-force levels provide the link between successive periods.

(*a*) Labour balance

$$W_t = W_{t-1} + H_t - L_t, \quad t = 1, \ldots, T \tag{1}$$

$$W_t \leqslant W_{t\,max}, \qquad t = 1, \ldots, T \tag{2}$$

$$\sum_i a_i P_{it} \leqslant \delta W_t, \qquad t = 1, \ldots, T \tag{3}$$

$$\sum_i a_i Y_{it} \leqslant \delta \beta_t W_t, \qquad t = 1, \ldots, T \tag{4}$$

$$H_t L_t = 0, \qquad t = 1, \ldots, T \tag{5}$$

Equations (1) ensure that the available labour-force in any period equals labour-force in the previous period plus labour-force change in the current period. (2) is used to set the limit of maximum available (or employable) labour-force in any period. This maximum can be dictated by labour market or available plant capacity. (3) and (4) limit the regular time and overtime production, respectively, to the available labour. (5) ensures that either net hiring or net firing of labour takes place in a period, but not both.

217

(b) *Product balance*

$$I_{it} - B_{it} = I_{it-1} - B_{it-1} + P_{it} + Y_{it} - S_{it} \qquad \begin{aligned} &i = 1, \ldots, N; \\ &t = 1, \ldots, T \end{aligned} \qquad (6)$$

$$S_{it\,\min} \leqslant S_{it} \leqslant S_{it\,\max}, \qquad \begin{aligned} &i = 1, \ldots, N; \\ &t = 1, \ldots, T \end{aligned} \qquad (7)$$

$$P_{it} + Y_{it} + I_{it-1} - B_{it-1} \geqslant S_{it\,\min}, \qquad \begin{aligned} &i = 1, \ldots, N; \\ &t = 1, \ldots, T \end{aligned} \qquad (8)$$

$$I_{it} B_{it} = 0, \qquad \begin{aligned} &i = 1, \ldots, N; \\ &t = 1, \ldots, T \end{aligned} \qquad (9)$$

Equation (6) ensures that the amount sold of each product in a period plus the inventory (or backorder) at the end of the period equals the total supply consisting of inventory (or backorder) from the previous period plus the regular and overtime production in the current period. The upper- and lower-bound on the sales of each product in a period is provided by (7). Equation (8) ensures that shipments are made for that portion of demand which must be satisfied in the current period and also that backorders are not carried over for more than one period. Equation (9) is used to ensure that either inventory or backorder will be in solution.

(c) *Production capacity balance*

$$\sum_i b_i P_{it} \leqslant \bar{M}_t, \qquad t = 1, \ldots, T \qquad (10)$$

$$\sum_i b_i Y_{it} \leqslant \alpha_t \bar{M}_t, \qquad t = 1, \ldots, T \qquad (11)$$

$$\sum_i b_i P_{it} \geqslant \bar{M}_{t\,\min}, \qquad t = 1, \ldots, T \qquad (12)$$

Total per period regular time and overtime production are limited by the available production capacity by (10) and (11) respectively. Equation (12) ensures that the utilization of production capacity will be at least up to a minimum level.

Depending on the actual problem one can add other resource balance constraints. If all the objective equations are linear, then (5) and (9) can be dropped.

Objectives

Of the objectives listed before, the following four have been included in the model. One can, of course, use a different set of objectives to suit the actual problem.

(i) Maximize contribution to profit and overhead,

(ii) Minimize capital investment in inventory,

(iii) Minimize backorders,

(iv) Minimize changes in work-force level.

$$\text{Max} f_1 = \sum_t \sum_i r_i S_{it} - \sum_t \sum_i c_{1i}(P_{it} + Y_{it}) - \sum_t c_{2t} W_t - \sum_t \sum_i c_{3t}(a_i Y_{it}) \qquad (13)$$

(revenue)   (production cost   (regular   (overtime
other than labour) labour cost)   cost)

This objective is for contribution to profit and overhead.

$$\text{Min} f_2 = \sum_t (H_t + L_t) \qquad (14)$$

This is to minimize the changes in work-force level.

$$\text{Min} f_3 = \frac{1}{T} \left\{ \sum_i \sum_t c_{4i} I_{it} \right\} \qquad (15)$$

This is to minimize the inventory investment.

$$\text{Min} f_4 = \frac{1}{T} \left\{ \sum_i \sum_t r_i B_{it} \right\} \qquad (16)$$

This is to minimize the backorders.

Comparison with other models

Table 1 shows a concise comparison of the principal features of the proposed model with two other models (Jaaskelainen 1969, Wallenius 1975). Additional differences between the models are also due to different mathematical equations used. The proposed model can be considered as a combination and extension of both these models. Two other MODM models in production planning related area are: a logistics planning model (Lawrence and Burbridge 1976) and a blending mix decision model (Lawrence and Burbridge 1977). However, these two models are completely different, in context, from the proposed model.

Numerical example

Tables 2–4 give numerical data of a hypothetical two-product, eight-period problem for the application of the model.

Results

The results from the three MODM methods is given in Table 5 which shows the achievements of the objectives. The first row shows the ideal solutions, that is, the optimum solutions considering each objective individually. In all the methods, the authors acted as Decision Maker (DM). All results were obtained by using LP package MPS/360 in an IBM 370/158 computer.

Four GP solutions were obtained using two sets of goals and two different priority structures. GP model 1 and 4 have different sets of goals but the same priority structure of goals. Model 1 and 2 have the same set of goals but different priorities; 3 and 4 also have the same goals but different priorities. Goals for f_3 (inventory) have been achieved in all four solutions. The achievement of goals in all GP solutions depend on the priorities as well as goal levels. Solution 4 of the GP is very similar, in terms of achievement of objectives, to the STEM and SEMOPS solutions. In GP,

Features	Jaaskelainen model	Wallenius model	The present model
No. of product	Multiple	Single	Multiple
No. of period	Multiple	Multiple	Multiple
No. of stages	Multiple	Single	Single (can be used for multiple stage)
Subcontracting	Considered	Not considered	Not considered (may be included)
Sales	Given fixed	Given fixed	Variable within upper and lower bounds
Work force	Not considered	Considered	Considered
Labour hiring	Not considered	Not allowed	Allowed
Labour lay-off	Not considered	Allowed (temporary only)	Allowed
Machine capacity	Considered	Considered (can be changed also)	Considered
Backorder	Not allowed (lost sales considered)	Allowed	Allowed
Objectives			
Cost (or profit)	Not considered	Cost	Profit
Inventory	Closing inventory	Included in cost objective	Considered
Changes in work force	Not considered	Lay-off only (in constraints)	Considered
Backorders	Lost sale considered	Considered	Considered
Overtime	Considered for machine centre	Considered for work-force in cost objective	Considered for work-force in profit objective (for machine centre considered in constraint)
Under-utilization	For machine centre	For work-force considered implicitly	For work-force considered implicitly

Table 1.   Features of three aggregate production planning models.

Product	Labour production time, a_i, hours/unit	Machining time, b_i, hours/unit	Production cost (other than labour) c_{1i}, $/unit	Value added c_{4i}, $/unit	Sales revenue r_i, $/unit
1	2	1·5	15	40	70
2	3	2·0	20	60	100

Table 2. Operating and cost data.

Period	1	2	3	4	5	6	7	8
$S_{1t\,min}$. lbs	4000	10000	4000	4500	9000	4500	3000	6000
$S_{1t\,max}$. lbs	12000	19000	15000	16000	18000	16000	10000	14000
$S_{2t\,min}$. lbs	3000	8000	7000	2000	6000	1500	4000	6000
$S_{2t\,max}$. lbs	6000	18000	15000	5000	12000	4000	10000	12000
$W_{t\,max}$, man-day	5000	4000	4500	3000	5000	5500	4500	4000
$\bar{M}_t$, machine-hour	32000	28400	29600	20000	32000	33600	29600	26400

Table 3. Sales, work force, and machine capacity data.

Period, $_t$	1	2	3	4	5	6	7	8
α_t	0·5	0·6	0·5	0·6	0·4	0·4	0·4	0·5
β_t	0·3	0·3	0·3	0·3	0·3	0·3	0·3	0·3

Table 4. Miscellaneous data. $c_2 = \$64$; $c_3 = \$15$; $b_{1,0} = 500$; $I_{2,0} = 500$; $w_0 = 3500$.

Method	Profit, f_1 ($)	Change in work-force, f_2 (man-day)	Inventory, f_3 $/period	Backorder, r_4 $/period
Ideal solutions	7657833	500	6000	0
Goal programming:				
Model 1: Goal	7250000(4)‡	2000(3)	80000(2)	150000(1)
Solution	6561750	2000	16250	150000
Model 2: Goal	7250000(1)	2000(3)	80000(4)	150000(2)
Solution	7250000	6310	41040	150000
Model 3: Goal	7250000(2)	3000(1)	60000(3)	150000(4)
Solution	6976750	3000	22750	359146
Model 4: Goal	7250000(4)	3000(3)	60000(2)	150000(1)
Solution	6836416	3000	23248	150000
STEM	6902601	3088	24298	163724
SEMOPS	6900000	3066	23332	165000

† All numbers have been rounded off to the nearest integer.

‡ Numbers in parenthesis indicate the preemptive priority. It is assumed that the constraints have been checked for consistency before.

Table 5. Objective function values in final solutions and the respective goals.†

there was not much difficulty in stating the goals because the ideal solutions were known beforehand; in the absence of known ideal solutions, statements of goals may not be as easy. The total number of problems solved for each GP solution was less than or equal to four (=number of priorities).

STEM requires sensitivity analysis, at each cycle, by systematically changing each objective function value individually. This sensitivity analysis helps the DM make the trade-off decisions. Thus, the total number of problems solved depends on the amount of sensitivity analysis done; for this example 32 problems in five iterations were solved. In addition, determination of the four ideal solutions are also explicitly required in STEM. However, because of the use of an LP package, the sensitivity analyses were easily done.

A total of 19 problems in three cycles were solved to get the solution using SEMOPS. Number of problems solved using SEMOPS can increase considerably because in some cycles one may find inconsistent constraints when solving for auxiliary problems. In such cases, a search for the new consistent set of aspiration levels have to be made. This condition happened in two cycles of the example. The number of problems solved to get consistency have not been included in the above count. Another serious drawback with SEMOPS is that even if all the original relations are linear, the resulting SEMOPS problem may become nonlinear when the dimensionless indicators (d_i) are defined. In the case of this example, the nonlinear d_i were converted to equivalent linear forms by mathematical simplifications. This was done to use the efficient LP package. For details of this conversion see Masud (1978).

One recurring problem in using the three methods is that under some circumstances the 'best' compromise solution can be a dominated solution. Special care needs to be taken in specifying the goals in GP. In STEM, dominance can be introduced when relaxations are specified to the satisfactory goals. In SEMOPS, dominance can occur in the solutions of the auxiliary problem. Thus, in all the above methods, the 'best' compromise solution must be checked for dominance. Other than that, the application of GP and STEM to the proposed problem has been straight-forward. For SEMOPS, the dimensionless indicators need to be redefined to use an LP alogrithm.

Since there is no 'optimal' solution to this example MODM problem, it is very difficult to compare the solutions with one another. All solutions are, however, non-dominated. The 'best' compromise solutions were moulded according to the goals or the trade-off information provided by the DM. Thus, for a different DM, a completely different compromise solution is possible. It should be noted that, in the interactive process, DM has more control over what the final compromise solution would be. In GP, the control is limited and somewhat indirect. However, by using various goals and priorities, similar to what was done in the example, the DM can explore various solutions before choosing the 'best' compromise solution. In this example, no such attempt at best compromise solution was made in using GP; only four possible solution options were generated.

The model has been able to serve its purpose of helping the DM make intelligent trade-off decisions. In GP, this has been possible by generating different solutions using different sets of goals and priorities. By generating all these solutions (four in the case of the example), the DM has been able to explore different trade-off options and decide which solution to select as 'best'. In STEM and SEMOPS, the DM is even more intimately involved. By using these methods, the model lets the DM guide the solution to his desired trade-off. This has been done by indicating the amount of relaxation in satisfactory objective values in each cycle of STEM or by reassessing the ALs in each cycle of SEMOPS. In contrast, if an equivalent single objective model was used, the DM would have to assess, subjectively, his trade-off in the form of unit costs even before he knew anything about his available trade-off options.

Concluding remarks

A multiple objective formulation of the aggregate production planning problem provides a more realistic modeling approach and affords the person in charge of production to make intelligent trade-off decisions about the different objectives. A variety of MODM methods are available for the solution of such a model.

Three MODM methods have been applied in this paper to a numerical example to provide an insight into what is involved in multiple objective production models. There is at present no 'the' best MODM method for solving such problems. More than one method can be used and the final choice will depend on such factors as personal preference, ease of use, and appropriateness of the method. Moreover, the level of involvement of the decision-maker (DM) can be tailored to the actual situation. In other words, the analyst can take up some of the DM's role and act for the DM to make the trade-off decisions, if necessary. For example, as shown in this paper, if GP is used then the analyst can solve a set of problems using different goals and priority structure and then let the DM make the final selection for implementation. In case of interactive methods, such as STEM and SEMOPS used in this paper, the analyst can provide the trade-off decision required in each iteration in lieu of the DM. Moreover, the analyst can also generate a set of solutions by providing different trade-off information and then let the DM make the final selection. However, it should be noted that many DMs may in fact want to get involved in the process of giving the trade-off information because it lets them explore the possible options available and also helps them learn more about the nature of the problem being dealt with. All such possible options in using MODM methods indicate that they are highly flexible and adaptable to different circumstances.

APPENDIX

Review of three MODM methods used

Mathematically, the MODM problems can be defined as:

$$\text{Max } [f_1(\mathbf{x}), f_2(\mathbf{x}), \dots, f_k(\mathbf{x})]$$
$$\text{s.t. } g_j(\mathbf{x}) \leqslant 0, \quad j = 1, 2, \dots, m \tag{17}$$

where $\mathbf{x}$ is an n dimensional decision variable vector.

Any or all of the above functions may be nonlinear. Because of the conflicting nature, there is usually no solution of (17) which optimizes all k objectives simultaneously. Thus, for MODM problems, one is interested in selecting one of the possible 'non-dominated' solutions as the 'best' compromise solution. A solution $\mathbf{x}^1$ is said to be dominated by $\mathbf{x}^2$ iff

$$f_i(\mathbf{x}^1) \leqslant f_i(\mathbf{x}^2), \quad i = 1, 2, \dots, k$$

and

$$f_i(\mathbf{x}^1) < f_i(\mathbf{x}^2)$$

for at least one i.

Goal programming (GP)

Goal programming requires that the decision maker (DM) set goals (or targets) for each of the k objectives. DM is also required to provide an ordinal ranking of the objectives in order of their importance. The GP formulation of (17) is:

$$\text{Min} \{P_1 h_1(\mathbf{d}^-, \mathbf{d}^+), \ P_2 h_2(\mathbf{d}^-, \mathbf{d}^+), \ldots, P_l h_l(\mathbf{d}^-, \mathbf{d}^+)\} \tag{18}$$

$$\text{s.t.} \ g_j(\mathbf{x}) \leqslant 0, \quad \forall_j$$

$$f_i(\mathbf{x}) + d_i^- - d_i^+ = b_i, \quad \forall_i$$

$$d_i^- d_i^+ = 0, \quad \forall_i$$

$$d_i^-, d_i^+ \geqslant 0, \quad \forall_i$$

where b_i, $i = 1, 2, \ldots, k$, are the goals set by DM for the objectives, and d_i^- and d_i^+ are, respectively, the under- and over-achievement of the ith goal. $h_r(\mathbf{d}^-, \mathbf{d}^+)$, $r = 1, 2, \ldots, l$, are linear functions of the deviational variables and are called achievement functions. The only restriction in forming an achievement function is that it should include only the deviational variables of those goals which are of the same priority and of the same units. The P_rs are preemptive priorities such that $P_r \ggg P_{r+1}$. This implies that no number W, however large, can make $W * P_{r+1} \geqslant P_r$.

The solution algorithm for (18) consists of first minimizing $h_1(\mathbf{d}^-, \mathbf{d}^+)$; let min $h_1 = h_1^*$. Next, $h_2(\mathbf{d}^-, \mathbf{d}^+)$ is minimized but always holding $h_1 = h_1^*$. Thus, a lower priority achievement function (and, hence, goals) can not be satisfied to the detriment of a higher priority achievement function. This process continues until $h_l(\mathbf{d}^-, \mathbf{d}^+)$ is minimized.

Step method (STEM)

STEM is an 'interactive' method where the DM is a part of the solution process. At each iteration, DM indicates his/her local preference information on the basis of results of the current iteration. Based on this new information, calculations of a new iteration are performed. The process stops when specified stopping rules are satisfied. Interactive methods, thus, progressively define the DMs preference along with the exploration of the objective space of the problem.

STEM is, however, applicable to (17) when all functions are linear: that is, for Multiple Objective Linear Problems (MOLP). At the lth cycle, a feasible solution to the LP problem (19) is sought which is the 'nearest', in the MINIMAX sense, to the ideal solution:

$$\text{Min} \ \lambda \tag{19}$$

$$\{\mathbf{x}, \lambda\}$$

$$\text{s.t.} \ \lambda \geqslant \{f_i^* - f_i(\mathbf{x})\} \cdot \pi_i, \quad \forall_i$$

$$\mathbf{x} \in X^l$$

$$\lambda \geqslant 0$$

where X^l includes $g_j(\mathbf{x}) \leqslant 0$, $\forall_j$, $\mathbf{x} > 0$ plus any constraint added in the previous $(l-1)$ cycles; π_i gives the relative importance of the distance to the ideal solution, but is only locally effective. f_i^*, $\forall_i$, is called ideal solution associated with ith objective when the following k problems are solved:

$$\text{Max}\, f_i(\mathbf{x}) \tag{20}$$

$$\text{s.t.} \quad g_j(\mathbf{x}) \leqslant 0$$

$$\mathbf{x} \geqslant 0$$

$$i = 1, 2, \ldots, k$$

The compromise solution $\mathbf{x}^l$ of (19) is next presented to DM who compares its objective vector f^l with f^*, the ideal solution. If some objectives are satisfactory and others are not, DM relaxes a satisfactory objective f_i^l by Δf_i to allow improvement of the unsatisfactory objectives in the $(l+1)$th cycle. For the $(l+1)$th cycle the feasible region is modified as:

$$X^l + 1 = \begin{cases} X^l \\ f_i(\mathbf{x}) \geqslant f_i(\mathbf{x}^l) - \Delta f_i \\ f_j(\mathbf{x}) \geqslant f_j(\mathbf{x}^l); \qquad j = 1, 2, \ldots, k \text{ and } j \neq i \end{cases} \tag{21}$$

The weight π_i is set equal to zero and the calculation phase of $(l+1)$ cycle starts. The process stops when DM is satisfied with all the achieved objective values in a particular cycle.

Sequential Multiple Objective Problem Solving (SEMOPS)

SEMOPS is also an 'interactive' method. It is, however, applicable to both linear and nonlinear MODM problems. SEMOPS cyclically uses a 'surrogate' objective function based on the DM's aspirations toward achieving the objectives. Aspiration levels (ALs) are attainment levels of the objectives which the DM desires to achieve. ALs change as each iteration cycle progresses. Let $\text{AL} = (\text{AL}_1, \text{AL}_2, \ldots, \text{AL}_k)$ be the DM's aspiration levels. Depending on the type of the objective, e.g., at least or at most, a corresponding dimensionless indicator of attainment, $d_i, i = 1, \ldots, k$, is defined. For each case, values of $d_i \leqslant 1$ imply the objective has attained the AL_i.

For the lth cycle, the following 'principal problem (PP)' and a set of 'auxiliary problems (AP)' are solved.

$$\text{PP:} \quad \text{Min}\, S_l = \sum_{t \in T} d_t \tag{22}$$

$$\text{s.t.} \quad \mathbf{x} \in X$$

$$f_j(\mathbf{x}) \geqslant \text{AL}_j, j \in (T - T')$$

$$\text{AP}_i: \text{Min}\, S_{li} = \sum_{\substack{t \in T \\ t \neq i}} d_t \tag{23}$$

$$\text{s.t.} \quad \mathbf{x} \in X$$

$$f_j(\mathbf{x}) \geqslant \text{AL}_j, j \in (T - T')$$

$$f_i(\mathbf{x}) \geqslant \text{AL}_i, \text{ for one } i, i \in T'$$

where,

$X = \{\mathbf{x} | g_j(\mathbf{x}) \leqslant 0, \forall_j\}$

$d_t = $ dimensional indicator for tth objective

T = set of objectives in first cycle

$T' = T - l + 1$

AL_j = Aspiration level for jth objective as decided prior to lth cycle

The resulting solutions are presented to DM, who then reassesses the ALs and a new aspiration for an objective is set. In the next cycle, the PP and APs are solved holding this objective at least to the new aspiration level. The process terminates when DM is satisfied with either the PP solution or one of the AP solutions in any cycle.

Cet article présente une formulation par objectifs multiples du problème de planification globale de production de produits multiples à périodes multiples. Le modèle proposé permet l'évaluation individuelle des objectifs multiples conflictuels sans se limiter à des décisions d'échange a priori après évaluation subjective des coûts. Un exemple numérique est résolu par application de trois méthodes de prise de décision à objectifs multiples.

In dieser Abhandlung wird eine Mehrfachzielformulierung des Multiprodukt-, Multiperioden-Gesamtproduktionsplanungsproblems vorgestellt. Das vorgeschlagene Modell sieht eine individuelle Berücksichtigung der zueinander in Konflikt stehenden Mehrfachziele vor, ohne über eine subjektive Kostenschätzung auf von vornherein getroffene Alternativentscheidungen zurückzugreifen. Ein numerisches Beispiel wird unter Anwendung von drei Mehrfachziel-Entscheidungsmethoden gelöst.

References

EILON, S., 1975, Five approaches to aggregate production planning, *A.I.I.E., Trans.*, **7**, 1.

HWANG, C. L., and MASUD, A. S. M., 1979, *Multiple Objective Decision Making: Methods and Application—A State of the Art Survey* (New York: Springer-Verlag).

JAASKELAINEN, V., 1969, A goal programme model of aggregate production planning, *Swed. J. Econ.*, **71**, 1.

LAWRENCE, K. D., and BURBRIDGE, J. J., 1976, A multiple goal linear programming model for coordinated production and logistics planning, *Int. J. Prod. Res.*, **14**, 2.

LAWRENCE, K. D., and BURBRIDGE, J. J., 1977, Multi-objective linear programming models for the blending of materials problem, Fourth International Conference on Production Research, Tokyo.

MASUD, A. S. M., 1978, A Study of Multiple Objective Decision Making—Methods and Applications, Ph.D. Dissertation, Kansas State University.

SILVER, E. A., 1967, A tutorial on production smoothing and work force balancing, *Ops. Res.*, **15**, 6.

WALLENIUS, J., 1975, *Interactive Multiple Criteria Decision Methods: An Investigation and an Approach* (Helsinki: Helsinki School of Economics.)

MULTIPLE-CRITERIA OPTIMIZATION IN PRODUCTION PLANNING: AN APPLICATION FOR A LARGE INDUSTRIAL GOODS MANUFACTURER

Lee Krajewski
Academic Faculty of Management Sciences
Ohio State University[1]

ABSTRACT

Recent competitive pressures from overseas companies have emphasized the need for organizations in this country to develop efficient production plans. The basic premise of this paper is that the formal production planning methods proposed in the literature have not received great acceptance by practicing managers because they do not incorporate considerations for criteria other than total costs. Customer service, utilization of resources, stable employment levels, and inventory investment are examples of criteria that management considers in addition to total production costs. A formal production planning method is proposed and applied to the problem of a large industrial-goods manufacturer. A complicating factor in this application is the need to consider major setups between product family production runs. The model, with 120 binary setup variables, 762 continuous variables, and 722 constraints, is solved with a heuristic that is based on the concept of repeated rounding of the binary variables. The heuristic is shown to be effective for the case data and saves considerable computer time compared to existing branch-and-bound codes.

Management can use the methods proposed in this paper to develop production plans that recognize various criteria, including production costs. A payoff table, showing the values of all the criteria for production plans generated by using each criterion as the sole objective, identifies the trade-offs that management must make when developing a compromise production plan. Two compromise plans generated by adjusting the criterion weights are presented. Management can continue adjusting the weights until an acceptable plan is generated.

There are also some side benefits from the multiple-criteria analysis of alternate production plans. For the case data, the desirability of multiperiod lot sizing, the number of setups, and the product mix were found to be functions of the relative importance of the various criteria. Additionally, it was found that capacity-related costs, such as undertime and overtime, should be considered in making lot-sizing decisions. Such information is useful for modifying outdated and inefficient manufacturing strategies and policies.

INTRODUCTION

In recent years, U.S. manufacturing companies have been experiencing increasing competitive pressure from overseas companies. This competition has led to an increasing awareness of the need to produce more efficiently, at better quality, and with good customer service. One way to begin satisfying this need is to develop more efficient production plans. According to Wight (1974), the production plan, usually stated in aggregate quantities such as hours, dollars, or units of product families, establishes a production rate that will raise or lower inventories or backorders as desired and keep production relatively stable. The production plan is then used to develop the master production schedule, which specifies the timing and sizing of specific finished-good quantities. Without a good production plan, component production schedules, workforce schedules, and purchasing plans will not achieve the goals of management.

[1] Invited review paper.

Formal Production Planning Methods

Although the number of formal aggregate production-planning models proposed in the literature is legion, a handful are representative of the methodologies suggested. Holt, Modigliani, and Muth (1956) derived linear decision rules for the monthly levels of workforce and production rate for a paint factory. One of the major assumptions was that the total cost curve is quadratic. Jones (1967) and Taubert (1968) suggested computer search methods to derive rules similar to those of Holt, Modigliani, and Muth (1956) without the restrictive assumption of a quadratic cost function. The linear-programming models suggested by Haussman and Hess (1960), Krajewski and Thompson (1978), and many others offered the realism of recognizing various linear resource constraints at the cost of assuming a linear objective function. In general, regardless of the solution methodology, the traditional objective for the aggregate planning models has been cost minimization.

Unfortunately, aggregate production planning models have not been extensively used in practice. Although ease of use and understanding the model or solution method have been suggested as major managerial concerns, a deficiency of most aggregate planning models is the assumption that a plan that minimizes total production costs is the best plan. However, several criteria, such as customer service, utilization of resources, and production costs, are typically considered by managers when designing a production plan. Most of the methods in the literature require the manager to temper the minimum-cost plan to account for the other important criteria.

Multiple Criteria and Production Planning

Although procedures for recognizing multiple criteria have been applied to many different planning problems, they have not been extensively explored for the aggregate production planning problem. Goodman (1974) applied goal programming to the quadratic cost problem of Holt, Modigliani, and Muth (1956); however, goal programming was suggested as a solution technique for quadratic cost-curve problems, as opposed to a technique for incorporating goals other than total cost. Krajewski and Bott (1978) demonstrated the nature and magnitude of the trade-offs that must be made among various goals when devising an acceptable production plan for a case example. Krajewski and Bradford (1977) made some observations for a related problem that have some relevance for production planning problems. They found that changes in a master schedule are a direct consequence of the rank orderings of the relevant goals, and a reordering of the goal priorities can reduce total production costs. Consequently, the relative importance of the goals or criteria would seem to be an important consideration in production planning.

Based upon these few studies, it is apparent that a formal production planning method recognizing multiple criteria has an advantage over other approaches. It can enable management to identify the trade-offs between various criteria such as costs, service, and utilization of resources and arrive at a compromise production plan. This paper proposes a multiple-criteria production planning procedure and demonstrates its usefulness for the production planning problem of a large industrial-goods manufacturer.

THE PROBLEM

The Krabott Co. produces truck axles for a national market.[2] Management indicated a need to develop a five-month aggregate production plan for each of two plants producing axle components. The plan must specify the monthly production quantities of each of twelve product families at each plant given the current labor plan. Each plant has its own shift schedule for each machine center; however, the plant in Chicago has very few third-shift operations, whereas the plant in Saint Cloud, Minnesota, has considerably more.

---

[2] For purposes of confidentiality the name of the company, its location, and the numerical data are disguised. However, the problem structure, size, and all conclusions are real.

Product Structure

The twelve product families represent ninety individual finished goods of varying sizes and gear ratios. For both plants, a finished item consists of a matched gear-and-pinion set. Figure 1 shows the simple bill of material. The raw materials are R1 and R2. Material R1 must pass through six machinery operations, if the parent is a single-speed gear, or seven operations, if the parent is a two-speed gear. Material R2 must pass through eleven operations to produce a pinion, no matter which finished item is being produced. Both gear and pinion must pass through two operations to make the finished pair F. Lead times for all components are much less than one month, the planning interval for the aggregate plan.

Figure 1. Bill of material for a gear-pinion set

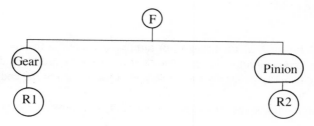

A major complicating factor in developing the production plan for the product families is that there must be a major setup of the machinery operations when production is switched from one family to another. The setup time averages eight hours. Setup times between items within a family are negligible by comparison. The aggregate production plan, recognizing setup between family changeovers, must schedule the production of the twelve product families at the two plants for a given level of capacity under varying production requirements.

Multiple Criteria

Discussions with management revealed four criteria that are considered in developing the production plan at Krabott. Without regard to order of preference (management could not agree on an ordinal ranking), the criteria to consider are

1. Total production costs—These consist of material, labor, undertime, overtime, inventory carrying, and setup.
2. Customer service—Customer service is defined in terms of the current safety stock policy. Optimal customer service would result when the desired safety stocks have been maintained.
3. Utilization of the Chicago plant—Utilization is measured in terms of the average aggregate number of units of finished gear-and-pinion sets produced per day.
4. Utilization of the Saint Cloud plant.

The Krabott Co. has a unique situation with regard to the two plants, necessitating separate criteria for each. The Chicago plant is unionized; the Saint Cloud plant is not. Consequently, the cost of production is considerably higher at Chicago. Taken at face value, it would seem that Saint Cloud should be scheduled to its capacity, leaving the residual, if any, for Chicago. However, reducing the manpower level at Chicago is not desirable for two reasons. First, the machinists at many of the operations are highly skilled and to release them, only to want them back later, would be costly. Most of these skilled people would have found jobs elsewhere. Second, reducing manpower levels means that the typical ''bumping'' process takes place when positions are left vacant. This can severely affect factory productivity for an extended period, not to mention the bad effect on morale. On the other hand, it is also undesirable to underutilize Saint Cloud if that plant is to remain nonunionized. Management has a good degree of flexibility in production scheduling at Saint Cloud and would like to keep good relations. Herein lies the basis for the conflicting multiple criteria faced by this company.

THE MODEL

The model seeks to minimize the weighted deviations from certain stated targets subject to a series of constraints. The technical and goal constraints will be presented first, followed by the objective function.

Technical Constraints

The inventory identity constraints are given by

$$I_{it}^l = I_{it-1}^l + X_{it}^l - D_{it}^l \qquad \begin{aligned} &l = \text{Chicago, Saint Cloud} \\ &i = 1, 2, \ldots, 12 \\ &t = 1, 2, \ldots, 5 \end{aligned} \qquad (1)$$

where

I_{it}^l = finished-goods inventory of family i at plant l at the end of month t

X_{it}^l = production lot size of family i at plant l to be produced during month t

D_{it}^l = quantity of family i to be shipped from plant l at the end of month t.

The total system requirements for family i in month t, D_{it}^T, must be allocated to each plant l.

$$\sum_l D_{it}^l = D_{it}^T \qquad \begin{aligned} &i = 1, 2, \ldots, 12 \\ &t = 1, 2, \ldots, 5 \end{aligned} \qquad (2)$$

The total system requirements are actually forecasts; however, for purposes of planning they are assumed to be known with certainty.

Overtime is limited to 50 percent of the regular-time hours assigned to each work center. The production routings of gears and pinions are separate except for the final two operations. Therefore, there are twenty work centers to recognize at each plant: seven for gears, eleven for pinions, and two for the pair.

$$d_{jt}^{l+} \leq .5 H_{jt}^l \qquad \begin{aligned} &l = \text{Chicago, Saint Cloud} \\ &j = j, 2, \ldots, 20 \\ &t = 1, 2, \ldots, 5 \end{aligned} \qquad (3)$$

where

d_{jt}^{l+} = hours of overtime scheduled for workcenter j at plant l in month

H_{jt}^l = regular time hours assigned to workcenter j at plant l in month t.

Finally, the product family production variables must be constrained to ensure that if there is no setup of family i at plant l in month t ($s_{it}^l = 0$), there is no production of family i at plant l in that month. This is accomplished in (4) where the setup variables s_{it}^l are binary integer variables.

$$X_{it}^l \leq s_{it}^l \sum_{m=t}^{5} D_{im}^T \qquad \begin{aligned} &l = \text{Chicago, Saint Cloud} \\ &i = 1, 2, \ldots, 12 \\ &t = 1, 2, \ldots, 5 \end{aligned} \qquad (4)$$

The summation term in (4) is a constant equal to the total system requirements for family i from month t to the end of the horizon. If $s_{it}^l = 1$, production of family i at plant l can be scheduled in month t but cannot exceed the remaining system requirements for family i.

Goal Constraints

The utilization of work hours in the production of gears, pinions, and the matched pair is presented in expression (5)

$$\sum_{i=1}^{12} p_{ij}^l X_{it}^l + d_{jt}^{l-} - d_{jt}^{l+} = H_{jt} \quad \begin{array}{l} l = \text{Chicago, Saint Cloud} \\ j = 1, 2, \ldots, 20 \\ t = 1, 2, \ldots, 5 \end{array} \tag{5}$$

where

p_{ij}^l = productivity expressed in hours per unit of family i at workcenter j in plant l.

The variable X_{it}^l can be used here because each finished item (matched pair) requires only one gear and one pinion and the production lot size of the family is the production lot size for the gears and pinions. The underutilization of work hours is given by d_{jt}^{l-}. The overtime has been defined in (3). These deviation variables will be used in the cost goal constraint to be presented later.

The Krabott management was more comfortable in expressing utilization in terms of units of output per day. For this reason, a separate goal constraint was constructed. With the exception of the last two operations on the matched pair, the production process of gears and pinions can be considered to be arranged in separate flow shops. The pinion production time at a given work center can be safely assumed to be independent of the product family. Because of this simplification, a reasonable goal for the maximum output in a day can be stated in terms of pinion production. Given the available regular-time and maximum overtime hours and productivities at each work center in the pinion routing, the maximum daily output of pinions is determined by the capacity of the *limiting* work center. The final two operations on the matched pairs were never bottlenecks. Let P_t^l denote the maximum output of pinions for plant l in month t (the maximum daily output multiplied by the number of working days in month t). The goal constraint then becomes

$$\sum_{i=1}^{12} X_{it}^l + d^{lU-} = P_t^l \quad \begin{array}{l} l = \text{Chicago, Saint Cloud} \\ t = 1, 2, \ldots, 5 \end{array} \tag{6}$$

where

d^{lU-} = deviation variable to be minimized.

The customer-service criterion is defined in terms of deviations from a stated safety-stock policy. Presently, the policy is to maintain an ending inventory in month t equal to a proportion α of the total system requirements in month $t + 1$. The goal constraint becomes

$$\sum_{l} I_{it}^{l} + d_{it}^{S-} - d_{it}^{S+} = \alpha D_{it+1}^{T} \qquad \begin{aligned} l &= \text{Chicago, Saint Cloud} \\ i &= 1, 2, \ldots, 12 \\ t &= 1, 2, \ldots, 5 \end{aligned}$$

where $0 < \alpha \leq 1$ and the deviation variables d_{it}^{S-} and d_{it}^{S+} measure the deviation from the target safety level.

Finally, the goal constraint reflecting total production costs is given by:

$$\sum_{t=1}^{5} \left\{ \sum_{i=1}^{12} \sum_{l} v_{i}^{l} X_{it}^{l} + \sum_{j=1}^{20} \sum_{l} c_{1}^{l} d_{jt}^{l-} + c_{2}^{l} d_{jt}^{l+} \right.$$

$$\left. + \sum_{i=1}^{12} \sum_{l} c_{i3}^{l} s_{it}^{l} + \sum_{i=1}^{12} \sum_{l} c_{i4}^{l} I_{it}^{l} \right\} + d^{c-} - d^{c+} = \beta \qquad (8)$$

where

$$\begin{aligned} v_{i}^{l} &= \text{variable labor plus material cost per unit of family } i \text{ at plant } l \\ c_{1}^{l} &= \text{labor cost per hour of undertime at plant } l \\ c_{2}^{l} &= \text{labor cost per hour of overtime at plant } l \\ c_{i3}^{l} &= \text{setup cost for family } i \text{ at plant } l \\ c_{i4}^{l} &= \text{inventory holding cost per month for family } i \text{ at plant } l \\ \beta &= \text{total cost target (which would be set equal to zero if the objective is to minimize costs).} \end{aligned}$$

The total cost function is the sum of material and labor costs, undertime and overtime costs, setup costs, and inventory carrying costs. The total cost target β can either be set by management at some desired level or be made zero to find the minimal cost plan.

Objective Function

The objective function can be stated as:

$$\text{Minimize} \quad Z = w_{1} d^{c+} + \sum_{t=1}^{5} \left\{ w_{2} \sum_{i=1}^{12} d_{it}^{s-} + \sum_{l} w_{3}^{l} d_{t}^{lU-} \right\} \qquad (9)$$

The first term relates to total production costs; the second relates to underachieving the service goal. The last term relates to the underutilization at the two plants. Each term is multiplied by a weight that reflects the relative importance of the criterion it represents.

The objective is to minimize (9) subject to the technical constraints (1) through (4) and the goal constraints (5) through (8). The complete model is a mixed-integer program consisting of 882 variables (including 120 binary setup variables) and 722 rows.[3]

---

[3] The size of the model reported here is smaller than that implied by the constraint set presented. Sixty overtime variables and sixty capacity constraints can be eliminated by taking advantage of the simplification that pinion production time is independent of product family. The details are omitted here for simplicity of presentation. The number of rows includes 120 upper-bound constraints for the setup variables.

ANALYSIS

The model was applied to the Krabott data to identify the nature of the trade-offs in the four criteria resulting from various production plans (including two compromise plans). It was also used to learn the effects of various criteria on production strategy. However, before these managerial benefits are addressed, the more technical aspects of the solution strategy and the solution quality must be discussed.

Solution Strategy

The procedure used in this application might be termed a quasi-utility approach. The decision-maker supplies weights for the criteria in an iterative fashion until a satisfactory solution is found. The Krabott managers were comfortable with this approach. Consequently, it did not seem necessary to use a more structured approach. In addition, the procedure enabled the managers to learn a considerable amount about the effects of the current workforce schedule and safety-stock policies on the major criteria.

Theoretically speaking, the solution of the model is straightforward. A number of efficient mixed-integer programming codes have been developed. However, there are two reasons that a mixed-integer code could not be used in this case. First, such a code was not readily available to Krabott Co. The purchase price or rental fees required were considered excessive for the application for which the code would be used. Second, and perhaps more important, the computing time required for such a code would be excessive. Krabott Co. has a limited amount of computer time that can be devoted to this application. Past experiences of the author with IBM's MPSX mixed-integer code for a smaller problem with about the same number of binary variables indicated that run times in the range of 30 to 50 minutes might be expected. As such, it was decided to use a heuristic approach to solve the model.

The heuristic procedure is shown in figure 2. It is based on the concept of repeated rounding of the binary setup variables. Repeated rounding of binary variables was found to be a good approach by Wagner et al. (1964), although their problem involved mutually exclusive constraints on their binary variables. The production planning problem is much more complex, since there could be a setup of a product family in each month for a given plant..

Initially, the iteration (month) count Y is set to zero. In step 2, the continuous (relaxed) solution is found for the desired weights in the objective function using a standard linear-programming code. The setup variables are free to take on any value on the interval $(0,1)$. Step 3 checks to see if all 120 of the setup variables are integer-valued. If they are, the heuristic is finished and the management reports are generated. If some setup variables are noninteger, increase the iteration count by one in step 4. In step 5, constraints are added to force the setup variables in month Y to be either zero or one. Any setup variable in month Y that has a nonzero value in the last linear-programming solution is forced equal to one; any setup variable in month Y that has a zero value is constrained to equal zero. All setup variables in months $Y + 1, \ldots, 5$ are left to take on a value anywhere on the interval $(0,1)$. A new linear-programming solution with the added setup constraints in months $1, 2, \ldots Y$ is computed in step 6. In step 6, if Y is less than 5, the heuristic branches back to step 3. Otherwise, the management reports are generated in step 8. In addition, cost ranging data can be made available to show how much the weights must be adjusted to achieve a new basis.

Solution Quality

The usual procedure for evaluating the merits of a heuristic procedure is to compare its solution to an optimal solution or some other benchmark. In this case, optimal solutions were not available. Nonetheless, useful comparisons on the performance of the heuristic can be made if bounds on the criteria values can be found. For example, a lower bound on total production costs can be found by setting w_1 equal to a very large value relative to the other weights in the objective function and solving the model, allowing the setup variables to take on any value on the interval $(0,1)$. The choice of value for w_1 would be such that larger values of w_1 would not result in a lower-cost solution. Similarly, the heuristic in figure 2 can be used with the same value of w_1 to provide an upper bound on total production costs.

233

Obviously, the *optimal* solution with total production costs as the sole criterion will fall somewhere between the two bounds or will be equal to the bound generated by the heuristic. If these bounds are reasonably close, we can be confident that the heuristic has generated a good solution. A similar process can be followed for the other three criteria.

Figure 2. Heuristic procedure for solving the mixed-integer program

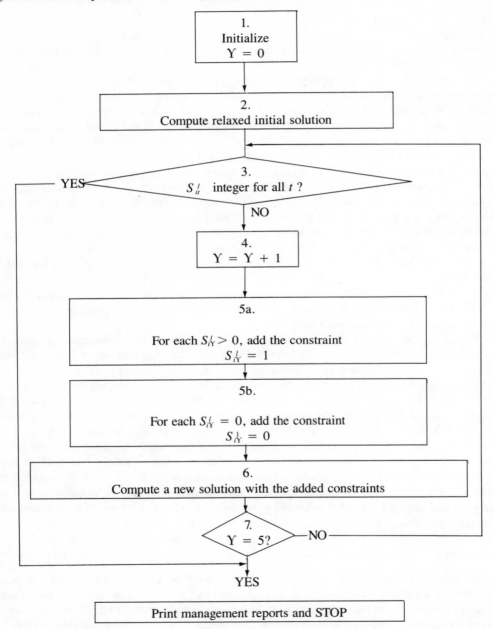

TABLE 1

HEURISTIC PERFORMANCE RESULTS

Criterion	Continuous solution	Mixed-integer solution	Deviation, percent
Total cost	$8,583,533	$8,601,565	0.2
Customer service	100 %	100 %	0
Chicago utilization	406/day	395/day	3
Saint Cloud utilization	823/day	821/day	0.2

Table 1 contains the results from the continuous and mixed-integer solutions for each of the four criteria for the Krabott data. The computations of the customer service and plant utilization criteria, however, need explanation. The service criterion is based on λ_t, the aggregate average proportion of underachievement of the safety stock target in month t.

$$\lambda_t = \frac{\sum_{i=1}^{12} d_{it}^{S-}}{\sum_{i=1}^{12} \alpha D_{it+1}} \quad t = 1, 2, \ldots, 5 \tag{10}$$

The value of α, the proportion of next month's requirements to keep in safety stock, is 0.75 for the Krabott Co. The five values of λ_t are averaged and subtracted from 1 to yield the aggregate average proportion of safety stock requirements met over the planning horizon, reported as a percentage in table 1.

$$\text{Customer Service} = 1 - \frac{1}{5} \sum_{t=1}^{5} \lambda_t \tag{11}$$

The results in table 1 indicate that the heuristic generated good solutions. Only one of the solutions deviated as much as 3 percent from the theoretical upper bound. In addition, the average run time for each continuous solution is 90 seconds on an IBM 370. Consequently, the maximum run time for each mixed-integer solution is 7.5 minutes of CPU time, only a fraction of that required to run a branch-and-bound code.

Managerial Use

The overall intent of the multiple-criteria production planning process presented here is to provide management with the information required to design the production plan. This process begins with the creation of a report similar to table 2. Each criterion is used as the sole objective in the heuristic solution method by placing a very large weight on the particular criterion and very small weights on the other three criteria.[4] For example, the MIN cost production plan is generated by setting $\beta = 0$ and w_1 equal to a value much larger than the weights of the other criteria. After the solution is obtained using the heuristic, the value of the major criterion and the values of the other criteria are entered into a matrix like that of table 2. The resultant matrix, sometimes called a payoff table, contains the optimal values (within the limitations of the heuristic) of each criteria along the diagonal and the attendant values of the other criteria in each row. Except in extraordinary circumstances, finding a feasible solution to the problem that yields the optimal values of all the criteria is not possible.

[4] Very small positive weights are needed for the other three criteria to ensure that each criterion takes on its best value when there are multiple optimal solutions for the major criterion.

TABLE 2

	Criteria			
Production plan	Production cost, $	Customer service, percent	Chicago utilization, units/day	Saint Cloud utilization, units/day
MIN cost	8,601,565	13	61	650
MAX service	9,541,083	100	139	687
MAX Chicago utilization	9,687,988	25	395	343
MAX Saint Cloud utilization	9,604,106	69	6	821

None of the plans represented in table 2 are very palatable. The MIN cost plan does not do well with respect to customer service or Chicago utilization. The MAX service plan, although costing about $940,000 more than the MIN cost plan, still does not do very well with respect to Chicago utilization. The plan that maximizes the utilization of Chicago does poorly with respect to costs and service. Finally, the MAX Saint Cloud utilization plan essentially calls for the shutdown of the Chicago plant.

Given the data in table 2 that indicated the trade-offs between the criteria for various plans, management can generate compromise plans by adjusting the weights on the criteria. For example, table 3 contains the results of two compromise plans. The first plan has the effect of placing equal emphasis on the utilization of Chicago and the utilization of Saint Cloud. The second plan has 50 percent relative weight on minimizing total production costs, 30 percent on maximizing service, and 20 percent on maximizing Saint Cloud utilization.[5] The second plan, compared to the first, shows the degradation in Chicago utilization that must be traded for the improvements in total production costs, customer service, and Saint Cloud utilization. Other values for the relative weights could give additional trade-offs to consider.

TABLE 3

EXAMPLE COMPROMISE PLANS

	Criteria			
Production cost	Production cost, $	Customer service, percent	Chicago utilization, units/day	Saint Cloud utilization, units/day
MAX Chicago and Saint Cloud utilization	9,513,150	81	242	593
50% costs, 30% customer service, and 20% Saint Cloud utilization	9,376,809	100	130	707

[5] Initially, the weight for each criterion was set equal to the inverse of the average deviations computed from the plans represented in table 2. This had the effect of equalizing the importance of each criterion in the objective function. The weights were then multiplied by appropriate constants to achieve the desired relative weightings for the respective compromise plans.

Effects of the Criteria on Production Strategy

Another benefit of the analysis performed with this approach is that it sensitizes management to the effects of emphasizing various criteria in constructing a production plan. This section discusses the effects of the criteria on multiperiod lot sizing, total system setups, and product mix for the plans reported in table 2. In addition, some insight into the consideration of capacity-related costs in the lot-sizing decisions can be gained.

Multiperiod Lot Sizing. Tables 4 through 7 contain the production plans represented in table 2. A multiperiod lot size is defined as any production quantity that covers more than one month's requirements. The different production plans indicate that considerable multiperiod lot sizing takes place when total production costs are minimized or Saint Cloud utilization is maximized. Alternately, if customer service is maximized or Chicago utilization is maximized, very little multiperiod lot sizing is required. From these data, it is apparent that the degree to which multiperiod lot sizing is advantageous depends on the major criterion to be considered.

TABLE 4

Minimize Total Production Costs

Family	Month 1 C	Month 1 SC	Month 2 C	Month 2 SC	Month 3 C	Month 3 SC	Month 4 C	Month 4 SC	Month 5 C	Month 5 SC
1		3039								
2	134		337		393		432		432	
3	1281		1932		2132		2172		2172	
4		727		367		794		884		884
5		470		1666		1835		2082		2082
6		1122		2012		2141		2126		2126
7		1152								
8		601								
9		1026								
10		1033								
11		2931		6584		7507		6892		6420
12	313		1024		1017		1112		1112	

TABLE 5

MAXIMIZE CUSTOMER SERVICE

Family	Month 1		Month 2		Month 3		Month 4		Month 5	
	C	SC	C	SC	C	SC	C	SC	C	SC
1		741		666		714		735		734
2	387		383		418		432		432	
3		2730		2082		2162		2172		2172
4	887	804		861		884		884		884
5		1720		1792		2021		2082		2082
6	2631		2109		2137		2126		2126	
7		304		563		498				
8		153		123		141		147		147
9		271		`232		233		237		237
10	261		238		238		237		237	
11	1301	6123	1097	5297	1317	6112	1168	6468	1043	5988
12	1081		1019		1088		1112		1112	

TABLE 6

MAXIMIZE CHICAGO UTILIZATION

Family	Month 1		Month 2		Month 3		Month 4		Month 5	
	C	SC	C	SC	C	SC	C	SC	C	SC
1		212		705		653		735		734
2		134		337		393		432		432
3	2730		2082		2162		2172		2172	
4		265		830		794		884		884
5		470		1666		1835		2082		2082
6	1961		2165		2529		2297		2075	
7		112		256		214		285		285
8		60		124		123		294		
9		107		219		236		232		232
10		93		224		242		237		237
11	4101		3725	1095	4101	2427	3913	3528	2735	3716
12		313		1024		1142		1117		980

TABLE 7

MAXIMIZE SAINT CLOUD UTILIZATION

Family	Month 1 C	Month 1 SC	Month 2 C	Month 2 SC	Month 3 C	Month 3 SC	Month 4 C	Month 4 SC	Month 5 C	Month 5 SC
1		741		829			1286		734	
2		2052								
3		2258		2271		2443		2172		2172
4		887		804		861		884		884
5		470		1666		3397		2082		2082
6		1122		2012		2214		3654		2126
7		1366								
8	60		124		123		147		147	
9		1026								
10		1033								
11		4615		5173		9278		8854		7280
12	3219									1112

Total System Setups. Tables 4 through 7 reveal that the plans that minimize total production costs or maximize Saint Cloud utilization require a total of forty setups over the five-month horizon; the plans that maximize customer service or maximize Chicago utilization require a total of 63 setups. This is consistent with the findings on multiperiod lot sizing. Although the a priori philosophy of management was to reduce setups as a matter of course, the analysis indicates that the number of setups required is a function of the major criteria to be considered.

Product Mix. Another observation from the Krabott data is that the product mix at the two plants depends on the major criterion. Table 8 contains the product mix at each plant for the four criteria. Although the total mix at Saint Cloud changes with each criterion, Saint Cloud always produces families 1, 4, 5, 7, and 11, no matter what the criterion is. No such consistency exists for Chicago. It would seem that Chicago should be flexible in its schedules if emphasis on the various criteria change over time.

TABLE 8

PRODUCT MIX AT THE TWO PLANTS

Criterion	Product Mix Chicago	Product Mix Saint Cloud
Total cost	2, 12	1, 3, 4, 5, 6, 7, 8, 9, 10, 11
Customer service	2, 10, 11, 12	1, 3, 4, 5, 6, 7, 8, 9, 11
Chicago utilization	3, 6, 11	1, 2, 4, 5, 7, 8, 9, 10, 11
Saint Cloud utilization	8	1, 2, 3, 4, 5, 6, 7, 9, 10, 11

Capacity-Related Costs. Traditional lot-sizing literature emphasizes the consideration of only setup and inventory holding costs. The experiments with the Krabott data suggest that this notion is not valid when capacity costs are important. Consider table 4, which shows the minimum-cost plan. Chicago is producing only families 2 and 12. The economic order quantity was calculated for these two families, using the cost structure for Chicago to determine the optimal number of setups for each family. Family 2 should have only two setups and family 12 only three. In both cases, the plan calls for five setups. A similar analysis conducted for Saint Cloud is shown in table 9. Notice that the number of setups for families 1, 4, 5, 7, 9, and 10 differs from the optimal number of setups. The fact that this plan is the minimum-cost solution indicates that costs other than the typical setup and holding costs are important in the lot-sizing decisions. From table 2, it is apparent that both plants are producing well below their capacities, so capacity *limitations* are not a factor here. Of course, these results must be tempered with the fact that the heuristic was used to generate the minimum-cost plan; however, the evidence indicates that other costs such as undertime and overtime are important in the lot-sizing decision.

TABLE 9

SAINT CLOUD LOT-SIZING ANALYSIS

Family	Optimal number of setups	Actual number of setups
1	3	1
3	5	5
4	3	5
5	4	5
6	5	5
7	2	1
8	1	1
9	2	1
10	2	1
11	5	5

CONCLUSION

One of the reasons that most aggregate production planning methodologies reported in the literature are never used in practice is that they fail to formally recognize the relevant criteria for a good production plan. This paper has presented a multiple-criteria methodology for aggregate planning and demonstrated its use with the data from a large industrial-goods manufacturer. An essential ingredient of the methodology is a heuristic for solving a mixed-integer linear program. The heuristic was shown to provide good solutions for the case data.

The methodology can be used to generate a series of alternate production plans for various values of the relative weights for the criteria to be considered. Given a payoff table such as table 2, management can try different relative weights to generate compromise plans for evaluation. Two example compromise plans were presented for illustrative purposes.

Although the heuristic solution procedure can be fully automated, the opportunity exists to allow managerial intervention at any iteration Y of the solution process. For example, the decision-maker may wish to deviate from the prescriptions of step 5 in figure 2 to avoid unnecessary setups. Suppose the plan calls for a small lot size of a given family at Chicago and a large lot size of the same family at Saint Cloud at iteration (month) Y. Even though the setup variable is greater than zero for that family at Chicago, it could be set to zero, forcing the entire production of that family at Saint Cloud in that month.

Other managerial benefits from the use of a procedure incorporating multiple criteria come from the analysis of various alternative plans. It was shown that, for the Krabott data, the advantages of multi-period lot sizing depend on the criteria to be emphasized. It was also shown that the total number of setups and the product mix at each plant are functions of the emphasis on the major criteria. Finally, the data suggest that capacity-related costs should be considered when making lot-sizing decisions.

REFERENCES

Goodman, D. A. 1974. A goal programming approach to aggregate planning of production and work force. *Management Science* 20(12):1569-1575.

Haussmann, F., and S. W. Hess. 1960. A linear programming approach to production and employment planning. *Management Technology* (1):46-51.

Holt, C., F. Modigliani, and J. Muth. 1956. Derivation of a linear decision rule for production and employment scheduling. *Management Science* 2:159-177.

Jones, C. H. 1967. Parametric production planning. *Management Science* 13(11):843-866.

Krajewski, L. J., and K. Bott. 1978. Goal programming for multi-plant schedules: A case application. *Proceedings of the Midwest American Institute of Decision Sciences:* 26-28. Cincinnati: Institute of Decision Sciences.

Krajewski, L. J., and H. E. Thompson. 1975. Efficient employment planning in public utilities. *The Bell Journal of Economics* 6 (1):314-326.

Taubert, W. H. 1968. A search decision rule for the aggregate scheduling problem. *Management Science* 14(6):B343-B359.

Wagner, H. M., R. J. Giglio, and R. G. Glaser. 1964. Preventive maintenance scheduling by mathematical programming. *Management Science* 10 (2):316-334.

Wight, O. 1974. *Production and inventory management in the computer age.* Boston, Mass.: Cahners Books.

Reprinted, by permission, from International Journal of
Production Research, *Vol. 14, No. 2, 1976.*

A multiple goal linear programming model for coordinated production and logistics planning

K. D. LAWRENCE† and J. J. BURBRIDGE‡

Of utmost importance to the firm is the achievement of the most efficient utilization of its available resources while adhering to the restrictions of its economic environment. One of the inherent difficulties with present linear programming formulations of the coordinated production and logistics planning problem is the failure to include the multiple goals intrinsic to the planning of the firm. The model to be presented in this paper will consider three commonly occurring goals of the firm in coordinating production and logistics planning. These are (1) the maximization of total sales revenue for a specific location and customer; (2) the minimization of total production and distribution costs; and finally, (3) the maximization of production for a particular item at a particular location. This model structure will also include capacity, budget, demand and volume constraints for each production facility. The solution technique for this model will be a computerized multiple objective analogue of the revised simplex method.

Introduction

The problem of interest involves deciding what products should be produced, how much of each product to produce, and where production should take place. The decision-making process utilized in this paper considers several key objectives of the firm: (1) maximizing total sales revenue for a specific location and customer, (2) minimizing total cost of production and distribution, and (3) maximizing production of a particular item at a particular location. Since these objectives may be mutually incompatible, it may be impossible to optimize with respect to all three goals. Thus, the decision process will concern itself with trying to find the best possible solution given the existing conditions. The technique of multiple objective linear programming was developed for such a situation (Cochrane and Zeleny 1973).

In addition to the objectives associated with this problem, the model structure for this complex decision process will consist of the following general constraint types:

(1) total demand for each item at each customer location,

(2) available production capacity at each production location,

(3) maximum shipping weight for all items from each production location,

(4) total budget for production and transportation for all locations and all items.

Presented at the 3rd International Conference on Production Research (Amherst) August 1975.

† Management Information Services, Hoffmann La-Roche Inc., New Jersey, U.S.A.
‡ Department of Mechanical, Industrial and Aerospace Engineering, Rutgers University, New Brunswick, New Jersey, U.S.A.

Published by Taylor & Francis Ltd, 10–14 Macklin Street, London WC2B 5NF.

The multiple objective linear programming problem

Multiple objective linear programming enables an optimization problem to be analysed in terms of the separate and often conflicting objectives inherent in many real world decision problems. Moreover, the value of each effectiveness measure or criterion can be compared and contrasted amongst the candidate solutions because of the explicit treatment given to each of the objectives in the analysis. Rather than seeking a single solution and thus imposing inflexibility on the decision maker, this procedure will produce a set of alternative solutions to be evaluated by the decision maker with respect to political, social, legal, moral, or any other criteria of this modern complex world.

The linear multiple objective programming problem takes the following form:

$$(M) \max (Cx = Z | x \in S); \quad S = (x \geqslant 0 | Ax = b)$$

where $x \in R^n$, $Z \in R^k$, C is $k \times n$, and A is $m \times n$. A solution to (M) is an efficient point. A point $\bar{x}$ is defined to be efficient if and only if there does not exist an $x \in S$ such that $Cx \geqslant C\bar{x}$.

The device for finding the extreme point solutions for the multiple objective linear programming problem is the FORTRAN computer programme MOLP74 developed by Steuer (Evans and Steuer 1973, Steuer 1973). MOLP74 uses a multiple objective analogue of the revised simplex technique.

In Phase I of the computational procedure, a special objective function is formed to minimize the sum of the artificial variables.

Next, in Phase II efficient extreme point solutions are found. The efficient point solutions are found by a sequential maximization procedure in which individual objectives are successively maximized subject to reduced constraint sets formed by the intersection of the original constraint set and optimal level curves of objectives previously maximized. The rule used for the selection of the ordering of the objective function is the following:

Select, as the next unmaximized objective to be maximized, the objective with the fewest number of negative elements in its reduced cost row.

Finally in Phase III all efficient extreme point solutions are enumerated.

The model structure

The decision variables in this multiple goal linear programming model for production and logistics planning:

x_{ijk}: amount of the ith item to be produced at the jth production location for transportation and sale at the kth customer location.

The objectives of this problem are as follows:

(1) Maximize total sales revenue of the ath production location to the bth customer location

$$Z_1 = \sum_{i=l}^{m} r_{iab} x_{iab}$$

where

r_{iab}: revenue per unit of the ith item produced at the ath production location for the bth customer location.

(2) Minimize the sum of the total costs of production at all plant locations and to also minimize the total cost of transporting the items from all plant locations to all customer locations

$$Z_2 = \sum_{i=1}^{m} \sum_{j=1}^{n} C_{ij} x_{ijk} + \sum_{i=1}^{m} \sum_{j=1}^{n} \sum_{k=1}^{l} t_{ijk} x_{ijk}$$

where

c_{ij}: total unit cost of producing the ith item at the jth production location.

t_{ijk}: total unit cost of transporting the ith item from the jth production location to the kth customer.

(3) Maximize the total production of the rth item at the sth production location. This objective seeks to have the sth location as the primary production facility for product r.

$$Z_3 = \sum_{k=1}^{l} x_{rsk}$$

The constraint set for the model is as follows:

(i) The total demand for the ith item at the kth customer location is equal to D_{ijk}

$$\sum_{j=1}^{n} x_{ijk} = D_{ik} \qquad \text{for all } i \text{ and } k.$$

(ii) The available capacity for the ith item at the jth production location is less than or equal to P_{ij}

$$\sum_{k=1}^{l} x_{ijk} = P_{ij} \qquad \text{for all } i \text{ and } j.$$

(iii) The maximum shipping weight for all the items shipped from the jth production location to all customer locations is equal to W_j

$$\sum_{i=1}^{m} \sum_{k=1}^{l} w_i x_{ijk} \leqslant W_j \qquad \text{for all } k$$

where

w_i: weight of one unit of the ith item.

(4) The total budget for the production and distribution of all items is less than or equal to B

$$\sum_{i=1}^{m} \sum_{j=1}^{n} C_{ij} x_{ijk} + \sum_{i=1}^{m} \sum_{j=1}^{n} \sum_{k=1}^{l} t_{ijk} x_{ijk} \leqslant B \qquad \text{for all } k.$$

The overall model will have the following form:

$$\max Z_1 = \sum_{i=1}^{m} r_{iab} x_{iab}$$

$$\max Z_2 = -\left(\sum_{i=1}^{m} \sum_{j=1}^{n} C_{ij} x_{ijk} + \sum_{i=1}^{m} \sum_{j=1}^{n} \sum_{k=1}^{l} t_{ijk} x_{ijk} \right)$$

$$\max Z_3 = \sum_{k=1}^{l} x_{rsk}$$

Subject to:

$$\sum_{j=1}^{n} x_{ijk} = D_{ik} \tag{1}$$

$$\sum_{k=1}^{l} x_{ijk} = P_{ij} \tag{2}$$

$$\sum_{i=1}^{m} \sum_{k=1}^{l} w_i x_{ijk} \geq W_j \tag{3}$$

$$\sum_{i=1}^{m} \sum_{j=1}^{n} C_{ij} x_{ijk} + \sum_{i=1}^{m} \sum_{j=1}^{n} \sum_{k=1}^{l} t_{ijk} x_{ijk} \leq B \tag{4}$$

$$x_{ijk} \geq 0 \qquad \text{for all } i, j \text{ and } k.$$

Example

The following problem was formulated and solved. The input data is given in the following tables:

Table 1. Shipping costs.

		Product 1			Product 2		
		Customer			Customer		
		1	2	3	1	2	3
Production location	1	4	5	7	3	3	5
	2	6	7	8	6	7	9

Table 2. Production costs.

		Product	
		1	2
Production location	1	20	24
	2	30	34

Table 3. Production capacity.

		Product	
		1	2
Production location		750	850
		740	860

245

Table 4. Selling prices.

		Customer location		
		1	2	3
Product	1	40	42	45
	2	58	62	65

Table 5. Estimated demand.

		Customer location		
		1	2	3
Product	1	300	225	275
	2	330	300	250

Table 6. Other pertinent data.

Total budget (production and transportation)	=	$60 000
Weight of product No. 1	=	30 lb
Weight of product No. 2	=	40 lb
Capacity for all items shipped—production location 1	=	75 000 lb
Capacity for all items shipped—production location 2	=	70 000 lb

In order to facilitate further discussion of this problem, the following objective criteria were utilized. Also, the variables of interest were coded as in the following table.

Table 7. Objective criteria.

Z_1: Criterion no. 1—Minimize total cost of production and transportation.

Z_2: Criterion no. 2—Maximize number of units of product 1 produced at production location 1.

Z_3: Criterion no. 3—Maximize number of units of product 2 produced at production location 2.

Z_4: Criterion no. 4—Maximize sales revenue for production location 1 and customer location 1.

Z_5: Criterion no. 5—Maximize sales revenue for production location 2 and customer location 2.

Table 8. Definition of variables.

	Product	Production location	Customer location
x_1	1	1	1
x_2	1	1	2
x_3	1	1	3
x_4	2	1	1
x_5	2	1	2
x_6	2	1	3
x_7	1	2	1
x_8	1	2	2
x_9	1	2	3
x_{10}	2	2	1
x_{11}	2	2	2
x_{12}	2	2	3

The example problem can now be formulated as follows:

$$\max Z_1 = -24x_1 - 25x_2 - 27x_3 - 30x_4 - 31x_5 - 32x_6$$
$$- 33x_7 - 33x_8 - 35x_9 - 40x_{10} - 41x_{11} - 43x_{12}$$

$$\max Z_2 = x_1 + x_2 + x_3$$

$$\max Z_3 = x_{10} + x_{11} + x_{12}$$

$$\max Z_4 = 40x_1 + 50x_4$$

$$\max Z_5 = 30x_8 + 34x_{11}$$

$$\text{s.t.} \quad x_1 + x_7 \geqslant 300$$

$$x_2 + x_8 \geqslant 225$$

$$x_3 + x_9 \geqslant 275$$

$$x_4 + x_{10} \geqslant 330$$

$$x_5 + x_{11} \geqslant 300$$

$$x_6 + x_{12} \geqslant 250$$

$$x_1 + x_2 + x_3 \geqslant 750$$

$$x_4 + x_5 + x_6 \geqslant 850$$

$$x_7 + x_8 + x_9 \geqslant 740$$

$$x_{10} + x_{11} + {}_{12} \geqslant 860$$

$$30x_1 + 30x_2 + 30x_3 + 40x_4 + 40x_5 + 40x_6 \geqslant 75\,000$$

$$30x_7 + 30x_8 + 30x_9 + 40x_{10} + 40x_{11} + 40x_{12} \geqslant 70\,000$$

$$24x_1 + 25x_2 + 27x_3 + 30x_4 + 31x_5 + 32x_6$$
$$+ 33x_7 + 33x_8 + 35x_9 + 40x_{10} + 41x_{11} + 43x_{12} \geqslant 60\,000$$

$$x_i \geqslant 0 \qquad i = 1, 2, \ldots, 12$$

After a computer run using MOLP74 the following set of 24 efficient extreme points were obtained.

247

Table 9. Efficient extreme point solutions.

Efficient basis	Amount of product produced											
	x_1	x_2	x_3	x_4	x_5	x_6	x_7	x_8	x_9	x_{10}	x_{11}	x_{12}
1	300	175	275	333	270	225	0	500	0	0	0	0
2	300	0	275	330	270	250	0	225	175	0	0	0
3	300	175	275	330	520	0	0	500	0	0	0	250
4	300	175	275	11	589	250	0	50	0	319	0	0
5	300	0	275	402	0	118	0	225	175	0	0	0
6	235	0	275	330	270	250	65	225	240	0	0	0
7	300	0	275	195	406	250	0	225	175	0	0	0
8	300	115	275	330	520	0	0	110	60	0	0	0
9	300	175	275	267	590	0	0	50	0	0	0	250
10	300	175	275	0	585	250	0	50	0	330	0	0
11	300	0	275	451	555	250	0	225	0	285	0	0
12	136	0	275	330	0	250	164	225	339	0	164	0
13	66	0	275	330	270	250	234	225	0	0	234	0
14	300	0	275	0	343	250	0	225	175	0	0	0
15	300	0	275	0	540	250	0	225	0	0	0	0
16	250	225	275	0	518	250	50	0	0	330	50	0
17	0	0	275	330	0	250	300	225	144	0	300	0
18	175	0	275	0	0	250	125	225	300	330	125	0
19	0	0	275	330	163	250	300	225	0	300	0	0
20	0	0	275	0	56	250	300	225	0	0	300	0
21	61	225	275	0	0	250	239	0	189	330	300	0
22	0	225	275	0	115	250	300	0	0	330	300	0
23	0	0	275	0	0	250	300	225	50	330	300	0
24	0	225	275	0	0	250	300	0	101	330	300	0

Table 10. Values associated with example problem objectives
for efficient extreme point solutions.

Efficient basis	Z_1	Z_2	Z_3	Z_4	Z_5
1	46 920	750	0	28 500	1 500
2	54 445	575	0	28 500	6 750
3	57 420	750	250	28 500	1 500
4	60 000	750	319	12 549	1 500
5	60 000	575	132	28 500	6 750
6	60 000	510	65	25 886	8 972
7	60 000	575	135	21 726	6 750
8	60 000	690	250	28 500	3 300
9	60 000	750	313	25 354	1 500
10	60 000	750	330	12 000	1 500
11	60 000	575	285	14 256	6 750
12	60 000	411	164	21 947	12 320
13	60 000	314	234	19 156	14 692
14	60 000	575	330	12 000	6 750
15	60 000	575	330	12 000	6 750
16	60 000	750	380	10 000	1 700
17	60 000	275	300	16 500	16 950
18	60 000	450	455	7 000	11 000
19	60 000	275	300	16 500	16 950
20	60 000	275	630	0	16 950
21	60 000	561	569	2 447	8 120
22	60 000	500	630	0	10 200
23	60 000	275	630	0	16 950
24	60 000	500	630	0	10 200

Conclusion

In this paper the use of multiple objective linear programming has been used to decide alternate production schedules for a group of products. The results of this optimization process on a relatively simple problem have produced a series of production and logistic schedules and their objective function evaluations. These alternative solutions can now be evaluated by appropriate decision makers with respect to other possible decision criteria. In Table 10 the decision maker is given the values associated with the objective criteria for the efficient extreme point solutions. Table 9 shows the values associated with the variables of interest for these same efficient extreme point solutions. The decision maker can now weigh the efficient extreme point solutions with respect to other qualitative factors that also exist. The decision maker can then make the decision concerning the production schedule that best satisfies all possible objective criteria.

Un des facteurs d'importance primaire pour l'entreprise est celui qui consiste à réaliser l'utilisation la plus efficace de ses ressources disponibles tout en respectant les restrictions imposées par son environnement économique. Une des difficultés associées aux définitions actuelles de la programmation linéaire de la production coordonnée, ainsi que la planification logistique, résident dans le fait qu'il est impossible d'y inclure les objectifs multiples à atteindre qui sont intrinsèques à la planification générale de l'entreprise. Le modèle à présenter par cette thèse examinera trois des objectifs constants de la société en matière de coordination de la production et de la planification logistique. Ces objectifs sont: (1) la maximisation du revenu total des ventes pour une situation géographique et un client spécifiques; (2) la minimisation de la production totale et des coûts de distribution et, finalement, (3) la maximisation de la production pour un article donné dans une position spécifique. Cette structure de modèle comprendra également les contraintes de capacité, budget, demande et volume pour chaque facilité de production individuelle. La solution technique du modèle sera représentée par l'étude analogique des objectifs multiples par ordinateur de la méthode révisée simplex.

Die Erzielung der wirksamsten Ausnutzung ihrer verfügbaren Mittel unter gleichzeitiger Einhaltung der Restriktionen ihrer wirtschaftlichen Umgebung ist von allergrößter Wichtigkeit für die Firma. Eine der inhärenten Schwierigkeiten bei gegenwärtigen linearen Programmierformulierungen des koordinierten Produktions- und Logistikplanungsproblems ist das Versäumnis, die der Planung der Firma innewohnenden Mehrfachziele einzuschließen. Das in dieser Abhandlung zu präsentierende Modell wird drei gewöhnlich auftretende Ziele der Firma in der koordinierten Produktions- und Logistikplanung erwägen. Diese sind (1) die Maximierung der Gesamtverkaufseinnahmen für einen spezifischen Standort und Kunden; (2) die Maximierung der Gesamtproduktions- und Vertriebskosten, und schließlich (3) die Maximierung der Produktion für einen speziellen Posten an einem speziellen Standort. Diese Modellstruktur schließt ebenfalls Kapazitäts-, Etats-, Nachfragen- und Volumenbeschränkungen für jede Produktions-einrichtung ein. Die Lösungstechnik für dieses Modell wird ein computerisiertes Mehrfachzielanalog der revidierten Simplexmethode sein.

REFERENCES

COCHRANE, J. L., and ZELENY, MILAN, 1973, *Multiple Criteria Decision Making*, (Columbia, South Carolina: University of South Carolina Press).

EVANS, J. P., and STEUER, R. E., 1973, A revised simplex method for linear multiple objective programming, *Math. Prog.*, 5, 1.

LAWRENCE, KENNETH D., KOCH, HOWARD, and BURBRIDGE, J. J., 1975, A good programming model for the transshipment of goods problem, *Proceedings of the 1975 Northeastern Regional Meeting of the American Institute of Decision Sciences*, Amherst, Massachusetts.

STEUER R.E., 1973, Generating efficient extreme points in linear multiple objective programming theory and computational experience, Doctoral Dissertation, University of North Carolina.

Reprinted, by permission, from International Journal of
Production Research, *Vol. 18, No. 6, 1980.*

Chemical production planning via goal programming

STELIOS H. ZANAKIS† and JAMES S. SMITH‡

Production planning in a chemical plant requires determination of production
quantities for several intermediate and final products. The production plan must
satisfy several absolute requirements (material balances, production capacities,
etc.) and conflicting objectives (profits, costs, sales limits, environmental
pressures, equipment utilization and other engineering objectives). A goal
programming approach for chemical production planning is presented and
illustrated by means of an industrial case study example along with implications
and extensions of the basic model. The presentation is kept simple so that it is
understood by students and practitioners interested in chemical process
planning.

Introduction

The total planning function in a continuous process industry, e.g. chemical, may
be viewed at different hierarchical levels (similar to those described by Royce
(1970)):

(i) *Plant unit design*: Determine equipment capacities and process design
characteristics (usually to maximize return on investment). This phase
occurs only at the initiation or modification of a plant unit.

(ii) *Production planning*: For a given plant and assumed steady-state operating
conditions, determine production quantities for each product that will
maximize total profits (or revenues) to meet market forecasted demands
while satisfying various technological and other restrictions. The planning
horizon may be long (a few years, strategic planning) or intermediate
(several months, tactical planning).

(iii) *Production scheduling*: In a multiproduct unit, determine the production
sequence and run lengths to produce quantities specified in phase (ii) above,
while balancing the storage costs against the set-up (product switching)
costs. The planning horizon may vary from several hours to a few days
(operations planning).

(iv) *Process operation*: Frequent (e.g. hourly) change of process operating
conditions to minimize operating costs or feedstock (input) consumption, or
to maximize yield (output). This is more of a control rather than a planning
function.

This article presents a new approach to level (ii) planning, a subject seldom
discussed in the chemical literature.

Levels (i) and (iv) have been addressed in many literature publications, primarily
chemical. Due to the inherent complex nonlinear relationships of the problem

Received 13 July 1978.

† Florida International University, School of Business and Organizational Sciences,
Division of Management, Miami, Florida 33199, U.S.A.

‡ Clarke Printing and Packaging, San Antonio, Texas 78205, U.S.A.

variables and constraints (flowrate, temperature, pressure, capacity, costs, etc.) nonlinear optimization is a natural approach (see for example Jen *et al.* 1968, Weisman *et al.* 1965). Several such applications are described in a workshop proceedings (Blakemore and Davis 1964) and a few books (e.g. Himmelblau 1972). Computational difficulties, however, have caused many practitioners to use other methods, such as simulation (Fowler and Harvey 1978); simple stagewise search/ranking rules (White 1971) or systematic random sampling (Jaakola and Luns 1973); linear/integer programming (LIP) applied to the original problem after linearizing it by means of linear regression (Flanigan *et al.* 1972), assumed local or piece-wise linear approximations (Gambro *et al.* 1972, Horn 1978, Kellogg 1971, Royce 1970), or derivative approximation from repeated application·of the method of steepest ascent (Schrage 1958).

Level (iii) type problems have been addressed extensively in the sequencing/scheduling operations research literature, but reported applications in the chemical industry are scarce (Prabhakar 1973).

Finally level (ii), chemical production planning, is an important yet seldom publicized activity in the chemical industry. A major search of chemical and operations research journals produced only a couple of references on this subject. A few large companies have developed integrated large-scale (multi-plant) LP models for intermediate and long-range production planning (Ahrsjoe and Svedunger 1973, Prabhakar 1973). These have been designed mostly by corporate operations research teams. Such teams seldom function at the plant or specific process level of large chemical companies and they hardly exist in smaller organizations. Consequently, production planning in a single plant is usually based on *ad hoc* and/or traditional chemical engineering procedures of limited scope rather than operations research models.

In this article we present a *single*-plant (or unit) linear *goal* programming model for planning production quantities of various intermediate and final chemical products in the presence of multiple-conflicting objectives. The few chemical production planning articles mentioned previously employ aggregate LP models at the multi-plant level and fail to consider the conflicting goals that exist in a real operating environment. We believe the approach presented in this article to be innovative and promising for the chemical industry and interesting to students and practitioners. For better understanding, the presentation is kept simple and illustrated by means of an industrial case study example.

A chemical process example

The process under study is shown in the figure. Cell liquor (CL) is produced in two production units, cell room (1) and cell room (2). The first can only pump to production unit 47, while the second can pump directly to production unit 46, to transfer tank 108, or to another company where it is sold as a final product (not to exceed 25 tons per day). Two tanks act as transfer storage buffers: T108 from cell room (2) to unit 47, and T104 between production units 46 and 47.

Four products A, B, C and D are produced in this chemical process. Production unit 46 makes product A for sales only. Unit 47 makes product B for sales and as an input to unit 49 for the production of product D. A minimum amount of 32·6 tons/day of product D is required for the operation of another corporate plant. The remainder of product D from unit 49 is used as feed stock for unit 48 (small amounts

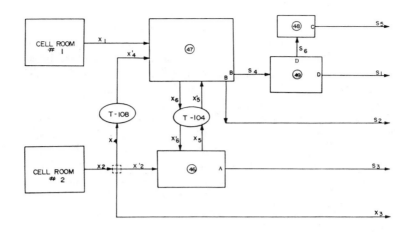

may also be sold). Unit 48 concentrates product D to product C, which is made for sales only.

Production and sales data for the above chemical process are shown in Table 1.

A production plan is required for the process of this example. This must specify the production quantity and intended use of each product, byproduct and cell liquor (see the figure) that will best satisfy several conflicting objectives dictated by managerial, technological and social considerations (as explained in the next section). Production is expressed in tons/day and the planning horizon is typically a month.

Department	46	47		48	49		CR_1	CR_2	
Product	A	B		C	D		CL	CL	
Quantity (ton/day)	S_3	S_2	S_4	S_5	S_1	S_6	X_1	X_2	X_3
Production capacity (ton/day)	409	284		73	179		354	400	—
Max. sales (ton/day)	130·1	335		106·7	963·3		—	—	25·0
Price ($/ton)	72·93	78·17	0	84·82	76·79	0	0	0	43·85
Cost ($/ton)	65·86	56·11	1·5†	68·40	69·92	1·5†	—	—	42·39
Profit ($/ton)	7·07	22·06	−1·5	16·42	6·87	−1·5	—	—	1·46
Conversion ratio (CL equiv.)	3	2·5	2·5	3·75	3·5	3·5	1	1	1

† Pumping costs only. The remaining cost figures include all production costs allocated to each product according to standard engineering costing procedures.

Table 1. Production and sales data.

Basic model development

A brief description of the linear goal programming approach is given in the appendix. In our example, we first identify the decision variables for the chemical production plan (see also the figure):

S_1: production of product D for sale (tons/day)
S_2: production of product B for sale (tons/day)
S_3: production of product A for sale (tons/day)
S_4: production of product B from 47 as input to 49 (tons/day)
S_5: production of product C for sale (tons/day)
S_6: production of product D from 49 as input to 48 (tons/day)
X_1: production of cell liquor from cell room (1) (tons/day)
X_2: production of cell liquor from cell room (2) (tons/day)
X_3: part of X_2 to be sold to another company (tons/day)

The remaining six variables (X_4, X_4', X_5, X_5', X_6 and X_6') represent CL transfers (tons/day) between tanks and production units. These are needed to increase the capacity of one unit (at the expense of another) in a planned or emergency situation (e.g., if one unit is not operating).

The next step is to generate the goals dictated by production capacities and sales ceilings, desires of managers, unit supervisors and technical assistants, etc. Once these goals are identified, they are ranked by preemptive priorities. The first priority is given to the goals that must be satisfied for the solution to be implementable (absolute goals). The remaining goals are assigned other priority levels and possibly different weights within the same priority.

The following goal programming model was initially developed (after eliminating redundant goals, which were not immediately obvious). The variables n_i and p_i denote the negative (underachievement) and positive (overachievement) deviation from the ith goal.

PRIORITY 1 (absolute)

G_1: *Do not exceed CL production capacity*   *Goal*

CR$_1$: $X_1 + n_1 - p_1 = 354$ Minimize p_1

CR$_2$: $X_2 + n_2 - p_2 = 400$ Minimize p_2

G_2: *Satisfy material balances*

Unit 46: $X_2' + X_6' - X_5 - 3S_3 + n_3 - p_3 = 0$ Minimize $n_3 + p_3$
          Where the coefficient of 3 converts S_3 to CL
            equivalent. Similarly,

Unit 47: $X_1 + X_4' + X_5' - X_6 - 2 \cdot 50 S_4 - 2 \cdot 50 S_2 + n_4 - p_4 = 0$ Minimize $n_4 + p_4$

Unit 48: $3 \cdot 50 S_6 - 3 \cdot 75 S_5 + n_5 - p_5 = 0$ Minimize $n_5 + p_5$

Unit 49: $2 \cdot 50 S_4 - 3 \cdot 50 S_1 - 3 \cdot 50 S_6 + n_6 - p_6 = 0$ Minimize $n_6 + p_6$

Split
    node: $X_2 - X_2' - X_3 - X_4 + n_7 - p_7 = 0$ Minimize $n_7 + p_7$

Tank
     104:   $X_6 + X_5 - X_5' - X_6' + n_8 - p_8 = 0$ Minimize $n_8 + p_8$

Tank
     108:            $X_4 - X_4' + n_9 - p_9 = 0$ Minimize $n_9 + p_9$

Note: Zero right-hand sides and not the tank capacities should be used in the above two equations (i.e. a steady state solution is sought); otherwise, the tanks will produce one way flows, i.e. they will act as a source or sink.

G_3: *Do not exceed production and sales limits*

Unit 46:	$S_3 + n_{10} - p_{10} = 130 \cdot 1$	Minimize	p_{10}
Unit 47:	$S_2 + S_4 + n_{11} - p_{11} = 284 \cdot 0$	Minimize	p_{11}
Unit 48:	$S_5 + n_{12} - p_{12} = 73 \cdot 0$	Minimize	p_{12}
Unit 49:	$S_1 + S_6 + n_{13} - p_{13} = 179 \cdot 0$	Minimize	p_{13}

PRIORITY 2

G_4: *The outside company can only take up to 25 tons/day of CL*

$$X_3 + n_{14} - p_{14} = 25 \qquad \text{Minimize} \quad p_{14}$$

G_5: *Meet the other corporate plan requirement for at least 32·6 tons/day of D*

$$S_1 + n_{15} - p_{15} = 32 \cdot 6 \qquad \text{Minimize} \quad n_{15}$$

PRIORITY 3

G_6: *Maximize profits*

$$6 \cdot 87 S_1 + 22 \cdot 06 S_2 + 7 \cdot 07 S_3 - 1 \cdot 50 S_4 + 16 \cdot 42 S_5$$
$$- 1 \cdot 50 S_6 + 1 \cdot 46 X_3 + n_{16} - p_{16} = 11000 \text{ (a very}$$
high value) $\qquad$ Minimize $\quad n_{16}$

PRIORITY 4

G_7: *Minimize transfers of CL*

Besides additional costs incurred (which are difficult to estimate) there is always the possibility of overflowing the system with a resultant discharge to the environment.

$$X_4 + X'_4 + X_5 + X'_5 + X_6 + X'_6 + n_{17} - p_{17} = 0 \qquad \text{Minimize} \quad p_{17}$$

PRIORITY 5

G_8: *Avoid underutilization of cell room capacities (n_1 and n_2)*

$$\text{Minimize} \quad n_1$$
$$\text{Minimize} \quad n_2$$

G_9: *Sell as much 'product' as possible*

$$3 \cdot 5 S_1 + 2 \cdot 5 S_2 + 3 \cdot 0 S_3 + 3 \cdot 75 S_5 + n_{18} - p_{18} = 800 \qquad \text{Minimize} \quad n_{18}$$
$$\text{(a very high value)}$$

where the coefficients convert each product to CL equivalent.

The achievement function for this goal programming model is

$$\text{Min} \{ (p_1 + p_2 + n_3 + p_3 + n_4 + p_4 + n_5 + p_5 + n_6 + p_6 + n_7 + p_7 + n_8 + p_8 + n_9 + p_9$$
$$+ p_{10} + p_{11} + p_{12} + p_{13}), (p_{14} + 7 \cdot 0 n_{15}), n_{16}, p_{17}, (2 \cdot 0 n_1 + 2 \cdot 4 n_2 + 3 \cdot 0 n_{18}) \}$$

where the commas separate adjacent priority levels. Note the following non-unit coefficients (weights) in the above achievement function: In the second priority, $7 \cdot 0$ is the product of $3 \cdot 5$ (to convert n_{17} to CL equivalent units as p_{16}) times 2 (which expresses management's feeling that it is twice as important to satisfy their own corporate plant needs, G_5, than the outside company demand, G_4). In the last priority, the three weights reflect management's assessment of the corresponding goals and that a ton of CL from cell room (1) costs 20% more than a ton from cell room (2).

One may observe that satisfaction of the first priority (absolute) goals requires that the corresponding deviational variables be zero (here p_1 to p_{13} and n_3 to n_9). Therefore, they could be omitted from the model, thus treating the corresponding equations as real constraints. Typical linear goal programming codes do not handle real constraints, but try to achieve them in the first priority minimization phase, which usually is only a small portion of the total computation effort. Treating first priority goals as real constraints will be computationally advantageous if they are many, but may cause difficulties if all of them cannot be satisfied simultaneously (analogous to an infeasible LP solution).

Discussion of model results

Case 1

The above linear goal programming model has 16 decision variables, 18 objectives (rows) and 5 priorities. It was solved using a simplex code for linear goal programming (Ignizio 1976). Two alternative solutions were obtained with CL input to unit 47 via tank 104 or 108 respectively. The results are summarized under Case 1 in Table 2 (along with some additional calculations at the bottom of the table).

	Variable	Case 1		Case 2	Case 3	Case 4
Product	S_1	32·60		32·60	32·60	32·60
	S_2	238·36		95·96	187·96	141·46
	S_3	14·67		130·10	56·67	53·33
	S_4	45·64		45·64	45·64	92·14
	S_5	0		0	0	31·00
	S_6	0		0	0	33·21
CL Flow	X_1	354·00		354·00	354·00	354·00
	X_2	400·00		400·00	400·00	400·00
	X_2'	44·00	400·00	390·30	265·00	255·00
	X_3	0		9·70	0	10·00
CL Transfers	X_4	356·00	0	0	135·00	135·00
	X_4'	356·00	0	0	135·00	135·00
	X_5	0	356·00	0	95·00	95·00
	X_5'	0	356·00	0	95·00	95·00
	X_6	0		0	0	0
	X_6'	0		0	0	0
	CL flow	798·00	1154·00	1144·30	1019·00	1009·00
	CL transfers	712·00		0	460·00	460·00
	Cost of CL flow, $	638·40	923·20	915·44	815·20	807·20
	Cost of transfers, $	1495·20		0	966·00	966·00
	Profit G_6, $	5517·43		3206·37	4702·53	4057·33
	Profit G_6', $	3383·83	3099·03	2290·93	2921.33	2284·03

Table 2.   Goal programming solution results.

255

It was felt that the solution to the above model does not really maximize profits, since G_7 did not include the cost of all CL pipe flows, which are difficult to estimate. In order to gain a feeling for this 'suboptimization', the following *rough* cost estimates were extracted from unit supervisors:

For X_1, X_2 and X_2' a variable cost of \$0·80/ton (less than that of the more corrosive products B and D) representing a direct pumping cost;
For the CL transfers X_4, X_4', X_5, X_5', X_6, X_6' a variable cost of \$2·10/ton representing pumping, maintenance, storage and power expenses;
Then, the profit goal G_6 becomes

$$G_6': \quad 6·87S_1 + 22·06S_2 + 7·03S_3 - 1·50S_4 + 16·42S_5 - 1·50S_6 + 1·46X_3$$
$$-0·80(X_1 + X_2 + X_2') - 2·10(X_4 + X_4' + X_5 + X_5' + X_6 + X_6') + n_{16} - p_{16} = 11000$$

Interesting enough, the *same* two alternative solutions were obtained as before (listed under Case 1 in Table 2). This solution robustness suggests that improved estimates of transfer costs are really not necessary in the above model.

Case 2

Another important concern of plant management relates to G_7. Recent environmental pressures place increased importance on the minimization of environmental discharges that may result from temporarily excessive transfers overflowing the capacity of the tank system. In order to gain some insight in this direction, a new run was made with the transfer minimization goal elevated to priority 3 and the profit maximization goal relegated to priority 4. The solution results (again identical for either G_6 or G_6') are listed under Case 2 in Table 2. The transfers are now completely eliminated at the expense of \$808·10/day (26%) reduction in profits (G_6'). This is a stiff price for a very tight discharge protection.

Case 3

The technique of goal programming is ideally suited for investigating comprom- ise trade-offs between conflicting goals. Case 3 results in Table 2 indicate such a compromise between G_6 and G_7:

G_6: Achieve at least \$5000/day profit (at priority 4)
G_7: Reduce transfers to no more than 190 tons/day through tank 104 and 270 tons/day through tank 108 (at priority 3). Management felt that these levels would provide adequate discharge protection with the existing alarm system.

The results indicate that G_7 achieved its upper limit, while profits G_6 fell short only by \$297·47 a day from the goal of \$5000 a day. It would cost more to improve the present alarm system. Adding for instance one maintenance mechanic to patrol the pumps and lines in each shift would cost approximately \$500/day for a continuous operation.

Case 4

Two interesting results became clear in all previous cases: (*a*) Although product C has the second highest profit (see Table 1), all previous solutions indicate that it should not be produced at all. This unexpected result raises questions on continuing the production of product C. (*b*) Sale of CL to the outside company is not beneficial ($X_3 = 0$), at least at the current price.

The above results initiate re-examination of some production policies. For the short run, however, management felt that client rapport dictates minimum sales of 31 tons/day for product C and 10 tons/day to the outside company (both at priority level 2). Adding these two goals into the Case 3 model produced the results shown under Case 4 in Table 2. The two minimum sales requirements were achieved exactly, at the expense of over $600/day reduction in profits.

Many other case runs can be made by changing goal levels and priorities in order to evaluate different 'what if' questions that management may want to evaluate. Goal programming is ideally suited for this analysis. The decision maker will then select the case results that best satisfy his objectives.

Summary

Production plans in a chemical process can be determined through a series of goal programming models. As the results of a model solution are fed back to management, additional inputs (data, goals, priorities, etc.) are created. In our study, this interactive modelling revealed the price paid by moving from an ideal Case 1 to the more realistic, at least for now, Case 4; evaluated some trade-offs between profit maximization and environmental protection; unmasked hidden unprofitabilities for some product sales; and generated production plans that best satisfied all management goals and objectives. Furthermore, management can gain a deeper insight into this process by examining the necessary information (some of which may have never been quantified before) and evaluating the proposed alternative courses of action.

It should be emphasized that any model is the means and not the end. The manager will be *aided* by the model in making a decision, viz. selecting a specific production plan. In doing so, he may alter the model results by considering factors that were not or could not be included in the model; these may be political and social pressures, company policies, etc. They will have to be addressed for the implementation of a solution along with data collection accuracy versus detail, solution validation and control, frequency of model revision, and other operational details (Fiore and Rozwadowski 1968). The proposed model would be maintained by the process engineering group; input would come from plant accounting ($ data), marketing department (sales levels) and plant operations (technological information).

This article presented an innovative application of goal programming to chemical production planning. The authors are not aware of any such approach published in the literature or practised by the chemical industry (where often production plans are simply the result of several meetings between sales and production managers, with no model support). Similar goal programming models could be developed for short-term and intermediate (1 week to a few months) production planning in other continuous process industries.

APPENDIX

The general linear goal programming model

Linear programming is a well known operations research method that is widely used in production management (Ledbetter and Cox 1977, Zanakis and Lawrence 1980). It can determine the optimal solution according to a single linear objective (e.g. cost minimization or profit maximization) that satisfies also various linear restrictions (e.g. resource and market limitations). However, many management problems, including chemical production planning, must address not one but many objectives that are often conflicting. Goal programming is an extension of linear programming methodology that attempts to hierarchically satisfy various conflicting objectives in a priority dictated by the user.

The general linear goal programming model can be stated as follows:

Find $\bar{X} = (x_1, x_2, \text{-----}, x_n)$ that minimizes

$$Z = \left\{ \sum_{l \in K_1} (w_l^- n_l + w_l^+ p_l), \ldots, \sum_{l \in Ks} (w_l^- n_l + w_l^+ p_l), \ldots, \sum_{l \in Kp} (w_l^- n_l + w_l^+ p_l) \right\} \quad (1)$$

$$\left. \begin{array}{ll} \text{s.t.} \sum_{j=1}^{n} a_{ij}x_j + n_i - p_i = b_i & i = 1, 2, \ldots, m \\ n_i, p_i \geqslant 0 & i = 1, 2, \ldots, m \\ x_j \geqslant 0 & j = 1, 2, \ldots, n \end{array} \right\} \quad (2)$$

where

x_j: the jth decision variable
b_i: the right-hand side (target) of the ith goal
a_{ij}:   the coefficient of the jth decision variable in the ith goal
n_i: the amount of underachievement of the ith goal
p_i: the amount of overachievement of the ith goal
w_l^-:   the weight of the lth priority underachievement (usually equal to 0 or 1)
w_l^+:   the weight of the lth priority overachievement (usually equal to 0 or 1)
K_s: the set of goals in the sth priority level ($s = 1, 2, \ldots, p$)
Z: the achievement function, a row vector of goal attainment at each priority level (separated by commas)†

The appearance of both or only one deviational variable at each term of the achievement function Z is dictated by the desirable direction of the corresponding goal. If we desire a goal type $\leqslant b_i$ we minimize the overachievement p_i; we minimize the underachievement n_i if we desire a goal type $\geqslant b_i$; and we minimize the sum $(n_i + p_i)$ if we want to approach b_i as closely as possible from above or below (i.e. a goal type $\simeq b_i$).

Priorities are preemptive in that each level is infinitely more important than the next lower level. Hence, a higher priority objective must be satisfied as closely as possible, before a lower priority objective is considered. Thus, a typical linear goal programming solution algorithm sequentially applies the simplex method of linear programming to problem (2) with each objective function of (1), without worsening the previously attained higher priority achievement values. It should be noted that all terms within a priority level must be expressed in the same unit of measurement. This, however, is not necessary for the first priority (absolute) objective, because for the solution to be implementable all terms of the first priority objective must be zero.

---

† We prefer this separation by commas, introduced by Ignizio (1976), to the traditional expression (Lee 1972) of connecting different priority goals with a '+' sign preceded by P_k to indicate the kth preemptive priority level. The latter is mathematically incorrect and misleads non-technical readers to think of P_k as a scalar (weight of the kth objective), thus reducing Z to a single weighted objective function.

Goal programming has become increasingly popular in quantitative decision making due to its simplicity and inherent capability of finding the best compromise solution to a problem with many conflicting objectives—as most real world problems are. Two major textbooks have been written exclusively on goal programming (Lee 1972, Ignizio 1976) and many goal programming applications have appeared in various scientific journals over the last few years. For a quick review of the goal programming approach and applications see Ignizio (1978).

La planification de la production dans une usine chimique nécessite la détermination de quantités de production pour plusieurs produits intermédiaires et finals. Le plan de production doit satisfaire plusieurs exigences absolues (balances de matériaux, capacités de production, etc . . .) et objectifs conflictuels (bénéfices, coûts, limites de vente, pressions liées à l'environnement, utilisation de l'équipement et autres objectifs techniques). Une approache pour la programmation d'objectifs dans le cas de la planification d'une production chimique est présentée et illustrée par un exemple qui est une étude d'un cas industriel, et les implications et extensions du modèle de base seront indiquées. La présentation est simplifiée de manière à être comprise par les étudiants et les professionnels intéressés par la planification de processus chimiques.

Die Produktionsplanung in einem chemischen Werk erfordert die Bestimmung von Produktionsmengen für verschiedene Halb- und Fertigprodukte. Der Produktionsplan muß verschiedene absolute Anforderungen (Materialausgeglichenheit, Produktionskapazitäten usw.) und damit in Konflikt stehende Ziele (Gewinn, Kosten, Verkaufsgrenzen, Umweltschutz, Anlagenausnützung und andere technische Ziele) erfüllen. Es wird eine Methode der Zielprogrammierung für die chemische Produktionsplanung vorgestellt und anhand einer industriellen Fallstudie unter Heranziehung von Konsequenzen und Erweiterungen des Grundmodells näher erläutert. Die Erklärung ist einfach gehalten, damit sie auch für Studenten und Praktiker, die sich für die chemische Prozeßplanung interessieren, verständlich ist.

References

AHRSJOE, G., and SVEDUNGER, S., 1973, A production planning system based on linear programming, *Omega*, **1**, 499.

BLAKEMORE, J. W., and DAVIS, S. H., 1964, Optimization techniques, *Chem. Engng Prog. Symp. Series*, **60**, 50.

FIORE, G. F., and ROZWADOWSKI, R. T., 1968, The implementation of process models, *Mgmt Sci.*, **14**, 350.

FLANIGAN, O., WILSON, W. W., and SULE, D. R., 1972, Process-cost reduction through linear programming, *Chem. Eng.*, Feb. 7, 68.

FOWLER, J. R., and HARVEY, D. J., 1978, Dynamic simulation of a PVC process, *Chem. Engng Prog.*, **74**, 61.

GAMBRO, A. J., *et al.*, 1972, Optimize ethylene complex, *Hydrocarbon Proc.*, March, 73.

HIMMELBLAU, D., 1972, *Applied Nonlinear Programming* (New York: McGraw-Hill).

HORN, B. C., 1978, On-line optimization of plant utilities, *Chem. Engng Prog.*, June, 76.

IGNIZIO, J. P., 1976, *Goal Programming and Extensions* (Lexington, Mass.: Lexington Book Co.).

IGNIZIO, J. P., 1978, A review of goal programming: a tool for multiobjective analysis, *J. Ops Res. Soc.*, **29**, 1109.

JAAKOLA, T. H., and LUUS, R., 1973, A note on the application of nonlinear programming to chemical process optimization, *Opns Res.*, **22**, 415.

JEN, F. C., *et al.*, 1968, Optimal capacities of production facilities, *Mgmt Sci.*, **14**, 573.

KELLOGG, M. W., 1971, Linear programming model picks best process scheme, *Chem. Eng.*, Dec. 13, 1971.

LEDBETTER, W. N., and COX, J. F., 1977, Operations research in production management: an investigation of past and present utilization, *Prod. Inv. Mgmt*, (3), 84.

LEE, S. M., 1972, *Goal Programming for Decision Analysis* (Philadelphia: Auerbach Publ.).

PRABHAKAR, T., 1973, Some scheduling applications in chemical industry, in *Symposium on the Theory of Scheduling and Its Applications*, edited by S. E. Elmaghraby (New York: Springer-Verlag), 69.

ROYCE, N. J., 1970, Linear programming applied to production planning and operation of a chemical process, *Opl Res. Q.*, **21**, 61.

SCHRAGE, R. W., 1958, Optimizing a catalytic cracking operation by the method of steepest ascents, *Opns Res.*, **6**, 498.

WEISMAN, J., WOOD, C. F., and RIVLIN, L., 1965, Optimal design of chemical process systems, *Chem. Engng Prog. Symp. Series*, **61**, 55, 50.

WHITE, C. H., 1971, Optimizing production rates, *Chem. Eng.*, June 14, 86.

ZANAKIS, S. H., and LAWRENCE, K. D., 1980, *Mathematical Programming Applications in Production Planning and Scheduling*, A.I.I.E. Research Monograph (in preparation).

Reprinted, by permission, from Multiple-Criteria Decision Making: Theory and Application, *Springer-Verlag, Heidelberg, 1979.*

MULTIPLE GOAL OPERATIONS MANAGEMENT PLANNING AND

DECISION MAKING IN A QUALITY

CONTROL DEPARTMENT

Kenneth D. Lawrence
Planning & Analysis
AT&T Long Lines
Bedminster, New Jersey U.S.A.

Joachim I. Weindling
Operations Research Program
Polytechnic Institute
of New York
Brooklyn, New York U.S.A.

ABSTRACT

This paper discusses the development of an operations management planning model for a quality control department in a typical large-scale, multi-product chemical firm. This model will serve as a management planning aid for the management of the firm. It serves as a tool which can be used to allocate the firm's available resources to the required tasks of quality testing the various production batches of the firm's numerous products. Additionally, a methodological extension of traditional goal progarmming will be used to evaluate various non-certain aspects of the goal structure.

I. THE PLANNING MODEL

   This paper will focus on the development of an operations management planning
model and its associated solution methodology for a quality control department in a
typical large-scale multi-product chemical firm. This model will develop a planning
device which will help the firm's management allocate its available resources to the
required tasks of quality testing the various production lots of the numerous products
of the firm (keeping in mind the numerous goals of the management of the firm.) Previous research work in operations management models under multiple goals can be found
in Goodman (1974), Lee (1971, 1978), and Lawrence (1976, 1977).

   It is quite typical for such a chemical firm to produce a substantial number
of products requiring a number of testing procedures and sequences to verify the
quality level of the products of the firm. In order to perform effectively the testing of the product line of the firm, it is necessary to sample statistically specified
amounts of the finished product from each production lot for use in current and in
potential future testing procedures. Depending upon the demand for the firm's products, production schedules for the items are developed and implemented for each product. Therefore, the magnitude and composition of the quality control workload is
linked directly to the production schedule of the firm, and, therefore, to the demand
for its product. Thus, to insure the efficient quality testing of the firm's products, the quality control department needs to allocate its available resources in a
most effective fashion.

   There are a number of objectives under which the quality control department of
the firm wishes to operate. These include the following:

   1. <u>Minimization of the over-attainment of the goal level for the</u>
      <u>total operational costs of sampling and testing the products of</u>
      <u>the firm</u>. This goal reflects the desire of the firm not to in-
      vest in laboratory equipement, or other laboratory facilities,
      which are directly tied to only a small part of the product line
      of the firm and not yet been proven to be a stable portion of
      the sales of the firm. Thus, this goal reflects the use and man-
      agement of the current resources of the firm, the allocation of
      various personnel, equipment, and laboratory storage.

   2. <u>The minimization of the over-attainment of the goal level for</u>
      <u>the use of outside quality testing and storage</u>. The management
      of the firm believes that the use of outside facilities should be
      minimized.   It believes that testing work performed by out-
      side laboratories does not measure up generally to the stand-
      ards and experience that is associated with in-house testing.
      Furthermore, such use creates logistical and operational diffi-
      culties to the company, as well as opening its product proprie-
      tary information to security violations. Thus, outside facili-

ties should be primarily used **during overtime** periods.

3. <u>Minimization of the over-attainment of the goal level for the</u> <u>amount of quality testing not completed within a short period</u> <u>after production of a batch of items</u>. If the quality testing work is not completed within a short period of time, (i.e., two weeks) deliveries to customers are delayed. Furthermore, a number of products have a limited shelf-life, and delay in quality tests may result in batches of the product being scrapped.

4. <u>Minimization of the over-attainment of the goal level for the</u> <u>amount of quality testing done in internal facilities during</u> <u>maintenance period</u>. In order to maximize the efficiency and effectiveness of the maintenance program for testing facility laboratories, all facilities are closed off from testing out-going products to the maximum extent possible.

Furthermore, the planning model will contain sets of operational constraints on testing capacity and for requiring all item batches to be tested.

II. GOAL PROGRAMMING

In the typical real-world situation, goals set by the decision-maker are achievable only at the expense of other goals. Furthermore, these goals are often incompatible. Thus, there is a need to establish a hierarchy of importance among these incompatible goals so that the most important goals are satisfied or have reached the point beyond which no further improvements are possible. If the decision-maker can provide an ordinal ranking of goals in terms of their contribution or importance to the organization, the problem can be solved by using goal programming.

Goal programming is an extension of linear programming. It is capable of handling decision problems dealing with a single goal and multiple goals and subgoals. The basic concept of goal programming involves incorporating all managerial goals into the model of the system (Charnes, Cooper (1961), Ignizio (1976), Kornbluth (1973), and Lee (1972)). In goal programming, instead of trying to maximize or to minimize the objective criterion directly (as in done in linear programming), the deviations between goals and achievable limits dictated by the set of system constraints are minimized. These deviational variables, which are known as "slack" variables in linear programming, have a slightly different meaning in goal programming. They are divided into positive and/or negative deviations from each goal or subgoal. The objective then becomes the minimization of these deviations within the pre-emptive priority structure assigned to these deviations.

Developing the goal programming model is similar to developing a linear programming model. The first step is defining the decision variables (i.e., X_1 X_2 X_3). Then all managerial goals must be specified and ranked as to priority. Even though it is generally not possible for management to relate to the various goals on a cardinal scale, they can usually associate an ordinal ranking with each of their goals or objectives. The distinction of goal programming is that is provides for the solution of the problems involving multiple (often conflicting) goals arranged according to the management's priority structure.

The general goal programming model can be expressed mathematically as follows

$$\text{Minimize } Z = \sum_{i=1}^{m} (d_i^+ + d_i^-)$$

$$\text{Subject to } AX - D^+ + D^- = B$$
$$X, D^+, D^- \geq 0$$

where m goals are expressed by an m column vector $B = (b_1, b_2, \ldots, b_m)^T$, A is an m x n matrix which expresses the relationship between goals and subgoals, $X = (x_1, x_2, \ldots, x_n)^T$ represents the variables involved in the subgoal, and D^+ and D^- are the m-component vectors of the variables representing deviations from goals, d_i^+ and d_i^-.

If over-achievement is completely acceptable, the over-achievement deviation d_i^+ can be elimianted from the objective function; similarly, if under-achievement is completely acceptable, d_i^- can be eliminated from the objective function. If deviation in either direction is undesirable, both d_i^+ and d_i^- must be included in the objective function and ranked according to their pre-emptive priority weights.

In goal programming, the most important goal is "optimized" to the extent possible before the second goal is considered. Next, the second goal is optimized. This procedure is followed within the given system constraints of the problem until all goals are fulfilled to the extent possible.

III. SOME DIFFICULTIES ASSOCIATED WITH GOAL PROGRAMMING

While goal programming offers a great deal of flexibility in solving operational management problems, there are a number of nagging difficulties associated with its use. One such difficulty is the manner in which the pre-emptive priority structure is chosen and the effect this ordering has upon the solution produced. Even though considerable care is exercised in developing the priority structure, there still may be uncertainty regarding the assignment of priority levels in a manner that actually reflects the objectives of the manager. While the effect of reordering these priorities can be investigated by solving all such permutations of priority structures, this would be highly inefficient. Moreover, it would typically produce a large number of solutions, many of which would be highly similar and overlapping in nature. Therefore, in order to insure correct or even rational solutions to the goal programming model, changes in the priority assignments of the various goals need to be investigated in a logical, computationally efficient manner.

Basically, the linear goal programming problem is a set of dependent, ordinally ranked linear programming problems, where the ordinal ranking is developed through the use of a set of pre-emptive priority levels. Since these pre-emptive priority factors imply that the higher order goals must be optimized before lower order goals can be considered for optimization, a solution to the overall linear goal programming model can be found by solving a nested series of the subproblems of the overall goal programming model.

Due to the enormous amount of computational effort needed to solve the entire set of goal programming problems posed by all of the permutations of ordering of goals and by the various levels of targeted goals, a stratified random sample of these sets should be selected for solution and examination.

A second difficulty typically associated with goal programming is determining proper values for the target level goals. Estimates of these target level goals should allow for their potential variation, by including both upper and lower bounds for each target goal level.

Finally, there is a need to prune the set of solutions obtained to a managable size. This pruning can be logically accomplished through the multivariate statistical technique of clustering analysis. The clustering analysis develops natural grouping among the many solution sets. It also allows for the presentation of a representative set of distinctive solutions to the decision-maker for his evaluation.

The use of these procedures will be highlighted in Section V.

IV. MODEL STRUCTURE

The decision variables in this goal programming model are as follows:

X^N_{ijk}: the number of bathces tested in the ith period in internal laboratory facilities during normal work periods in the ith product produced in the jth period

X^0_{ijk}: the number of batches tested in the kth period in internal facilities during overtime work periods in the ith product produced in the jth period

Y_{ijk}: the number of batches tested in the kth period in external laboratory facilities of the ith product produced in the jth period

The goal constraints of the model are as follows:

1. The first goal seeks to minimize the over-attainment of the goal level for the total operational costs of sampling and testing the products of the firm. These goals take the following form:

$$\sum_{j=1}^{k} \sum_{i=1}^{I} (C^N_{ijk} X^N_{ijk} + C^0_{ijk} X^0_{ijk} + C^E_{ijk} Y_{ijk}) + d^-_{TC_k} - d^+_{TC_k} = TC_k \tag{1}$$

for k=1,2,...,K

(K: planning horizon)

C^N_{ijk}: cost of the sampling and testing in the kth period of the ith product produced in the jth period in internal laboratory facilities during normal work periods

C^0_{ijk}: cost of sampling and testing in the kth period for the ith product produced in the jth period in internal laboratories during overtime work periods

C^E_{ijk}: cost of sampling and testing in the kth period for the ith product produced in the jth period in external laboratory facilities

TC_k: budget level for operational costs of testing the firm's products in the kth period

$d^-_{TC_k}$: under-attainment of the budget level for operational costs of testing the firm's products in the kth period

$d^+_{TC_k}$: over-attainment of the budget level for operational costs of testing the firm's product in the keth period

2. The second goal seeks to minimize the over-attainment of the goal level for the

amount of quality testing done in external facilities. These constraints take
the following form:

$$\sum_{j=1}^{k} \sum_{i=1}^{I} Y_{ijk} + d_{OT_k}^- - d_{OT_k}^+ = OT_k \qquad (2)$$

$$k=1,2,\ldots K$$

(K: planning horizon)

OT_k: goal level of the number of batches of items for quality
testing done in external facilities in the kth period

$d_{OT_k}^-$: under-attainment of the goal level of the number of batches
of items for quality testing done in external facilities
in the kth period

$d_{OT_k}^+$: over-attainment of the goal level of the number of batches
of items for quality testing done in external facilities
in the kth period

3. The third goal seeks to minimize the over-attainment of the goal level for the
amount of quality testing not completed within the period in which items are
produced due to their short period in which their effectiveness diminishes
seriously. This constraint takes the following form:

$$\sum_{k=1}^{K} \sum_{j=1}^{K-1} \sum_{i=1}^{I} (X_{ijk}^N + X_{ijk}^0 + Y_{ijk}) + d_B^- - d_B^+ = B \qquad (3)$$

B: goal level of the number of batches of items for quality
testing not completed within the period in which they
are produced

d_B^-: under-attainment of the goal level of the number of batches
of items for quality testing not completed within the period
in which they are produced

d_B^+: over-attainment of the goal level of the number of batches
of items for quality testing not completed within the
period in which they are produced

4. The following goal seeks to minimize the over-attainment of the goal level for
the amount of testing done in internal facilities in normal and overtime working hours during the maintenance period (M). This constraint takes the following
form:

$$\sum_{j=1}^{m} \sum_{i=1}^{I} (t_i X_{ijm}^N + t_i X_{ijm}^0) + d_M^- - d_M^+ = M \qquad (4)$$

268

t_i: time per batch needed for testing a batch of the ith item in internal facilities

M: goal level of the amount of time available for testing of all items in internal facilities during the maintenance period, M

d_M^-: under-attainment of the goal level of the amount of time available for testing of all items in internal facilities during the maintenance period, M

d_M^+: over-attainment of the goal level of the amount of time available for testing of all items in internal facilities during the maintenance period, M

The objective function for this goal programming problem is as follows:

$$\text{Min } Z = P_1 \sum_{k=1}^{K} \left[d_{TC_k}^+ \right] + P_2 \sum_{k=1}^{K} \left[d_{OT_k}^+ \right] + P_3 \left[d_B^+ \right] + P_4 \left[d_M^+ \right] \tag{5}$$

P_1, P_2, P_3 P_4 are pre-emptive priority factors

The regular constraints of the model take the following form:

1. To assure that the number of items of product are produced and tested meets the demand for these items: (Since they cannot take the risk of deterioration, the items must be shipped out in the same period that they are tested.)

$$\sum_{j=1}^{k} (x_{ijk}^N + x_{ijk}^0 + Y_{ijk}) = D_{ik} \tag{6}$$

$$i=1,2,\ldots,I; \ k=1,2,\ldots,K$$

D_{ik}: demand for the ith product type in the kth period

2. To set maximum capacity levels on the availability of internal laboratory facilities during normal working hours:

$$\sum_{j=1}^{k} \sum_{i=1}^{I} t_i x_{ijk}^N \leq T_n^N$$

$$k=1,2,\ldots,K$$

T_k^N: total testing time available in the kth period during normal work hours

3. To set maximum capacity levels on the availability of internal laboratory facilities during overtime working hours

$$\sum_{j=1}^{k} \sum_{i=1}^{I} t_i X_{ijk}^0 \leq T_k^0$$

$$k=1,2,\ldots,K$$

T_k^0: total testing time available for items in the kth period during overtime working hours

About the Authors

Kenneth D. Lawrence *is Group Manager in Strategic Planning and Financial Analysis in the Marketing Department at AT&T Communications. He has previously held positions with the U.S. Army Munitions Command, Prudential Insurance, Hoffman-La Roche, Inc., AT&T Long Lines, and AT&T. His articles have appeared in many scientific and professional publications. Dr. Lawrence is a senior member of IIE where he has held several positions in the Production and Inventory Control Division. He has also served as a referee for* Operations Research, Naval Logistics Quarterly, IIE Transactions, *and the* Sloan Management Review. *Currently he is co-editor of a special report in* IIE Transactions *entitled "Multiple Criteria Decision Making in Production Planning and Scheduling." His research interests concentrate on the application of multiple criteria decision making to problems in operations and financial management economic planning; optimization in statistics; and new product forecasting. Dr. Lawrence received his B.S. in computer science and statistics from the University of Delaware; masters degrees in industrial engineering from West Virginia University, in business administration from Pennsylvania State University, in statistics from the Rochester Institute of Technology, in operations research from Rutgers University; and a doctorate in statistics and operations research from Rutgers University.*

Stelios H. Zanakis *is Chairman and Professor of Decision Sciences, College of Business Administration, Florida International University. Prior to joining F.I.U., Dr. Zanakis was Associate Professor and Director of the Industrial Engineering and Systems Analysis Program at the West Virginia College of Graduate Studies. He has authored over thirty articles in scientific and professional journals and has edited a special volume of* Management Science *on "Optimization in Statistics." Dr. Zanakis is listed in* American Men and Women of Science, Who's Who in Engineering, Personalities of the South, Men of Achievement, Forensic Services, *and* Lawyer to Lawyer Consultation Panel *Directories. Dr. Zanakis has served as the chairman or invited speaker at various national and regional meetings, as well as the ORSA/TIMS Visiting Lecturer Program. He was the program chairman for production and inventory control at the Spring and Winter 1982 National Conferences of the AIIE. His abiding interest is the development and implementation of manual and computerized decision support systems to solve real-world problems. Dr. Zanakis holds a Ph.D. in management science, a M.A. in statistics, and a M.B.A., all from Pennsylvania State University. He also holds a M.S. in mechanical/electrical engineering from the National Technical University of Athens, Greece.*